M

6/23/94   12/26/95   16 T

THE
LAST
CAVALIERS

THE
LAST
CAVALIERS

CONFEDERATE AND UNION CAVALRY
IN THE CIVIL WAR

BY

Samuel Carter III

ST. MARTIN'S PRESS   NEW YORK

Maps by Clarice Borio, New York City

Library of Congress Cataloging in Publication Data

Carter, Samuel.
  The Last Cavaliers: Confederate and Union Cavalry in the Civil War

  Bibliography: p.
  Includes index.
    1. United States—History—Civil War, 1861–1865—
Cavalry operations.   I. Title.
E470.C24   973.7′4   76-62758
ISBN 0-312-12553-4

To
Burnham and Peggy

Modern skepticism has destroyed one of the most Beautiful creations of epic ages, the belief that the spirits of dead warriors meet daily in the halls of Valhalla, and there around the festive board recount the deeds they did in the other world. . . . a man in my command may be forgiven for thinking that, in this assembly of heroes, he will not be unnoticed in that mighty throng.

JOHN SINGLETON MOSBY
to veterans of his partisan rangers

CONTENTS

FOREWORD

IT HAS BEEN SAID THAT PREFACES TO BOOKS ARE OFTEN VEILED apologies for the author's failures and omissions. If so, this introduction may be guilty of that charge.

For there are many things this book is not. It is not a history of the Civil War; its limitations are deliberate. Nor is it a definitive record of the wartime cavalry in all its manifold dimensions. Rather, it is an introduction to a few of the men, most of them outstanding, some more obscure, who brought a rare light of chivalry to a dark time in our past.

Frank Burr of the 2nd Michigan Cavalry states in his biography of General Sheridan: "About the man who fights on horseback the romance of war has always centered." War has ceased to be romantic, and the cavalry, in all but name, has vanished. But the names of the Civil War cavaliers, both Union and Confederate, should be engraved in granite, for their like will not be seen again—men like Jeb Stuart, Bedford Forrest, John Hunt Morgan, Sheridan, Wheeler, Ashby, Custer, Hampton, and the many others who composed the "mighty throng" assembled in John Singleton Mosby's vision of Valhalla.

It is impossible here to do full justice to all of them. Their characters were too complex; the deeds they did too numerous. An attempt is made, nevertheless, to consider them one by one in a chronology conforming to the progress of the war. For the sake of narrative flow this sometimes means overlooking, for the moment, the actions and achievements occurring on another corner of the stage, as well as omitting much detailed statistical data found in conventional histories.

The focus of this narrative is strictly on the cavalry. For this reason it may seem to slight other branches of the service, though no one is suggesting that the Civil War was largely fought on horseback. The presence of infantry and artillery, and sometimes gunboats, was often a decisive backdrop to a cavalry engagement; and the infantry's role in such battles as Five Forks and Saylor's Creek was indispensable to victory.

There is no such thing as selective history. The term itself is a contradiction; history is not selective. Because, however, we are focussing on the highlights of the cavalry, one may find gaps in geography as well as history. Little attention, for example, is given to the Trans-Mississippi theater, since most of the major action pertinent to this narration took place east of the river, between the Mississippi and the Appalachians and the Appalachians to the coast.

There are two controversial areas in a narration such as this. One is the matter of military figures and statistics. The precise size of a given army or a certain regiment, the precise numbers of casualties in an engagement, vary according to the source. Each side had its own method of tabulation. There was a difference, for instance, between the number present and the number of "effectives;" the South often did not list as "casualties" those wounded who later recovered and rejoined their units. The qualifying words "approximate" or "estimated" are good handles to apply to figures.

A second controversial area is that of eye-witness accounts of a battle or event. These lend a sense of immediacy to the story, and a valuable human touch. Except that—true to eyewitnesses everywhere—no two of them agree. There are several versions of John Hunt Morgan's entrapment and death in the fall of 1864, as there are of Mosby's capture of General Stoughton in the spring of 1863. One can only choose the version that seems to fit the circumstances best, aware that others may not agree with the choice or interpretation.

No book is ever finished—nor sometimes ever started—without the encouragement and help of individuals for whom an author feels enduring thanks. A blanket of gratitude must serve to cover the advisers and staff members of the Yale University Library, the Mississippi Department of Archives and History, the Library of Congress and the National Archives. And a special measure of thanks to Dr. Edwin C. Bearss for his patient and thorough reading of the manuscript, and his corrections and suggestions before publication. If faults and omissions still remain, they can be attributed only to the author.

Finally, my thanks to John Brennan of Laurel, Maryland, for his constant forwarding of otherwise unobtainable material; to Virginia Canfield for her expert typing of the manuscript; to Alison Carter for her careful reading of the proofs; and to Thomas L. Dunne of St. Martin's Press who is the true father of this work, having suggested it in the first place and having nurtured it to its conclusion.

1

RALLYING OF THE SABERS

THROUGHOUT THE LONG WAR YEARS TO FOLLOW, WHEN THEY thought of home and happier times as soldiers will, they remembered different things. To Wade Hampton of South Carolina the past was enshrined in the clean white-porticoed frame of Millwood, the Columbia plantation manor, and long hours in the saddle riding to hounds across the Piedmont hills.

In the West, John Hunt Morgan's thoughts returned to the Blue Grass region of Kentucky, where horses were a man's religion akin to cards and women; to days spent in the game-filled wilderness with Bowie knife and hunting rifle—where wellborn lads (and wellborn did not mean well-educated) were taught to ride properly, sitting the "dragoon seat" and not rising to fire from the saddle.

And in the North, George Armstrong Custer remembered the bustling mercantile town of Monroe, Michigan, where he learned a trade and watched the militia drilling on the village green. Remembered too the saucy pig-tailed Libby Bacon who swung on the front gate of her father's house and hailed him as he walked to work with "Hyuh, Custer boy!" For common to all soldiers was The Girl They Left Behind Them.

Not far from Custer, as American distances were measured, was L. Clayton's dry goods store in Somerset, Ohio, which bandy-legged Phil Sheridan would remember as the place he got his start in life. Luckily one of Clayton's customers was an Ohio congressman who, chatting with the young clerk, was able to fulfill his boyhood dream by appointing him to West Point. ("Not that!" the family pastor told young Sheridan's father. "Rather, take him behind the chickencoop and cut his throat!")

These, sketchily, were the backgrounds from which they rode or tramped to war in 1861, a pattern repeated many thousandfold on both sides of the Mason-Dixon line. And these backgrounds determined the early stages of their war careers. On a different time schedule, all four were to become larger-than-life leaders of Confederate or Union cavalry, a rare breed of men that will not come again. Their moment in history was brief; the deeds they did were long remembered. For a flash in time, it seemed, chivalry and romance rode to battle in the eighteen-sixties—never to return.

In no American conflict prior to the Civil War did cavalry play so significant a role. Though a nation of horses and horsemen, there was little cavalry tradition in the United States. The nature of preceding conflicts had not required or fostered one. Mounted troops played only a minor role in Colonial wars with the Indians and French, since the heavily forested wilderness curtailed their movements. Colonel George Washington, an excellent horseman, preferred to fight on foot.

The Revolutionary War had heroes on horseback—Light Horse Harry Lee and the "Swamp Fox," Francis Marion, for two examples. But these were essentially land-roving privateers, waging war on their own, by standards of their own. Though often effective as guerillas, especially in the South, they were an accidental breed compared with the disciplined troopers of Banastre Tarleton or the Civil War cavalry that followed later.

And one could forget the War of 1812. Though Congress authorized money for two regiments of dragoons, these were never organized, and American mounted militia from Kentucky and Tennessee only twice performed significant service, at the Battle of Thames and in the Creek campaign of 1814. The British brought over a company of Light Dragoons, used them principally for escort service, and put their faith in infantry, artillery, and ships.

Coming, however, to the years immediately preceding the Civil War, Northerners and Southerners with previous military service had one thing in common: Limited cavalry experience in the war with Mexico and, more important, Indian fighting on the plains. The latter, especially, involved mounted troops—but they were mounted for mobility, and generally fought dismounted when they reached the site of battle. A lieutenant at Fort Dodge complained that the Comanches could ride rings around his troopers, using their horses' bodies as shields, "as my men have never learned to do."

This limited experience did not, of course, apply to cavalry alone.

Americans entered their tragic, fratricidal war almost totally unprepared in every branch of military service. But in other areas the odds
seemed overwhelming in favor of the North. The twenty-four states of
the Union outnumbered by more than two to one the available man-
power of the 11 Southern states—by more than three to one if the slave
population were discounted. The North had three-quarters of the
Nation's wealth; and more than five times the manufacturing capacity
of the South.

And along with a larger land area, the North had nearly three times
the railroad mileage of the South, a waterways transportation system,
and a network of generally well-surfaced highways. All important to
the movement of troops, munitions, and supplies—but to which there
is a significant footnote: except in some Western rural areas, the
average Northerner traveled by carriage, railroad car, or steamer. The
Southerner got where he wanted to go on horseback.

Which gave the South an initial advantage, inherent to its way of life.
Rich or poor, the youth of the South were born to the saddle and
learned to ride in infancy. The hunt, the steeplechase, the gymkhana,
or tournament, were the popular diversions. The Southerner conducted his business in the saddle, whether overseeing a plantation,
trading in the rural market, or touring the professional circuit as
doctor, lawyer, preacher, or government agent.

Only in California and certain northwestern states were men as
familiar with horses as in the South. In general, in the North, the horse
was a draft animal, used for pulling the plow, the carriage, and the
street car, and rarely used for sport or pleasure. In military exercises,
the horse was a means of getting troops and artillery to one place or
another, for escort or courier duty, or for carrying officers to and from
the scenes of action. Generals did not lead on horseback: they directed
from the saddle; mounted troops were simply mobile infantry.

All of which is to say that, when the war came, the South had instant
cavalry material. Tactical training might or might not be imposed, and
often wasn't; Southern cavalry rode and maneuvered as later fighter
pilots flew—by the seat of their pants. By contrast, most of the Northern cavalrymen, often arbitrarily assigned to that branch of the service,
knew horses only by proximity—"clerks and tailors on horseback,"
Southerners referred to them derisively. It would take two years of
training to turn them into accomplished troopers; and, looking ahead,
those two years were sufficient. Basically, what the South had was a
head start, not a permanent monopoly, not, in the final years of war,
even an adequate fighting edge to see them through.

The Southern equestrian fraternity—for want of a better term—
developed a rare breed of men akin to the war aces of the air force in

more modern times. It was more than riding ability and knowledge of the use and care of horses. It was a sense of being part of the machine — in this case a four-legged animal machine. Observers noted of Turner Ashby, idol of the Shenandoah Valley, that as he leaped a stream, both horse and rider moved as one, and the only visible movement in the rider was the settling of Ashby's cape as he landed on the other side.

Horsemanship also developed qualities of daring, innovation, and independence in thought and action. A fence or ditch could not be cleared according to studious planning in advance. It could only be cleared with dash; and if that proved insurmountable, another approach would have to be instantly improvised. The same with facing an unpredictable enemy in this fast-moving fluid means of waging war. Advance orders were of little use; precise goals must depend on opportunities; slate-board strategy was a waste of time when speed and split-second decisions were the ultimate deciding factors.

While the cavalry was regarded by the foot soldier, somewhat enviously, as a bunch of deadbeats — "buttermilk rangers" and "critter boys" — there was also a think-gap between the cavalry and the top command. For one thing, many of the generals were West Pointers. They understood the use of cavalry as prescribed in the *Trooper's Manual* by Captain Lucius Davis, himself a West Point cavalry instructor. Cavalry was a useful tool, but only as a servant of the army, not as a combat unit in itself. There were exceptions to this attitude, and the exceptions grew; and in time the use of cavalry as a striking force became part of the Confederate and Union strategies.

Still, throughout the war there was an undercurrent of friction between cavalry leaders and army generals, born largely of the cavalryman's sense of pride and independence — Robert E. Lee provoked by Jeb Stuart's tardiness at Gettysburg, Braxton Bragg outraged at John Hunt Morgan's absence on the road to Chattanooga, Bedford Forrest refusing to accept orders from his immediate superior, General Joe Wheeler. There were few chiefs of cavalry such as Wheeler who dutifully followed army requisitions — and even Wheeler, during the campaign for Atlanta, went off on his own on a wild goose steeplechase.

And in the North, when Philip Sheridan took command of the mounted branch of the Army of the Potomac, he faced the same persistent problem, writing in his *Memoirs*:

> Heretofore, the commander of the Cavalry Corps had been, virtually, merely an adjunct at army headquarters . . . I knew that it would be difficult to overcome the custom of using the cavalry for the protection of trains and the establishment of cordons around the infantry

corps, and so far subordinating its operations to the movements of the main army that in name only was it a corps at all. . . .

From the civilian standpoint, however—important to recruitment—the cavalry was the privileged, romantic branch of military service. For this was the age of Sir Walter Scott and *Ivanhoe*, and the popular English novelist Charles Lever whose Napoleonic masterpiece, *Charles O'Malley, the Irish Dragoon*, did more to spur enlistments, North and South, than all the pronouncements and recruiting posters of the separate War Departments. For here was glory to which every youth aspired, as portrayed in the framework of Wellington's Peninsula Campaign:

> "Forward! Close up; charge!"
> The words were scarcely spoken, when a loud cheer answered the welcome sound, and at the same instant the long line of shining helmets passed with the speed of a whirlwind; the pace increased at every stride, the ranks grew closer, and, like the dread force of some mighty engine, we fell upon the foe. I have felt all the glorious enthusiasm of a fox-hunt, when the loud cry of the hound, answered by the cheer of the joyous huntsman, stirred the very heart within, but never till now did I know how far higher the excitement reaches when, man to man, saber to saber, arm to arm, we ride forward to the battlefield. On we went, the loud shout of "Forward" ringing in our ears.

Both mill hands in Michigan and farm boys in the Carolinas saw themselves among those gallant cavaliers, sweeping over the foe and earning the praise of their commander:

> "Well done, Fourteenth!" said the old gray-haired colonel, blood trickling from his sabered cheek. "Gallantly done, lads!"

Here was such stuff as dreams are made on, as enduringly glorious as Waterloo or Balaklava. One had only to mount a horse—his own horse if he was a Southerner, a farm horse if he were a Yankee—and ride forth to join the ranks of the immortals.

None hesitated when the call came, in response to either Lincoln's request for 75,000 volunteers or Jefferson Davis' appeal for a force not to exceed 100,000. But even before the fall of Sumter, the Southern cavalry had begun to organize, and in this regard Virginia was foremost of the Southern states. In time the Old Dominion would contribute 27 regiments and 17 battalions of sabers to the Cause.

Some were already established companies of local reputation. The Black Horse Cavalry of Fauquier County was formed in June of 1859, composed, according to its Captain, John Scott, "of young gentlemen of the first respectability, either themselves planters or the sons of planters." At about the same time Turner Ashby and his brother Richard organized the Ashby Rangers, similarly comprising planters or the wellborn sons of planters. Both units saw service as guardian escorts at the hanging of John Brown at Charleston; and both provided a pattern for the volunteer companies rising in Virginia in the spring of 1861.

They called themselves Dragoons, Lancers, Hussars, Light Horse, Mounted Chasseurs (anything but cavalry), until the War Department gave them regimental numbers. They created their own uniforms in every shade of blue and gray, with a penchant for gold and scarlet trimmings—braided jackets, silk-lined capes, soft broad-brimmed hats, and hussar boots. They brought their personal black grooms and body servants, provided their own horses, supplied their own arms from often antiquated family stores, and preferred the light, curved, French-style saber of domestic or imported manufacture.

The rallying point in the spring of 1861 was Richmond, and the volunteer cavalry companies came from virtually all the counties of Virginia, as well as from the Carolinas. From Abingdon came William E. ("Grumble") Jones, ex–U.S. Army officer, with his Washington Mounted Rifles, among whom was a rising young country lawyer named John Singleton Mosby. In the Shenandoah Valley ex–Indian fighter Angus MacDonald—who thought that hatchets (2½ lbs. in the head) were superior to sabers for cavalry combat—organized ten companies of mounted volunteers to patrol the bluffs of the Potomac. And in South Carolina, gentleman-planter Wade Hampton advertised in the Charleston *Courier* for 1,000 recruits to form the Hampton Legion, which would join the universal march to Richmond.

While the infantry traveled to Richmond by rail or trudged along dusty backroads, the cavalry rode from town to town with spurs and sabers jangling, gaily uniformed and plumed beneath silk battle flags created by the girls they left behind. And if Southern belles threw kisses or strewed flowers in their path, and the proud cavaliers acknowledged this homage as appropriate, it was all in keeping with the age of Ivanhoe and the Southern legend that all girls are beautiful and all men brave.

In the white-tented camps around Richmond the assembled companies elected their officers, read the manuals, drilled dutifully and kept themselves in riding trim, leaving the dirty work of camp life to their body servants. For they were more concerned with the entertainment so freely offered in Richmond homes and neighboring plantations, in the cotillions, balls, charades, and dinners; the mock battles staged for visiting belles, who obligingly swooned at the sound of the guns and the murderous charge of the saber. Though the enemy was scarcely a hundred miles away, this was no cause for concern. It was well known that one Confederate was the equal of six Yankees and the Union cavalry were simply a bunch of bungling amateurs.

If the light-hearted carnival atmosphere seemed adolescent and unrealistic, foreboding disaster when the fighting started, there was another side to this fledgling cavalry, noted by one of their severest adversaries, William Tecumseh Sherman:

> The young bloods of the South, sons of planters, lawyers about town, good billiard players, and sportsmen—men who never did work nor never will. War suits them, and the rascals are brave, and bold to rashness. . . . They hate Yankees *per se*, and don't bother their brains about the past, present or future. . . . They are splendid riders, first-rate shots, and utterly reckless . . . the most dangerous set of men which this war has turned loose upon the world.

In the Confederate West, the spirit and enthusiasm were the same among the flood of cavalry recruits. There was not a great deal of difference in the composition and *esprit* of Virginia's Black Horse Troop and John Hunt Morgan's Lexington Rifles of Kentucky. But, though both attracted the wellborn youths of a horse-oriented aristocracy, there was a certain pioneer toughness in the Western volunteers. Among other factors, conflict with such marauders as the Border Ruffians developed an early familiarity with violence.

So that in the Confederate cavalry camps at Bowling Green and elsewhere south of the Green River, there was not the time for formal training, for camp festivities, and gentlemanly pastimes. The troops were trained in the field, on raids upon enemy outposts, and foraging expeditions into Union territory. But the lure of adventure was the same, as was the magnetic attraction of the cavalry; and both east and west of the Appalachians, men rode from camp to the rhythm and chorus of the same song:

> If you want to have a good time,
> If you want to have some fun,
> If you want to catch the devil,
> Jine the cavalry!

If Confederate cavalry enrollment was spontaneous, enthusiastic, and relatively unplanned, the organization of cavalry in the Northern states was sluggish to the point of negligence. In May 1861, President Lincoln, calling for an increase in the regular army, asked for only one new regiment of mounted troops, to be added to the five already in existence. If all six were up to standard strength, they would have aggregated 6,500 men in all.

General-in-Chief Winfield Scott, now in his seventy-fifth year and unable to mount a horse without assistance, believed that in the impending war the role of cavalry would be "unimportant and secondary," and that the existing regiments would be sufficient. Which ignored the fact that many of the regular cavalry officers had gone over to the Southern side. The First and Second U.S. Cavalry Regiments, formed by War Secretary Jefferson Davis in 1855, spawned such Confederate leaders as Robert E. Lee, Jeb Stuart, Joseph Johnston, Kirby Smith, Albert Sidney Johnson, John Bell Hood, and Fitzhugh Lee. The North got a decent share, of course, in such officers as George H. Thomas and George Stonemen, and few if any enlisted men went over to the South.

The regular cavalry, too, was widely scattered in the West when war broke out, engaged in fighting Indians, protecting settlers, and guarding such routes of trade as the Santa Fe Trail. Only one unit, the Second Dragoons under Captain Alfred Pleasonton, was able to make the long ride from Utah to Washington, to arrive in the autumn of 1861 after the first major battle had been fought. Many others remained at their outposts, exiles of the Civil War, fearful of renewed outbreaks of Indian attacks.

So for all practical purposes the Union had to start from scratch to build whatever it wanted in the way of cavalry. Though George B. McClellan, who succeeded Winfield Scott as General-in-Chief, was himself a veteran of the ?nd U.S. Cavalry and inventor of the "McClellan Saddle" used by the mounted troops of both sides, he too was slow to see the cavalry in more than an auxiliary role. Moreover, despite an ample supply of horses in the Union, the federal government refused to provide the necessary mounts, leaving it up to the states to furnish horses and equipment at their own expense.

Pennsylvania was one of the first of the states to raise a substantial force of cavalry, with recruits selected, "for the intelligence and energy to become good cavalrymen," from a host of applicants. The 9th Pennsylvania Cavalry which served throughout the war from 1861 to 1865, in both the East and West, was as typical as any in the field. As catalogued by John W. Rowell, the roster of one company in the regiment (Company C) showed 36 civilian occupations represented, among them: artist, blacksmith, carpenter, mason, chemist, civil engineer, railroad worker, printer, shoemaker, teacher, merchant, tailor, gunsmith, physician, teamster, weaver, clerk. Of the 156 men in Company C , roughly 60 percent came from the trades and professions, with 20 percent from farms—a low figure for the latter category, farmers often making up half the average cavalry enrollment.

This diversified background was part of the problem. Recruits were plentiful enough; young men volunteered for the sabered arm with the same enthusiasm as their Southern counterparts. But, noted John K. Herr and Edward S. Wallace in their *Story of the U.S. Cavalry*, "There were some handicaps in the raising of Union cavalry regiments. The men in the industrial areas of the Northeast were largely office workers or factory laborers who had grown away from the rigors of outdoor life." On the other hand, "they were used to a certain amount of discipline and were easier to handle than the highly individualistic Southerners." So it would take time—time prolonged by inexperience in horsemanship and the care of horses that came naturally to the South. According to Herr and Wallace:

> It took two years to train a cavalryman, for the duties required a higher order of intelligence and initiative than the other branches, and a good trooper had to be equally efficient mounted or dismounted. The wastage during this time was fabulous. . . . One swallow too much of water allowed to heated horses on long marches, by the thousands of green Union troopers in the early part of the war, meant losses of millions of dollars—and it happened all the time. It was in things like this the experienced Confederate horseman had such an advantage at the start.

Uninitiated recruits, plus inexperienced commanders and inept officers of ordnance, led to early, temporary chaos in the Union training camps. Maverick horses had to be broken in by green recruits who had never handled a horse before except from behind a plow. Equipment was provided or selected without regard for practicality or need. A captain of the 10th New York Cavalry, just mustered into service, described his company's initial ride from camp on escort duty:

> Many men had extra blankets, nice large quilts presented by some fond mother or maiden aunt (dear souls), sabers and belts, together with the straps that pass over the shoulders, carbines and slings, pockets full of cartridges, nose bags and extra little bags for carrying oats, haversacks, canteens, and spurs—curry-combs, brushes, ponchos, button tents, overcoats, frying-pans, cups, coffee pots, etc.

Adding their own weight to the overburdened horses brought predictable results:

> Such a rattling, jingling, jerking, scrabbling, cursing, I never heard before. Green horses—some of them had never been ridden— turned round and round, backed against each other, jumped up or stood up like trained circus-horses. Some of the boys had a pile in

front of their saddles, and one in the rear, so high and heavy it took two men to saddle one horse and two men to help the fellow into his place.

Many of the green troops, the captain observed, had never ridden anything but childhood hobbyhorses, and, clasping their legs too tightly, unwittingly drove their spurs into the horses' sides, causing the animals to sheer and buck with consequent disaster:

> Blankets slipped from under saddles and hung from one corner; saddles slipped back until they were on the rumps of horses; others turned and were on the under side of the animals; horses running and kicking; tin pans, mess-kettles—flying through the air; and all I could do was to give a hasty glance to the rear and sing out at the top of my voice. "C-L-O-S-E U-P!"

The proper employment of cavalry was slow in gaining recognition. For almost two years, noted Herr and Wallace, "the great resources of the North were wasted by incompetence and the cavalry was dissipated by detail. It was initially attached to infantry commands and rather futilely used on petty defensive assignments such as outposts and patrols, as orderlies, messengers, and grooms for staff officers, and as guards for slow-moving wagon convoys which infantry could have done equally well."

The assembly point of Union cavalry in the East was Washington, and here the secondary role was evident. Troopers were used to guard the Potomac bridges, and for courier service and picket duty. A few veteran regulars kept their eyes on the south bank of the river where Confederate flags and campfires marked the locations of the enemy. But the majority were loosely scattered in camps along the Seventh Street Road and generally idle.

The crowning indignity was to find themselves without mounts shortly after they arrived, relegated to what was known as "Company Q"—cavalry without horses who were assigned to intermediate duties or transferred to infantry. The cause was often the requisition of horses for the artillery, considered a more important branch of service. A Maryland cavalry company strolling the streets of Washington was asked by a passing regiment of Connecticut artillery, "Where are your horses?" and receiving the embittered answer, "Gone to fetch your heavy guns."

British officer Garnett Joseph Wolsely, touring Washington as a neutral observer, compared the Union horsemen with the Confederate cavalry he had previously visited. The Southerners, he noted, were magnificent riders:

In which particular they present a striking contrast to the Northern cavalry, who can scarcely sit their horses, even when trotting. Indeed, I have no doubt but that all who have seen Northern troops on duty in Washington, will agree with me in thinking them the greatest scare-crows under the name of cavalry that they ever saw. . . . Every man in the South is at home in the saddle; whereas to be on horseback is a most disagreeable position for a Yankee, and one in which he rarely trusts himself.

Picturing the Union cavalry, however, as a clumsy, untrainable bunch of amateurs, never to rise above the level of incompetence, would, of course, be both inaccurate and ludicrous. To a large extent the South was tricked into making that mistake. The North, for reasons noted, simply started at a disadvantage it would take two years to overcome. And looking ahead, overcome they did.

They were slower in starting, slower to get organized, and seemingly infected by a great inertia. But, noted Herr and Wallace, when the Union cavalry "finally picked up momentum it became a veritable juggernaut and crushed everything before it. By the end of the war, under superb leadership . . . it became the best arm of the service and probably the most efficient body of soldiers on earth. . . ." The story of the cavalry, covering both sides, is directed by a swinging pendulum that moves from South to North.

Now it was close to mid-July in 1861.

Mobilization of both Union and Confederate armies in the West was proceeding haltingly, but in northern Virginia, between the capitals of Washington and Richmond, the battle lines were being drawn. While Horace Greeley's New York *Tribune* raised the cry of "Forward to Richmond!" Lincoln prodded his armies into motion, concerned that the three-month term for volunteers would expire in a few more weeks. Near Harpers Ferry, Union General Robert Patterson, having earlier crossed the Potomac with 14,000 troops, confronted Joseph E. Johnston's Army of the Shenandoah farther up the Valley.

The main Union army of Irvin McDowell, 35,000 strong, was mov-ing westward from Alexandria to meet and destroy the Confederate Army of the Potomac under General Pierre G. T. Beauregard sta-tioned at Manassas Junction. With barely 20,000 troops in his com-mand, Beauregard was outnumbered by more than three to two. He was awaiting reinforcements, including Wade Hampton's 600 South Carolinians on their way from Richmond, but these would add only small patches to his thin line west of Bull Run.

But if Johnston could break loose from Patterson at Harpers Ferry, and join him with all or a large part of his infantry, Beauregard would have a force nearly equal to McDowell. In addition, he would have the 1st Virginia Cavalry now attached to Johnston's army. The regiment numbered only 500 troopers; but all were peerless horsemen, honed to a keen fighting edge and trained to the pattern of their commander, the *beau sabreur* of the Confederacy, Colonel James Ewell Brown Stuart. . . .

2

GOLD   SPURS   AND   ROSES

LOOKING BACK, IT WAS MONDAY, OCTOBER 17, 1859.

"There is trouble of some sort at Harpers Ferry," began the bulletin reaching Secretary John B. Floyd of the War Department. A group described as "Kansas Border Ruffians" had taken possession of the United States Armory and Arsenal, and were holed up in the fire house with several captured citizens as hostages.

This meager news had little bearing on the affairs of young cavalry lieutenant J. E. B. Stuart, waiting in the anteroom for an interview with Floyd. Twenty-six years of age with five years of service in the field behind him, Stuart had invented a device for attaching the horseman's saber to his belt (U.S. Patent Office No. 25,684). Considering the importance of the saber to the cavalry, he hoped to sell the invention to the War Department.

The opportunity never came. An aide appeared to ask him, as a favor to the Secretary, to deliver an urgent message to Robert E. Lee at the colonel's home in Arlington House.

Stuart jumped at the chance. Lee had been superintendent of West Point when Stuart was there, and the lieutenant would be happy to renew the contact. He delivered the message and awaited a reply. Learning that Lee had been ordered to Harpers Ferry to quell the disturbance with any troops that he could muster, Stuart begged to go along as his aide. Lee consented.

The next morning ninety United States Marines, commanded by the colonel, surrounded the fire house where the insurgents were making a last stand. Concerned with the safety of the hostages, Lèe was reluctant to storm the place. Instead he dispatched Lieutenant Stuart with a note to their leader, a man who called himself Smith, demanding that they surrender in return for their lives.

There was to be no bargaining, Lee told his volunteer aide. Just a simple yes or no. If the answer is no surrender, just come to the door and wave your hat and the marines will move in on the double.

Hammering on the fire house door and calling for Mr. Smith, Stuart was suddenly confronted with a face from the past, gaunt, bearded, and fanatical, with eyes like glowing embers. "Osawatomie," John Brown, the man he had chased over half of Kansas as a cavalry lieutenant during the bloody days of 1856.

He might have guessed what the old man's reply would be to Lee's surrender message. No. War, fire, and blood by preference! Stuart stepped to the door and waved his hat.

Lieutenant Israel Green, who led the marines who overwhelmed Old Osawatomie and his disciples, remembered the lieutenant's signal in some detail. It was a soft felt hat, he noted, with a feather fastened to the crown. He could not know, nor did Stuart, that the hat and the feather would become a guidon of victorious cavalry charges in countless battles yet to come, a trademark of the King of Southern Cavaliers.

There was fighting blood in Stuart's veins for sure. If one searched back far enough, one might find him descended from the Stuarts of England, dating from a time when knighthood was in flower. There was a bit of Wales, a bit of Scotland, and a bit of Ireland in his background. Though not wealthy, his forebears came from the landed gentry of Virginia. His great-grandfather, Alexander, fought under Nathanael Greene in the Revolution. His father, Archibald, served with distinction in the War of 1812. His mother was related to Virginia's Governor John Letcher and could trace her family's battle records back to William the Conqueror at Hastings.

Yet he had not plunged precipitously into military life. Youngest son and seventh of eleven children born at the family's "Laurel Hill" plantation in southwestern Virginia, he had been tutored at home and later attended Emory and Henry College where the emphasis was strongly on the classics. A self-acknowledged love for "the beauties of Ovid" inclined him toward a career of teaching, until family influence steered him into West Point, class of 1854.

Among his fellow cadets were many he would long remember: Philip Henry Sheridan, of Irish lineage, whose combativeness earned him a year's suspension from the academy; William Wood Averell of Steuben County, New York; the Scotch-Irish David McMurtrie Gregg of Pennsylvania; Alfred T. A. Torbert of Delaware; and Fitzhugh Lee, a nephew of Robert E. Lee and grandson of "Light Horse Harry" Lee of Revolutionary fame. His classmates saw the seventeen-year-old Stuart as a green cadet who was all arms and legs, with a jaw too long and a chin too short. They dubbed him "Beauty" Stuart—a sobriquet whose true significance, wrote Fitzhugh Lee, "was in inverse ratio to the compliment implied." It was agreed, however, that he sat to good advantage on a horse.

Graduating thirteenth in a class of forty-six, with a notable record of fighting everybody in the academy at any welcome provocation, he was commissioned a second lieutenant with the Mounted Rifles serving on the western frontier. Such was the training of many of his kind, and Indian fighting, noted William Tecumseh Sherman, was "the hardest kind of fighting in the world." Later Stuart transferred to one of the two regiments formed by Jefferson Davis, the 1st United States Cavalry, stationed at Fort Leavenworth, Kansas.

It was in bleeding Kansas, policing the war between the Border Ruffians and the Abolitionists, that he was thrown with many fellow officers whom he would later meet as friend or foe: bantamweight, gentlemanly Joseph E. Johnston of Virginia, Kirby Smith, Alfred C. Iverson, and Albert Sidney Johnson. And it was at Fort Leavenworth, too, that he met and married Flora Cooke, daughter of Colonel Philip St. George Cooke commanding the 2nd United States Dragoons.

He would love Flora devotedly for the balance of his life, and his capacity for love was great, and often generously spread. He would gladly have clobbered or captured his father-in-law at any time during the Civil War, tried hard enough, and almost succeeded.

Even before Virginia left the Union in mid-April 1861, Stuart applied to Jefferson Davis "as one likely to exercise a large control in the organization of the Army of the South." He wanted "a position in that Army," and gave as references Robert E. Lee, Joe Johnston, and (knowing no better at the time) his father-in-law Colonel Cooke. Four months later, having resigned from the U.S. Army, he was commissioned a lieutenant colonel in the forces of Colonel Thomas Jackson, stationed then at Harpers Ferry.

When Joe Johnston superseded Jackson, Stuart was given command of the 1st Virginia Cavalry, composed of a number of volunteer companies, such as the Washington Rifles under W.E. "Grumble" Jones. It was a perfect marriage. Six years of campaigning in the West had rounded out his character and frame. From the undistinguished chin there now flowed a distinguished russet-colored beard, and above it a scimitar-shaped mustache of similar hue, described poetically as "flaming." His eyes were a bright and piercing blue. A lofty forehead and Roman nose gave him the air of a Gallic gladiator, and his booming voice, in speech and song, had the resonance of beaten bronze.

He was every inch the cavalier *par excellence*. And he dressed the part as well, with an extravagant fondness for color and show. The sweeping cape worn over his double-breasted jacket was lined with scarlet. Around his waist curved a yellow sash, tied at the sides with golden tassels. The brim of his soft felt hat, worn slightly atilt, was pinned to one side by a star that held the proverbial ostrich plume. From his sash, within reach of the elbow-length gauntlets, hung a curved French saber. On his boots were gold spurs, suitable for battle or ballroom; and in his buttonhole always a rose, given him, more often than not, by some female admirer.

More than his appearance, however, was a temperament eminently suited to his calling. To Stuart, according to his aide John Esten Cooke, war "seemed to be a splendid and exciting game, in which his blood coursed joyously. . . . A single look at him was enough to convince anybody that Stuart loved danger and adventure, and that the clear blue eye of the soldier, 'with a frolic welcome took the thunder and the sunshine.' " When action impended:

> He swung himself into the saddle, at the sound of the bugle, as the hunter springs on horseback; and at such moments his cheeks glowed, and his huge mustache curled with enjoyment. The romance and poetry of the hard trade of arms seemed first to be inaugurated when this joyous cavalier, with his floating plume and splendid laughter, appeared upon the great arena of the war in Virginia.

The 1st Virginia, nucleus of what would become one of the more famous cavalry units of the Civil War, was an undermanned regiment of some 300 volunteers. It was, like so many of the early companies, a *corps élite* composed of the blue bloods of Virginia aristocracy— "beautiful, high-bred young men, in fine linen and high stocks," mounted on beautiful, high-bred horses and attended by their personal black servants. Stuart considered them pretty good officer material. Given time, he could break down their hauteur and vanity and turn them into soldiers.

But there was not much time to get the regiment in shape. There was never enough time in the late spring of 1861; impatience rode the soft winds like a pestilence. While the Virginia cavalry chafed like quarter horses at the starting gate, Stuart drilled his troopers mercilessly, changing them from gentlemen equestrians to deadly cossacks. And when Federal troops began to cross the Potomac, to establish a bridgehead for invasion, this training took the form of death-defying exercises.

Discovering the location of a Union battery mounted on a hill, he invited his troops to join him in "some fun," and led them in a wild charge almost to the muzzles of the guns. As they circled back, he halted them, within tantalizing range of the still flaming battery, and lectured them like schoolboys.

"You see?" he said. "Cannon! They make a lot of noise, but they always fire too high."

Then, another maxim to remember: "Always gallop toward the enemy. Trot away."

The inference was clear. When you galloped toward the enemy, you could afford to trot away. Because you left no enemy behind you.

As the invasion threat increased in early June, Johnston pulled his army back to Winchester, a little way up the Valley, and Union General Robert Patterson led a Federal force into Harpers Ferry. Farther east at Manassas Junction, on what the Confederates called the "Alexandria line," General Pierre Gustave Toutant Beauregard's 20,000–22,000 troops guarded that key point on the route to Richmond.

In response to the demanding cry of "Forward to Richmond!" the Union leaders conceived a master plan. Patterson would keep Joe Johnston pinned down in the Shenandoah Valley, while the main Federal army under General Irvin McDowell would move from Arlington Heights to Manassas Junction to overwhelm Beauregard with a numerical superiority of nearly two to one, provided Johnston was kept from joining his Creole ally.

President Davis and his staff had the same plan in reverse. Johnston would see to it that Patterson was pinned down around Harpers Ferry while he moved east to join with Beauregard in presenting, with his added army of 10,000 men, a united front to the Union forces moving on Manassas Junction. And who would do the pinning down?—Jeb Stuart's cavalry, with an assist from Turner Ashby's rangers and any other volunteer companies available.

Seeing Turner Ashby's name in reports of this operation revives a problem all too common in the cavalry: conflict of temperament and personality. One can assume that Ashby and Stuart were very much alike, both peerless horsemen, brilliant, brave beyond a doubt, with pride in prerogative and fiercely independent. What a team they would have made! But two such men cannot be placed in joint command, nor can one be made subservient to the other.

So that when Stuart became Jackson's chief of cavalry, Ashby refused to submit to this new command, and offered to resign. The problem was resolved by forming a second regiment under Angus MacDonald. Ashby served in this second unit, at the head of his own company.

Now, however, all worked together in screening Johnston's withdrawal from the Shenandoah Valley. Raise plenty of noise, Johnston instructed Stuart; make Patterson think that there are a lot more of you than a single regiment. And deception became the name of the game, with less than a thousand troopers to intimidate a Federal army of more than 18,000.

Stuart used every trick in the book, and added others. Spacing his cavalry in single file, he rode them back and forth and in and out, in sight of Patterson's outposts, each rider dragging a broken branch behind him, to add to the dust kicked up by horses' hooves. Bugles sounded, men hallooed, the valley echoed with the din of small-arms fire. At night, enough campfires blazed to cheer the armies of Napoleon.

The grand charade was properly effective. Patterson, urged by his superiors to take the offensive, reported to Washington that he faced an enemy of 35,000 or more, and "it would be ruinous to advance, or even to stay here, without immediate increase of force." He stayed there; while Johnston sneaked his army, unit by unit, down to Manassas Junction to join Beauregard. As soon as the last of the infantry had left, Stuart followed with the 1st Virginia Cavalry, leaving Turner Ashby and others to keep Patterson in check at Harpers Ferry.

Sunday, July 21. Sunny and warm, and, except for the dust, a perfect day for a picnic or a pageant. Down from Washington came the congressmen and their wives, the newspaper correspondents, the photographers with their curtained wagons, the sightseers with their buggies and blankets and picnic baskets. They congregated on the high ground overlooking Bull Run, in anticipation of the spectacle, for here was to be staged the greatest battle ever witnessed in the western hemisphere.

There was little doubt about the outcome. For General McDowell had brought a mighty army to Manassas Junction, 38,000 strong, to smother Beauregard's meager force of 23,000—and Patterson would surely see to it that Johnston sent no reinforcements from the Valley. Most of Johnston's infantry, however, was already there or on the way, and Stuart's cavalry was in position.

Stuart's 1st Virginian Cavalry was stationed in reserve on the Confederate right, west of Bull Run Creek, where the infantry of Generals Richard S. Ewell and Theophilus Holmes guarded against a flank attack. A flank attack was precisely what McDowell had planned—on the opposite end of the line however, and with no knowledge of Johnston's arrival from the Valley. Beauregard had a similar design in mind, to swing around the Union left and come at McDowell from his rear.

Thus the two armies might have pinwheeled inconclusively upon a common center, had not McDowell got the jump on the Confederates and launched his attack while Beauregard was still preparing. So that initially the Federal forces were successful, crossing Bull Run at Sudley's Ford and driving back the men in gray, until by noon a Union victory seemed certain.

By midafternoon, however, the green and ill-conditioned Yankees had run out of steam; and several hours after General Edward Bee had rallied the Confederates with his premonitory cry, "See Jackson standing like a stone wall!" they recoiled from that collision like a wave rebounding from a cliff—and Stuart with the 1st Virginia Cavalry charged into the melee.

They clashed first with a column of New York Fire Zouaves whose crimson coats and turbans Stuart mistook for the similar uniform of the Louisiana Tigers. Seeing them coming from the opposite direction and assuming they were fleeing, Stuart shouted, "Don't run, boys! We're here!"

The Zouaves knelt and opened fire. Eleven horses screamed and reared, and nine men toppled from their saddles. Shocked by his error, Stuart signaled the Black Horse Troop to charge. Thunder of hooves, death rattle of carbines, and the flash of sabers slashing at the turbaned heads. The Zouaves unable to escape were cut to ribbons. A newspaper correspondent on the scene—noting with what terror the Federals reacted to the charge of the Black Horse Troop—believed that here originated the enduring myth that all Confederate cavalry rode mounts the color of the ace of spades, a mortal omen in itself.

By now the Stone Bridge and the several fords of Bull Run were spillways turned blue with the retreating Federals. A correspondent for the New York *World*, uncertain "whether we had won or lost," reported, "The question was quickly decided for us. A sudden swoop, and a body of cavalry rushed down upon our columns near the Bridge." John Imboden, commanding a Confederate battery, was equally certain of the outcome when he saw that "Colonel J. E. B. Stuart, at the head of a body of yelling cavalry, was sweeping around the base of the hill we were on, to cross the run and fall upon the enemy."

Thus it might be said that Stuart's cavalry played a vital role in that first major battle of the war. But the impression would be false. Though adding greatly to the terror and confusion of the Union rout, it was Jackson's stand and the infantry's response that blunted and shattered the Federal attack. Though the mounted Virginians continued their pursuit for some miles down the Warrenton Turnpike— behind the chaotic column of soldiers, officers, and terrified sightseers fleeing back to Washington—it was after that a matter of rounding up and guarding the 1,400 prisoners taken in the final hours of the fight.

But if they had played no major and decisive role, a psychological effect had been achieved and one that would operate in East and West to the detriment of Federal morale. To the men in blue, the Confederate cavalry had registered as deadly, swift, and irresistible. Its sting was mortal; the Union cavalry, for now at any rate, could not compare. And it was at First Manassas that the terrifying cry of "Black Horse!" was first raised, to be applied to Confederate horsemen everywhere regardless of the color of their mounts.

The engagement also affected Stuart's career. The service his cavalry had rendered in screening Johnston's withdrawal from the Valley and holding Patterson in check, greatly impressed the general, as Stuart himself admired Johnston ("the dearest friend I have on earth . . . head and shoulders above every other general in the Southern Confederacy . . ."). "Little Joe" had already seen Stuart raised to the rank of colonel; only Jefferson Davis and the Confederate Congress could lift him higher.

Accordingly, three weeks after Bull Run or First Manassas—as the North and South, respectively, called the battle—Johnston wrote to the President urging that Stuart be again promoted:

> He is a rare man, wonderfully endowed by nature with the qualities necessary for an officer of light cavalry. Calm, firm, acute, and enterprising, I know no one more competent than he to estimate the occurrences before him at their true value. If you add a real brigade of cavalry to this army, you can find no better brigadier-general to command it.

His commission came through on September 24, 1861: James Ewell Brown Stuart, brigadier general of cavalry. Grumble Jones succeeded him as colonel of the 1st Virginia. Five more regiments made up the brigade, among them the 4th Virginia with its famous Black Horse Troop, hitherto not directly under his command; the 2nd and 6th Virginia; the Jeff Davis Legion of Mississippians, Alabamans, and Georgians; and the 1st North Carolina under Colonel Robert Ransom.

They aggregated less than 2,000, but to Stuart they made up in quality what they lacked in quantity. "We must substitute *esprit* for numbers," he wrote to his brother William Alexander, adding, "It is considered the handsomest command in the service."

The pride was reciprocated. The troopers began cultivating whiskers similar to the general's—a difficult feat for some of the younger men. They aped their commander's style of dress, added color to their uniforms and feathers to their caps, chicken feathers if they could not get an ostrich plume. And his aides presented him with a handsome charger, named Star of the East, which prompted him to write to Flora, "I am now better mounted than any general in the army."

For his staff he picked men who would later make brigade commanders, stealing them from other units if he had to. From Johnston's staff came Fitzhugh Lee, nephew of the general, who had been with Stuart at West Point. Along with "Fitz" Lee came one of Lee's lifelong friends, Lunsford Lindsay Lomax, who had served with Stuart in the West. And later, from the Washington Artillery, came young Thomas Rosser, a Texan just out of the Academy who was good with guns and horses both.

A brigade, felt Stuart, was entitled to a battery, and he added this Civil War innovation to his cavalry. In November of 1861 he formed the Stuart Horse Artillery, a light three-gun battery commanded by Lieutenant John Pelham whom Stuart enticed from the regular army. While Stuart is often given credit for this innovation, widely accepted by the Southern cavalry, he was not the first commander to adopt it. Some weeks earlier Turner Ashby had conceived and formed a similar unit for his wide-roving rangers, captained by R. Preston Chew, late of Virginia Military Institute.

There was nothing new about horse-drawn artillery accompanied by mounted gunners. But these fast, mobile batteries were altogether new. The guns and carriages were light, the horses fleet. They could turn on a dime, keep pace with a charge, or cover a retreat. They added an extra dimension to the saber-wielding, carbine-carrying Virginia cavalry.

Throughout the late fall the brigade encamped near Fairfax, fifteen miles west of Washington and the Potomac, and in sight of Union pickets guarding Arlington and Alexandria. Stuart's adjutant, John Esten Cooke, declared that the colonel's motto should be *joie de vivre*, and so the bivouac was christened "Camp Qui Vive" and lived up to the motto. Though Stuart maintained discipline, patrolling every road in the vicinity, the nights were generally for relaxation.

From a minstrel troupe stranded by the war in Richmond, Stuart imported Sam Sweeny, a banjo player dear to the colonel's heart. Sweeny's music brought the local belles to camp to dance with the officers; and around the campfires at night Sweeny led the troops in singing the lilting Southern favorites, "Listen to the Mocking Bird," "Sweet Evalina," "The Old Gray Horse," and "If You Want to Have a Good Time, Jine the Cavalry."

In this good-humored atmosphere the troopers began calling their commander "Jeb," eliding the initials of his name, and Jeb he would be for all time left to him. His faithful devotion to Flora did not preclude a liking for the ladies, very much reciprocated. They came to the camp from as far away as Maryland, bearing gifts for the troops and once a fine spy glass for the commander. And the camp in turn provided generously for its guests, keeping a festive open house, staging mock battles and dress parades, and making the visitors feel that their very presence and participation were helping win the war. Wrote Virginia-born Constance Cary Harrison of one such occasion:

> Then were the gala days of war, and our proud hosts hastened to produce home dainties dispatched from the far-away plantations — tears and blessings interspersed amid the packing, we were sure; though I have seen a pretty girl persist in declining other fare, to make her meal upon raw biscuit and huckleberry pie compounded by the bright-eyed amateur cook of a well-beloved mess. Feminine heroism could no farther go.

The local belles were generally staunch rebels, but not above keeping company with Union officers one night, and Confederates the next. Thus flexible, they provided Stuart with useful information: Colonel William Averell's 3rd Pennsylvania Cavalry was camped on the Warrenton Pike; a Federal troop train had arrived at Alexandria. He rewarded these lovely Mata Haris with commissions as "Honorary Aide-de-Camp," supplying them with parchment certificates, signed and witnessed, and sealed with the impression of his signet ring.

He was, wrote the worshipful John Esten Cooke, "the gayest of companions; full of fun, frolic, laughter, hope, buoyance, and a certain youthful joyousness which made his presence like the sunshine. . . . The war was evidently like play to him — and he accepted its hardships with the careless abandon of a young knight-errant seeking adventure." He was able to joke with the troops and they with him, on rough and equal terms. They followed him by inspiration, not by order. "Jeb never says to us, 'Go on!' What he says is 'Come on, boys!' He leads us — he don't send us."

Even in camp diversions he did everything, as he wrote to his brother, William Alexander, to "inculcate the spirit of the chase" in his command. A simple horse race was not enough; it needed an element of risk to give it zest. The thing to do was to hold the race close to the Federal picket line, so that riders sought to outstrip both competitors and bullets. On one such steeplechase, when the openmouthed blue jackets fired wildly at them, Stuart returned to camp with his companion, exhilarated but inquisitive. "What do you suppose our time was for that distance," he inquired.

Any form of military action, any challenge, offered a promise of excitement and diversion. From a Union camp across the strip of no man's land, near Washington, came a taunting invitation from cavalry Captain Orlando Poe, a comrade of Stuart's at West Point:

"My Dear Beauty: I am sorry the circumstances are such that I can't have the pleasure of seeing you, although so near you." Poe suggested that they meet for dinner at Willard's Hotel in Washington the following Saturday night at five o'clock. He urged Stuart meanwhile to "keep your Black Horse off me, if you please."

Stuart accepted the offer with zest, and somewhat earlier than Poe expected. The following day, with the banjo-strumming Sweeny by his side, he led a detachment of singing cavalry in a raid on Poe's camp, scattered the Federal horsemen "to at least three quarters of the compass," and sent Poe's message of invitation to Johnston's headquarters with the notation: "From the manner in which Captain Poe left here, he was going in to get that dinner without waiting for Saturday night."

There was only one incident of serious fighting by the troops at Camp Qui Vive that year. As winter approached, the question of forage became severe for the cavalry and horse artillery of both sides. Stuart was called upon to guard a wagon train sent out from Centerville, where Johnston's army was encamped, to collect fodder and forage in the fertile farmland around the hamlet of Dranesville, south of the Potomac. For this mission, he was placed in command of 1,450 infantry, plus his own detachment of 150 cavalry.

On that same day, December 20, fate decreed that Union General E. O. C. Ord should have the same idea. Ord was also informed of Confederates in the vicinity, and dispatched three brigades of Pennsylvania infantry to get there first, drive off the Southerners, and appropriate the forage for themselves.

Stuart would learn an important lesson from the impending clash. He should have scouted the area more thoroughly before he let the wagon train advance. As it was, the train and its escort rolled into a nest of blue-clad riflemen, 6,000 strong, who emerged from concealment to block their approach. Though outnumbered more than two to one, there was only one thing to do—what Stuart always did—attack first. Two hours of fierce fighting saved the wagon train, and enabled Stuart to withdraw in reasonable order; but it cost him 194 men compared with the enemy's 68, losses that he acknowledged as "severe."

In writing to Flora of the engagement, the first battle he had seen since Manassas, he exaggerated the enemy's numbers as "4 times larger than mine" and concluded that "our side therefore came out first best." He added: "I was never in greater personal danger & men & horses fell around me like ten-pins, but thanks to God to whom I looked for protection, neither myself nor my horse was touched."

Stuart's seeming immunity to bullets would become a legend. He seemed to bear a magic life. "It was hard to realize," wrote John Esten Cooke,

> that death could ever come to him; and the perilous positions from which he so often escaped unharmed, appeared to justify the idea of

his invulnerability. Although he exposed his person recklessly in more than a hundred hot engagements, he was never wounded in any. . . . Death appeared to shrink before him and avoid him; and he laughed in the grim face, and dared it for three years of reckless fighting, in which he seemed every day to be trying to get himself killed.

Cooke sentimentally suggested that perhaps it was the rosebud in his buttonhole, given him by some admirer as he rode to battle, that protected him. Or perhaps the Bible, always carried in his jacket—for indeed a large number of Confederates throughout the war were known to survive from "Testament wounds," or bullets that had been stopped by Bibles carried in their breast pockets.

The unhappy affair at Dranesville threw no lasting pall of gloom on Camp Qui Vive. To boost morale, and occupy the winter months, Stuart held numerous brigade reviews, for which horses were groomed to a brilliant sheen, boots and sabers polished, dress uniforms exhibited. Of one of these he wrote to Flora, "It meant extra work, but it appealed to the men's pride . . . it went off splendidly, all hands seemed delighted. All the Generals were out to witness them, & expressed themselves highly gratified."

His wife came to visit him that Christmas with the children, little Flora and her brother. The boy had been christened Philip after Flora's father, Colonel Cooke; but the way things had worked out, with Cooke commanding a Union brigade in the Washington defenses, it was felt mandatory to change the name to James Ewell Brown, Jr.

After the holidays Stuart moved his family to a house in nearby Warrenton, and though he devoted every available moment to their company, for Flora it was not enough. Perhaps she was jealous of his zest for military life, for he felt obliged to explain to William, "I have told her that if I neglect the higher duties of the patriot to be a daily companion to her, I would make a husband to be ashamed of hereafter."

During the winter months the camp near Manassas settled down to tedious routine, and Stuart and his staff and officers debated what might lie ahead. In the East, the first year of the war had been a good year for the Confederacy, one of frustration for the Union. But now George B. McClellan was General-in-Chief of Union forces, succeeding Winfield Scott, and McClellan was raising and training his Army of the Potomac, more than 100,000 strong, near Washington. From what direction would he eventually strike and toward what goal? Stuart believed he knew the answer: Between the James and York rivers, the southern peninsula offered the most likely route to Richmond.

"I think we shall hear from him there, come spring," Stuart told his staff.

3

HELLION ON HORSEBACK

WILLIAM TECUMSEH SHERMAN, OFTEN THE HARSHEST AND FAIREST OF critics, called him "that devil Forrest," and elaborated with less printable phrases. Yet after the tumult and the shouting died, the Union general declared that Forrest was "the most remarkable man our Civil War produced on either side," while Sherman's superior Ulysses S. Grant, pronounced him "about the ablest general in the South."

So much for the opinions of his enemies. But what of his friends, and more particularly those who rode with "Old Bedford" throughout four long years of war?

It is easy to admire, even to love, one who leads you to repeated victories and glory. The test comes at the moment of disaster. And in the retreat of Forrest's cavalry from Middle Tennessee, before the end came, a private in the ranks observed the bone-weary general turn his horse over to a barefoot soldier, borrow a lesser mount, and ride down the line with words of encouragement to each and every man of his defeated corps. "On that day," the private remembered, "he rode into my heart as well . . . and rides there still."

Loved, hated, feared, admired, Nathan Bedford Forrest was perhaps the most controversial figure in the wartime cavalry, and surely one of the most complex. Yet he came from the humblest, least pretentious of beginnings.

He was born in 1821 in Bedford County, Tennessee, from which he got his middle name. In the background was a great-grandfather, Shadrach Forrest of Virginia, who started the family's migration from

North Carolina west to Mississippi and then Tennessee. Bedford's father William was a blacksmith, an honorable trade on the frontier, but his early death left the teen-age son to provide for six brothers, four sisters, and a mother, cutting short his rudimentary education.

Perhaps it was this need to fight for everything the family possessed, including the crude log cabin in the wilderness, that gave young Forrest his fierce sense of competition. There was not much chance at first to do more than clear the land and raise crops for survival, working at night to make buckskin clothing for the children. But once he had the family on a solid footing, he went out on his own—to Hernando, Mississippi, and then Memphis—to make his fortune as a trader in cotton and tobacco, slaves and cattle.

Later he added real estate to his commercial ventures, accumulating three thousand acres of plantation land in Mississippi, planted principally to cotton. He was not ruthless in his dealings, but his wrath was quick. In a gun fight that led to the killing of his uncle, Bedford's partner at the time, Forrest tracked down the four assassins, wounded two and forced the other two to flee. With similar boldness, he rescued the innocent target of a lynch mob, singlehandedly holding the crowd at bay until the victim could be delivered to the law.

He was twenty-four when he accidentally met his future wife, Mary Ann Montgomery, whose carriage was mired in a creek, resisting the Negro driver's efforts to release it while two local gallants simply stood by in amusement. Forrest, in his Sunday best, plunged through the creek and carried the lady to firmer ground. Not long after he had seen her safely home, he had made up his mind to propose to Mary Ann and before long she accepted.

Happily married, wealthy, elected to the board of aldermen in Memphis, Forrest had much to sacrifice when the war broke out in 1861. He would later write that he went to war as a millionaire and returned a pauper. It was not war damage alone that stripped him of everything he owned, but the fact that, like Wade Hampton of South Carolina, he spent much of his fortune in providing horses, arms, equipment, and provisions to the men he led to battle.

There is a natural inclination to compare Forrest, the Westerner, with Hampton of South Carolina. By 1861 both had reached or passed the age of forty; both were extremely well-to-do and independent; both had married well, were fathers of families; owned land and slaves, and served their communities in public office. Neither had had any military experience, though while Hampton had had a liberal education, Forrest had had none at all, and could only spell phonetically.

Their principal differences, however, arose from the background and social climates of the East and West. Though both men were essentially of pioneer stock, in the sense that their Scotch-Irish-English ancestry had carved a new life in a new world, Bedford Forrest, disdainful of status and privilege, stuck to the rough manners of the frontier—light years away from the cultured refinement and *noblesse oblige* of South Carolina aristocracy.

Their attitude toward the war was different, a sacred duty for Hampton, a stirring adventure for Forrest. And geographically the war itself was different. In Virginia the fighting, for want of a better word, was "tidy." The battle lines were clearly drawn, the issues well defined. West Point generals faced West Point generals to fight for precise small zones marked out, as on a playing field, between the symbolic goal posts of their capitals at Washington and Richmond.

West of the Appalachians, overlooking for the moment the Trans-Mississippi, it was a wide-ranging, sprawling war, as devious as the Western rivers. There was no single arena, and no clear-cut and unshifting goals, beyond the general objective of gaining control of the Mississippi River. The people themselves were ambivalent in their emotions, with Kentucky and Missouri symbols of that ambivalence. Hostility was often more local than national, often an exercise of personal grudges, more concerned with family feuds, states' rights, and social jealousies. And the land itself was an untidy land of forests, prairies, mountains, swamps, and rivers, the latter both barriers and highways governing the conduct of the war.

So the role of the cavalry would be different, too. The quick, decisive saber charge as part of the Eastern strategy of battle, and the close cooperation between mounted troops and infantry, was less important in the West than the long raids, more often called "expeditions," into enemy-held territories for purposes of plunder, terrorism, and destruction.

Mobilization was immediate. In June of 1861, when his was the last state to secede from the Union, Forrest sought to enlist in Memphis as a private in the Tennessee Mounted Rifles. His reputation, like Wade Hampton's, virtually excluded his acceptance as a lowly private. According to John Allen Wyeth, whose regiment later served under the Tennesseean, "Forrest's high character as a man of probity and courage, his success in business, and the position he had obtained in Memphis were too well known to permit him to remain in the ranks." Governor Isham Harris, conferring with General Leonidas Polk, obtained authorization for Forrest to raise a battalion of cavalry with himself as colonel.

It would have been hard to accord him anything less. He was, said one of his colleagues, a natural fighter as others were natural poets or artists. And his appearance, his manner, his commanding presence, could not be easily overlooked—by either friend or enemy. As one of his antagonists, Byran McAllister, recorded, "Forrest was a man of fine appearance, having piercing eyes, carefully trimmed mustache and chin-whiskers, dark as night, with finely cut features and iron-gray hair. His form was lithe, plainly indicating great physical power and activity."

Colonel George W. Adair of Atlanta, one of Bedford's more intimate friends, wrote of Forrest: "He was more than six feet high, well proportioned, with hands tapering like those of a woman, small feet, exceedingly graceful in his movements, a swarthy complexion, and a look of the eye that indicated absolute fear of nothing." Others noted his fierceness of expression, and a face that turned crimson when pricked by anger.

Yet his habits were civilized and temperate. He neither smoked nor drank, and he was deeply though not patently religious. No preachers rode with his regiments except as officers or soldiers; but when a Federal army chaplain was captured on a raiding expedition, Forrest invited the man of God to sit with him and his officers at dinner and invoke a blessing on the meal. Later, before returning the chaplain to the Union ranks, he told him, "Parson, I would keep you here to preach for me if you were not needed so much more by the sinners on the other side."

He set about at once to garner recruits for his battalion. At the time that Wade Hampton was mustering his Legionnaires through the columns of the Charleston *Courier*, the Memphis *Daily Appeal* published Forrest's call for "five hundred able-bodied men, mounted and equipped with such arms as they can procure (shot-guns and pistols preferable), suitable to the service. Those who cannot entirely equip themselves will be furnished arms by the State." The *Appeal* supported the notice in its editorial columns:

> To Arms! We invite attention to the call of Col. N. B. Forrest in today's paper. There are still hundreds of young men in the country anxious to engage in the military service. Those whose fancy inclines them to the cavalry service will find no better opportunity to enlist under a bold, capable and efficient commander. Now is the time.

Despite his promise that arms would be furnished by the state, Forrest himself would have to purchase most of the pistols, shotguns, carbines, saddles, and other equipment with money of his own. Leaving Captain David C. Kelley, an early volunteer who had been a preacher in civilian life, to handle recruitment in Memphis, Forrest traveled to Kentucky on a buying spree while agents traveled through northern Alabama, Mississippi, West and Middle Tennessee to enlist recruits. He sometimes had to smuggle his purchases by camouflaged wagon back through pro-Union territory. He also collected volunteers.

In one Louisville livery stable, six teenage youngsters who helped to load the wagon climbed on top of the cargo to ride back to Memphis as recruits.

Back in that city in August he found that Kelley had welcomed more support than called for: eight independent companies, which had ridden in from Alabama, Kentucky, Tennessee, and Texas, numbering 650 eager, ambitious Westerners. They were, according to railroad president Sam Tate, "as fine a body of men as ever went to the field," and Tate wrote to Western commander Albert Sidney Johnson, "Give Forrest a chance and he will distinguish himself."

General A. S. Johnson, commander of the Confederate armies in the West, had a long frontier to guard, made more precarious when Kentucky sided with the Union. At his disposal were some 45,000 troops to defend a line that stretched 700 miles from Cumberland Gap to the Mississippi, and an almost equal distance on beyond that river into the Indian Territory.

Union forces held the mouths of two key rivers, the Tennessee and Cumberland, thrusting like a forked tongue into the heart of the Confederacy; and at Paducah, Union forces were assembling to spearhead the first great Federal invasion of Confederate territory in the West.

Only two small bastions of resistance blocked that threat: Fort Henry on the Tennessee and Fort Donelson on the Cumberland, both close to the Kentucky border, both incomplete and undergunned as well as under manned. Johnson rushed these to completion, better to guard the gateway to the Southern heartland, and Forrest's battalion was ordered to patrol the vulnerable area between the Cumberland and Green rivers, with Bowling Green one of the few remaining Confederate bases in Kentucky.

It was on this patrol that Forrest's scouts brought news of the Federal gunboat *Conestoga* operating on the Cumberland, raiding Confederate depots some miles west of the Confederate camp. Forrest led his battalion on an all-night march to Canton, likely target for the Union raider, and positioned his troops in ambush above and below the landing. When the *Conestoga* appeared at Canton the dismounted troopers hid behind trees and, supported by a small detachment of artillery, "fired at the open portholes of the gunboat with such effect that she was compelled, after a few hours, to close them, up-anchor and steam down the Cumberland—amid the jubilation of Forrest's men."

It was a little like Jeb Stuart's exposure of his cavalry to the guns of Federal batteries near Fairfax. Though the action was insignificant in itself, it served to overcome a psychological impediment. The gunboats were something of a secret weapon in the Federal armament, feared by the Confederates as much as the Southern cavalry was feared by the Union rank and file. The encounter with the *Conestoga* helped to squelch that bugaboo; and it also gave Forrest's troopers a foretaste of future expeditions in the West.

After the Canton affair Forrest pulled his troops back to Hopkinsville, where they set about building huts and erecting shelters for the winter. Here Adam Johnson, a hard-riding Texan, joined the regiment and found "the whole command very comfortably fixed with good floored tents and good beds, and the commissary department most abundantly supplied." Forrest's wife and his young son Willie, now a private in the Rangers, were spending the Christmas holidays in the commander's private tent. Johnson himself would not be with them long; he was destined in a few more months to serve with another western cavalier, considered by some the equivalent of Forrest, John Hunt Morgan.

The winter bivouac was aroused when Forrest's scouts reported a Federal advance to the Green River, fifty miles north of Hopkinsville. The bugle sounded "Boots and Saddles" and Forrest led his regiment, 300 strong, at a fast pace toward Sacramento. When advance scouts reported that a column of 500 Federal troops was just outside the village, Forrest ordered his regiment forward at a gallop, to which the troops responded with "jubilant and defiant shouts, which reached the height of enthusiasm as the women from the houses waved us forward."

In this exhilarating spurt toward battle they were joined by the sort of rebel Joan of Arc that was frequently encountered by the cavalry. According to John Allen Wyeth, later Forrest's biographer, as they neared Sacramento, the regiment:

> was augmented by an unexpected volunteer in the person of a Kentucky belle, who, mounted on a magnificent horse, with more enthusiasm than discretion, galloped by his side and cheered him and his soldiers on to the conflict. The gallant *sabreur* so far forgot the strict business of his official report as to embody in that document the acknowledgment that "her untied tresses, floating in the breeze, infused nerve into my arm and kindled Knightly chivalry in my heart."

He recovered his military sense as he approached the enemy deployed across the road below Sacramento. Outnumbered three to two, he resorted to a tactic that would become his trademark—keeping half his cavalry on the enemy's front, he sent two detachments, right and left, to descend upon the Union flanks. It worked like a miracle. On hearing shots from the flanking parties, signaling that the wings were in position, Forrest rose in the saddle, waved his saber, and gave the order, "Charge! Charge!"

The men followed him without formation, in a hell-for-leather race to keep up with their leader who, according to Wyeth, " standing up in his stirrups, his saber in the left hand, looked a foot taller than any of his men." And from the woods on both sides of the enemy, the flanking columns tore into the Union ranks. The results were recorded in Forrest's report:

> The enemy . . . broke in utter confusion, and, in spite of the efforts of a few officers, commenced a disorderly flight at full speed, in which the officers soon joined. We pressed closely on their rear, only getting an occasional shot, until we reached the village of Sacramento, when, the best mounted men of my companies coming up, there commenced a promiscuous saber slaughter of their rear, which was continued at almost full speed for 2 miles beyond the village, leaving their bleeding and wounded strewn along the whole route.

Perhaps innate modesty prevented the colonel from recounting his own deeds in the affair. During the final melee he was attacked by three men at once, a private and two officers. He shot the private, swung around and sabered the officer on his front, then turned and shot the other pouncing on him from behind. By that time, another officer had joined the fight. Forrest charged him head-on and knocked him from his horse, at which point his own horse reared, pitching him twenty feet through the air and landing him with a dislocated shoulder.

It was the colonel's first taste of blood, and he would sample it voraciously in years to come. There is no official count of the number of foes who fell to his saber thrust or pistol shot. Wyeth claimed, however, that "he placed *hors de combat* thirty Federal officers or soldiers fighting hand to hand"; while Confederate General Richard Taylor, with whom he would later serve, observed, "I doubt if any commander since the days of the lionhearted Richard killed as many enemies with his own hand as Forrest."

Sacramento was a small affair, yet General Charles Clark, commander at Hopkinsville, officially reported, "It was one of the most brilliant and successful cavalry engagements that the present war has witnessed, and gives a favorable omen of what that arm of the service will do in the future on a more extended scale."

And there were side benefits to the encounter. Except for the engagement with the *Conestoga*, it was the first test of the troops in action, and their first chance to observe their leader under battle stress. They noticed his fierce primeval expression as the blood rushed to his face from the excitement, the wild look in his eyes, the impetuous recklessness with which he rode to the attack. "It seemed certain," wrote his subordinate, Captain Kelley, "that whenever he should meet a skilful opponent his command would be utterly cut to pieces." And Kelley noted:

> So fierce did his passion become that he was almost equally danger-
> ous to friend or foe, and, as it seemed to some of us, he was too wildly
> excitable to be capable of judicious command. Later we became aware
> that excitement neither paralyzed nor misled his magnificent military
> genius.

Kelley found in all of this a lesson: "In the short period since its organization, this command found that it was his single will, impervi-ous to argument, appeal, or threat, which was ever to be the governing impulse in their movements." They were Forrest's men, and there was nothing bigger in the world than that. Wherever he led them, they would go, come hell or high water; and in the postwar years there would be no prouder boast than: "Me, I rode with Old Bedford!"

In February 1862, under Grant's direction, Flag Officer Andrew H. Foote's gunboat flotilla started up the Tennessee, imperilling Fort Henry guarding the approaches to the Southern base at Nashville. Grant, with twenty-three regiments of infantry, several batteries of artillery, and assorted cavalry, planned to spearhead the attack. He made his purpose plain in a dispatch to Major General Henry W. Halleck, "I will take Fort Henry, on the Tennessee, and establish and hold a large camp there."

Grant would not need his infantry and artillery. General Lloyd Tilghman, holding Fort Henry with 3,400 men and 16 antiquated guns, was a realist. When the seven gunboats appeared on February 6, bringing their concentrated fire to bear upon the fort, Tilghman sent his garrison across the twelve miles of intervening land to Fort Donel-son, while he and a handful of artillerists covered their withdrawal. Then he surrendered. Grant wired Halleck, "Fort Henry is ours. I shall take and destroy Fort Donelson on the 8th. . . ."

Confederate troops were rushed to Donelson, raising the fort's gar-rison to 17,500, and Sidney Johnson sent three brigadier generals— Gideon Pillow, Simon Buckner, and John Floyd—to take command. As the senior, Floyd was in charge of the defense. At the same time General Clark sent Bedford Forrest, whose "dashing affair" at Sac-ramento he had noted, to take command of all Confederate cavalry at Donelson, with Forrest's own regiment and four additional companies of Tennesseeans and Kentuckians.

Johnson had no great hope that Donelson could stand for long. Hard pressed in Kentucky by Union forces under Don Carlos Buell, he planned to abandon his bases at Hopkinsville and Bowling Green and concentrate his troops at Nashville, a principal Southern depot and capital of Tennessee. His hope, as he told his generals at Fort Donelson, was that they could keep Grant and Foote at bay long enough to cover his withdrawal from Kentucky.

Foote's gunboat flotilla, circling down the Tennessee and up the Cumberland, arrived opposite Donelson on February 13. Meanwhile, Grant's troops from Fort Henry moved overland toward the fort. Forrest's cavalry rode out to meet them and delay their progress. After five hours of skirmishing against superior numbers, Forrest reported, "The enemy . . . did not move to the attack that day, satisfying themselves with planting a few cannon and commencing at long range a slow cannonade."

Foote's flotilla was also in action, bombarding Donelson with more than fifty guns, and receiving fire from the smaller guns within the fort. Watching this duel, Forrest turned to the former pastor, Captain Kelley, and pleaded, "Parson, for God's sake pray! Nothing but God Almighty can save that fort!" But his spirits lifted as three of the four gunboats, and then finally the fourth, were forced to withdraw by superior Confederate marksmanship. "More determination could not have been exhibited by the attacking party, while more coolness and bravery never was manifested than was seen in our artillerists."

Despite this initial success the generals commanding the fort held a grave council of war that night. Grant's 27,000 infantry and artillery had them pinned against the river, with Foote's gunboats just downstream. Word had come from Johnson that Confederate forces had successfully withdrawn to Nashville. Donelson had served its purpose. It was time to abandon the stronghold and, with the garrison intact, withdraw to the rendezvous at Nashville.

To do this, however, meant breaking the iron ring which Grant had thrown around the fort, and this would be a job for Pillow's and Buckner's troops with the help of Forrest's cavalry. Pillow would advance against the Federal right, southeast of the fort, pushing back the Union line like opening a door, and clearing the principal roads to Nashville. Forrest's cavalry would support the attack, riding and slashing on the army's left flank.

Both infantry and cavalry moved out at dawn of February 15. Forrest led the advance through "undergrowth so thick horses could scarcely press through it," and had driven the enemy's pickets back before the infantry arrived. Pillow's troops followed, meeting and crushing stubborn Federal resistance. As the enemy was reeled back to their artillery support, Forrest charged a battery of six guns, captured all, then charged another battery farther to the right and captured three more guns.

In each of these sallies his horse was shot from under him, the first two of twenty-nine mounts that he would lose in months to come. To be ridden by Old Bedford, it was generally agreed, was the kiss of death for any horse throughout the war.

By early afternoon, reported Forrest, "We had driven the enemy back without a reverse from the left of our entrenchments to the center, having opened three different roads by which we might have retired if the generals had, as was deemed best in the council of the night before, ordered the retreat of the army."

But now occurred an extraordinary breakdown of command. Pillow declared that "the object of opening the way has been accomplished." He ordered his troops to return to the fort. The ground that had been gained was lost, the door that had been opened would be closed when and if the Federals returned to their positions following the Confederate withdrawal. From the jaws of victory Floyd and Pillow had snatched defeat.

A future Congressional Investigation would not reveal the reasons for their conduct, other than Pillow's statement that the troops had been fighting all day and "were tired." Even the enemy was puzzled. General Lew Wallace, later author of *Ben Hur*, who had fought on the Union right, declared that the Confederate general "could have put his men fairly *en route* for Nashville before the Federal commander could have interposed," and that now that road "was again effectually shut."

That night the three Confederate generals, Pillow, Floyd, and Buckner, held another conference, this time with an angry Forrest present. Buckner declared that it would be "wrong to subject the army to virtual massacre" by holding out. The other two agreed. Then Forrest spoke.

"I did not bring my cavalry here for the purpose of surrendering," he said.

Then he turned on his heel and left the room, reporting later, "I am clearly of the opinion that two-thirds of our army could have marched out without loss, and that, had we continued the fight the next day, we should have gained a glorious victory, as our troops were in fine spirits, believing we had whipped them. . . ." As it was, the cavalry alone would have to cut its way out of the trap and somehow make its way to Nashville, risking the threat that Grant's surrounding troops presented. That evening, Forrest recorded:

> I sent for all the officers under my command, stated to them the facts that had occurred and my determination to leave, and remarked that all who wanted to go could follow me, and those who wished to stay and take the consequences might remain in camp. All of my own regiment . . . said they would go with me if the last man fell.

Three of the four attached companies from Tennessee and Kentucky chose, however, to remain.

That night the cavalry slipped past the right flank of Grant's line, crossed Lick Creek "saddle skirt deep," and filed onto the road to Nashville. Here Forrest ordered Captain Kelley "to remain at the point where we entered this road with one company, where the enemy's cavalry would attack if they attempted to follow us. They remained until day was dawning. . . . More than two hours had been occupied in passing. Not a gun had been fired at us. Not an enemy had been seen or heard."

They had beaten by just twelve hours Buckner's submission to Grant's terms of "Unconditional Surrender," which gave the Union general his enduring sobriquet.

One can, with little risk, refer to almost any battle, any cavalry engagement, as "decisive" in a war. Within limits, any battle is decisive. But the loss of Fort Henry and Fort Donelson marked a turning point in Confederate fortunes, one that the editor of *Harper's Weekly* captioned "The Beginning of the End." It was the first Confederate debacle in the West. It left untenable the critical Southern base at Nashville, and more important outflanked Columbus, Kentucky, the Confederate bastion on the Mississippi.

In fact, all of Middle and West Tennessee were opened to invasion. "Unconditional Surrender" Grant became a national hero; more than that, a major general. With Fort Donelson's capture, followed by Nashville's evacuation, the Western Confederacy was pierced by an arrow that pointed directly at Johnson's army at Corinth, where Beauregard, transferred from Virginia, was second in command.

After the flight of his cavalry from Fort Donelson, Forrest paused at Nashville to supervise the evacuation of provisions from that city, then went on to Huntsville, Alabama, to reequip and enlarge his forces, bringing his regiment back up to strength. It was Forrest's scouts that brought word to Albert Sidney Johnson that General Buell's army from Nashville was approaching and would soon rendezvous with Grant at Pittsburg Landing. Forrest himself joined Johnson and Beauregard in the advance to confront the Union forces of Grant at Shiloh.

With Johnson's army was a squadron of Kentucky cavalry under a rising new captain, John Hunt Morgan. It was the first time the two leaders had fought on the same battlefield, and though Forrest outranked Morgan, he left the captain on his own. As a matter of fact, he himself was given no instructions. "I shall charge on my own orders," he concluded. That he did. During the first Confederate assault that morning, April 6, he later helped to surround and capture Brigadier General Benjamin Prentiss and 3,000 of Grant's army. Up until nearly sundown Shiloh was a Southern triumph, costly to both sides. Then two among several things began to turn the tide. Albert Sidney Johnson was mortally wounded and replaced by Beauregard; and Forrest's scouts brought word of General Buell's approach with 20,000 Union reinforcements.

The cavalry colonel sought out Beauregard to inform him of Buell's approach with reinforcements . . . "and if this army does not move and attack them between this [hour] and daylight, and before other reinforcements arrive, it will be whipped like hell before ten o'clock tomorrow." As at Fort Donelson, his opinion was disregarded. Rather than attack and clinch the victory, Beauregard would retreat toward Corinth.

On the following day, Sherman started pursuing Beauregard down the Corinth Road, with Forrest covering the retreat, and near the Monterey crossroad the cavalry turned on their pursuers like a pack of snarling wolves. They were joined at this point by two companies of Morgan's Kentucky cavalry, and even the veteran Sherman was astounded at the force and fury that this combination generated.

Forrest was at the head of the charge, and as the Confederate cavalry routed the first body of pursuers, the colonel's horse kept right on going, infected with battle fever. In a few seconds Forrest was alone, well behind enemy lines, with startled Federal infantry shouting, "Kill him!" "Grab his horse!" A musket ball pierced his left hip and lodged against his spinal column, two minié balls mortally wounded his horse. But the dying horse refused to fall before it had carried its master to safety.

Sherman's pursuit was stopped cold by the charge, as he reluctantly admitted in his "After Action Report." But Forrest's wound was so severe that he was carried to his home in Memphis for treatment. He wasted no time while convalescing, inserting a notice in the local paper: "Wanted: able-bodied men . . . with good horse and gun. I wish none but those who wish to be actively engaged . . . Come on, boys, if you want a heap of fun and to kill some Yankees." It echoed an old refrain:

> If you want to have a good time,
> Jine the cavalry!

CHAPTER

4

A TEAR FOR ASHBY

IN THE SHENANDOAH VALLEY HE WAS LONG REMEMBERED, NOT AS A character in textbook history but as one who epitomized the legendary chivalry, the grace and courage, of "the Indestructible Dominion." Turner Ashby's name endured not so much because of what he did, but because of what he was.

He seemed at times larger than life, and hard to compress into reality. John Esten Cooke, who knew him as the *beau sabreur* of Southern cavalry, expressed it well:

> His career was all romance—it was brief, splendid, and evanescent as a dream—but, after all, it was the man Turner Ashby who was the real attraction. It was the man whom the people of the Shenandoah Valley admire, rather than his glorious record. There was something grander than the achievements of this soldier, and that was the soldier himself.

And as another saw him: "Along the trails Ashby blazed for military history, fact and fable were so intertwined that no one bothered to try to separate them. He became a phantom, a soldier with a charmed life, a rider who appeared always at the right moment and in the right place, a knight on a charmed horse, a gladiator who found romance in war. . . ."

A contemporary Southern poet, Frank Ticknor, defined Ashby in his verses as:

> The knightliest of the knightly race,
> Who since the days of old,
> Have kept the lamp of chivalry
> Alight in hearts of gold. . . .

The same superlatives would have applied to Turner's younger brother Richard, for both were cut from the same skein that stretched back nine hundred years to the Norman Conquest. Since Ashbys first settled in Virginia, in 1635, four generations of ancestors had left their mark in history, in the Colonial wars, in the Revolution, and in the War of 1812. Surviving the latter conflict the boys' father, Colonel Turner Ashby, sired three sons and three daughters at the family seat of "Rose Bank" in the picturesque Piedmont country.

Turner's education was limited to what he learned at his mother's knee, and later at Major Ambler's Academy in Fauquier County. His schoolmates recalled that he "was remarkable for his contempt of danger . . . exhibited nearly every day. Whenever the creek was swollen by heavy rains, he might be seen in it, breasting the torrent above the waterfalls, where a failure would dash him to pieces on the rocks below. Whenever a colt was found too wild and vicious to be ridden by any one else in the neighborhood, it was his pleasure to mount and tame him."

He had no formal military training; but the life of the hurdle race, the foxhunt, the local tournaments, developed invaluable skills for military life. Passionately fond of horses, in beautiful control as rider, he seemed to float over fence and stream. "So perfect was Ashby's seat," wrote a family acquaintance, Bishop Charles T. Quintard, "and so exactly did his movements coincide with those of his horse, that the only motion visible in the noble rider was the settling of the folds of his cape as he landed on the opposite bank."

As horsemen akin to centaurs, Turner and his brother Richard were outstanding figures in the local tournaments, or medieval-type gymkhanas, so popular throughout that section of Virginia. It was during one of these events that Turner won the somewhat fatuous title of "Knight of Hiawatha." As recorded by the Reverend James B. Avirett who knew both Ashbys well:

> During the contest, a horseman rode up in the full costume of an Indian chief, painted and feathered, and calling himself Hiawatha. He rode an unbroken colt, without saddle or bridle; and without noticing the music or the crowd, he uttered the war cry of his race, and passing like a flash along the line, he lifted the ring from its rest as if it were child's play, and continuing at full speed to the outer extremity of the plain, bounded over a high stone wall, and disappeared.

His good looks, his grace, his courtly manners, made him the darling of the women of the Valley; but he kept them at a distance. Unlike the wild colts he was fond of taming, he would not be tamed. He loved the Piedmont country, and his mistress was Virginia; sewn to the crown of his hat was a square of silk on which the shield of Virginia was painted. He was content to remain a bachelor and to be known only as "the son of a gentleman, a hard rider, a good companion, and the kindest-hearted of friends."

Shortly before John Brown's raid in October 1859, Ashby had organized a company of mounted vigilantes which he later took to Harpers Ferry in the fall of 1859 to help quell the fear of further insurrection. After the hanging of Old Osawatomie the group stayed together as Ashby's Mountain Rangers, or more popularly "Ashby's Men," and with Virginia's secession from the Union they again rode out to reinforce the Virginia militia assembled at Harpers Ferry.

Beyond patrolling the Potomac from Harpers Ferry to Point of Rocks there was not much, at first, for this free-lance cavalry to do. But when Federal troops crossed the river to occupy Alexandria, Turner Ashby discovered his true career and mission as defender of Virginia's soil. He became the terror of Federal pickets and of troops at Union outposts. They felt the sting of his bullets, and sometimes the prick of his saber, but they could not catch him. He came and went, they complained, "like a dream."

On April 28, when dour Thomas Jackson, fresh from his professor's chair at V.M.I., took command at Harpers Ferry, he looked to Ashby for information on General Patterson's positions north of the Potomac. Turner dressed himself in a borrowed homespun suit, hired a plowhorse, and rode into the Union lines disguised as a country veterinarian. With his saddlebags filled with remedies, he rode from one Federal camp to another, treating Patterson's horses for spavin and ringbone, and returning to Jackson with an immense amount of military data. From that point on, wrote then Captain John D. Imboden, "the affection and confidence of the two men were remarkable."

Only one thing threatened briefly to come between them. When Jeb Stuart reported to Jackson for assignment, Jackson ordered all companies to be consolidated under Stuart's command. "The order," wrote Imboden, "was very offensive to Captain Turner Ashby, at that time the idol of all the troopers in the field, as well he might be, for a more brave and chivalrous officer never rode at the head of well-mounted troopers." Ashby threatened to resign.

Jackson patched up the rift with wisdom, recognizing that two such volatile personalities could not combine. He relieved Ashby of the "obnoxious" order, and assigned him to the new regiment then being organized by Colonel Angus McDonald. McDonald himself had already indicated his intention of retiring because of ill health, and Ashby would shortly be in full command. On June 5, 1861, the 7th Virginia Cavalry came into being, with Turner's brother Richard in command of one of its ten companies, and Turner himself promoted to lieutenant colonel of the regiment.

Regimental chaplain James B. Avirett described with some hyperbole the appearance of the brothers as they accompanied their regiment to the cavalry camp at Winchester, southwest of Harpers Ferry: "Lieutenant Colonel Turner Ashby, now a little past 32 years of age, with his lithe figure gracefully balanced in the saddle, lightly touched the reins of his milk-white steed . . . while the effect of Capt. Richard Ashby's port and mien, not quite 29 years of age, splendidly mounted on the stallion as jetty black as the raven's wing, was no less imposing."

In the figure of Turner Ashby, John Esten Cooke saw "a man rather below the middle height, with an active and vigorous frame, clad in plain Confederate gray. His brown felt hat was decorated with a black feather; his uniform was almost without decorations; his cavalry boots, dusty or splashed with mud, came to the knee; and around his waist he wore a sash and plain leather belt, holding pistol and saber." Of Ashby's features, Cooke observed:

> His complexion was dark as that of an Arab; his eyes of a deep rich brown, sparkled under well formed brows; and two-thirds of his face was covered by a huge black beard and mustache, the latter curling at the ends, the former reaching to his breast. There was thus in the face of the cavalier something Moorish and brigandish; but . . . the brown eyes, which would flash superbly in battle, were the softest and most friendly imaginable; the voice, which could thrill his men as it rang like a clarion in the charge, was the perfection of mild courtesy. . . . but under the soldier, as plainly was the gentleman.

One of the regiment's first missions was to raid the Baltimore & Ohio Railroad, connecting Washington with the west, destroying bridges and trestles. Following separate routes, Turner's brother Richard was ambushed by a band of Federals. In attempting to escape, the captain's horse stumbled on a cattle-guard, throwing its rider to the ground; and Richard, shot several times and bayoneted, was left dying where he fell.

It was an hour later that Turner caught up with his mortally wounded brother. Assigning a squad to carry him to a nearby house, he and eleven troopers pursued the Federals to the south bank of the Potomac. Here they killed three of them, before the rest escaped to an island in the river.

At the home of Colonel George Washington, nursed by Chaplain Avirett, Richard survived for eight days, a remarkable fight for life "for one so cut to pieces." Afterwards, Turner had him buried at a cemetery east of Romney where, according to one unreliable eyewitness, "He stood over the grave, took his brother's sword, broke it, and threw the pieces in the opening . . . then, pressing his lips together in bitterness, he turned without a word, mounted his horse and rode away."

There were those who refuted the legend of the broken sword, but all agreed that from that moment Turner was an instrument of vengeance. He and Richard, noted Avirett, had been as close as Damon and Pythias, and the grief that Turner himself described as "all but unbearable" drove him to a reckless, almost suicidal fury in the months to come.

It was this disdain of death that spawned the legend of his indestructibility. On a ridge near the Potomac, the Union pickets saw him on his snow-white charger, silhouetted against the sky, calmly observing through his glass the enemy camp below. They fired at him with their long-range rifles. He remained as quiet as a statue until, satisfied with his scrutiny, he waved his hat at the enemy in arrogant disdain and disappeared.

Later, as Joe Johnston and Jackson rode to join Beauregard at Bull Run, Ashby's cavalry alone was left to confront General Patterson south of Harpers Ferry. The odds of more than twenty against one bothered Ashby not at all. His gray-clad rangers could be everywhere at once, and were. "I can't catch them, sir," a Federal cavalry officer complained to Patterson. "They leap fences and walls like deer; neither our men nor our horses are so trained."

That fall, during the calm that followed First Manassas or Bull Run, Ashby introduced a new arm to the cavalry, one that would give the Confederate horsemen a further advantage over their Union counterparts. It was Chew's Horse Artillery led by eighteen-year-old Captain R. Preston Chew, formerly of the Virginia Military Institute and two lieutenants, seventeen and eighteen, also ex-cadets of V.M.I.

Unlike heavier field artillery, this was a battery designed to go wherever cavalry could go, over stream or wall, through thicket and morass, drawn by swift horses that could keep up with a charge. It featured a little English Blakely Gun, and ah! what a sweet sound it made! Even women and children learned to recognize its rifle-sharp report, and the people of the Shenandoah, hearing it echo from the Blue Ridge, would turn to one another with a smile of satisfaction. "Listen! Hear that? Ashby's coming! That's Ashby's little gun."

Knowing that for a while at least their Valley was secure.

In early November 1861 as Jackson, now major general, arrived at Winchester to command the Shenandoah Valley District, Ashby's cavalry became an integral part of Stonewall's Army of the Valley. They made a contrasting pair, one writer noted, as they rode together:

"The praying, shabby general with the inner fire, and the magnificent colonel on the magnificent steed, plume floating, beard floating, speaking as gently as a woman, with the softness in his eyes hiding the killer's gleam."

Yet for all their differences—and for one thing, Jackson was sorely troubled by his cavalry commander's lack of army discipline—the bond was strong between them. To Jackson, the dedicated ubiquitous Ashby was the eyes and ears of his small army. If Ashby said go, they went—headlong into a startled enemy whose weak points Ashby had discovered. If they had to fall back, they could do so in confident order, knowing that Ashby's horsemen would discourage any hot pursuit.

English military commentator Colonel G. F. R. Henderson wrote of the cavalry leader at this time:

> Ashby was the *beau-idéal* of a captain of light horse. His reckless daring, both across country and under fire, made him the idol of the army. Nor was his reputation confined to the Confederate ranks. "I think even our men," says a Federal officer, "had a kind of admiration for him, as he sat unmoved upon his horse, and let them pepper away at him as if he enjoyed it."

During the late fall and early weeks of winter, his duties and those of the army were routine, patrolling the south bank of the Potomac. But, noted Henderson, "of excitement and adventure there was enough and to spare. Scarcely a day passed without shots being exchanged at one point or another of the picket line. There were the enemy's outposts to be harassed, prisoners to be taken, bridges to be burnt, and convoys to be captured."

By the time March 1862 arrived, all the sluggish armies that had hibernated in Virginia, Union and Confederate, set shoulders to their spring campaigns. As McClellan made plans for invading the Peninsula, Nathaniel Banks, a politically-oriented general, crossed the Potomac with 37,000 troops to challenge Jackson in the Valley, his army outnumbering Jackson's about eight to one.

With Winchester threatened by this overwhelming force, Jackson appealed for reinforcements. *"If this Valley is lost, Virginia is lost."* But neither Johnston nor Davis advocated sparing any men, with McClellan's Army of the Potomac aimed at Richmond. Jackson must not only survive with his force of 4,600, but must use it adroitly enough to keep Banks, and the troops that he commanded, from moving to team up with McClellan.

Reluctantly Jackson abandoned Winchester to move farther up the Valley, with the 7th Virginia Cavalry bringing up the rear. Ashby was the last to leave, sitting his horse in the center of town as the enemy poured in. Puzzled by the sight of this lone rider, Federal officers dispatched two mounted men to circle around by back streets to cut off his retreat.

"Ashby either did not see this maneuver," wrote John Esten Cooke, "or paid no attention to it. He waited until the Federal column was nearly upon him, and had opened a hot fire—then he turned his horse, waved his hat around his head, and uttering a cheer of defiance, galloped off."

Eyewitnesses from both sides, hypnotized by this little drama, agreed on Ashby's subsequent performance:

> All at once, as he galloped down the street, he saw before him the two cavalrymen sent to cut off and capture him. To a man like Ashby, inwardly chafing at being compelled to retreat, no sight could be more agreeable. Here was an opportunity to vent his spleen; and charging the two mounted men, he was soon upon them. One fell with a bullet through his breast; and, coming opposite the other, Ashby seized him by the throat, dragged him from his saddle, and putting spur to his horse, bore him off.

Jackson's withdrawal from Winchester lulled Banks into a false sense of security. He decided to leave a small force under Brigadier General James Shields to press the Confederate retreat, while he himself prepared to join McClellan with the rest of his army. Then he changed his mind. He would leave Shields with his entire division in the Valley, to make certain Jackson did not return.

Ashby had been scouting the operation. If there was only a small detachment under General Shields, left to contend with in the Valley, now was the time to attack. On March 23, as the 7th Virginia launched a frontal attack on the advancing Union forces on the Valley Pike, Jackson sent his infantry to attack and turn Shield's right.

For once, and for the only time, Ashby's intelligence was woefully deficient. At the first shot, Federal troops swarmed over valley and hills like an overwhelming tide. This was not the vanguard of Shield's forces, but his entire 9,000-man division! Fighting behind every tree and rock, shooting from every wall and doorway, the Confederates gave ground. Recalling that fierce encounter, Avirett later wrote:

> It is doubtful whether there was a more desperate and hotly contested engagement through the whole period of the war than that of Kernstown. Ashby was in his glory as, mounted on his white charger, he rode at full speed, clearing every obstacle, whether post-and-rail or stone fence ... animating his men with his peculiarly expressive, "Drive them, boys! Drive them!" ... So well ordered was his

withdrawal from the field, that neither a man nor gun was lost on that part under his immediate eye.

Nevertheless, when darkness ended the three-hour fight, with Shields in possession of the field, Jackson had lost a quarter of his army, killed or wounded. Only his fierce resistance snatched an element of victory from the defeat. Plainly his Army of the Shenandoah was a factor to be reckoned with. Banks was pulled back to the Valley, and Lincoln ordered McDowell to stay put at Manassas Junction. With less than 5,000 men Jackson had immobilized, more than 50,000 Federal troops that might have joined McClellan in the Richmond campaign. The Confederate Congress tendered him and his army a vote of thanks, to which Joe Johnston added his praise for their "admirable conduct, by which they fully earned the high reward bestowed."

Now began Jackson's long withdrawal up the Valley, not so much a retreat as the retraction of an arrow in the bow, gathering strength with each inch of compression. Ashby covered the rear, never letting the enemy out of his sight. Near Mount Jackson, Henry Kyd Douglas of Jackson's staff surveyed a blue column pressing close behind. He was puzzled to see that the officer in the lead was dressed in trim Confederate gray and rode a white horse. Then he realized it was Ashby, leading the Federals toward an ambush at a bridge across the North Fork of the Shenandoah. Paraphrasing Douglas's report:

> At the bridge Ashby reined up to set fire to the combustibles which had been placed there, but two of the Union troopers reached him before he could succeed. One of them fired at close quarters and wounded the horse. Ashby cut him down with a sword stroke, the white stallion plunged on as though it understood danger, and did not fall until it reached the Confederates. Then Ashby knelt beside it stroking its mane and looking into its eyes until it died.

"Thus," wrote Douglas, "the most splendid horseman I ever knew lost the most beautiful war-horse I ever saw."

But as the army continued its retreat, Ashby mounted another horse, as white as its predecessor, and with Chew's Battery "barking and biting," continued to plague his pursuers and to guard the Confederate bivouacs at night. Recalled Major R. W. Hunter of the 2nd Virginia Infantry, "I never slept more soundly in my life than when in sight of the enemy's campfires, with Ashby between us, for I knew it was well nigh impossible for them to surprise him."

Urged by President Lincoln and Secretary of War Edwin M. Stanton to keep pressing Jackson up the Valley, Banks pursued the Confederates first to Rudes Hill and then to Harrisonburg. Here he paused. The 7th Virginia Cavalry was ranged along the south bank of the waterway, the grays and butternuts blending with the pastel shadings of the trees. For six days, 19,000 bluecoats stared across the creek at the 600 mounted men in gray. When an exasperated president demanded of Banks just what was stalling him, Banks replied with three small words that tolled like Poe's alarum bells:

"Ashby is here."

It was the third week of April at Jackson's camp near Swift Run Gap in the upper Shenandoah, last stop on the long retreat. Pausing here, the Valley Army regained its strength, with new recruits replacing the Kernstown battle losses. More than that, General Robert E. Lee, who was advising President Davis, had promised to reinforce Jackson with a full division under Richard Ewell, which would bring his forces up to about 17,000 men. It would take three weeks for Ewell to reach him, time enough to plan his campaign to retake the Valley.

Ashby's cavalry, too, had grown from ten companies of roughly 60 each to 22 companies of nearly 1,400 troopers overall. There could have been more, except for lack of horses. For the cavalry command attracted the young men of the Valley like a magnet. Ashby himself, wrote James Kendall Hosmer in the Confederate *Appeal to Arms*, "was the ideal and hero of the whole region; on his white charger he was the most familiar of figures. His dash was full of wild fascination, and every youth along the Shenandoah burned to be among his riders."

Jackson alone was troubled by this sudden rise in Ashby's numbers. Fourteen hundred high spirited horsemen, independent and exuberant, were hard to keep in hand. He thought of dividing Ashby's cavalry up into more manageable units, then wisely withdrew the order when Ashby threatened to resign, convinced that "if I persisted in my attempt to increase the efficiency of the cavalry it would have produced the contrary effect, as Colonel Ashby's influence, who is very popular with his men, would be thrown against me."

Now it was Jackson's hour to strike back at Banks. He had been reinforced by General Ewell's division, plus another brigade. The arrow had been drawn back to its full extent, ready to release its force against the invaders of the Valley. The troops would march back the way they came, sweeping the enemy before them, until only the ruins of the vanquished Union army would remain to mar the Valley floor.

It was not a direct march down the Valley, but a wide sweep, back and forth between the bordering ridges, striking first at enemy forces in the village of McDowell, then switching back through Harrisonburg and up to New Market, driving the Federals before them. Frantically, Banks called on General John C. Frémont to press down from the west on Jackson's flank. But Frémont could not keep pace with the movement of the gray-clad troops that, racing ahead at twenty miles or more a day, were earning the sobriquet of "Jackson's Foot Cavalry."

By May 23 the Confederates were approaching strategic Front Royal, where Belle Boyd, eight weeks away from imprisonment as a Southern spy, dashed through the Federal lines to direct them into town. The Union garrison took to its heels, losing almost 800 killed, wounded, or captured, and exposing Banks's army at Strasburg to a flank attack.

At Strasburg, Banks briefly wrung his hands, fearing that "from any cleft between the mountains Ashby's cavalry might, at any time, sweep down upon his trains of wagons, his hospitals, and his magazines." His own cavalry, he moaned, was "weak in numbers and spirits, much exhausted, . . . and greatly inferior to the enemy." He headed for Winchester, ordering his mounted troops to make a stand at Newtown, half way up the turnpike.

But by the time the Federals had formed their battle line at Newtown, Confederate cavalry was already bearing down upon the village. Penned in the narrow streets, the Union horsemen made a desperate effort to escape, but were cut off by a squadron of hard-riding Virginians. Wrote Jackson in his report:

> In a few moments the turnpike, which had just before teemed with life, presented a most appalling spectacle of carnage and destruction. The road was literally obstructed with the mingled and confused mass of struggling and dying horses and riders. Among the surviving cavalry the wildest confusion ensued, and they scattered in disorder in various directions, leaving, however, some 200 prisoners, with their equipment, in our hands.

"There was reason to believe," wrote Jackson, "if Banks reached Winchester, it would be without a train, if not without an army."

He was right. A few miles up the pike from Newtown, Ashby's cavalry captured the Union wagon trains, breaking off their pursuit of Banks long enough to revel in the plunder. Then on to Winchester, where the forces of Jackson and Ewell combined to drive the Federals from the town in a battle described by one Union soldier as "hell—or at least about as good an imitation of it as is often produced in the upper world." This time it was Banks who lost a quarter of his army, over 2,000 killed or captured. Banks fled north toward Harpers Ferry, while Jackson's Foot Cavalry raised the war cry, "On to the Potomac!"

The capital was in a state of panic. The Stonewall Brigade, racing ahead of the army, was at Harpers Ferry; Ashby's horses were reported drinking from the river. Lincoln advised McClellan either to attack Richmond immediately or "come to the defense of Washington." Frémont was ordered to march from Franklin, and Irvin McDowell to shift part of his troops from Fredericksburg, to try to cut off Jackson in

the lower Valley. With McDowell's cavalry was Colonel Sir Percy Wyndham, English soldier of fortune, whose declared ambition was "to bag
Ashby." He would have his chance.

With the threat of being cut off in the lower Valley by Federal
divisions coming from the east and west, Jackson began his swift retreat, and Ashby faced the acid test of his career. If he could delay the
Federal pursuit, Jackson would have a chance to slip from the Valley
and join Joe Johnston in his fight to drive McClellan from the gates of
Richmond. It would take speed to beat the enemy forces closing in, and
Jackson's Foot Cavalry lived up to its name. Evacuating Winchester on
May 31, Jackson began his famous retreat up the valley. By the end of
five days the Confederates had marched and fought a distance of
nearly a hundred miles, from one end of the Valley to the other.

The feats that were added to the Ashby legend in that swift retreat
were countless as the stars. "On every hill, in every valley, at every
bridge," wrote John Esten Cooke, "he swore to hold his ground or die.
He played with death, and dared it everywhere."

The Confederate command did not waste words of praise on Ashby.
Before he left Harpers Ferry he was raised to brigadier general. With
the promotion went Jackson's advice to be less reckless in the face of
danger. Ashby only smiled; the bullet had not yet been molded that
could touch him.

On June 6, the Army of the Valley rested briefly at Cross Keys, south
of Harrisonburg, and Ashby's cavalry occupied a wooded ridge commanding all approaches from the north. In close pursuit came Percy
Wyndham with 800 mounted Federals, intent on "bagging Ashby."
Ashby waited till Wyndham's troops were halfway to the crest, then
turned loose his cavalry. By the time the bluecoats had escaped the fury
of that charge, they had lost four officers and 63 prisoners. One of the
captured officers was Wyndham.

In Jackson's camp they heard the sounds of fighting to the northwest, the high rebel yell that signaled Ashby's charge, then silence, then
the file of Union prisoners being escorted to the rear. Sir Percy Wyndham rode at the head of the latter column, humiliated by his capture,
but proudly disdainful of his captors. A Maryland infantryman
shouted with delight, "Look yonder boys; there's a Yankee colonel!"
Upon which Wyndham rose in the saddle and told the man with scorn,
"I'm not a Yankee, you damned rebel fool!" He demanded to be taken
to the general in command.

More prisoners arrived, including the wounded Lieutenant Colonel
Thomas L. Kane of the Pennsylvania "Bucktails." Talking with his
captors, Kane claimed to have saved the life of General Ashby, "a man I

admire as much as you do. He was today within fifty yards of my skirmishers, sitting on his horse, unconscious of the danger he was in. I saw three of them raise their guns to fire, but I succeeded in stopping two of them and struck the gun of the third as it went off.

"Ashby is too brave to die that way."

Kane's gallantry was only a reprieve. Smarting from his previous defeat, Frémont threw a still stronger force of Union infantry and cavalry against the Confederate position. Ashby saw his men begin to waver before their overwhelming numbers, rode forward, waving his saber, and called on them to rally for a charge. His horse was shot from under him, but he rose to his feet, still crying, "Charge, men! For God's sake, charge!" As the men responded, sweeping past him toward the enemy, a Federal marksman shot him through the heart.

He was carried to the rear by four cavalrymen riding abreast, their faces streaked with tears. "Who is it?" they were asked of the body beneath the blanket; and at the reply, "General Ashby," infantryman McHenry Howard recalled that "men who had borne without tears the horror and sorrow of battle," wept unashamedly at those two words.

In the house in Port Republic where he lay that night, attended by a guard of honor, the troops passed through in silent file to pay last tribute to their fallen chief. One of Ashby's scouts tried to improvise a eulogy. "We shall miss you mightily, General. We shall miss you in the camp. We shall miss you when we go out on a scout. But we shall miss you most, General, when—" Then his voice broke, and the words were left unfinished.

When word reached the main camp, Jackson was in his room, meeting with Colonel Wyndham. "Dismiss him," he told the corporal of the guard. Then he finished the dispatch he was sending to John Imboden, adding beneath it in a shaky hand: "Poor Ashby is dead. He fell gloriously—one of the noblest men and soldiers in the Confederate army." Imboden wrote later, "I carried that slip of paper till it was literally worn to tatters." Avirett remembered that Jackson was not seen by his staff again that night. "He remained beside Ashby's body, asking only to be left alone. . . ."

Later Jackson would write to his superiors: "An official report is not an appropriate place for more than a passing notice of the distinguished dead, but the close relation with General Ashby bore to my command, for most of the previous twelve months, will justify me in saying that as a partisan officer I never knew his superior. His daring was proverbial, his powers of endurance almost incredible, his tone of character heroic, and his sagacity almost intuitive in divining the purposes and movements of the enemy."

More eloquent, in a way, than Confederate tributes were those of the enemy, to whom his very name had been anathema. One of Frémont's officers wrote of "the brilliant leader of the enemy cavalry, a man worth to them *regiments*, a blast upon whose horn was worth a thousand men. When we found the brave Ashby was slain, there was no rejoicing in our camps."

Even throughout the North, Ashby was apotheosized, hailed by the New York *Herald* as "one of the most brilliant generals developed on either side during the war." Frémont reported to War Secretary Stanton on the fallen general's "admirable audacity and incomparable skill." And in the revealing diary that she kept in Richmond, Mary Boykin Chesnut wrote her entry for the day: "Drop a tear for Turner Ashby, the hero of the Valley."

All Virginia shed a tear for Ashby, knowing his like would not be seen again. Mary Preston, sister-in-law of Stonewall Jackson, known as the "Poetess of the Confederacy," was one of the first to express her grief in verse:

> Hear ye that solemn word,
> Accent of dread . . .
> Ashby, our bravest one!
> Ashby is dead!

And many followed suit, Arthur Peticolas concluding his poem on Ashby:

> Sadly sweet the bugle's calling
> Over Ashby's bier . . .
> Matchless horseman of the Valley!
> Knightly horseman of the Valley
> That we loved so dear.

Screened by the saddened but determined cavalry, Stonewall Jackson was able to slip from the closing forces of the enemy, and join Robert E. Lee, new commander of the Army of Northern Virginia, in the victorious defense of Richmond. For a blessed while the Valley was free of the tramp of feet, the clouds of dust and smoke, the rattle of rifle fire, and the sound of "Ashby's little gun." But as the people rebuilt their fences and reclaimed their fields, the skies seemed somehow darker overhead, the hills more solemn, for,

> Ashby, our paladin!
> Ashby is dead!

CHAPTER

5

KENTUCKY CAVALIER

IN KENTUCKY, AS ON THE PLANTATIONS AND FARMS OF VIRGINIA AND the Carolinas, Southern women, reading their Sir Walter Scott, cherished the image of young Lochinvar coming out of the West, and they found its reality in John Hunt Morgan. For faithful in love and dauntless in war he was indeed, and more besides.

Tall, fair, and handsome, with a high forehead, neat Van Dyke, and cavalry mustache, "his form was perfect and the rarest combination of strength, activity and grace." So wrote his brother-in-law, comrade-in-arms and biographer Basil Duke, who added, "In some indefinable way he became intimately identified with the fortunes and aspirations of the Southern people." And this, perhaps, because he was so much of a product of the land from which he came.

Life in the Bluegrass region of Kentucky was not dissimilar to life in the tidewater counties of Virginia. Wellborn lads were taught to ride properly, sitting the "dragoon seat," not rising from the saddle. They early learned to handle firearms and, because of the forested nature of the game-filled land, put more emphasis on marksmanship than did their Eastern counterparts.

Otherwise, the same emphasis on chivalry and courtly manners, the same quick impetus to fight for honor, the same love of freedom, independence, and outdoor pursuits, prevailed—in Kentucky, Tennessee, and the western Confederate states in general. There was, however, more of a frontier slant to Western living. The social codes were not as absolute; the gallantry at times a little tarnished by the rough necessities of frontier life. Externally, John Morgan was a different breed of man than Turner Ashby. Basically, however, they were brothers.

Though born in Huntsville, Alabama, in 1825, Morgan was raised from the age of four in Lexington, Kentucky. Like his slightly older western colleague, Bedford Forrest, he and his five brothers were of Virginia ancestry, their father being, in fact, a former Virginia merchant. Educated at Transylvania College, Jefferson Davis' alma mater, John got a year's military training in the War with Mexico, serving as a lieutenant with the 1st Kentucky Cavalry.

Returning to Lexington when this stint was up, Morgan entered the family's textile business. Six feet tall, blue eyed, with Viking-blond hair, he became a conspicuous figure in the community for reasons other than his business acumen. For horses were almost a religion in the Blue Grass, second only to cards and women, and Morgan was devoted to all three. Nonetheless, because of his looks and breeding he was welcomed in the homes of blue-blood matrons and their marriageable daughters, who forgave his fashionable peccadillos.

So, in 1848, he married Rebecca Gratz Bruce, daughter of a wealthy Lexington family, whose mother was said to be the prototype of Scott's Rebecca in the novel *Ivanhoe*. The marriage harbored sorrow. The couple's first child died a few years after birth, and Rebecca never recovered from the loss. Morgan expunged his grief in a feverish pursuit of pleasure mixed with business, and when Rebecca died in July of 1861 he mourned respectfully and hardly missed her. He had married not a girl of flesh and blood but a romantic image, and to a degree he would always be pursuing images where women were concerned.

In 1857, a few years before Rebecca's death, Morgan organized the Lexington Rifles, a gaudily uniformed militia composed of Kentucky bluebloods whose principal activities were ceremonial and social. It is doubtful that the Rifles had in mind the war to come; they confined themselves to semiweekly drills and meetings, formal dinners, balls, and serenades. But events caught up with them with ruthless swiftness, as Kentucky strove futilely to preserve neutrality at the outbreak of the Civil War.

Strict neutrality for a state that could produce two native sons like Abraham Lincoln and Jefferson Davis, and occupied such a strategic position, was impossible to maintain. Even after neutrality ended in September, and Kentucky sided with the Union, the state remained divided, becoming a battleground of warring factions. On September 20, 1861, on word that the Lexington Rifles and similar pro-secession units were to be disarmed by Federal order, Morgan called a secret meeting of his men at the armory. They loaded their arms and equip-

ment onto wagons and crept out of town, headed for the rendezvous of
Confederate forces at Bowling Green, Kentucky.

His sudden departure for the wars evoked one of many stanzas in the
Morgan ballad appearing in a Western paper:

> But Fame, of John's expanding mind,
> Possession full had gotten,
> And so he left his woolen mills,
> To go and save King Cotton.

At Bowling Green the company was sworn into the Confederate
service. Morgan was elected captain and the newly arrived Basil Duke
was chosen first lieutenant. Duke, a young Missouri lawyer, had married John's sister three months earlier, and from intimate association
he would later become his brother-in-law's biographer. Since Morgan
wrote few letters and kept no diary, Duke's narrative offers a sympathetic portrait of his subject, seen, however, through rose colored
glasses. But if Duke attributed to Morgan virtues few men could pos-
sess, it may be just as well; for Morgan would be branded in his time as
bandit, bushwhacker, and horse thief—epithets not wholly deserved.
So perhaps the two views balanced out.

In early November, Morgan's company was ordered to Bowling
Green which was almost the center of the Confederate defense line that
ran from Cumberland Gap to the Mississippi. Charged with defending
that line as commander of Confederate armies in the West, Albert
Sidney Johnson had hoped somehow to draw Kentucky back from the
Union, despite the fact that by year's end there were 27,000 Kentuckians serving Federal commanders, less than 8,000 in the Southern
armies.

Though never so clearly stated, this coercion was a major purpose of
Morgan's early raids into that state. They started that fall from Bowling
Green, more as sporting adventures or training exercises than sound
military expeditions. The cavalry burned a few bridges, plundered
enemy depots, raided Federal corrals, and made off with horses anywhere that they could find them—inspiring Union General Jacob D.
Cox to compose one of many ballads that their leader's name inspired:

> John Morgan's foot is on thy shore,
> Kentucky! O Kentucky!
> His hand is on thy stable door
> Kentucky! O Kentucky!
> You'll see your good gray mare no more,
> He'll ride her till her back is sore
> And leave her at some stranger's door,
> Kentucky! O Kentucky!

They evolved into something far different from the polished cadre of Lexington Rifles that Morgan started with. The abrasions of the raiders' life, of hard skirmishing and hours in the saddle, supplanted the cavalier sheen with something tougher and more durable. They wore what they liked in the way of uniforms ("their clothing was uniform only in its variety," wrote Basil Duke), and in place of the cavalry saber armed themselves with Bowie knives to supplement their rifles, muskets, and revolvers. And, with the other mounted troops, they exercised their right to act as fighting men, not as troopers on parade. As, for example:

> The camp at Bowling Green was a mad drunken hole, full of wild outfits, "Deadshots," "Hell-roarers," "Desperadoes," "Earthquakes," electing their own officers, impatient of drill or control. . . . Drunkenness was terrific, as it was through all the Southern armies, and in the Northern to but less degree. It is astonishing that the simplest principles of discipline were not used to control it.

The words "Deadshots" and "Hell-roarers" quoted by Duke were not descriptive epithets invented by the writer, but names chosen by the individual companies. Morgan, however, was indeed no disciplinarian, except insofar as he disciplined himself. Though he overlooked much in camp, he demanded total obedience to orders in the field.

Even Southern sympathizers in Kentucky had mixed feelings toward Morgan's raiders. They were accused of "having no more discipline than a cage of monkeys"—of stealing horses at every opportunity, looting barnyards, making off with chickens by the squawking armful. Many indulgent homeowners housed them, fed them, and gave them provisions, only to find their stables emptied of horses the next morning.

It is unlikely that Morgan participated in this thievery, any more than he shared the other vices of the cavalry, such as liquor and tobacco. He simply turned his back upon it. All was fair in love and war. And as for love, his raiders, passing from village to village, observed the Southern chivalry toward womanhood, though Kentucky belles were strongly attracted to the fair-haired, tall-in-the-saddle leader with his handsome features and "beautiful suit of hair."

His thoroughbred horse, "Black Bess," came in for similar admiration, a magnificent animal, according to Duke, of glossy black coat and "as agile as an antelope." At Pulaski, Tennessee, through which the raiders passed in May of 1862, she "almost stole the show, prancing high and tossing her beautifully shaped head." But when the ladies not only patted her and fed her tidbits, but insisted on scissoring souvenir strands from her jet black mane, Morgan drew the line. He had Black Bess stabled for the night, and locked the door.

As they rode through jittery Kentucky, part Confederate in sympathies, part Union, some of their Hallowe'en-type pranks bordered on the childish. Skillful at tapping telegraph wires, Morgan's telegrapher, George A. Ellsworth, was fond of intercepting Federal orders to commanders in the field, and replying to them in a manner destined to drive the senders to distraction. On one occasion General Jeremiah T. Boyle, commander of the District of Kentucky, received a wired message reading: "Good morning, Jerry! This telegraph is a great institution. My friend Ellsworth has in his portfolio all your dispatches for the last month. Do you want copies? Signed, John Morgan."

The beleaguered Boyle, finding Morgan's fake orders were sending his forces to all corners of Kentucky, demanded of Halleck that he be "driven out of the state with all his horse thieves." But Morgan had his own plans for moving on, and thoughtfully wired the Federal general, "Goodbye, Jerry. Regards to Mrs. Boyle."

If it added up to confusion and exasperation behind Union lines, that was sufficient in itself. Actual military victories were not Morgan's goal. Military victories meant army discipline and army orders, and Morgan was fighting his own brand of war. So it was, wrote Whitelaw Reid in the Cincinnati *Gazette*, that "in the early days of 1862 a new name was growing into popular favor and fear. . . . Morgan and his men occupied as much popular attention in Kentucky and along the border as Beauregard and Lee."

By means other than tapping telegraph wires he kept himself informed of enemy strength and operations. If, on scouting expeditions, he ran into a formidable Union force, he kept his riders in concealment while he approached the unit with a white flag. He would state that the forces with him were five times their actual number, and call on the Federal commander to surrender, "to avoid a useless effusion of blood." The white flag was, of course, a ruse; the surrender demand a bluff. But by getting this close to the enemy's front, Morgan was able to estimate his opponent's strength, and decide on the wisdom of attacking or retreating.

After Fort Donelson's fall, and the Confederate withdrawal from Bowling Green and Nashville to Murfreesboro, Morgan's raids became more daring. On February 26, 1862, the day after Forrest pulled out of Nashville and Federal troops began to occupy the city, Morgan with only fifteen men made his way into the outskirts. An unobservant Federal patrol was about to enter the city, and Morgan's nondescript troopers fell in behind them, using the bluecoats as a screen.

Inside the city, Morgan saw the steamer *Minnetonka* anchored in the river, and downstream from it several Federal gunboats. He had a brainstorm: set fire to the steamboat, cut it loose, and let it drift down with the current to ignite the transports. Three volunteers selected for the mission approached the vessel in a small skiff, overcame the crew by sheer surprise, and set the craft ablaze.

The vessel, however, was anchored at stem and stern not by ordinary hawsers of hemp but by chains of iron. After hacking at these cables for a while, sparks showering upon their heads, the three volunteers gave up and, their skiff overturning, made it ashore by clinging to a fence rail. The mission was thus a qualified success. The *Minnetonka* burned to the waterline, making "a beautiful blaze" wrote Basil Duke. After which, to the bedlam of shouting citizens and swearing Federals, Morgan fled the city with his band, a swarm of Yankees on his heels. He lost one man to the pursuers, but the Union lost a steamship; so things more than evened out.

When Albert Sidney Johnson evacuated Murfreesboro and headed for Corinth in Mississippi, to rendezvous with the forces of Braxton Bragg, Leonidas Polk, and Daniel Ruggles, Morgan hung around to pester Federal occupation troops at Nashville. He also had one more raid to undertake before rejoining Johnson. North of the Tennessee capital on the Louisville & Nashville Railroad lay the strategic town of Gallatin, astride Buell's Federal supply line. On March 15 Morgan's men descended on the village, and their captain entered the telegraph office to inquire of the operator if he had any news of Morgan's whereabouts. He had not, but—

"Let him come; I for one am ready for him," said the operator, patting his revolver.

Morgan placed his pistol against the operator's head. "Give me that gun," he said. "I'm Morgan."

Morgan stayed several days at Gallatin where the telegrapher, still with a pistol at his head, collected information on the strength and whereabouts of Union troops, at the same time imparting false information on the movements of John Hunt Morgan. During that time, the troops took possession of a Federal supply train, toured the countryside awhile, then burned the cars and wrecked the locomotive by running it over a bank. After tearing up tracks on both sides of the town, interrupting railroad operations for a week or more, the Kentuckians headed south and west to Johnson's base in Mississippi.

Events were shaping up that would bring together as fighting allies the two great cavalry commanders of the West—for the first time, but not the last. After the capture of Fort Donelson, Grant moved south to link up with the forces of Don Carlos Buell coming down from Nashville; and the first week in April, Johnson and Beauregard marched eastward from Corinth to meet the combined forces of the enemy at Shiloh Church near Pittsburg Landing.

Bedford Forrest was with Johnson's army. So, of course, was Morgan, having been promoted to colonel three days before. In this bloodiest of battles in Tennessee, where, for two days, green, untested infantry of both sides fought and killed each other cruelly to no satisfactory conclusion, one would expect the cavalry to be critically involved. They barely were; it was not that kind of fight. Wrote Colonel William P. Johnson, the general's son, of the role played by the combined forces of Morgan and Forrest: "The cavalry, about 4,300 strong, guarded the flanks or was detached on outpost duty; but, both from the newness and imperfection of their organization, equipment, and drill, and from the rough and wooded character of the ground, they could do little service that day."

As an aide-de-camp, Johnson could be forgiven such words as "newness" and "imperfection." What was not new or imperfect at this stage of the war? But otherwise the comment was correct. Morgan's troops were most of the time held in reserve on the fringes of the battle. Though Confederate corps commander William J. Hardee considered sending them against a Union battery, he canceled the order and told Morgan to "charge the first enemy he saw."

The first visible target was a Louisiana regiment that, because of its blue uniforms, was often mistakenly fired on by fellow Confederates. The Louisianans had grown used to it, and were ready to take on Morgan should he provoke them. "We fire at anybody who fire on us, god-damn!" said their Creole colonel. Morgan was able to restrain his troops in time to prevent a wholesale slaughter among friends. Later there was an impulsive charge on a Union battery, which Morgan's men put out of commission, and during which Basil Duke was wounded.

Somewhere in the midst of that blazing inferno was a young colonel of Alabama infantry named Joseph Wheeler, fighting with Braxton Bragg's corps of Johnson's army. It was said of most raw troops that they could be counted on to "run like the devil or fight like hell," and the Alabamans were relatively green. The fact that Wheeler's regiment lost a third of its men in a hard-held covert known as "the hornet's nest" suggests that they "fought like hell."

Probably neither Morgan nor Forrest knew Joe Wheeler, nor were they likely to have noticed him. He was difficult physically to see, five and a half feet in height. And he was not a showy commander given to rash, spectacular action. But when the Confederates lost heart with the killing of General Albert Sidney Johnson, and the second day's battle saw Grant, reinforced by Buell, advancing to the attack, Wheeler fought a rear-guard action that aided Beauregard's withdrawal to Corinth.

Morgan and Forrest also aided the withdrawal in their separate ways, Morgan's cavalry screening Beauregard's return march into Mississippi. Though the Kentuckian's role at Shiloh had been relatively minor, his handling of men in battle did not go unnoticed. "Can you not infuse some of Morgan's spirit in the other cavalry commanders?" Kirby Smith asked of the Richmond War Department. General Beauregard, replacing the fallen Johnson, offered more than praise. He authorized Morgan, since promoted to colonel, to increase his squadron to regimental size, gave him $15,000 for expenses, and instructed the colonel to raid behind enemy lines in Tennessee.

Thus encouraged, Morgan set out on April 26 for a raid into middle Tennessee, to wreak havoc on enemy communications and supplies. The first eight days went beautifully, riding at a pace of only twenty miles a day, with the troopers acquiring more supplies than they destroyed. A festive spirit pervaded the expedition, enhanced by plenty of applejack accumulated on the way and by the hospitality of the citizens in towns through which they passed. At one home where Morgan stopped, the daughter of the household later wrote, "I felt that night as if I were living in the time of Robin Hood."

> There was much revel in the lovely spring [wrote Basil Duke]. What more romantic, what more theatrical for the girls of Tennessee than to have these lads, just out of the Shiloh fighting, come riding into town, the dusty fours wheeling at the bugle, dismounting, laughing, dancing, making divine love under the blossoms, with the vedettes in grim vigilance up the pike only lending another thrill. It was the time, as someone has pointed out, for many *morganatic* alliances.

By the time the battalion reached Lebanon, Tennessee, on May 4, the skylarking nature of the expedition and the general lack of discipline began to take effect. The weather turned rainy and cold for May, and the good people of the town not only housed the raiders but plied them with food and drink as well. A few pickets were posted on the major highways, but these too were proffered whiskey as an antidote to the chilly rain and soon sought refuge in the nearby barns. The roads into Lebanon were empty and wide open.

Most of the troops were either sleeping or celebrating in the village inn when the First Kentucky Cavalry, U.S.A., 600 strong, galloped into town, commanded by Colonel Frank ("Old Meat Axe") Wolford. It was not an isolated irony that brought Kentuckians into conflict with Kentuckians, but one common to the border states. Morgan had known Wolford well before the war, and many of those in the ranks of both sides would have recognized one another, but for the confusion. As it was, Morgan's men had barely time to seize their weapons, no time to organize for battle.

The fighting raged at first from house to house and street to street. According to one newspaper correspondent, fortuitously present and trying to follow the action, "little could be seen except flashes from the muzzles of guns. The din was terrible. Amid the crack of rifles, the reports of pistols, and the clatter of hoofs on hard wet streets, could be heard hoarse shouts of fighting men, and at times the shrill shrieks of frightened women and children in the houses."

It was hard to distinguish between friend and foe in that surging, seesaw battle. Wounded in the side, Colonel Wolford continued to charge his rival Kentuckians until, weak from loss of blood, he fell from the saddle into the arms of one of Morgan's men. "Old Meat Axe!" cried his captor in delighted recognition. "Well, this is glory enough for one day!" Morgan himself greeted the prisoner warmly, but refused to keep him captive, leaving the wounded Wolford to the care of his own troops.

By now the Confederates were retreating in the face of overwhelming numbers. More than 120 raiders were captured, scores killed and wounded, as the retreat became a rout. "We were on the wildest race a soldier ever experienced. Sometimes we would jump clear over a fallen horse, and horses would sometimes shy around a man on hands and knees struggling to escape from the road." In what became known as "The Lebanon Races" the Federal cavalry kept up its pursuit as far as the Cumberland River, where Morgan's men were briefly halted.

A single ferry across the river was not large enought to carry men and horses both. Reluctantly the survivors dismounted, slapped the rumps of their mounts, and watched the animals disappear as they poled themselves to the opposite shore. It was a bitter moment as Morgan saw Black Bess, "head high, mane flying," running back and forth along the receding shoreline, indignant at being left behind. "She was the most perfect beauty I ever beheld . . . broad tilted loins, and thighs—all muscle . . . her head as beautiful as a poet's dream . . . wide between the eyes, it tapered down until her muzzle was small enough to have picked a lady's pocket."

The rout at Lebanon had been an inexcusable and humbling defeat. Basil Duke reported that it was the first and only time that he saw Morgan reduced to tears.

With Federal forces investing Beauregard's base at Corinth, Morgan led what was left of his depleted band of cavalry to Confederate-occupied Chattanooga. Here he set about rebuilding his regiment, with marked success. The men he had lost at Lebanon were more than compensated for by new recruits. He enlisted 200 men of the 1st Kentucky Infantry who had served out their 12-month term of enlistment. One mounted company from Alabama, and another from Mississippi joined the force, along with two companies of Texans. Back to more than full strength, over 800 men, the unit was designated the 2nd Kentucky Cavalry.

In mid-June the regiment moved to Knoxville, headquarters of Confederate troops in East Tennessee. Here Morgan was joined by an extraordinary figure in the hagiology of Southern cavalry: George St. Leger Grenfell, British soldier-of-fortune, fifty-four years of age, fresh from the Sepoy Mutiny and the Crimean War. He arrived from Richmond, having crossed the Atlantic on a blockade runner, with a letter of recommendation from Robert E. Lee, in which the Virginia general stated, "His information is so extended & his experience so varied, that there is hardly any position in which he could not be useful."

On his way West, Grenfell learned of the exploits of John Hunt Morgan, and decided that the Kentuckian was a man of kindred heart. In characteristic fashion he ignored his assignment to the Army of the Mississippi, now under Braxton Bragg, and rode to Morgan's camp at Knoxville. He had never intended to enlist, and never did. It was his custom to go wherever there was fighting in the world, and side with whichever faction he found most appealing. "If England is not at war, I go elsewhere to find one," he explained.

No one could quite believe "St. Lege's" stories. To hear him talk, according to Basil Duke, he had, at sixteen, run away from the aristocratic family seat in Cornwall to pursue a life of military buccaneering. He had joined a French regiment in Algeria, then shifted allegiance to side with the Emir Abd-el-Kader against the French. He had fought the Riff pirates off the coast of Morocco, and then served with Garibaldi in South America.

After a few drinks in the course of this narration, he would claim to have ridden with the Charge of the Light Brigade at Balaklava, to have fought in the Opium War in China, to have left a half dozen wives pining in Morocco, and to have followed various careers of smuggling, gunrunning, and privateering that had outraged British authorities around the world.

And in red tasseled turban with a giant saber belted to his waist, he looked the part of the swashbuckling buccaneer. As he rode into the camp at Knoxville, with two hunting dogs at his horse's heels, the troopers saw

> . . . a ramrod-straight six-footer, a man no longer young, but with a spare, wiry, angular figure, and an erect, soldierly bearing. The newcomer had a stern, weather-beaten bronzed face framed in dark hair and sidewhiskers, with a look in his eye that was sometimes fierce and hawklike, sometimes coldly aloof and supercilious.

Among Morgan's men brought up on the novels of Sir Walter Scott, many saw in Grenfell a remarkable resemblance to "Sir Brian de Bois Guilbert," the grim Templar of *Ivanhoe*.

There was an instant rapport between Morgan and Grenfell, and the Kentuckian subsequently made him his adjutant general, to which

Grenfell appended the title of "Colonel." There was less instant rapport between the Britisher and Morgan's men, whom Grenfell saw as a band of undisciplined ruffians wearing anything they chose, with broadbrimmed hats pinned up at the side by a star or crescent, oversized spurs that jangled loudly on their boots, irregular but deadly Bowie knives thrust into beltless trousers. In the Crimea, Grenfell had commanded a Turkish irregular cavalry company, "whose atrocities and unruliness were a byword in the army," and by breaking them into shape had won the rank of major. He would apply the same pressure to these promising but raw Kentuckians.

In that effort he failed miserably, unable at first to understand the easy camaraderie of the Southern cavalry, in which every man was of equal rank, and officers' titles were meaningless. Morgan recognized, as had Stonewall Jackson in the Valley, that the Confederate cavalryman, cocky and independent, was not easily controlled. He differed from the infantryman, according to Duke, in that "he was harder to catch. It is more difficult to regulate six legs than two." Grenfell concurred. "I never encountered such men," he confessed, "who would fight like the devil, but do as they please, like this damned Rebel cavalry."

Confederate cavalry leaders, as Grenfell learned, commanded by example, not by orders. Riding always to the forefront of their regiments, they inspired their men by the fury of their skill in combat. In that respect Grenfell admitted some months later to a British colleague that

> . . . the only way in which an officer could acquire influence over the Confederate soldiers was by his personal conduct under fire. They hold a man in great esteem who in action sets them an example of contempt for danger; but they think nothing of an officer who is not in the habit of *leading* them. In fact such a man could not possibly retain his position. Grenfell's expression was, "every atom of authority has to be purchased by a drop of your blood."

Grenfell had blood to spare and, given future opportunity, would prove of tremendous value to the 2nd Kentucky Cavalry and to other mounted Confederate units he would later lead.

He was of immediate value in imparting to Morgan's regiment all he had learned from experience in cavalry tactics and maneuvers. These were areas that Basil Duke excelled in, and Duke found Grenfell an "efficient officer, energetic and constant in his attention to duty," while Morgan would later write that "I feel indebted . . . especially to Colonel St. Leger Grenfell for the assistance which his experience offered me." One of Morgan's biographers enlarged on this by comparing Grenfell's assistance to Morgan to that of Baron von Steuben's aid to General Washington in the Revolutionary War.

In contrast to the year before, when Manassas had started things off so promisingly for the South, Confederate fortunes seemed on the wane in the spring of 1862, with all of Kentucky lost to the Union along with much of west and middle Tennessee. Beauregard had been replaced by Braxton Bragg, and little Joe Wheeler, colonel of infantry at Shiloh, was slated in mid-July for a new post, commander of cavalry in Bragg's newly constituted Army of the Mississippi.

Morgan and Forrest were bound by considerably more than their joint dislike of Wheeler, and that autumn, at Murfreesboro, Tennessee, they got together to compare notes and discuss their operations. Basil Duke was present at that conference, and reported: "Each seemed far more concerned to learn what the other had done and how he did it than to relate his own performances; and it was interesting to note the brevity with which they answered each other's questions and the eagerness with which they asked them."

They had much to talk about, because no two men became more active in so short a time in Confederate cavalry operations in the West. It was on this occasion, noted Duke, that, asked by Morgan the secret of his success against superior numbers, Forrest answered modestly:

"Oh, I just . . . got there first with the most men."

Because of his use of the colloquial, and his phonetic spelling, which shortened "head" to "hed" and "though" to "tho," his subsequent biographers distorted the phrase to "Git thar fustest with the mostest," which was passed down through the years. Though lacking in education (he once remarked, "I never see a pen without thinking of a snake") Forrest would not have been guilty of that double superlative; he understood words without concern for their alphabetical architecture just as he understood women without concern for their mathematical dimensions.

And in any event "fustest with the mostest" or "first with the most men," whichever, was not Forrest's only secret. Nor was it Morgan's. Both were born leaders and strategists when it came to cavalry; they shared a common pedestal.

For Morgan's troops there were several months of training in the camp at Knoxville, training that for once the men took seriously, for there were rumors of a big raid in the offing. Everything big was happening that spring. In the West, New Orleans had fallen to Farragut, and the whole Mississippi Valley, with Vicksburg the key to its control, was threatened. It was more important than ever to keep the Federals off balance in Kentucky and distract them from the campaign against Vicksburg; and Kirby Smith, Confederate commander in East Tennessee, had ideas of that sort for Morgan's cavalry.

In the East, Stonewall Jackson had completed his campaign in the Shenandoah Valley, sending the Federals scampering across the Potomac, and was preparing to join Lee, who had succeeded Joe Johnston, in the defense of Richmond. For the Confederate capital was facing the first crisis of its year-long life; and as Lee bolstered his defending forces, and McClellan called for reinforcements before launching an all-out attack, Jeb Stuart prepared his troops for a routine assignment that would turn into one of the war's more astonishing feats of cavalry.

CHAPTER

6

RING AROUND AN ARMY

"I THINK WE SHALL HEAR FROM HIM ON THE PENINSULA THIS SPRING," Jeb Stuart had prophesied of McClellan's plans for taking Richmond. And in mid-March of 1862 the word came. The Army of the Potomac was on the move. Prodded by Lincoln ("If General McClellan does not want to use that army, I would like to *borrow* it"), McClellan had loaded 85,000 troops on 400 motley transports and had shipped them down the Chesapeake to Hampton Roads. His intention, obvious to both sides, was to land at Fort Monroe and march up the Peninsula, between the York and James, to the Southern capital.

Johnston, with Stuart's cavalary brigade, broke camp at Manassas Junction and headed south for the defense of Richmond. With the Confederate troops already on the Peninsula, his forces numbered only slightly more than 50,000, or approximately two-thirds of McClellan's strength, but those were odds the South was getting used to. Contesting mile by mile the Federal advance, checking it for a month before the Yorktown lines and blunting its advance at Williamsburg, the Army of the Peninsula was pressed back to a line just seven miles east of Richmond where, on May 31, Johnston was severely wounded in the battle at Seven Pines.

He was replaced by Robert E. Lee, a somewhat unknown quantity, referred to as "Evacuation Lee" by critics of his earlier reversals. Jeb Stuart doubted his qualifications, even though Lee had once been a lieutenant colonel of the 2nd U.S. Cavalry, and had a son and a nephew serving under Stuart. "With profound personal regard for Gen'l Lee,"

Stuart had written a few months earlier, "he has disappointed me as a general."

At first, but only at first, the rank and file shared Stuart's bias. In contrast, they loved Joe Johnston. There was a funny difference between the two men, better expressed in manners than in words. (One officer was known to have put his arm around Little Joe's shoulders and to have patted the general's graying dome with comradely affection. You could never put your arm around the shoulders of Lieutenant General Lee.)

Heavily outnumbered by McClellan, Lee had two choices: to withdraw his army, henceforth known as the Army of Northern Virginia, from Richmond or to launch an offensive that would drive McClellan from the city's gates. The first was unthinkable; the second was risky—unless, he could strike at the Union force between the Pamunkey and the Chickahominy, and come upon McClellan's flank and rear, possibly bringing Stonewall Jackson from the Shenandoah to add muscle to the blow.

For this he would need information on the strength and disposition of the Union forces; and on June 10 he sent for his former cadet at West Point, and requested that Stuart "make a scout movement to the rear of the enemy now posted on the Chickahominy, with a view of gaining intelligence of his operations, communications, etc. . . . [and] to destroy his wagon trains." To these instructions, Lee added a note of caution:

> You will return as soon as the object of your expedition is accomplished; and you must bear constantly in mind, while endeavoring to execute the general purpose of your mission, not to hazard unnecessarily your command . . . be content to acomplish all the good you can, without feeling it necessary to obtain all that might be desired.

Lee must have known his cavalry commander well, by reputation if not by direct association. Self-restraint—any kind of restraint—was not Jeb Stuart's forte. And there was one among many factors in this mission that could overstimulate his natural aggressiveness. Guarding McClellan's right, with General Fitz-John Porter's corps, was the Federal cavalry reserve commanded by General Philip St. George Cooke. When his father-in-law had chosen to side with the Union, Stuart had declared "he will live to regret it—continuously." Here was the chance to make Cooke start regretting it. Possibly they might even meet, face to face, in battle.

For what was to be his ride to fame, Stuart selected his expeditionary force with care. Four selected regiments would go along, including those of Fitzhugh and Rooney Lee and the Jeff Davis Legion, numbering in all 1,200 sabers. There would also be two light guns from

Pelham's Horse Artillery, commanded by Lieutenant James Breasted, and a few volunteers from other units such as John Singleton Mosby and an extraordinary gladiator from abroad: Heros Von Borcke, late 3d Dragoon Guards of the Prussian Army.

There were to be many of these foreign heroes in the cavalry of both sides in the Civil War—St. Leger Grenfell was a good example— gentleman soldiers of fortune from the European armies, seeking to relive past glories, impelled by the clarion call of clashing sabers. Sometimes they applied at Washington or Richmond and formally enlisted. More often than not, they simply showed up where the action was, wearing British shakos or hussar caps or Turkish turbans, and took their place in line. It could happen only in America.

Von Borcke had run the blockade into Charleston, and had made his way to Richmond. He had no papers or letters of introduction; he had thrown them overboard, he said, when a Yankee frigate chased and boarded the blockade runner. Not knowing what to do with him, the Confederate War Department sent him on to Stuart. He arrived at the cavalry camp near Richmond wearing a pink and white riding habit, white breeches and top boots, swinging at the air with his oversized dragoon sword. Stuart accepted him on sight; then happily discovered that he had an excellent singing voice.

At 2 A.M. on the morning of June 12, Stuart roused his command with the order, "Gentlemen, in ten minutes every man must be in his saddle." And in ten minutes every man was mounted, jubilant at the thought of action, curious as to their destination. Stuart rode to the head of the column with the banjo-playing Sweeny, and led them north toward Ashland, convincing the troops that they were headed for Stonewall Jackson in the Valley to help drive the Yanks into the Potomac.

To the questions of those left behind and the envious pickets that they passed—"Where are you off to, boys?" "How long will you be gone?"—Stuart and Sweeny responded in duet:

> Oh, it may be for years
> And it may be forever . . .

And the ranks would join in, sending a chorus of voices across the sleeping Virginia countryside:

> Kathleen, Mavourneen, the gray dawn is breaking,
> The horn of the hunter is heard on the hill . . .

They bivouacked near Taylorsville for the night, and the next morn- ing the temper of the expedition changed, from carnival lightness to grim purpose. No fires were lit for breakfast, no bugles sounded "Boots and Saddles," and no voices were raised in song as the mounted column turned in direction from north to east and headed for Hanover Court House. They were not joining Jackson in the Valley; they were riding directly toward the enemy, and enemy scouts had already spotted their advance.

On the road from Hanover Court House to Old Church they made contact. Two squadrons of the 5th United States Cavalry, 100 strong, were ranged across their path. Rooney Lee, commanding the lead regiment in the column, gave the order to charge and, recorded Captain W. T. Robins of that unit, "the men dashed forward in fine style. The onset was so sudden that the Federal cavalry broke and scattered in confusion. The latter had a start of barely two hundred yards, but the Confederate yell that broke the air lent them wings, and only a few fell in our hands. The rest made their escape after a chase of a mile and a half."

By the time the main column under Stuart had reached Rooney Lee's position, the Federals had reformed in force a little farther down the road, drawn up in column of fours, and prepared to charge. These were more of the Union Fifth under Captain W. B. Royall, not yet the natural riders of the Southern cavalry, but ready at least to have their mettle tested. Again Lee ordered an attack, this to be spearheaded by a squadron commanded by Captain William Latané of the 9th Virginia.

It was a spirited thrust in which both squadrons met head on, in a clash that resulted in widespread confusion. Advancing Confederates were caught in a swirl of retreating Federals, each on all sides of the other. "Soon," wrote Robins, "we were pushed by foes in our rear into the ranks of those in our front, and a series of hand-to-hand combats ensued. To shoot or cut us down was the aim of every Federal who neared us." Riding by Robins's side, Captain Latané tumbled from the saddle, shot by Union Captain Royall. He was dead before he hit the ground. Simultaneously Captain Royall fell, cut down by a Southern saber.

Latané's death bequeathed him a certain immortality, and "Remember Latané!" became the battle cry of the brigade throughout the balance of the raid. The fallen captain also became the subject of a eulogy by John R. Thompson, a Richmond poet who more than any reflected the lyrical traditions of Virginia; in fact Lord Tennyson considered "the Burial of Latané one of the great poems of the Civil War." A sample verse:

> One moment on the battle's edge he stood,
> Hope's halo like a helmet round his hair,
> The next behind him, dabbled in his blood,

Prostrate in death, and yet in death how fair!
Even thus he passed through the red gate of strife,
From earthly crowns and palms to an immortal life.

The Federals did not try another stand until they had reached Old Church, where they rallied to defend their camp. Here at long last Philip St. George Cooke, Stuart's father-in-law, had a chance to score against his relative in gray. Stuart, according to Robins, allegedly sent Cooke "a polite message" by courier, but what it contained was not revealed. It resulted, however, in Cooke's withdrawal. After a fleeting skirmish, the Federals retired down the road to Cold Harbor, and the Confederates occupied, plundered, and burned the Union Camp.

The column rested briefly at Old Church where, according to Robins,

> . . . the people of the neighborhood, hearing of our arrival, came flocking out to greet us and wish us God-speed. They did not come empty-handed, but brought whatever they could snatch up on the spur of the moment, rightly supposing that anything to allay hunger or thirst would be acceptable to us. Some of the ladies brought bouquets, and presented them to the officers as they marched along. One of these was given to General Stuart, who, always gallant, vowed to preserve it and take it into Richmond.

But could he keep that promise? Stuart was now deep in enemy territory. He had penetrated the Federal line, discovered the weakness of the Union flank, and was faced with Lee's instructions to "return as soon as the object of your mission is accomplished." But as the Confederate cavalry was well to the rear of Fitz-John Porter's army corps, so it was reasonable to guess that Porter's cavalry was almost automatically on *their* rear, between them and Richmond.

Stuart's ordnance officer, John Esten Cooke, asked the question for him:

> "How was he to return? He could not cross the Pamunkey, and make a circuit back; he had no pontoons. He could not return over the route by which he had advanced. As events afterward showed, the alarm had been given, and an overpowering force of infantry, cavalry, and artillery had been rapidly moved in that direction to intercept the daring raider. Capture stared him in the face, on both of these routes—across the Pamunkey, or back as he came; he must find some other loophole of escape.

Stuart debated just five minutes, then came to his decision. He would make a circuit of McClellan's army—head south and east instead of west, somehow cross the Chickahominy to Charles City on the James, and follow the New Market road northwest to Richmond. "If on his way he encountered cavalry," Cooke reported, "he intended to fight it; if a heavy force of infantry barred his way he would elude, or cut a path through it; if driven to the wall and debarred from escape, he did not mean to surrender."

But if he would not surrender, Cooke inquired, what other course was left?

"To *die game*," Stuart told him.

In his official report Stuart called his decision "the quintessence of prudence." Apparently not all his officers concurred. They were not averse to risk, but they were opposed to suicide. "While none accorded a full assent," wrote Stuart, "all assured me a hearty support in whatever I did." Thus on the second afternoon out from his base, he led his column deeper into enemy territory, heading for Tunstall Station on the York River Railroad which linked McClellan's army to his base of supplies at White House on the York.

"The gayest portion of the raid now began," wrote Lieutenant Cooke. "From this moment it was neck or nothing, do or die. We had one chance of escape against ten of capture or destruction"; while Stuart, maintaining "an abiding trust in God," found that "there was something of the sublime in the implicit confidence and unquestioning trust of the rank and file in a leader guiding them straight, apparently, into the very jaws of the enemy, every step appearing to them to diminish the faintest hope of extrication."

By now Stuart knew the enemy were in his rear, and on his flank, and surely on his front. Closest and of most concern were his father-in-law's forces, which included a brigade of infantry, some artillery, and at least six squadrons of mounted troops, including the 5th Pennsylvania Cavalry, Colonel Richard H. Rush commanding, distinctively equipped with lances.

How close these pursuers were, it was hard at any time to know. Stuart kept the guns of the Horse Artillery tight on the rear of his column, ready to wheel about at the first sign of the enemy and lay down a screen of exploding shells until the main body of the cavalry could rally to the charge.

There was a critical moment when one of the guns became mired in deep mud, buried to the axle. The horses strained until they nearly broke the traces; the cannon did not budge. An ingenious sergeant approached Lieutenant Breasted, and pointed to a keg of whiskey on a wagon captured from a Union train. "Just put that keg on the gun, Lieutenant," he suggested, "and tell the men they can have it only if they pull through."

The troops responded, noted Cooke, with "herculean muscularity. . . . With eyes fixed ardently upon the keg, they waded into the mudhole up to their knees, seized the wheels of gun and caisson loaded down with ammunition, and just simply lifted the whole out, and put them on firm ground. The piece whirled—the keg had been dismounted—the cannoneers revelled in the spoils that they had earned."

It was an eventful day. Scouting and flanking parties, led by the resourceful scout Mosby, overtook Union wagon trains and either plundered them or burned them. One wagon was found loaded with champagne, which the troopers eagerly consumed. Others, Cooke found, contained "excellent army stores," from which he himself got "a fine red blanket, and an excellent pair of cavalry pantaloons for which I still owe the United States."

They were nearing Tunstall's Station now, and expecting at any moment to meet enemy resistance. Captain Robins's company, riding in vanguard, was first to come face to face with a squadron of Union cavalry approaching from the opposite direction. It was a curious encounter:

> As soon as the Federal officer in command saw us he called a halt, and, standing still in the road, seemed at a loss to know what to do. His men drew their sabers, as if about to charge, but did not come on . . . Our men were hastily mounted and formed into columns of four, with drawn sabers, ready for any emergency. There we stood, eyeing each other, about two hundred yards apart, until the head of the main Confederate column came in sight, when the Federals retreated down the road leading to the White House.

Robins assumed that the bluecoats were speeding to sound the warning and assemble troops at Tunstall Station. He later learned that the officer had led his troops galloping through Tunstall without stopping, and when asked what was happening, had shouted enigmatically, "There's all hell happening"—and disappeared.

The taking of Tunstall, garrisoned by a platoon of infantry, was no hard problem. As Stuart's vanguard approached the station, a Union officer, perhaps unfamiliar with the Confederate cavalry uniform, genially waved them on. Ignoring the welcome, Stuart ordered "Form platoons! Draw sabers! Charge!"—and, "at the word the sabers flashed, a thundering shout arose, and sweeping on in columns of platoons, the gray riders fell upon their blue adversaries, gobbling them up, almost without a shot."

The raiders were almost in time to capture a Union train coming down from Richmond. Seeing the graycoats ranged along the depot platform, the engineer sounded his whistle, put on all steam, and pluckily prepared to race through. The cavalry fired at the trainmen and soldiers riding the flatcars as at moving targets in a shooting gallery, and Captain Will Farley of Stuart's staff took aim and shot the engineer. The train rocketed past, and escaped down the tracks to White House.

At this point, straddling the railroad only five miles from McClellan's base at White House, Stuart must have been sorely tempted to raid that Federal depot where enormous stores were kept. But the odds, as he properly guessed, were prohibitive. Too many hounds were on his trail; his men had been riding and/or fighting almost ceaselessly for two days; and troops at White House Landing would be thoroughly alerted.

Prudent for once, he settled for a thorough wrecking of the railroad, telegraph wires, sutlers' stores, and rolling stock. Tracks were torn up; men with axes ranged up and down the line felling the telegraph poles across the roadbed. The only accessible bridge across Black Creek was destroyed; loaded freight cars were burned or plundered; Tunstall's Station appeared struck by a tornado before the column formed again to move southeast toward the Chickahominy.

The full haversacks with which the cavalry had started out were long since empty. There had been no time for foraging; men and horses both were hungry and exhausted. From scattered houses along the way the people ran out with what meat and bread they had to spare, but the lifesaver was a Yankee sutler store at Talleysville that catered to McClellan's troops passing to and from the landing. The proprietor saw his stock of cheese, fruits, beef-tongue, sausages, molasses candy, and canned meats disappear in sixty minutes—after which, Robins observed, the cavalry seemed like "new men."

At midnight the march was resumed, the column heading for the Chickahominy. "The highway lay before us," wrote Captain Austen Cooke, "white in the unclouded splendour of the moon." But what lay ahead was definitely clouded, for "The critical moment was yet to come. Our safety was to turn apparently on a throw of the dice, rattled in the hand of Chance." More than one enemy was pressing them. Rush's Lancers were two hours behind. And Stuart's brigade had reached the point of total exhaustion. Recorded Cooke:

> Whole companies went to sleep in the saddle, and Stuart himself was no exception. He had thrown one knee over the pommel of his saddle, folded his arms, dropped the bridle, and—chin on breast, his plumed hat dropping over his forehead—was sound asleep. His sure-footed horse moved steadily, but the form of the General tottered from side to side, and for miles I held him erect by the arm.

They came to Sycamore Springs Ford on the Chickahominy at dawn, and the chill light revealed a still more chilling scene. Recent rains had turned the normally tranquil stream into a raging torrent that over-flowed the banks and swirled around the trunks of toppled trees. There was no means of measuring its depth or strength, but Rooney Lee, arriving with the vanguard, tried to do so. Accompanied by several men, he plunged into the river, was caught by the current, and nearly drowned as his horse became tangled in submerged debris and branches.

He barely made it back to shore, where Captain Cooke asked him, "What do you think of the situation, Colonel?"

"Well, Captain, I think we are caught," Lee told him cheerfully.

The rest of the cavalry arriving took one look and shared Lee's estimation. More dead than alive they slid from the saddle and sprawled wherever there was dry ground, too tired to care what hap-pened to them. Until Jeb Stuart rode up, no longer the dapper smartly uniformed figure with the rose in his lapel, but muddy, gaunt-eyed, and disheveled, with only the plumed cap marking the dauntless cavalier who had led them forth from Richmond.

One thing was obvious to Stuart. They could not remain where they were, with the enemy behind them and no way to cross the river. The general ordered the weary column to remount and led them a mile down stream to a point known as Forge Bridge. The bridge had been destroyed, but two large stone abutments still remained, some thirty or forty feet apart, between which the river flowed deep and narrow and contained by steep banks.

Under Stuart's direction, a stranded barge was floated and anchored in midstream between the twin abutments. A nearby warehouse was torn apart to furnish timbers, which were laid between bank and barge on one side, between skiff and bank on the other. Over this footbridge the men were able to cross, leading their swimming horses by the bridles. So far so good, but there remained the Horse Artillery. More planks and timbers were brought from the dismantled warehouse, and in less than two hours a bridge was thrown together solid enough to bear the horse-drawn guns.

Colonel Fitz Lee headed the detail left behind to cover the transit of the battery. When the last man was over, Captain Robins set fire to the bridge piled high with tinder, and waited for flames to consume the structure. "I was seated under a tree on the bank of the river," Robins noted, "and at the moment that the hissing of the burning timbers of the bridge let me know that it had fallen into the water, a rifle-shot rang out from the other side, and the whistling bullet cut off a small limb over my head."

They had been not a minute too soon. Rush's Lancers came galloping to the far side of the burning bridge, as frustrated by the river as the Confederates had been two hours earlier. With a cheerful wave of his hat, Robins bade them farewell—and galloped off to rejoin the column of gray raiders.

They were now about forty miles from Richmond, and grateful for the swollen river at their backs. Stuart had missed the hoped-for showdown with his father-in-law, but Philip St. George Cooke would be humiliated nonetheless. Fitz-John Porter officially complained that he had seen "no energy or spirit in the pursuit by General Cooke," and Cooke was ordered to submit a written explanation as to why he had allowed the rebels to escape.

The raiders followed the James River Road toward the capital, the only hazard being Federal gunboats on the James and troops of General Joseph Hooker's division covering their northward route. Stuart galloped on ahead to reach Richmond before sunrise on the 15th and report to General Lee. The cavalry had taken 165 prisoners, 260 horses and mules, and destroyed telegraph wires, supplies, and ammunition dumps, and damaged the York River Railroad. More important, they had established that the right of McClellan's line was "in air," weak and relatively unprotected.

Having delivered this information, Stuart rode back to lead his weary but triumphant raiders into Richmond. The capital turned out to give the dirty, weary, and unshaven troopers a triumphant welcome:

> The colonels are at the heads of their regiments—brisk compact Fitz Lee, with the jolly gleam of white teeth in his dark beard; big Rooney Lee, with his heavy, dependable air, tall on his tall horse; Lieutenant-Colonel William Martin, hard and competent. Then the troopers—the smart soldiers, their gray jackets buttoned, sitting up in their saddles—the dull, tired soldiers, slouching on their weary horses—the gay soldiers, with keen, roving eyes for the pretty Richmond girls.

In war-weary Richmond, as well as in the North, Stuart's ride around McClellan's army was hailed as the greatest cavalry maneuver, so far, of the war. "This was service after the true Marion and Ashby fashion," wrote the editor of the Richmond *Dispatch*; while Colonel William Averell of McClellan's thwarted cavalry was forced to admit, "This raid of Stuart's added a new feature to cavalry history . . . The expedition was appointed with excellent judgment, and was conducted with superb address."

Stuart himself distributed the credit with largesse. He recommended Von Borcke for promotion, and singled out many of his officers and troops for special praise, among them John Singleton Mosby who had served as scout throughout the raid. He gave Mosby a letter to War Secretary George W. Randolph, commending the scout as one "who for months past has time and again rendered services of the most important and valuable nature, exposing himself regardless of danger, and, in my estimation, fairly won promotion." The letter would do much for Mosby's future.

There was no question that Stuart's ride around the Union army had given a mighty boost to Confederate morale. It had demonstrated, to public satisfaction, that the Southern cavalry could ride better, shoot better, and wield the saber with more dexterity than its Northern counterpart. And this would be true for at least a year to come.

More than that, Stuart had given Lee the sought-for information that McClellan's flank was vulnerable. Strangely enough, though McClellan shifted his base from White House to Harrison's Landing on the James as a result of Stuart's penetration of his line, he did little to strengthen the weaknesses that Stuart's raid exposed. The right of his line was still "in air," unprotected by adequate fortifications or troop concentrations.

Guided by this information, Lee summoned Stonewall Jackson from the Shenandoah Valley and launched his counteroffensive against the Union army in front of Richmond. Stuart covered the front and flank of Jackson's forces as they advanced to attack the Union right. In the Seven Days' Battle that followed, June 25 to July 1, 1862, Jeb's horsemen were constantly but never critically engaged. There were frequent skirmishes with General George Stoneman's Union cavalry, but in no instance did the Federals offer any strong resistance.

Out West, where Farragut's fleet was beginning its attack on Vicksburg on the Mississippi, the Union had introduced a weapon more fearful to the Confederates than the Southern cavalry was fearful to the Union: heavily armored ironclads and gunboats. Riding down to White House, now being abandoned by the Federals, Stuart had his first encounter with this nemesis of the inland rivers. Standing off the Landing was the U.S.S. *Marblehead*, loaded with infantry that had been engaged in the destruction and evacuation of the Union base.

Gunners on the *Marblehead* sighted the gray-clad cavalry on shore and opened fire with their 11-inch naval rifles. Determined "to expose this Yankee bugaboo called gunboat," Stuart ordered his troops to return the fire and sent a hasty call for Pelham's Horse Artillery. As the dismounted horsemen ducked shells and spattered the deck of the *Marblehead* with bullets, the gunboat launched two cutters loaded with infantry for a land assault on the arrogant Confederate cavalry.

They had reached shore, bayonets bristling above the deck rails of the cutters, when Pelham brought one of his howitzers to bear upon the

Marblehead. His aim was, as always, flawless. Shells burst above the vessel's crowded deck; the two cutters churned about to seek the safety of the mother ship—one capsizing as she was hoisted in; and the *Marblehead* hastily weighed anchor and steamed down the York. Probably no victory gave Stuart greater satisfaction than this encounter with the Union navy.

Back in Richmond early in July, with the capital free of immediate danger from McClellan's army, the Stuart legend waved like a flag above the city. This god of battles had even defeated a Union gunboat! The gray-clad troopers strutted like conquerors through the streets, and envious infantrymen had a glimpse of the new Confederate hero:

> He was on his horse, backed against a wall and held close prisoner by a group of pretty girls in crinoline and little bonnets. They had thrown a wreath of red roses around his charger's neck, and bestowed a great cluster of red roses that blazed now in the crook of his arm, against his new gray jacket. He sat, bareheaded, a willing captive, beaming down onto their flushed, merry faces, and he was—Infantry observed, as its leading files came around the corner—reciting poetry to the ladies.

He won more than admiration. On July 25 he was promoted to major general in command of the cavalry division of Lee's Army of Northern Virginia. Fitzhugh Lee headed one of the brigades, and forty-four-year-old Wade Hampton, twice wounded as infantry commander, was placed in charge of the other as Stuart's senior brigadier. It had been a year in coming, but Hampton was at long last with the cavalry, where he belonged.

Stuart made his summer headquarters at Timberlake's farm, near Atlee's Station, north of Richmond, where Flora and his son and daughter joined him. To the newly commissioned Major Von Borcke, the family group was reminiscent of a Rembrandt painting, full of soft lights and pleasing contrasts. But this domestic bliss was interrupted when Major General John Pope was put in command of the newly formed Federal Army of Virginia.

Pope was one of the early known generals to appreciate the proper use of cavalry, and he had good officers in that department, among them Brigadier General John Buford. To take the pressure off McClellan and screen his impending withdrawal from the Peninsula, Pope moved south to the Rappahannock, while Stuart's cavalry rode north to support Stonewall Jackson and harass the enemy's communications. Fitzhugh Lee led the cavalry's advance. In fact, Fitz Lee rode so far in advance that Stuart lost track of the brigade, and stopped for the night of August 17, with his staff and a small escort, at the tiny village of

Verdiersville, a few miles south of the Rapidan. Here they spread out and catnapped on the porch of a neighborly house, while Mosby and another scout rode out to reconnoiter the surrounding country.

At dawn came a sudden burst of pistol shots, the clatter of hooves, and Mosby's cry of "Yankee cavalry!" Stuart leaped to the saddle, jumped his horse over the garden wall, and took to the woods, just seconds before a column of Union horsemen stormed into the village. He was followed by the rest of his staff; and from concealment in a grove of trees they watched with chagrin while the Federals looted their belongings—one blue trooper rode off waving Stuart's plumed hat like a captured regimental flag.

Stuart and his staff were safe, as was Fitzhugh Lee's brigade, too far away to know of the attack. But Stuart's near capture and the loss of the plumed hat rankled beyond measure—somewhere between a catastrophe and a regimental joke. As the grapevine carried the news through the rest of the army, Stuart complained to his wife, "I am greeted on all sides with the banter, Where's yer hat? . . . I intend to make the Yankees pay dearly for that hat."

In late August, with McClellan pulling out of the Peninsula, Lee raced to intercept Pope before the returning troops could reinforce the Federal Army of Virginia. Stuart got General Lee's permission to sever the Orange & Alexander Railroad on Pope's rear and cut off the flow of Federal supplies. Heading for the railroad line, he ran into five regiments of Union cavalry, commanded by General Buford near Brandy Station.

It was a brief but furious clash of sabers, with the Federals retreating across the Rappahannock. The encounter decided nothing—except that the Yankee horsemen were exhibiting more spunk. And it put Brandy Station on the war maps, a name that in time would be proudly stamped on regimental banners. But the engagement left Stuart dissatisfied, and he led his regiments across the Rappahannock in pursuit. If he could find where Pope's army was, he could possibly make a swift raid on their supplies, and further upset that general's plans for reaching the Potomac unassailed.

So on to Warrenton, where the troops paused for refreshment in the taproom of the local tavern. Stuart tried to gain information on the whereabouts of General Pope, but could gather from the local citizens only that the Federals were somewhere to the east. It was night by now, misty and rainy, and Stuart was well behind the Union lines. The mission began to seem foolhardy, but he led his column gropingly to Catlett's Station farther down the line.

Then the raiders got a break. Among the prisoners taken in their ride from Hanover to Brandy Station and beyond, was a black teamster who had been impressed by the Federals. He was a Virginian and recognized Jeb Stuart, the most easily recognized Virginian of them all. Yes, he knew precisely where Pope's headquarters were—right here in the vicinity of Catlett's Station. He would be glad to lead the gentlemen to the general's tent, to the troop encampment, the wagon park, the horse corrals, and all.

Stuart consulted with his brigadiers. It might be a trap, but it was worth the chance, and they agreed to let the teamster be their guide. On the way they planned their attack; it must be quick, it must be coordinated. One of the regiments, under Rooney Lee, would descend on Pope's headquarters and take the general prisoner, while the other two created a diversion with a hit-and-run raid upon the camp. Of what followed, Captain John Thomason wrote:

> They moved swiftly and in close order, the rain covering all small sounds. Rooney Lee led quietly up to the tents occupied by the convivial members of General Pope's Staff, and charged, shooting and yelling. Sleepy sentries, sheltering against the wet, lay discreetly low, or ran out to be ridden down. The camp guards fled or surrendered. The soaked gray troopers ravaged about, cutting tent-guys and upsetting wagons, rounding up prisoners and horses, and putting fire to everything that would burn.

But the prize target, General Pope, was absent. The raiders settled for capturing his quartermaster and the members of his staff, his horses and baggage, and most importantly his orders and correspondence file revealing much of the army's plans. And there was one more item among the booty: Pope's military frock coat, tailored for dress parade, with its gilt braid and buttons and the gold stars of a major general on the shoulders.

While Pope's correspondence file, delivered to Lee, helped the Confederates achieve victory at Second Manassas, the captured cloak and hat had particular significance to Stuart. He had them mounted on a frame and displayed around the Confederate camp, later to go on view in the State Library in Richmond. "I have had my revenge on Pope," he wrote to Flora. The Yankees had paid dearly for the hat.

There was a sequel to this plumed-hat-versus-dress-coat saga. Writing to Flora of the Battle of Second Manassas, August 29-30, Stuart boasted that his men had "knocked Buford's cavalry into Bull Run," and "won imperishable laurels." He also reported that a captured prisoner had brought him a personal message from Major General Pope.

"Pope told him to tell me that he would send me my hat if I would send him his coat. But I must have my hat first."

There, unsatisfactorily, the matter ended. Buford's cavalry clung to the hat, as a symbol of their rising proficiency, and Pope presumably sent to Washington for a new coat, perhaps remembering the words of his poet-namesake, "What mighty contests rise from trivial things!"

CHAPTER

7

THUNDERBOLT OF THE CONFEDERACY

JULY FOURTH, 1862.

Plenty of reason in Virginia to celebrate Independence Day, with Richmond free of danger from McClellan's battered army, and most of the Shenandoah free of Union occupation forces after Stonewall Jackson's victories.

Not much cause to celebrate in the West, with Henry Halleck and Don Carlos Buell keeping the Confederates on the defensive in north Mississippi and Alabama. The Cleveland *Plain Dealer* brightened the holiday for Northerners with the bannered headline, "Vicksburg Is Ours!"—then had to publish a retraction: Vicksburg was still holding out against Farragut's ocean-going fleet and Flag Officer Charles Davis' gunboats.

At Knoxville, Tennessee, however, John Hunt Morgan was about to launch his own spectacular display of fireworks, as he led his cavalry west on what would be known as the First Kentucky Raid. Though fifty or sixty men were left behind for want of horses, the brigade still numbered between 800 and 900 troops—Morgan's largest force to date; and though some were poorly armed they counted on getting fresh weapons from the killed, wounded, or captured enemy.

A few days later, on July 9, Nathan Bedford Forrest led 1,000 of his cavalry west from Chattanooga in a raid into Middle Tennessee. Both he and Morgan had a common purpose: to take the pressure off Braxton Bragg's and Kirby Smith's Confederate armies by disrupting enemy communications and supplies. Morgan, however, had another goal. He was confident that two-thirds of Kentucky was sympathetic to the South. Show the citizens the Stars and Bars, and they would rally to the colors. The Confederacy would gain a whole new army of recruits.

As Morgan's men headed northwest toward Kentucky their spirits soared, for as one of their number later wrote, "The cavalryman enjoys nothing more than a long raid into the enemy's country . . . the Kentuckian always had a longing eye for the Bluegrass region, and was never so happy as when marching in that direction." In keeping with that spirit, Basil Duke composed his "Song of the Raiders," intended to be chorused by the troopers on the march:

> Through the woodland's deep shade
>   By the meadow's green side
> Up the hill, down the valley
>   We steadily ride
>
> But hushed is the laughter
>   And silent the song
> As all night the squadrons
>   glide swiftly along.
>
> Then ho for the Bluegrass
>   And welcome the chance
> Whatever the danger
>   that bids us advance!

As the brigade passed through the Tennessee town of Sparta, they received disturbing information that altered their itinerary. It seemed that after the Lebanon Races a squadron of Pennsylvania Cavalry, pursuing Morgan's fleeing troopers, had entered the town and, disgruntled at not overtaking their quarry, had vented their wrath on the women of the village, using abusive language and advising them to "sew up the bottoms of their petticoats."

Their commander, Major Thomas Jefferson Jordan, had since repaired to Tompkinsville, where the Pennsylvanians were now encamped. Though Tompkinsville was some miles west of Morgan's planned invasion route, an insult to Southern womanhood must be avenged. Pausing at Celina only long enough for St. Leger Grenfell to take his daily dip in a local stream, enjoyed without removing his tasseled red silk turban, the column set out to chastise Major Jordan.

At Tompkinsville, with his 350-man battalion of the 9th Pennsylvania Cavalry, Jordan received word of Morgan's coming, feeling "little fears as to the result, as my men had met him before and felt sure of victory." He ranged his cavalry in line of battle, on high and wooded land above the road, and watched through his field glass the approach of what he referred to as "a band of guerillas."

What he saw was disconcerting. He had estimated Morgan's force as a single regiment; now he saw a whole brigade, which he estimated would outnumber his battalion six to one. In point of fact, some of Morgan's hopes for obtaining new recruits had been fulfilled. Between Sparta and Tompkinsville, two or more volunteer companies had joined the column—including Champe Ferguson, a renegade freebooter almost as infamous as William Quantrill—which had increased Morgan's force to more than 1,100 men.

Finding the enemy well in command of the highway, Morgan decided on a frontal assault across a belt of open fields. And in this attack St. Leger Grenfell made his bid for fame and recognition. He had bragged of his feats to the Kentuckians, remarking to Basil Duke on the way to Tompkinsville that the raid "reminded him of the expeditions made by Abd-el-Kader into the territory held by the French." Now came the opportunity to live up to his self-created image.

When they were still sixty yards from Jordan's line of Pennsylvanians, Grenfell suddenly spurred his horse forward at a gallop and, recorded Basil Duke, "risking the fire of the enemy, leaped a low fence behind which the enemy were lying, and began lashing at them right and left with his saber." The apparition of this scarlet-turbaned tartar gone berserk, roaring and rearing on his giant stallion, cutting at bluecoats as if shucking corn, was more than enough to spread terror through the Union ranks. The Pennsylvanians broke and fled, leaving behind them twenty-two dead, up to forty wounded, and thirty taken prisoner.

Among the latter was Major Jordan, who gave himself up, believing that "resistance would be madness." But, complained Jordan, "After I had surrendered I was fired upon at a distance of but a few feet, the charge, happily for me, missing its mark, but blackening the side of my face with powder." Brought before Morgan, Jordan was refused a parole, taken behind the Confederate lines, and eventually sent to Richmond, where he was formally charged with "insulting the women of Sparta and Celina"—and finally exchanged.

Grenfell had won his figurative spurs in the engagement, and the Kentuckians agreed with Duke that his "gallantry in battle was superb." In addition to the prisoners taken, the Pennsylvanians' camp yielded a substantial number of Federal horses and mules, as well as a goodly supply of coffee and sugar—but no reward so satisfying as seeing Major Jordan being escorted under armed guard to their rear. Moving north to Horse Cave, the colonel, along with Grenfell, telegrapher George ("Lightning") Ellsworth, and a few scouts, pushed on to the Louisville & Nashville Railroad. Here Ellsworth hooked his instruments up with the wires that paralleled the tracks and began sending messages up and down the line. "No rebels here," he reassured operators throughout central Kentucky, and "Morgan believed withdrawing into Tennessee." It was Ellsworth's whimsy that helped to create the legend that Morgan could be anywhere and everywhere at once.

Leaving the railroad, the group forded the Green River and closed in on Lebanon, Kentucky. At Lebanon the raiders easily routed the defending garrison of 200 Union infantry and took possession of the town. Flushed with success, Morgan tested some methods of winning Kentucky back into the Southern fold. He distributed a proclamation calling on citizens to "rise and arm and drive the Hessian invaders from the soil." The manifesto opened with the ringing lines of Yankee poet Fitz-Greene Halleck:

> Strike—for your alters and your fires!
> Strike—for the green graves of your sires!
> God—and your Native Land!

A continuing paragraph called for "the willing hands of fifty thousand of Kentucky's bravest sons" to join the fight.

Unfortunately for the purpose of this proclamation, the conduct of the cavalry at Lebanon was not such as to win unqualified support. The local correspondent for the Louisville *Journal* observed that Morgan "did not appear to care much for discipline, permitting his men to go as they please;" while the troops were "mostly of that class to which we apply the term 'sporting gentlemen.' "

On entering Lebanon, Morgan had promised the citizens that their rights and property would be respected. But his men, the Louisville reporter noted, took the order lightly. "The soldiers stole horses by the wholesale.... Indeed, whenever they wanted anything, they took it." Perhaps because the troopers later chased him out of town, the reporter added the vindictive footnote: "A big degenerate Englishman named Greenville [*sic*] burned down the depot and set fire to the courthouse."

With better horses than they had started with, and better weapons captured from the Pennsylvania Cavalry, the column moved on to Harrodsburg, a town noted for its Southern sympathies. It was Sunday, July 13, the day that Nathan Bedford Forrest captured Murfreesboro, aggravating a Northern fear that Confederate raiders were riding at will throughout the West. News of Morgan's arrival emptied the church of Sunday worshipers as the congregation flooded out in welcome. Villager Lizzie Hardin wrote in her diary of that memorable moment:

At last they came! Oh! the grand and glorious sight it seemed to us! Eleven hundred Southern horsemen, rushing on at full speed amid the waving of caps and the glancing of steel. . . . The men and boys rushed up the road to meet them, giving shout for shout. The ladies waved handkerchiefs and threw flowers, and wept and almost shouted, too, as among the troops they saw brothers and sons and husbands.

Maria Daviess watched the column pass her home and recorded: "It was a weird, wild cavalcade, horses of all kinds and colors; boys of all ages and sizes, and no uniforms, save the general grimy gray, that dust and wear had given. There were shaking of hands and tears and kisses, and such unsoldierly demonstrations, as never were shown." One young girl vowed she would never again wash the hands the men had kissed, another stole a button from Morgan's coat to wear on her watch chain, and a third announced that she intended to marry St. Leger Grenfell.

In polite response to this enthusiasm, Morgan paraded his troopers around the town to give all a view of these saviors of Kentucky. In turn, the brigade was treated to the greatest outdoor feast in local history. Maria Daviess noted that "the fat of the land was furnished in rich abundance . . . and the larders of the loyal yielded up their stores as freely as the most rabid secesh."

Only one thing marred this show of hospitality. When the feast was over, many of the civilian guests found that their horses had been replaced by animals that were lame, or sick, or generally inferior. Yet under the circumstances such "exchanges" were forgiven. Lizzie Hardin generously noted that "men were never kept in better order than Morgan's on that raid. After they left Harrodsburg even their enemies could say nothing of them except that they had taken horses as well as the letters from the post-office."

The raiders were only twenty-eight miles from Lexington, Morgan's home town, which meant that they were within striking distance also of both Louisville and Cincinnati. At the intervening village of Georgetown, the commander of the home guard gave his men a spirited address in which he warned that "Morgan, the marauder and murderer — the accursed of the Union men of Kentucky" was all but upon them, with twelve thousand bearded men with butcher knives. He advised immediate action: a wholesale flight to safety.

In Cincinnati the alarm approached hysteria, with the papers warning of imminent attack. "The enemy is at our doors!" A similar sense of panic prevailed at Federal headquarters in Louisville. Brigadier General Jeremiah T. Boyle, an earlier victim of Morgan's prankish telegrams, began sending frantic wires of his own — to Secretary of War

Stanton, generals Halleck and Buell, and even President Lincoln: "Morgan has over fifteen hundred men." . . . "Morgan is devastating with fire and sword." . . . "Send artillery and men without delay."

Lincoln himself took steps to ease the panic. Henry W. Halleck had just been appointed general-in-chief of armies of the United States, and to him the President wired, "They are having a stampede in Kentucky. Please look to it." At the same time Halleck received a dispatch from Boyle, in which the number of Morgan's troops was doubled by the author: "Morgan has invaded the state with 3,000 men, robbed the bank and is murdering and stealing everywhere."

Though Morgan intended no attack on Louisville or Cincinnati, he knew that the countryside was up in arms. He set his sights on a more modest target, the river-girt town of Cynthiana, thirty miles northeast of Lexington. No more than 800 Union soldiers held the town, half regulars and half militia, but they had one advantage in the river and the easily-defended bridge that spanned it.

Morgan resorted to familiar strategy: a frontal assault—in this case over the Licking River bridge—with flanking attacks on the enemy from both sides. But the latter meant fording the river under fire, one of the most hazardous feats of this or any war. Scores were killed or wounded struggling waist-deep in the water; others died on the banks; but the bridge was secured, and St. Leger Grenfell led a thundering charge across the planks and into the center of the town.

"I cannot too highly compliment Colonel St. Leger Grenfell," recorded Basil Duke, "for the execution of an order which did perhaps more than anything else to gain the battle. His example gave new courage to everyone who witnessed it." Grenfell "received eleven bullets through his horse, person, and clothes," but miraculously was only slightly hurt, though Duke noted, of a hole through St. Leger's scarlet cap, that "it fitted so tight upon his head that I previously thought a ball could not go through it without blowing his brains out."

The July 17 fight at the bridge and in the town lasted less than two hours, but the toll was heavy, roughly fifty killed or wounded on both sides, with many of the surviving Federals taken prisoner. And what had been gained? A small town entered, a depot burned, lives lost, and an already outraged section of Kentucky further mobilized against the raiders. Union Colonel Rutherford B. Hayes, future President of the United States, wrote of the affair at Cynthiana: "I am really jolly over the rebel Morgan's raid into the Blue Grass. It will do great good. The twitter into which it throws Cincinnati and Ohio will aid us in getting volunteers. Good for Morgan!"

On the return march to Tennessee there was only one minor incident. From behind distant trees, as the column was entering Crab Orchard, a bushwhacker fired at it. George Ellsworth and a companion, after the column had halted, leaped on the nearest horses and took after the offender. The horse Ellsworth borrowed happened to be St. Leger Grenfell's prize steed fitted with a valuable English saddle; and during the ensuing skirmish, the horse broke loose and disappeared.

When Ellsworth rejoined the column and reported the animal's loss, Duke reported that "St. Leger was like an excited volcano, and sought Ellsworth to slay him instantly. Three days were required to pacify Grenfell, during which time the great 'operator' had to be carefully kept out of his sight."

Arriving at Livingston on July 28, Morgan issued his own report of the whole expedition. In twenty-four days his men had ridden more than a thousand miles, "captured seventeen towns, destroyed all the government supplies and arms in them, dispersed about fifteen hundred Home Guards, paroled nearly twelve hundred regular troops." Basil Duke, in his account, noted also that Morgan had entered Kentucky with about nine hundred men and returned to Tennessee 1,200 strong. The troops, reported Duke, were "admirably mounted and well armed, and the new recruits were fully the equal of the original 'Morgan Men,' in spirit, intelligence, and capacity to endure."

Morgan had not, as he had hoped to do, persuaded Kentucky that her interests lay in siding with the South. But the generally successful expedition, coupled with the simultaneous raids of Bedford Forrest, convinced both Kirby Smith and Braxton Bragg that Kentucky could be won by a joint invasion of the state. Smith would march toward Lexington from Knoxville, threatening Cincinnati; Bragg would march from Chattanooga toward Louisville. As a prelude to this double-pronged campaign, Morgan was to cut the Louisville & Nashville Railroad, which supplied Buell's Federal army which was feeling its way toward Chattanooga.

Morgan struck the railway line near Gallatin on August 12. Here an 800-foot tunnel ran through a mountain seamed with veins of coal. Sides and roof were supported by wooden beams, which gave the raiders an inspired opportunity. A captured train was loaded with hay, the hay was set ablaze, and the cars were pushed through the tunnel igniting the anthracite along the way. The smouldering, smoking tunnel, part of which collapsed when the supporting timber burned, was impassable for weeks, and Morgan's Kentuckians established another "first" for Confederate cavalry: setting fire to a mountain.

Following the flaming mountain episode, Morgan moved his command to Hartsville, Tennessee, where it remained for six days. Here, with the discovery of an abandoned print shop, another first for the innovative cavalry was spawned: Volume One, Number One, of *The Vidette* —a company newspaper edited by Lieutenant Gordon Niles, a former journalist with the brigade. *The Vidette,* whenever and wherever similar facilities were found, was printed, according to Duke "on any sort of paper that could be procured, and consequently . . . it appeared at different times in different colors. . . . Sometimes a pale rose hue and once a delicate pea-green."

Niles filled his paper with both local and national news, including "some tremendous and overwhelmingly decisive Confederate victories, of which official records make no mention." Also "the horrors of Federal invasion were depicted in terms which made the citizen reader's blood freeze in his veins." There were legitimate accounts of the brigade's engagements, and patriotic contributions from Basil Duke, including his poetic plea for new recruits:

> Ye sons of the South, take your weapons in hand,
> For the foot of the foe hath insulted your land.
> Sound! Sound the loud alarm!
> Arise! Arise and arm!

Due notice by *The Vidette* was taken of the personal achievements of the cavalry, and in his second issue Niles reprinted a story from the Knoxville *Register* describing Grenfell's performance during the Kentucky raid in which

> . . . he commanded the respect and admiration of the entire command by his undaunted bravery, being always where bullets whistled thickest, and when, in the bloody streets of Cynthiana, his noble horse fell pierced by eleven bullets, his own clothing riddled, and himself wounded, he placed himself at the head of a small party detached from their command, and calling upon them to follow, he dealt such destruction among the enemy as to cause them to tremble at the sight of him.

Outraged by Morgan's escapades, General Buell ordered Brigadier General Richard W. Johnson to assemble such cavalry companies as he needed to "catch Morgan and bring him back in a bandbox." On August 21 the Union cavalry, 800 strong, approached Gallatin to which Morgan had returned. Duke formed his 2nd Kentucky Regiment in battle line to greet them. Three times the Federals charged that line, wasting their strength against a stone wall. When Duke was convinced that the enemy was played out, the Confederates countercharged, and the bluecoats broke and ran "in a style of confusion more complete than the flight of a drove of stampeded buffaloes."

In the engagement near Gallatin, 30 Federals were killed, 50 wounded, and some 75 captured, including Johnson and his staff. Confessed General Buell, who had prompted the misadventure, "Our cavalry was totally insufficient to cope with Morgan," while the dispirited Johnson called the performance of his horsemen "shameful in the lowest degree."

Kirby Smith's invasion of Kentucky was now under way, coordinated with that of Braxton Bragg, and Morgan received orders to join Smith at Lexington the first week in September. Lexington was Morgan's home town as well as that of a number of his men; so the troops were ordered to spruce up their attire, polish their boots, and curry their horses. They must demonstrate that they had kept faith with their Blue Grass heritage.

And as they marched into Lexington on September 4 the town turned out to welcome them in kind, with tumultuous crowds, flag-bedecked streets, and marching bands:

> The bells of the city pealed forth their joyous welcome—men, women and young boys and girls, with smiles, tears, shouts, and cheers rushed into the streets, waving white handkerchiefs and small Southern flags, and making the air resonant with the strains of wildest joy. Wives pressed husbands to their bosoms, parents clasped sons in affectionate embrace, and for hours the most intense interest everywhere prevailed.

"John Morgan could scarcely get to his home, the people almost carried him," Mattie Wheeler wrote in her diary; while one of Kirby Smith's infantrymen observed:

> The great chieftain, John Morgan . . . is a splendid type of the *genus homo*, and seems to be a perfect idol with the people. They gather around him in groups and listen with wondering admiration to the recital of his daring adventures. Recruiting is going on rapidly, and Kentucky is enlisted in the cause of freedom.

In the weeks to follow, however, Morgan's cavalry played no major role in the invasion, being assigned to diversionary raids behind the Union lines. Kirby Smith marched north toward Cincinnati, but did no more than frighten the residents before falling back to rendezvous with Bragg's army. Braxton Bragg raced Don Carlos Buell to Louisville, but was blocked and defeated at Perryville on October 8.

After that, all was downhill for Smith and Bragg, and Morgan was summoned to protect the rear of Bragg's retreating army. To a cavalry commander accustomed to acting aggressively and independently, with faith in hit-and-run tactics as a means of winning wars, no task could have been more unappealing. On top of that, it placed the colonel under the orders of General Joseph Wheeler, Bragg's chief of cavalry, whose ideas on the use of mounted troops were precisely the opposite of Morgan's.

The consequences were predictable. Somehow or other—and there is a suspicion that St. Leger Grenfell played some sleight of hand which Bragg's dispatches—orders got lost, mislaid or misinterpreted, and Morgan's Kentuckians went off on their own, "gadding about, no one knew where, among the Kentucky hills." In any event Morgan's command did not accompany Bragg's army on its retreat through Cumberland Gap.

But they would not be uninvolved for long. For his failure to pursue Bragg's damaged and retreating army, Don Carlos Buell was replaced by William S. Rosecrans; and as Bragg settled down at Murfreesboro, Rosecrans took a threatening position at Nashville. The left flank of "Rosey's" army was protected by a Union garrison at Hartsville, Tennessee: 2,500 troops commanded by Colonel Absalom B. Moore. Morgan's scouts reported this situation to their commander, and the Kentucky leader—who had been too long inactive—had a target.

Starting from Baird's Mill in bitter cold weather on December 9, Morgan marched for Hartsville with four regiments and one battalion of cavalry and, for this expedition, two regiments of infantry and two horse batteries—twenty-two hundred men in all. Speed and surprise were vital to success, and Morgan feared that the infantry would slow him down. He introduced another innovation, what was called a "ride and tie" procedure, in which the cavalry rode for five or six miles, then dismounted and gave their horses to the infantry. The infantry rode for five or six miles and returned the horses to the cavalry. The resulting brouhaha was critically appraised by one historian:

> It was an absurd, unmilitary arrangement. . . . The infantry, now mounted, found their soaking feet and legs almost frozen in the stirrups and were anxious to dismount. The erstwhile foot cavalry, on remounting, found their own dripping feet and legs unfitted for the comparative inaction of the stirrup. Worst of all there was terrible confusion in the early winter nightfall in getting the horses back to their owners. The snowy turnpike was hot with yelling, cursing men bellowing for the god-damned infantry to give them back their horses, and for the god-damned cavalry to take their horses, a trooper yelling that's not his horse . . . and another, upon remounting and finding his oilskin gone, calling to a comrade to shoot that god-damned soldier there, number three man in that four, he's got my oilcloth, and a general chorus of malediction on the snow that was wetting the guns and the ammunition.

Despite the confusion, the system worked. Crossing the Cumberland, the column reached Hartsville in time to strike at dawn the following morning, taking the garrison by surprise. In less than 90 minutes' fighting, in which 262 Federals were killed or wounded, Moore surrendered, and Morgan had 1,834 prisoners on his hands.

The prisoners served a logistic purpose. Lined up in the bitter cold, the order was given:

"One Hundred Fourth Illinois, attention! Come out of them overcoats!"

The captives peeled off their overcoats and boots and handed them over for worn-out Confederate clothing. Then, with a captured wagon train of Federal equipment and supplies, the jubilant column, with prisoners almost equivalent in number, headed back for Baird's Mill. The expedition had been "a brilliant feat," wrote General Joe Johnston, who recommended to President Davis that Morgan "be appointed brigadier general immediately. He is indispensable."

Davis acted on the suggestion. Morgan was raised to brigadier general, and Basil Duke was promoted to colonel. St. Leger Grenfell, as Morgan's adjutant, journeyed to Richmond and miraculously extracted from the War Department $250,000 for new horses and equipment, and for new recruits. The brigade became a division mustering 3,100, the largest force that Morgan had ever commanded. And as their numbers grew, so did the legend that surrounded Morgan's cavalry, expressed in the folk lyrics of the time:

> Morgan, Morgan, the raider, and Morgan's
> terrible men,
> With Bowie knives and pistols are galloping
> up the glen.

In Murfreesboro that autumn, as during most of her life, lived twenty-one-year-old Martha Ready, daughter of former U.S. Representative Charles Ready. A newspaper correspondent found her "a bewitching woman, belonging to the blood stock of the old South," and during her father's days in Congress she was remembered as "a favorite in society . . . the first girl in Washington to wear a curl upon her forehead."

How she and Morgan met is unclear. According to one version, shortly before Sidney Johnson evacuated Murfreesboro in the late winter of 1862, Morgan stopped at the home of Colonel Charles Ready to discuss his cavalry operations with his commander William J. Hardee. Not Martha but her sister overheard that conversation, in which Hardee cautioned the colonel to be more careful and avoid the risk of capture. "It would be impossible for anyone to capture me," said Morgan. But somehow Martha had, either then or later.

According to another account, when Murfreesboro was still in Union hands, a Yankee officer asked the young lady her name.

"It's Mattie Ready now," she said, "but by the grace of God one day I hope to call myself the wife of John Morgan."

Told of this romantic boast on arriving at Murfreesboro, Morgan sought the lady out and her capitulation was immediate. Their marriage on December 14 became a significant date in Tennessee wartime annals, with subsequent happenings often referred to as before or after Morgan's wedding. And what a wedding! The two-story Ready Mansion was barely large enough to hold the crowd of guests.

President Jefferson Davis barely missed attending, but plenty of prestige was supplied by the star-studded generals serving as ushers at the ceremony, among them William J. Hardee, Benjamin Cheatham, John C. Breckinridge, and Braxton Bragg. As Bishop of Louisiana, Leonidas Polk performed the wedding rites, wearing Episcopal robes over his lieutenant general's uniform. And following the ceremony, a Lucullan feast:

> Supplies were still plentiful, and the supper included turkeys, hams, chickens, ducks, and "all the delicacies and good dishes of a Southern kitchen," while Colonel Ready's cellars still had a sufficient stock of wine to provide for the drinking of many toasts. Two regimental bands were on hand, and after supper there was dancing until the hour grew late. On the street outside, hundreds of soldiers assembled and celebrated the wedding with bonfires and cheers for Morgan and his bride.

Basil Duke, of course, was at the party; and so also was St. Leger Grenfell, who later "in a high state of delight . . . sang Moorish songs, with a French accent, to English airs, and was as mild and agreeable as if someone was going to be killed." As it turned out, however, neither Duke nor Grenfell were in favor of the marriage, and both seemed to see it as a turning point in Morgan's life—and not one for the better.

To Grenfell, apparently, Martha Ready appeared as a Delilah, intent on shearing Samson's hair, or an early-day Scarlett O'Hara, consumed in self. Duke also disapproved, but, did not, of course, declare as much in writing, only that she "exercised over . . . [Morgan] the great influence which she was thought to have possessed."

Nor was Grenfell any more specific. He simply chose this occasion to start fading out of Morgan's orbit, seeming to believe a soldier's life was not compatible with marriage. Colonel James Fremantle, a British observer on leave from the Coldstream Guards, met Grenfell some months later and reported in his diary: "He talked to me much about John Morgan, whose marriage he had tried to avert, and of which he spoke with much sorrow. He declared that Morgan was enervated by matrimony, and would never be the same man as he was."

Morgan himself, however, seemed not to have compromised his battle instincts. Rather than wasting time on a honeymoon, he almost literally leaped from the nuptial bed to set out on another raid. Seven days after the wedding he was with his assembled troops at Alexandria, thirty miles northeast of Murfreesboro, tall in the saddle and back in his element. As he lined his men up on dress parade, prior to departure, Basil Duke recorded the words of an unidentified writer "whom I have frequently had occasion to quote":

> The men were never in higher spirits or more joyous humor; well armed, well mounted, in good discipline, with perfect confidence in their commander, and with hearts longing for the hills and valleys, the blue-grass and woods of dear Kentucky; they made the air vocal with their cheers and laughter and songs and sallies of wit. It was a magnificent body of men—the pick of the youth of Kentucky. No commander ever led a nobler corps—no corps was ever more nobly led.

The lyrical tone was not amiss, for perfection was the order of the day. Every sick soldier and disabled horse had been weeded out, so that only "stout men and serviceable horses were permitted to accompany the expedition." To this peerless company Morgan read his orders and explained the purpose of the expedition: to wreck Rosecrans' supply line, especially the Louisville & Nashville Railroad north of Bowling Green, destroy provisions and ammunition dumps, and generally raise hell with operations in the Union rear.

After the troops had listened in silence to "the stirring words of their beloved hero-chieftain," according to Duke's unnamed writer, "the woods trembled with the wild hurrahs of the half crazy men, and regiment answered regiment, cheer re-echoed cheer, over the wide encampment."

It took two hours for the last of the column of fours to clear the assembly point and strike out for the Kentucky border. And once on the march, General Morgan rode from the rear to the head of the column, cheered by the men as he passed, smiling and waving his hat in acknowledgment. Duke's anonymous writer could not resist another portrait:

> Did you ever see Morgan on horseback? If not, you missed one of the most impressive figures of the war. Perhaps no General in either army surpassed him in the striking proportion and grace of his person, and the ease and grace of his horsemanship. Over six feet in hight [sic], straight as an Indian, exquisitely proportioned, with the air and manner of a cultivated and polished gentleman, and the bearing of a soldier, always handsomely and tastefully dressed, and elegantly mounted, he was the picture of the superb cavalry officer.

On Christmas Eve the raiders captured a wagonload of holiday merchandise bound for the stores of Glascow. No great military feat;

but Morgan wanted a dress for Mattie. He found one and sent it back by a volunteer courier who, it happened, turned out to be a Union spy. Mattie got the dress, and wrote to her sister in Nashville:

> I wore it to the ball last Friday night, given in honor of 'the bandit and his bride.' It was magnificent and very much admired. I had a splendid time and of course was something of a belle . . . My life is all a joyous dream now, for I know my liege lord is devoted to me. . . .

To which the apt reply: "Dear Mattie, you think the honeymoon will never pass, don't you?"

No, the honeymoon would never pass for Mattie, and Morgan's letters to his bride were also tinged with starshine. The virile raider began greasing his hair with pomatum, and his staff observed that he was often lost in daydreams. Were Duke and Grenfell right, that marriage was slowing the old raider down?

No immediate evidence of that, however. Morgan led his galloping cavalry on a wide-ranging circle that crested at Elizabethtown on the Louisville & Nashville Railroad. At nearby Muldraugh's Hill they destroyed two enormous trestles, eighty feet high and nine hundred long, after capturing the garrisoned stockades protecting them. Then they turned east and south with scattered Federal units in pursuit.

Back they rode, tearing up miles of railroad track, pausing at Bardstown on December 30 to pillage the largest general store in town. Of this jubilant event Confederate scout John Allen Wyeth wrote:

> The men who crowded in through the doors they had battered down, found difficulty in getting out with their plunder through the surging crowd, which was pressing to get in before everything was gone. One trooper induced the others to let him out by holding an ax in front of him, cutting edge forward. His arm clasped a bundle of a dozen pairs of shoes and other plunder, while on his head was a pyramid of eight or ten soft hats, telescoped one in the other just as they had come out of the packing box.

From that point on, the retreating column was plagued by bitter cold and sleet, concerned not so much with the pursuing Federals as with the fight to stay awake, being sometimes forced to ride for thirty-six hours at a stretch. They crossed the Cumberland on January 2 and were back at their starting point near Alexandria on January 5. As summed up by Wyeth:

> This was Morgan's most successful expedition. The Louisville and Nashville Railroad was a wreck from Bacon Creek to Shepherdsville, a distance of sixty miles. We had captured about nineteen hundred

prisoners, destroyed a vast amount of Government property, with a loss of only two men killed, twenty-four wounded, and sixty-four missing. The command returned well armed and better mounted than when it set out. The country had been stripped of horses.

Was it really Morgan's most successful raid? During the bloody battle of Stones River, December 31 to January 2, Bragg had been sending him messages urging an immediate cavalry attack on Rosecrans' rear. The couriers had not been able to reach Morgan, and Bragg blamed his need to withdraw from Murfreesboro partly on the missing cavalry. Basil Duke defended his chief on the grounds that the raid, although perhaps unnecessarily prolonged, had diverted Federal troops that otherwise might have aided Rosecrans.

In appreciation, the Confederate Congress passed a resolution of thanks to Morgan and his men "for their varied, heroic, and invaluable services in Tennessee and Kentucky, immediately preceding the battle before Murfreesboro [Stone's River]—services which have conferred upon their authors fame as enduring as the records of the struggle which they have so brilliantly illustrated."

In Morgan's own estimation, however, his career was just beginning. Though Northern newspapers howled at his irregularities, branding him a "horse thief" and "guerilla," the South had begun to refer to him as the "Thunderbolt of the Confederacy." And the South's definition was not so much a tribute to his past accomplishments as an omen of the future.

8

THE GRAY GHOST

"QUIET TO QUICK BOSOMS IS A HELL," WROTE JOHN SINGLETON MOSBY in December of 1862, quoting as he was wont to do from Lord Byron's vibratory verse. For this was the winter of his discontent. It was partly, perhaps, because he had just turned twenty-nine, and the war was twenty months old and he not yet a hero. He had acted as Stuart's scout throughout part of 1862, had been on the fringes of many battles, had been captured and exchanged; but now the Virginia cavalry had settled into winter quarters south of Fredericksburg, with only boredom to contend with. Stuart had whimsically named the place "Camp No-Camp," since its principal characteristic was a lack of everything: no food, no tents, no forage for the horses. If one added to that list "no action," then the situation became unendurable.

Mosby was ready for a change; and it would be the fulfillment of a childhood dream going back almost as far as memory permitted — when he was four or five on the family's farm in Nelson County, Virginia. In his slight frame and fair and delicate complexion — his mother considered him "pretty" — he gave no sign of the dark tide of impatience that would rule his life, for good or ill. Yet action and danger were his personal imperatives. His hero was the "Swamp Fox" Francis Marion for whom, as he grew older, Turner Ashby was the modern counterpart.

His education was typical of the middle-class Virginian: first a country school; then classes in Latin, Greek, and Mathematics in nearby Charlottesville; then to the University of Virginia, where his classmates found him convivial, but "deep" and quiet, given to quoting poetry and the classics. This scholarly image was abruptly broken when, in an argument with a fellow student, George R. Turpin, he drew a revolver and shot and severely wounded the outspoken classmate who had made a "disagreeable allegation." Plainly there was a dark side to his fair complexion.

This tragedy, which resulted in a year's jail sentence and a $500 fine, had a recompensing aftermath. The prosecuting attorney took a liking to the well-bred, erudite, and smart young man. He invited Mosby, when finally released from prison, to read for the law in his Lynchburg office. One year later, he was on his own, hanging out his shingle—"John S. Mosby–Lawyer"—in the thriving Washington County town of Bristol. He also took a wife, Pauline Clarke, daughter of a Kentucky lawyer.

So he might have ended, a quiet, dedicated small-town lawyer, with two children and a pious wife—far removed from the role of his idol, Francis Marion. Even when war broke out, he at first was loyal to the Union; then, with Virginia's secession, followed the tide of volunteers that swamped such county seats as nearby Abingdon. Hence he rode, with his own horse and body servant Aaron, to enlist with the Washington Mounted Rifles under Captain William E. Jones.

Jones was a tough drillmaster for the callow, starry-eyed Virginians seeking romance in the cavalry. Nothing pleased him; hence the nickname "Grumble" Jones. A West Point graduate, he had resigned from the army after the death of his wife to live the life of a hermit in the Appalachian Mountains of Virginia. The threat of war brought him out of hiding, but he disdained the pomp of military life. Wearing only blue jeans, a hickory shirt, and a homespun jacket, he sought to dress his troops in clothes from the state penitentiary, as a sensible economy. Most of the aristocratic volunteers dumped the clothes in a pile before the captain's tent, preferring to wear whatever they had brought from home. Mosby wore the penitentiary uniform.

Mosby liked Grumble Jones, perhaps because the gritty commander showed no deference to the slight, 125-pound private in his ranks. And when, sometime later, six Sharp's carbines were rationed to the company, Jones parcelled them out as badges of honor, saying as he did so: "I shall always put these men in front. I shall always place them in the post of greatest danger." Mosby was flattered to find himself among these men.

Summoned to Richmond by Robert E. Lee, commander of military forces in the state, the company rode northeast at a leisurely pace, with voices raised in song; for this was to be a singing war, even in its sadder moments. "If Abraham Lincoln could have been sung out of the South as James the Second was out of England," wrote Mosby in his memoirs, "our company would have done it and saved the country all the fighting." Riding through village after village, young maidens threw roses and kisses at the handsome cavaliers, with probably scant notice of the slight, stoop-shouldered private in prison denim.

Stopping for two weeks near Richmond where Grumble Jones drilled his men further and whipped them into fighting shape, they were ordered to join Jeb Stuart's 1st Virginia Cavalry in the Shenandoah Valley, where Joe Johnston was keeping General Patterson in check near Harpers Ferry. It was Mosby's first sight of the bearded Stuart with the plume and gold star on his cap, so nearly Mosby's age yet becoming a legend in his time. He likened Stuart to his boyhood hero Francis Marion, and felt there was a certain destiny at work in their encounter.

Perhaps there was; but his service under Johnston and Stuart was mostly confined to scouting and picketing in the no man's land south of the Potomac. Even at First Manassas in July of 1861, Mosby saw little action, yet, "I was in the fight," he wrote to Pauline, "We at one time stood for two hours under a perfect storm of shot and shell." He saw plenty of shot and shell, but from a distance, for the Washington Mounted Rifles, to Grumble Jones' chronic dissatisfaction, was held in reserve throughout the battle and Mosby did no fighting and was never in real danger.

His time would come, however. Though for the next six months he was assigned primarily to picket duty, occasionally within sight of the Capitol dome in Washington, he stood up well in frequent brushes with the enemy, and Jones observed that "Private Mosby . . . has always been ready in the most active and dangerous duty, rendering brilliant service."

A curious, probably unrelated incident preceded his first promotion. Wherever Jeb Stuart headquartered, pretty girls appeared like flowers germinated by the sun. On a snowy day in February the colonel had two such ladies on his hands, who needed transportation home before the blizzard locked them in. Either Mosby volunteered or was elected for the honor; and on returning from this mission was invited to breakfast with Stuart, General Johnston, and other officers. That morning Grumble Jones summoned Mosby to his tent. The young ex-lawyer had just been commissioned first lieutenant and regimental adjutant.

In mid-march, General Johnston evacuated his winter camp at Centerville and withdrew behind the Rappahannock and Rapidan. Stuart, now brigadier general of cavalry, rode with him, with Grumble Jones now colonel of the 1st Virginia Regiment. Anxious to know the disposition of the enemy, Johnston asked for a scout to penetrate the Union lines, and Mosby volunteered. He returned the next day, bedraggled and wet from swimming the Rapidan, knowing more about Federal maneuvers than the Secretary of War in Washington.

"Adjutant Mosby . . . of the 1st Virginia Cavalry," Stuart wrote in his report to Johnston, "volunteered to perform the most hazardous service, and accomplished it in the most satisfactory and creditable manner." Stuart added that the adjutant was "worthy of promotion and should be so rewarded."

While the promotion failed to materialize, it was the first time Mosby had been accorded official recognition. It indicated he had Stuart solidly behind him, support that was worth its weight in gold. When Lee succeeded Johnston, after the latter's injury at Seven Pines on May 31, and Stuart planned his raid behind McClellan's army below Richmond, the cavalry general designated Mosby as one of his principal scouts for the expedition.

Mosby claimed more than that. After Stuart's famous ride around McClellan, Mosby wrote to Pauline: "I returned yesterday with General Stuart from the grandest scout of the war. I not only helped execute it, but was the first one who conceived and demonstrated that it was practicable." Stuart was not so generous. Nowhere did he write that Mosby had conceived the whole maneuver, though he did include the adjutant among those who had "rendered conspicuous and gallant service during the whole expedition." To General Lee he cited Mosby as one whose "distinguished services run back toward the beginning of the war, and present a shining record of daring and usefulness."

After the Seven Days' campaign, Mosby was back again at the business he was best at: scouting. And becoming restless. When Pope took over the newly-formed Federal Army of Virginia, to launch an offensive that would screen McClellan's flight from the Peninsula, he gratuitously offered Mosby an idea. The Union general proclaimed to his troops, "Let us look before us, and not behind." Which meant to Mosby that Pope would be less concerned with the army's rear and his supply lines, than with the enemy in front. So—raid the enemy's rear; raid his ammunition dumps; raid his communication lines; capture or destroy his wagon trains.

"I saw that here was a bountiful harvest to be gathered, and that the reapers were few."

He applied to Stuart for permission to go out on his own, with a select group of comrades, taking advantage of the Partisan Ranger Law passed by the Confederate Congress. Under the terms of this act, partisan cavalry could raid at will upon enemy forces and facilities, keeping whatever booty they captured apart from government supplies and being paid for captured arms and ammunition turned over to the U.S. Government. Better than anyone, from his months of scouting, Mosby knew the territory south and west of the Potomac, the likely military routes, the mountain passes. Given a dozen men like himself, he could wreak havoc on the enemy.

Stuart was sympathetic. He himself, however, could not spare even the handful of men that Mosby wanted, with both Pope and McClellan still a threat to Lee's Army. He suggested that Mosby apply to Stonewall Jackson, as one who might better be able to release some veterans from his "foot cavalry." And he gave Mosby a letter of recommendation to the general.

So on July 19, Mosby rode north to hunt out Jackson, then at Gordonsville collecting troops to guard the Virginia Central Railroad. Near Beaver Dam Station he paused to rest, tethering his horse to a tree and stretching out on the turf beneath the warm mid-summer sun, perchance to dream of the life ahead that promised freedom and adventure. He was awakened by a rattle of hooves, to find himself surrounded by a group of mounted men in blue: Federal cavalry from Fredericksburg on a raid against the Virginia Central Railroad.

Mosby has little to say in his memoirs of his capture and stay in Old Capitol Prison in Washington. A formula for the exchange of prisoners had just been agreed upon between the North and South, which cut short his stay in the capital's "bastille." In fact, he left the Old Capitol on the day, July 29, that one of its more famous prisoners arrived: Belle Boyd, the Confederate Mata Hari, who had aided Jackson's operations in the Valley and now entertained the prisoners with ringing choruses of "Maryland, My Maryland!"—coming down strong on the line, "Huzza! she spurns the Northern scum!"

From the Old Capitol, Mosby was transported by Union steamer down the Potomac and up the James to City Point, the place of exchange. His observant eye made good use of the voyage. He took note of Federal troop ships, heavily loaded, passing up the James from Hampton Roads. By judicious questioning of the vessel's crew he learned that the troops were reinforcements bound for Pope's Army of Virginia, about to launch its offensive against General Lee.

As soon as he was ashore and free, on August 5, Mosby walked the twelve miles to Richmond—sustaining himself through the heat with a sack of lemons—and appeared like a dusty scarecrow at Lee's headquarters in the city. He demanded to see the general, with important news. Nobody who looked like that, the guards decided, could be the bearer of important news; but the interloper made so much noise to get attention, that a staff officer finally brought him in to General Lee. Mosby spat out his information in a rush of words; Union troops, whole shiploads of them, bound for Pope's army on the Rapidan. Then he curbed his excitement and identified himself.

"You will know better what weight to attach to my information when

I tell you that I am one of the men mentioned in your general order in connection with General Stuart's ride around McClellan."

The chief's eyes softened with recognition. "Yes," he said, "I remember."

The news brought by Mosby prompted Lee to speed his counteroffensive against Pope, sending his troops across the Rapidan to attack the Union flank and rear. Jeb Stuart's cavalry prefaced the maneuver with a raid on Federal communications, during which his near capture at Verdiersville occurred. Mosby's earlier reconnoitering of the roads around the village enabled him to warn the general in the nick of time, and the scout escaped with the rest of Stuart's staff.

At Second Manassas and during Lee's invasion of Maryland, Mosby scouted on the fringes of the fighting, capturing, with the aid of a companion, seven Federal cavalrymen, two infantrymen, and for himself "a good Yankee horse, two fine saddles and two pistols." His own horse was shot, and some days later he himself narrowly escaped death when a bullet pierced his hat and creased his scalp. Like Stuart, however, he seemed impervious to that one fatal bullet that would stop him.

After Antietam he accompanied Stuart on the latter's Chambersburg raid into Pennsylvania, as detached scout for the cavalry. He rode like a one-man fury, dedicated to destruction of the enemy. Place names flashed past his saddle like signposts on a highway: Frederick, Sharpsburg, Chambersburg, and Hyattstown. After a Christmas raid on the Washington approaches, he returned with Stuart to Loudoun County where Lee's Army of Northern Virginia prepared to settle for the winter.

Mosby had been riding, scouting, and fighting almost steadily since his release from prison. But he still had not achieved his goal: to have and to lead his own company of partisans. He again attacked Stuart on the subject. Much as he hated to lose his scout and adjutant, Mosby had certainly earned the chance. All right, said Stuart; take nine men from Fitzhugh Lee's brigade, and try it.

Until Stuart's December raid, a drowsy complacency ruled the Federal outposts guarding Washington, from Dranesville, Virginia, through Centerville and down to the Potomac south of Alexandria. "All Quiet Along the Potomac" became both a stereotyped dispatch and the title of a song. Then, in the first two weeks of January 1863, a series of pixyish misfortunes plagued the perimeter of the defense line.

On January 10 at Herndon Station on the Alexandria, Loudoun & Hampshire Railroad pickets were surprised at a game of cards, and they and their horses were captured by a motley group of men in gray and butternut.

Several miles away, five mounted Union soldiers on patrol were pounced upon and added with their horses to the group of captives.

Two nights later a ten-man Federal patrol at Frying Pan Church was taken prisoner by men who seemed to come from nowhere.

And on January 15 Mosby appeared at Stuart's headquarters near Fredericksburg. He presented the general with 22 horses, the paroles of an equal number of Union prisoners, along with assorted rifles, pistols, saddles, and military equipment.

"I could do more with more men and more time," Mosby said.

"Very well," Stuart said. "You shall have them."

Three days later Mosby was off again, headed for Fauquier County with fifteen hand-picked men from the 1st Virginia Cavalry. Though it was not yet official, he had begun his career as leader of Partisan Rangers—the lonely life of which John Esten Cooke wrote, "The trump of fame will never sound for him. If he fails, it will be in the depths of some forest, where his bones will moulder away undiscovered; if he survives, he will return to obscurity as a rain drop sinks into the ocean and is seen no more."

He did not drop into obscurity, far from it. But thereafter Mosby did seem to vanish like a phantom in the morning fog and dusk of evening, becoming so elusive that an enemy-inspired sobriquet, "the Gray Ghost," clung to him throughout the remainder of the war.

In his mind he had already staked out the territory he would haunt, the area he knew best. Triangular in shape, it was bound roughly by the Blue Ridge Mountains on the northwest, by the Potomac on the northeast, with its base a horizontal line through Warrenton. Involving portions of three Virginia counties—Loudoun, Fauquier, and Fairfax—it would be known in time by both allies and enemies as "Mosby's Confederacy."

Besides being ideal country for any sort of cavalry maneuvers—rolling meadows and bare hills with occasional clumps of trees, segmented only by shallow streams and low stone fences—it was perfect for the operations Mosby had in mind. The groves and woodlands offered concealment and bases for ambush, while gaps in the Catoctin Mountains and the Blue Ridge offered avenues of quick escape to hiding places in the mountain hollows.

The partisans would have no regular headquarters, no established camp, though certain places like Warrenton made favorable points of rendezvous. Since the country people were generally friendly, they lived in farmhouses and barns, or, where these were lacking, in the field. To avoid being trapped, never more than two men spent the night in proximity—the whole group reuniting at some appointed place at dawn.

The organization was loose but loyal, with Mosby their unchallenged leader. The men rode their own horses, carried their own arms. They wore whatever they chose, careful not to approximate the uniform of either side. As time went on they exchanged their mounts for captured Union horses, often fresher and better nourished, and their guns for the Spencer repeating carbines or rifles carried by the Union cavalry. Like partisans everywhere, they were often better mounted, better shod, and better fed than the regular, army-attached cavalry.

A principal target for Mosby's early operations was Fairfax Court House, a central point in the defense of Washington, and headquarters for the Federal cavalry brigade of Colonel Percy Wyndham, the British soldier of fortune. Mosby automatically detested Wyndham as one who had badgered Turner Ashby in the Shenandoah Valley. So he set his sights on the forces concentrated around Fairfax.

"I began on the picket-lines," he later wrote. "My attacks were generally in the nighttime, and usually the surprise compensated for the disparity in numbers. They would be repeated the next, and often during the same night at a different point, and this created a vastly exaggerated idea of my force. Some conception of the alarm produced may be formed from the fact that . . . the planks on Chain Bridge [over the Potomac] were taken up every night to keep me out of Washington."

The first raid was on a nine-man picket of the 18th Pennsylvania Cavalry, at Old Chantilly Church. Mosby's men, crawling out from a grove of pines, surrounded and pounced on the group, capturing all nine and dividing the horses and weapons among the captors. Then they retreated up the road to Middleburg.

The attack aroused Wyndham to take off in pursuit. With a 200-man detachment he headed for Middleburg, where Mosby, informed of the move, secreted his men strategically around the village. As the Federal column rode through town, Mosby waited till it had almost disappeared, then pounced on its rear, capturing one trooper and three horses. When the news reached Wyndham, at the head of the line, he turned back in fury and warned the citizens of Middleburg that he would burn the town if he found them giving sanctuary to the raiders.

Mosby did not give Wyndham time to cool off. That night, January 30, while the colonel was searching for him around Middleburg, Mosby was already on his way back to Fairfax Court House for another attack on Union pickets. This time it was an outpost of ten men, surrounded and captured, with one killed while trying to escape. And again, on hearing of this second outrage, Wyndham threatened the town of Middleburg with burning if the partisan attacks continued.

A trap was set for the raiders — a train of covered wagons escorted by only a handful of Union cavalry. On the surface it made tempting bait; but huddled inside the wagons were hidden several squads of infantry, armed to the teeth, ready to spring at the first sound of ambush. Nothing passed through Mosby's domain without undergoing the partisan's scrutiny; Mosby had read his Homer in the original Greek and knew the fable of the Trojan Horse. He let the train pass, then followed it at a discreet distance; waited till the ruse was abandoned and the infantry dispersed; then swept down on the remainder.

"He [Wyndham] set a very nice trap a few days ago to capture me in," Mosby gleefully wrote to Stuart. "I went into it, but contrary to the colonel's expectation, brought the trap off with me, killing one, capturing twelve, the balance running." And he added: "The extent of the annoyance I have been to the Yankees may be judged by the fact that, baffled in their attempts to capture me, they threaten to retaliate on citizens for my acts."

He was being made aware of one snag in a partisan's career, opposition on the part of friendly citizens. The townsfolk of Middleburg appealed to him to halt his operations in their neighborhood, fearing for their lives and property. He rejected "any such degrading compromises with the Yankees." In late February he was reported as back in the vicinity of Middleburg, and Wyndham on March 1 sent Major Joseph Gilmer after him with 200 men of the 18th Pennsylvania Cavalry. Hearing of Gilmer's coming, the partisans slipped out, and according to Mosby's somewhat fanciful report:

> A certain major general came after me with a division of cavalry and a battery of artillery. After shelling the woods in every direction so as to be sure of my extermination, and destroying many bats and owls, he took off as prisoners all the old men he could find. He had the idea that I was a myth and that these old farmers were the raiders. One old man appealed to his crutch to show the physical impossibility of his being a guerilla. But the major-general was inexorable. He returned with his prizes to camp, but I was there almost as soon as he was.

In Washington, the partisans were vigorously denounced as violating all the rules of "civilized" war. Colonel Wyndham came in for his share of criticism. In one newspaper he was accused of "bungling," allowing his men to be "gobbled up through the careless and gross negligence of the officers he sends out in command of detachments." Wyndham in retaliation turned on Mosby, accusing him of being a common horse thief; in reply to which Mosby readily admitted stealing horses, but only those with Union riders on them.

In contrast to his castigation in the North, Mosby received warm praise from Stuart who wished him "great and increasing success in the glorious career on which you have entered." More to the point, Stuart sent Mosby's report of his operations on to General Lee, as "additional proof of the prowess, daring and efficiency of Mosby (without commission) and his band of a dozen chosen spirits." To which Lee added the note: "Respectfully forwarded to the Adjutant and Inspector General as evidence of merit of Captain Mosby."

"Captain" Mosby? A slip? A twist of courtesy? Or an augury of things to come. Lee straightened this out in a report at the end of February: "Lieutenant Mosby, with his detachment, has done much to harass the enemy, attacking them boldly on several occasions, and taking many prisoners." This time the "Lieutenant" was official; Mosby's commission had finally come through.

Raid after raid, by night and day, brought to Mosby's command more captured horses, more Yankee prisoners, and new recruits, the latter bringing his numbers up to twenty-nine. Among the newcomers was a Federal deserter, Sergeant James F. Ames of the 5th New York Cavalry. Ordinarily Mosby was wary of deserters, and his Confederates warned him that Ames might be a double agent. But he tended to trust the giant, frank-eyed Ames who had been alienated from the Union cause by Lincoln's Emancipation Proclamation. And Ames, Mosby observed, was "animated by the most vindictive hatred" of his former commander Wyndham, which was something in his favor.

He tested the sergeant in a trial raid on Wyndham's outposts in Fairfax County, in which Ames's advice and information proved reliable. The partisans captured all the horses at the post, took some prisoners, and made their getaway with Wyndham in pursuit. But all Wyndham accomplished, noted Mosby, "was to return to camp with a lot of broken down horses. Ames, like the saints, had been tried by fire; he was never doubted afterward. The time had now come for me to take a bolder flight. . . . "

He had never relinquished his intent to get rid of Wyndham, or get revenge on the arrogant Britisher who had dared to refer to him as a horse thief. What better revenge than a sneak attack on Wyndham's camp, and the capture and abduction of the colonel? Wyndham had four regiments of cavalry at Fairfax Court House, and several regiments of infantry at nearby Centerville—outnumbering Mosby's men a hundredfold. But Mosby believed with the meteorologist that the force of a storm is weakest in the center. Once inside the enemy lines, he would have only Wyndham's staff to deal with. And Big Yankee Ames could get him through those lines.

On the rainy evening of March 8 the column moved out from camp at Dover, taking none of the heavily picketed roads to Fairfax but threading a little known route selected by Ames and John Underwood which skirted the Federal danger points. A single picket challenged them with "Who goes there?" With the oilskins covering their motley uniforms, it was hard to distinguish them as friend or enemy. Ames rode forward, and more or less truthfully identified himself. "Fifth New York Cavalry," he said. Then getting closer still, Underwood drew his revolver and threatened to shoot the picket if he made a sound.

They moved on, quietly and single file, reaching the outskirts of Fairfax Court House in the early hours of the morning. The town was asleep, secure in the knowledge that no Confederate could penetrate the picket line. Ames silently pointed out the targets—the horse corrals, the telegraph tent, the officers' quarters, and Colonel Wyndham's house. Mosby split his force up in groups: one to round up the horses, another to silence the telegraph operator, a third to capture Wyndham's sleeping staff.

He sent Ames after Wyndham himself, at the sergeant's particular request. And met with bitter disappointment. Only that afternoon Wyndham had gone to Washington to answer repeated complaints of his failure to capture Mosby and his partisans. The other groups were more successful, capturing members of Wyndham's staff, all the horses, and bringing in one startled prisoner who claimed to be the headquarters guard of Brigadier General Edwin H. Stoughton, commander of the 2nd Vermont Brigade defending Washington. His house was yonder.

At that extraordinary piece of luck, Mosby's spirits soared. A brigadier general! Worth a dozen colonels.

General Stoughton was a long way from home, home being Chester, Vermont, until the family moved to Bellows Falls. From the local academy, he attended West Point, class of 1859, making him a fellow cadet of Fitzhugh Lee. Following service with the U.S. army, he resigned in March of 1861 to organize and lead a Union regiment from his native state, the 4th Vermont, which served with such credit under General McClellan on the Peninsula that Stoughton was raised to brigadier general in November, 1862, the youngest man to hold that rank in the U.S. Army.

The position he held in Fairfax, commanding the forward units defending Washington, was of vital importance but lacked the excitement of campaigning with McClellan. Perhaps for that reason he sent for his mother, Laura Clark Stoughton, and sisters Susan and Louise, to occupy the Ford house adjoining the home of Dr. Gunnell where Stoughton lived. On this dreary late winter evening of March 8 there had been a party at headquarters, with dancing and champagne. It was after midnight when the soiree ended and the guests departed. Stoughton donned his nightshirt and retired, smelling strongly of champagne, as attested by three empty bottles on the table.

He may not have slept too soundly, partly because of worries over

Washington security. Time and again he had complained of laxity in Wyndham's cavalry brigade; and a week before had called the attention of the War Department to enemy agents penetrating the defenses, noting that "our cavalry pickets do not keep up a connected line. . . . This should be remedied, as it gives free ingress and egress to any wishing to give intelligence to the enemy." There had been no reply. If he slept that night, he slept uneasily.

To be awakened rudely. Someone had lifted his nightshirt and slapped him soundly on the behind. He swung around and sat up sharply, outraged. A slight, soaked, sandy-haired figure in oilskins was standing over him, dripping water on the general's floor.

"What's the meaning of this! Do you know who I am, sir?" the general roared.

"I reckon I do, General. Did you ever hear of Mosby?" asked the unperturbed figure in oilskins.

Understanding and relief replaced the general's wrath. "You've caught him!" he shouted with delight.

"No," said the other, "but he has caught you."

Behind Mosby stood the dejected figure of Lieutenant Prentiss by whose means Mosby had gained access to the room. It had all been ridiculously easy. A knock on the door of Dr. Gunnell's house, Prentiss' response from an upstairs window, and Mosby's reassurance, "Fifth New York Cavalry with a dispatch for General Stoughton." Prentiss had opened the door, and with a pistol at his head, had led Mosby to the general's bedroom.

Stoughton was made to dress and join the train of captives and loot assembled on the street. The haul included, besides the general, two officers of Wyndham's staff, 30 other prisoners, arms, equipment, and 58 horses, captured without losing a man or firing a shot. The raiders withdrew the way they had come, skirting the Federal infantry at Centerville. Reaching Fitz Lee's headquarters at Culpeper, southwest of Warrenton, Mosby turned his prisoners over to Lee, who paid considered, if somewhat amused attention, to his former West Point comrade, General Stoughton.

The Union press and public were choleric at the news. "There is a screw loose somewhere," charged the Washington *Star*. "It is about time that our brigadier-generals at exposed points brightened up their spectacles a bit." But Mosby had no bone to pick with Stoughton; it was Wyndham he wanted to defame. "He [Stoughton] was entirely blameless," he insisted. "If any one was to blame it was Wyndham, who commanded the cavalry outposts and let me slip in."

Stuart hailed the raid and the capture of Stoughton as "a feat unparalleled in the war"; but of greater radiance were the words of Robert E. Lee: "Mosby has covered himself with honors." The partisan himself was more modest in his comments. His observation, on seeing the sun rise over his returning partisans, was simply "It seemed to me that it had never shone with such splendor before."

CHAPTER

9

THE YANKS ARE COMING

IF THE UNION CAVALRY WAS SLOW TO CATCH UP WITH THE BRILLIANT exploits of their rivals from the South, the spring of 1863 marked the beginning of a turnaround. It had been long in coming, since Stuart's Virginians had scored so heavily at First Manassas. But those two years, or a little less, had not been wasted. The Union horsemen had learned much from their Confederate antagonists; they had trained religiously, submitted to discipline, and profited from past mistakes. They were ready for their wings.

In the East, Fighting Joe Hooker had replaced Burnside as commander of the Army of the Potomac, and George Stoneman had supplanted Pleasonton as leader of the army's mounted arm. Facing Lee across the Rappahannock, during the late winter and early spring of 1863, Hooker sent Stoneman's cavalry corps on a raid toward Richmond behind the Southern lines to disrupt Lee's communications, "inflicting on him every possible injury which will tend to his discomfiture and defeat."

Stoneman's raid was something of a milestone, in that it marked the shift of Union cavalry to the offensive. Beyond that, its value was debatable. Though Stoneman started out in April with 10,000 of the ablest horsemen that the Union could provide—led by such promising division and brigade commanders as John Buford, William Averell, Judson Kilpatrick, Thomas Devin, John McIntosh, and David Gregg—luck and circumstances were against them.

Heavy rains delayed the start, forcing Hooker to revise his schedule of operations against Lee. What was done in the way of damage to Confederate communications was too little and too late. And Stoneman's absence at Chancellorsville, where Hooker and Lee collided during the first week in May, deprived the Union of much needed cavalry support. Still the raid raised Federal morale and gave the army's cavalry new confidence with which to face their greatest test to date at Brandy Station six weeks later.

It was in the West, however, that the Federals first edged toward equality with the Confederates. Southern leaders like Forrest and Morgan had set examples that the Northerners were not too proud to follow. And in the Western states "the men were more like the Southerners in their knowledge of horses and guns, and it was from this section that some of the best volunteer regiments were raised."

Even Confederate troopers began to concede a difference between the Yankees from the northeastern states and these tough Western riders who "will do more, go farther, strike deeper" than their Eastern counterparts. In fact, beyond the Appalachians the mounted Federals did not regard themselves as Yankees. They were Westerners.

No great attention was paid to the earliest Federal raid in the West, launched by Brigadier General S. P. Carter with three regiments of Ohio, Michigan, and Pennsylvania troopers numbering 980 men in all. It was a sixteen-day affair starting from southern Kentucky, in late December 1862, slicing deep into Tennessee and southwestern Virginia, and severing the East Tennessee & Virginia Railroad connecting Lynchburg with the West. Like Stoneman's raid, without great consequences, it boosted Federal morale, and prompted General-in-Chief Henry Halleck to report:

> The daring operations and brilliant achievements of General Carter and his command are without parallel in the history of the war and deserve the thanks of the country. This expedition has proved the capacity of our cavalry for bold and dashing movements which I doubt not will be imitated by others.

If the first sentence was largely hyperbole the conclusion was sound. In an otherwise dismal winter, with Rosecrans stalled at Murfreesboro, and Grant and Sherman frustrated in repeated strikes at Vicksburg, the raid demonstrated that the Union cavalry could now perform effectively.

Grant was quick to recognize this new potential. He had been given a painful lesson in the striking force of cavalry at the start of his campaign for Vicksburg in late 1862. This first of many plans involved a pincers movement, Sherman would bring his forces down from Memphis, supported by David Dixon Porter's gunboats, and assault the city from the river, while Grant moved south from Grand Junction, Tennessee, to march on Vicksburg from the east. He established his base of supplies at Holly Springs, Mississippi, and then pushed on to Oxford, farther south.

The chief nemesis of this campaign was Major General Earl Van Dorn, with a mighty assist from Nathan Bedford Forrest. In October, Lieutenant General John C. Pemberton had replaced Van Dorn as commander of the Confederate Department of Mississippi and East Louisiana, and Van Dorn became his chief of cavalry.

As Pemberton prepared his forces to check Grant east of Vicksburg, Van Dorn, on December 20, made a devastating raid on Grant's base at Holly Springs—"surpassed by none of its character achieved during the war," according to Western commander Joseph Johnston. His 3,500 grayclad horsemen destroyed or made off with more than a million dollars worth of provisions and munitions, and captured the entire garrison of 1,500 Union troops. Almost simultaneously, and with equal effect, Forrest's cavalry raided through West Tennessee, cutting Grant's communications and supply lines.

With the loss of his base, and his communications severed, Grant was forced to withdraw to Tennessee, leaving Sherman, uninformed and unsupported, to meet with disaster at Chickasaw Bluffs on December 29.

If Van Dorn had done nothing further in the war—and there was little time left to him; he would be murdered by a jealous husband in a few more months—this was almost enough. He had pulled the rug out from under Grant's projected thrust at Vicksburg, and bought precious time for the Confederates to strengthen their defenses against Grant's future strikes at the Gibraltar of the South.

The following May of 1863, with his troops seemingly checkmated on the Louisiana side of the Mississippi, Grant contemplated crossing the river south of Vicksburg. He looked for means of diverting Confederate forces from this operation and of disrupting the enemy's supply lines, much as Van Dorn and Forrest had wrecked his operations six months earlier. In February he had written to Major General Stephen Hurlbut, his subordinate at Memphis, to suggest that the cavalry of Colonel Benjamin Henry Grierson might be useful for this purpose:

> It seems to me that Grierson, with about five hundred picked men, might succeed in making his way south, and cut the railroad east of Jackson, Miss. The undertaking would be a hazardous one, but it would pay well if carried out.

Though he told Hurlbut, "I do not direct that this shall be done," he subsequently wrote him, "I look upon Grierson as being much better qualified" than other officers among the mounted troops to lead the expedition. And Major General Sherman, a harsh critic of the cavalry, agreed. In December 1862 he had written, "Grierson has been with me all summer. He is the best cavalry officer I have yet had."

Three years earlier no one, including Grierson himself, would have visualized this gangling, thirty-seven-year-old Scotch-Irishman from Jacksonville, Illinois, in the role of cavalry commander. He had had no military training apart from drilling as a youth with the Ohio militia during which, he wrote, "the men worked systematically to get the officers drunk"—after which they roguishly pushed them into the canal. His interest was in music, and at age thirteen he was conducting and composing musical numbers for his own band.

Graduating from local schools, Grierson won an appointment to the U.S. Military Academy. His mother persuaded him to turn it down, for a career in music. It proved an unwise decision when marriage obliged young Ben to earn a living. He failed in his aim as a music teacher, then entered a general merchandising business which brought him close to bankruptcy. When the war came along it promised at least a paying job, but he was jolted to find himself assigned to the one branch of service he detested most—the cavalry.

Horses! How he hated horses! At the age of eight he had been kicked in the face by a recalcitrant pony. Temporarily blinded by the blow, his cheek was scarred from chin to ear, a disfigurement he bore for life. From then on he distrusted horses and the men who rode them. When his appointment as major of cavalry came through he appealed directly to General Halleck for a transfer anywhere to avoid service in the mounted arm. The appeal was denied.

"General Halleck jocularly remarked," wrote Grierson, "that I looked active and wiry enough to make a good cavalryman."

Though his principal qualification seemed to be that he could play the jew's-harp mounted on a horse, he rose quickly from major to colonel of the 6th Illinois Cavalry. Serving in West Tennessee and northern Mississippi under General Sherman, a difficult commander for a cavalryman to please, he proved resourceful and efficient in pursuing Southern partisans and in raiding enemy supply lines. With a reorganization of Union cavalry in 1863, he was given command of the First Brigade, First Cavalry Division, of Grant's Army of the Tennessee.

Like Grierson, most of the 1,700 men in the brigade, encamped in April at La Grange in southern Tennessee, had had no formal military training. They came from midwest farms and schoolrooms, small town stores and offices; they had been bookkeepers, shoemakers, doctors, and ministers. Yet nearly a years' service in West Tennessee had made them veterans. They had begun to copy, and no longer fear, Confederate raiders like Bedford Forrest and John Morgan.

The principal goals of the raid, apart from diverting Confederate troops from the defense of Vicksburg, were the railway lines supplying that beleagured city with materials of war: the New Orleans, Jackson, & Great Northern which connected with the Mississippi Central, and the Mobile & Ohio, running north and south and paralleling one another, and the vital Southern Railroad running east and west. Cut these lines and the vaunted "Gibraltar of the West" would be sapped of its vitality.

Though his orders suggested he return by way of Alabama, Grierson was given considerable latitude on the route he chose to follow. Coming and going, he was "to use his own best judgment as to the course it would be safest and best to take." Besides a compass and a rough map, he carried a secret report from a loyal Mississippian (name undivulged) that "described routes by which a cavalry column might move through Mississippi, locations of well-stocked plantations, Confederate warehouses, the varying loyalties of the people in different sections of the state, the probable presence of guerillas, the geography of the country, and the distances between towns."

Leaving La Grange at dawn on April 17 and moving due south into Mississippi, the first three days were uneventful. To Sergeant Richard Surby of the 7th Illinois Cavalry they were beatific:

> The morning . . . was a beautiful one, with a gentle breeze from the south. The fruit trees were all in full bloom, the gardens were fragrant with the perfume of spring flowers, the birds sang gaily, all of which infused a feeling of admiration and gladness into the hearts of all true lovers of nature.

The first night was spent at a plantation east of Ripley near the home of William C. Faulkner, great-grandfather of the later American novelist. Colonel Faulkner, being currently employed in the defense of Vicksburg, was blissfully unaware of this unscheduled hospitality to a group of raiders bent on his destruction. A second night was passed south of New Albany where Grierson was accosted by an indignant housewife, Elizabeth Beach, who complained that the colonel's men "were searching all over my house and tearing up everything." Just high spirits, the colonel explained. However, he stationed a guard at Mrs. Beach's home. The next morning they proceeded south, still paralleling the Mobile & Ohio Railroad.

In his own account of the expedition Grierson does not say when he became aware of Confederate pursuers on his trail. But there had been a skirmish at New Albany, and on the following day a clash with a Southern cavalry patrol, in which the raiders took a number of prisoners who proved to be members of Colonel Clark R. Barteau's 22nd Tennessee Cavalry camped near Verona. The captives reported that

Barteau's 500 cavalrymen were supported by an equal number of militia, and were already less than 20 miles away.

Accordingly, Grierson began several decoy maneuvers to take the pursuers, real and potential, off his back. On April 20 at Pontotoc he weeded out "all men and horses in any way disabled or unfit for hard marching," numbering roughly 175. He grouped them with the Confederate prisoners and started them in column of fours back toward La Grange. They would leave tracks, and doubtless those who saw them pass would report to the Confederates that Grierson's cavalry was marching back to Tennessee.

The following day, south of Houston, he resorted to a more elaborate maneuver. He detached one regiment—Colonel Edward Hatch's 2nd Iowa Cavalry—for a diversionary strike at the Mobile & Ohio Railroad. With 600 troops and one gun from the horse artillery, Hatch would cut the railroad and telegraph line and then head back for the base camp at La Grange, presumably luring Barteau's Confederate cavalry to follow in pursuit.

Near Kilgore's plantation Hatch's regiment turned southeast onto the West Point road, spreading out to obliterate the hoofprints headed southwest to Starkville. The single gun was turned four times around, to suggest that the entire four-gun battery was going with them and that, in fact, all of Grierson's raiders were returning to La Grange.

"These detachments," Grierson wrote, "were intended as diversions, and even should the commanders not have been able to carry out their instructions, yet, by attracting the attention of the enemy in other directions, they assisted us much in the accomplishment of the main object of the expedition."

The main objective was the severing of the Southern Railroad between Vicksburg and Jackson supplying the war materials for Pemberton's survival in the hard-pressed city. Grierson would not know until all was over how well his diversionary tactics worked. Colonel Barteau had indeed been on his trail, and was getting close when he reached the point where Hatch's regiment had veered to the southeast and where four pieces of artillery had evidently turned around. He assumed that Grierson's main force was heading back for a raid on Columbus or the Mobile & Ohio, and took off in pursuit—leaving Grierson's main column free to move unmolested toward the target.

"A cavalry raid at its best," wrote Sergeant Stephen Forbes of the 7th Illinois, "is essentially a game of strategy and speed, with personal violence as an incidental complication. It is played according to more or less definite rules, not inconsistent, indeed, with the players killing each other if the game cannot be won in any other way; but it is commonly a strenuous game, rather than a bloody one, intensely exciting, but not necessarily very dangerous."

So it might seem at this point. But the two remaining regiments of the brigade, now reduced to less than a thousand men, were pushing ever deeper into hostile territory. Though Barteau's cavalry had been diverted from the scent, it was reasonable to suppose that other Confederate units had taken up the chase. Grierson needed scouts to patrol his front and flanks and keep an eye out for the enemy.

He appointed Lieutenant Colonel William Blackburn, commander of the 7th Illinois, to organize the scouts, and Blackburn selected eight men from the ranks, placing Sergeant Surby in command. The men adopted makeshift uniforms pieced together from captured or stolen clothing—gray slouch hats, gray shirts, and butternut dyed trousers—and dubbed themselves "The Butternut Guerillas." Since they could pass as either friend or foe, the brigade agreed on countersigns to distinguish them from the enemy.

Thereafter, complained the rest of the brigade, it was the Butternut Guerillas who had all the fun. Backcountry people, having had no news of the Union raiders, mistook them for Confederates, and cheered them on. Passing one plantation manor, Surby was flagged down by hands waving from the window. He ordered the squad to halt. "No sooner done than the front door flew open and three lovely looking females dressed in white appeared at the opening, their faces beaming with smiles, and in a voice soft and sweet invited us to dismount. . . ."

On learning that the scouts were hungry, the women ran back into the house "and soon returned with two black servants following, loaded down with eatables . . . half a ham, biscuits, sweet cakes, fried sausage, and peach pie, all in abundance were pressed upon us, while one of the young ladies plucked some roses and presenting one to each bade us adieu, with many blessings and much success in our 'holy cause.' "

At another mansion, they were welcomed by two Southern soldiers home on furlough. After much convivial drinking from a demijohn of rye, in which all toasted success to General Pemberton at Vicksburg, the two Confederates decided to join these apparent allies. Armed with shotguns they fell in with the Butternut patrol, bringing along a retinue of eight slaves, fourteen mules, and half a dozen blooded horses.

All was disarmingly friendly until, a mile down the road, Surby asked permission to inspect the young men's weapons. Once the guns were in his hands, he politely announced that the couple and their retinue were captives of Colonel Grierson's cavalry. Reportedly the Confederates laughed heartily at the good joke played upon them, but Surby confessed that later they looked "downcast" and "became uncommunicative."

Meanwhile, to the northeast of Grierson's southward moving raiders, Hatch's Iowans were leading Barteau on a merry chase. When the Confederates got too close, Hatch swung his single gun around and

peppered them with shrapnel. When he had them weaving and duck-
ing, he led his cavalry in a charge that sent the pursuers scampering for
shelter; then regrouped his forces and marched on. Though Barteau's
brigade undoubtedly outnumbered Hatch's, the colonel was loath to
press the attack, still believing he was following Grierson's full brigade
equipped with field artillery.

In Jackson, Confederate General Pemberton was getting worried.
What was going on behind his vulnerable rear? There had been destruction at Starkville and now the raiders appeared headed for the
Mobile & Ohio Railroad. On April 22 he telegraphed Joseph Johnston,
his immediate superior, "Heavy raids are making from Tennessee
deep into the State. . . . Cavalry indispensable to meet these raids. . . .
Could you not make a demonstration with a cavalry force in their
rear?" Like many such messages to Johnston it drew no satisfactory
response.

Grierson's column was now less than forty miles from the Southern
Railroad, with only the Pearl River intervening. The Butternut Guerillas reconnoitered the approaches to the only bridge across the river
and had a stroke of luck. Surby found a white-haired native by the
roadside, and asked him if the bridge was guarded. Yes, the old man
said, his son was part of an armed squad stationed at the crossing, with
orders to burn the bridge the minute that Federal raiders were reported in the neighborhood.

Surby told the old man, "It lies in your power to save your buildings
from the torch, to save your own life, and probably that of your son, by
saving the bridge." He ordered the man to carry that ultimatum to the
guards and insist that they withdraw.

It was a tense moment at the bridge, as the Confederate guards were
presented with this cruel choice. Surby's heart was in his mouth; were
the bridge destroyed, the whole mission would be thwarted. With
infinite relief he saw the Confederates mount their horses and reluctantly withdraw. It had been so easy, after all. An hour later, Grierson's
cavalry had crossed the river and was on its way to Decatur, last town
before Newton Station on the Vicksburg Railroad.

Anything could happen now. There was no knowing who was behind
them or what forces lay ahead. Though Decatur appeared deserted,
the inhabitants possibly frightened away by news of the approaching
raiders, the Butternut Guerillas took no chances. They checked the
town out in advance. Surby knocked on the door of a shuttered resi-
dence. Someone from within inquired, who was there?

"A Confederate soldier on important business," Surby answered.

"Come in," a voice invited.

Surby entered and found himself not many paces from a bed "from
beneath whose covering I could see a pair of sparkling, roguish black

eyes, traces black as the raven's wing, a mischievous mouth, belonging to a young and charming woman. Can it be possible, thinks I. . . .?"

The proprietor who had invited Surby in, answered the sergeant's questions with his head enveloped in a blanket. Yes, there were troops at Newton Station. Also a hospital with a hundred sick and wounded. Surby thanked the couple, and as he left "a sweet voice invited me to call if I came that way again."

Blackburn's battalion had no trouble clearing Newton Station of its seventy-five defenders before the rest of Grierson's cavalry arrived. And they had another stroke of luck. A locomotive whistle sounded in the distance. Telling the hospital convalescents not to come out "on peril of your lives!" they concealed themselves around the depot until the wheezing west-bound locomotive with its train of twenty-five cars pulled up to a stop.

The raiders had barely time to surround the train and capture the crew and engineer before another whistle sounded. From the opposite direction came a second locomotive towing passenger and freight cars. This too was captured by the same procedure. Cars containing ammunition and supplies for Vicksburg were rolled out of the depot and exploded; cars containing food and whiskey were appropriated by the troopers.

Hearing the explosions, Grierson hurried his cavalry forward to join the indicated battle. He found Blackburn's battalion in full possession of Newton Station, and devoting their attention to a keg of "confiscated" whiskey, but now the real work of the raid began. It was grim and fast and massively destructive.

Dismounted, blue-coated cavalry swarmed up and down the railway, toppling telegraph poles, tearing up the tracks, and building fires over which to heat and twist the rails. Bridges and trestles along the line were set ablaze; the two locomotives were blown up, and their wreckage left scattered on the roadbed. It would take the Confederates days or weeks to repair the damage, while Vicksburg hungered for provisions.

It was now Friday, April 24. Thirty miles below Vicksburg, nearly opposite Grand Gulf, Grant was assembling the transports and invasion barges that would take his troops across the river for the march on Vicksburg, confident that Grierson's raiders had severed the railroad, depriving the city of supplies and ammunition and, even more important, diverted Confederate forces that might otherwise challenge his advance.

In Jackson, General Pemberton had not yet heard of the raid on Newton Station. His concern remained focused on the Mobile & Ohio Railroad where Barteau was still pursuing the wrong quarry. Though

Barteau's superior, Daniel Ruggles, had wired that the Federals "are falling back before our cavalry," Hatch's Iowans were not "falling back" but moving north toward La Grange, their destination, having torn up miles of the Mobile & Ohio tracks. Luck stayed with them all the way. By the time Barteau's cavalry started closing in, and the Iowans had reached the point of exhaustion, the Confederates ran out of ammunition. Forty-eight hours later, free of pursuit, Hatch's regiment arrived home at La Grange.

Pemberton was left at wit's end. Grierson's raiders were reported here, there, everywhere and nowhere. Unable to get any satisfaction out of Johnston, he wired Richmond on April 23: "I have so little cavalry in this department that I am compelled to divert a portion of my infantry to meet raids in northern Mississippi. If any troops can possibly be spared from other departments, I think they should be sent here."

Before he could get a reply, news of the havoc at Newton Station reached him. His lifeline had been cut; the city faced lack of ammunition and starvation. Grant was threatening from one direction, Grierson's raiders from another. Pemberton had only one regiment of cavalry in the Vicksburg area, commanded by Wirt Adams, and it was needed at Grand Gulf to oppose Grant's forces if they tried to cross the river. He telegraphed Generals William Loring at Meridian, Simon Buckner at Mobile, and Johnston in Tennessee asking that they send all the troops that they could spare to help track down the raiders.

At Garlandville southeast of Newton Station, Grierson halted. He knew that his destruction of the railroad had roused a hornet's nest in Mississippi. To return to La Grange the way he had come was out of the question. Confederate cavalry would be swarming to the north and south of him, and from Columbus on the east. But he could hear the sound of artillery from Grand Gulf, and guessed that Grant was preparing to cross the river for the grand assault on Vicksburg. What better objective than to join Grant in that epoch-making venture?

First, however, he had one more railroad to destroy, the New Orleans, Jackson & Great Northern feeding Vicksburg from Louisiana and the Gulf. Leaving Garlandville the brigade headed southwest for the railway town of Hazlehurst. Only one major obstacle intervened: the Pearl River, a more formidable barrier here than farther north. There was no bridge, only a ferry by which to cross. To secure that ferry was, wrote Grierson, "a matter of life and death"; and on the night of April 26 he sent Colonel Edward Prince racing ahead with two battalions of the 7th Illinois.

Prince arrived at the Pearl after dark, to find no guard at the landing and the ferry tied up on the farther shore. A volunteer tried to swim the river and secure the ferry single-handed, but horse and rider were tumbled downstream by the galloping current. His shouts, however, aroused attention on the distant bank. A voice with a Mississippi drawl called through the darkness:

"You-all want across?"

"First Regiment, Alabama Cavalry from Mobile!" Prince shouted back.

There were tense moments of waiting, hearing the splash of the pole, seeing the bulk of the flatbottom boat crawl toward them. Then the ferryman stepped ashore, apologizing for the delay. No, he told Prince, there were no soldiers on the opposite landing. Why should there be? What would Yankees be doing in this neighborhood?

The ferry was small and could carry no more than two dozen men and horses at a time. With the rest of Grierson's cavalry catching up, it took all night to get the two battalions across — with only one interruption. A Confederate courier galloped up to the landing to warn the ferryman that Grierson's raiders were headed for the river. He was disarmed and invited to join the expedition. At daybreak Colonel Grierson arrived with the main column, and while they crossed, Prince and his two battalions headed westward for the railroad.

At Hazlehurst the same massive destruction took place as at Newton Station. Freight cars loaded with ammunition were fired, tracks were ripped up on both sides of the depot. But before tearing down the telegraph wires Grierson resorted to a prank he may have learned by hearsay from John Morgan. He sent a message to General Pemberton:

> The Yankees have advanced to Pearl River, but finding the ferry destroyed they could not cross, and have left, taking a northeasterly direction.

The harassed Confederate general concluded that Grierson was heading back for the Southern Railroad to further disrupt the department's lifeline. Frantically he tried to summon Colonel Barteau and his weary cavalry back from northern Mississippi, and sent another appeal to Johnston informing him of the raid on Hazlehurst. "I cannot defend every station on the road with infantry. Am compelled to bring down cavalry from North Mississippi here, and the whole of that section is consequently left open. Further, these raids endanger my vital position."

Then he resorted to a desperate measure. General John Bowen's Confederate forces were at Grand Gulf, ready to oppose the crossing of Grant's army. Now Pemberton wired Bowen to send Wirt Adams' Mississippi cavalry to intercept Grierson's raiders. "Follow them up without delay. Annoy and ambush them if possible. Move rapidly." Grierson's raid had achieved its vital objective: the diversion of troops

Nathan Bedford Forrest,
Confederate cavalry raider
in the West, whose daring
exploits matched those of
John Hunt Morgan.
(Library of Congress)

"Duel Between a Union Cavalryman and a Confederate Trooper" is the title of this painting by Civil War artist W. T. Trego. *(Battles and Leaders of the Civil War)*

Turner Ashby, Virginia cavalier and legendary leader in the Shenandoah Valley until his untimely death in the second year of the war. *(Library of Congress)*

Turner Ashby, with Jackson in the Valley, attacks and foils Union troopers pursuing him through Winchester, March 11, 1862. *(Library of Congress)*

ADVENTURE OF ASHBY AT WINCHESTER.

BATTLE OF BULL RUN, Va. July 21st 1861.
Gallant charge of the Zouaves and defeat of the rebel Black Horse Cavalry.

Currier and Ives depicted the "defeat" of the Black Horse Cavalry at Bull Run in July of 1861, reversing the facts to soothe ruffled feelings in the North. *(Library of Congress)*

John Hunt Morgan, Confederate raider in the West, and his bride Martha Ready, at the time of their marriage in December, 1862. *(Library of Congress)*

JOHN MORGAN'S HIGHWAYMEN SACKING A PEACEFUL VILLAGE IN THE WEST.—[See Page 555.]

Union propaganda drawing of John Hunt Morgan's raiders "sacking a peaceful village in the West." (*Harper's Weekly*)

Major General Fitzhugh Lee, nephew of Robert E. Lee, who shared briefly with Wade Hampton the command of Confederate cavalry in Virginia. (*Library of Congress*)

Colonel John Singleton Mosby,
Confederate partisan leader in
Virginia throughout all four years
of the war. *(Library of Congress)*

Charge of Cooke's Fifth United
States Cavalry at Gaines' Mill,
Virginia, June 27, 1862. From a
painting by W. T. Trego.
(Library of Congress)

James Ewell Brown Stuart, beau sabreur of Confederate cavalry in Virginia. Etched from a contemporary photograph. *(Library of Congress)*

Shooting of Confederate Captain William Latané in a skirmish with Union cavalry during Stuart's ride around McClellan, sketched by an eyewitness. *(Frank Leslie's Illustrated Newspaper)*

THE REBEL'S RAID—THE REBEL CAVALRY RAID TOWARDS THE WHITE HOUSE—DESPERATE SKIRMISH AT OLD CHURCH, NEAR TUNSTALL'S STATION, VA., BETWEEN A SQUADRON OF THE 5TH U. S. CAVALRY AND STEWART'S REBEL CAVALRY, JUNE 13TH—DEATH OF THE REBEL CAPTAIN LATANE.—FROM A SKETCH BY OUR SPECIAL ARTIST, MR. WM. WAUD.

Major General John Buford, Federal division commander at Brandy Station and throughout the Gettysburg campaign. (*Library of Congress*)

Charge of John Buford's Union cavalry on Stuart's Confederate troopers in the major battle of Brandy Station, Virginia, June 9, 1863. (*Harper's Weekly*)

CHARGE OF GENERAL BUFORD'S CAVALRY UPON THE ENEMY NEAR KELLY FORD, ON THE RAPPAHANNOCK.—Sketched by Mr. A. R. Waud.—[See Page 437.]

Jeb Stuart leads his cavalry in a sweep around McClellan's army on the Peninsula in June of 1862. From a painting by H. A. Ogden. *(Library of Congress)*

INVASION OF MARYLAND—GENERAL BUFORD'S ACTION WITH STUART'S REBEL CAVALRY AT BOONSBORO', JULY 9.—FROM A SKETCH BY OUR SPECIAL ARTIST.

Buford's Union cavalry clashes with Stuart's Confederates during Lee's retreat through Maryland from Gettysburg, July 9, 1863. *(Frank Leslie's Illustrated Newspaper)*

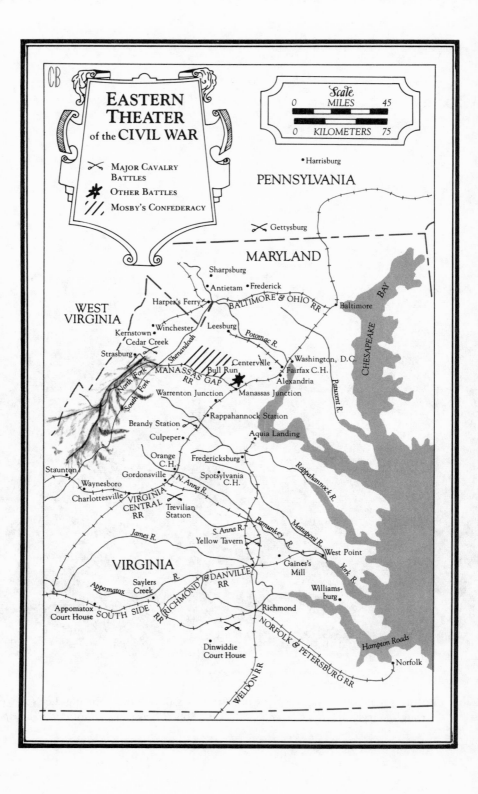

EASTERN
THEATER
of the **CIVIL WAR**

✕ MAJOR CAVALRY
  BATTLES
✱ OTHER BATTLES
/// MOSBY'S CONFEDERACY

Scale
MILES
0   45

0   KILOMETERS   75

•Harrisburg

PENNSYLVANIA

✕ Gettysburg

MARYLAND

•Sharpsburg
•Antietam •Frederick

WEST
VIRGINIA

Harper's Ferry•
•Winchester   Leesburg•
Kernstown•   BALTIMORE & OHIO RR   •Baltimore
Cedar Creek•
Strasburg•   Shenandoah   Potomac R.

Washington, D.C.•
Centerville• Bull Run Fairfax C.H.•
MANASSAS GAP   •Alexandria
RR
Warrenton Junction•   Manassas Junction

Brandy Station•   •Rappahannock Station
Culpeper•
Orange   •Aquia Landing
C.H.•   Fredericksburg•
Staunton•   Gordonsville•   Spotsylvania
Waynesboro•   C.H.•
Charlottesville• VIRGINIA   N. Anna R.
CENTRAL   Trevilian
RR   Station
James R.   S. Anna R.   Pamunkey R.
Yellow Tavern•

VIRGINIA   •West Point

Saylers   Gaines's
Creek   Mill•
Appomatox R.   Williams-
Appomatox   SOUTH SIDE RR RICHMOND & DANVILLE RR burg•
Court House   •Richmond

•Dinwiddie   Hampton Roads
Court House   •Norfolk
WELDON RR   NORFOLK & PETERSBURG RR

CHESAPEAKE BAY

Patuxent R.

Rappahannock R.

Mattaponi R.

York R.

North Fork
South Fork

from the defense of Vicksburg. Within 72 hours Grant crossed the Mississippi unopposed.

Grierson, however, was now threatened by pursuing cavalry from almost all points of the compass. Enemy scouts were everywhere, wrote Sergeant Surby, reporting on their movements. "Rebel forces were concentrating and sent to intercept us, hem us in, and annihilate us . . . Retreat was impossible, even if such an idea had occurred to us, we having destroyed our only hope in that quarter—bridges and ferries."

Heading west toward the Mississippi, Grierson awaited news that Grant had crossed the river and was in possession of Grand Gulf. Hearing no word by April 28, he halted the column temporarily at Union Church—and here he ran into the first determined opposition since the raid began: a detachment from Wirt Adams' Mississippi Cavalry. In a brief, fierce fire-fight, they dislodged the graybacks and took possession of the village. But Grierson knew that Adams was now close behind, and that the routed Confederates would spread the information on his whereabouts.

The trap was closing from all sides. Grierson had planned on joining Grant by way of Port Gibson or Fayette. Now the Butternut scouts reported that seven companies of cavalry were setting up an ambush for the raiders on the route west. Forces at Carthage and Okolona were ready to intercept them if they moved north. Two infantry brigades had assembled at Meridian to close the door on escape routes to the east.

That General Gardner at Port Hudson in Louisiana, on orders from Pemberton, was establishing a cordon to keep the raiders from slipping through the Union base at Baton Rouge, Grierson did not know. But he estimated that some 20,000 Confederate troops, infantry and cavalry were out to get him. And he still did not know if Grant had crossed the Mississippi. He abandoned hope of reaching Grand Gulf, and at daybreak on April 29 he turned his column east—"A straight line for Baton Rouge, and let speed be our safety"—while one battalion covered their withdrawal with a thrust at Adams' roadblock.

They were a hundred miles from Baton Rouge, due south from Union Church, most of it through enemy-held territory, with Gardner's cavalry and a generally hostile population between them and the Union lines. Grierson's men had been in the saddle for two solid weeks, with only snatches of food and rest. The byroads through the Mississippi and Louisiana bottom lands were belly-deep in mud from the excessive April rains. After dark the route was barely discernible. "We lost several animals drowned," wrote Grierson, "and the men narrowly escaped the same fate."

But their luck so far had been phenomenal. Of the 900 men in the two regiments only one had been killed—a Butternut Guerilla ambushed on the way to Newton Station. Four had been wounded; several were missing and presumably captured. Nowhere had they met with serious reversal or defeat. Sergeant Surby remained in a lyrical mood, writing of that May Day morning as they started out for Baton Rouge:

> A gentle breeze floated through the trees, causing a rustling among the green leaves of the oaks. Perched among the branches was the mocking bird, singing a variety of notes, the whole impressing the beholder with a sense of the Creator of all this beauty. . . . We little dreamed what a change would be produced in a few hours.

The change was produced at Wall's Bridge over the Tickfaw River, three miles north of the Louisiana border. Here Sergeant Surby and his scouts in their tatterdemalion uniforms encountered three Confederate pickets.

"We're reinforcements for Adam's cavalry," Surby told them.

With surprising willingness the Confederates stepped aside to let them cross the bridge, at which point the scouts raised their carbines and took the three men prisoner. Blackburn rode up, followed by the advance company. His arrival brought disaster that might have been avoided if, as Grierson later wrote, Blackburn had been "as discreet and wary as he was brave."

> The passage of the Tickfaw might have been a complete surprise and accomplished without loss but for the accident of the firing and alarm. Unfortunately, Lieutenant-Colonel Blackburn, calling on the scouts to follow him, dashed forward to the bridge without waiting for the column to come into supporting distance.

Seemingly the sight of the open bridge persuaded Blackburn to throw caution to the winds. He raced over the planks with Surby at his heels. Halfway across the bridge a rifle snapped. The horse reared, screamed, and tumbled, pinning Blackburn, bleeding profusely, beneath its twitching body.

Surby reined up to aid his commander. "Go on! Go on!" yelled Blackburn. The sergeant leaped his horse over the sprawling bodies, felt a burning pain in his side as the saddle gave beneath him—and remembered nothing more.

Now the whole company was thundering over the bridge, hallooing and firing as they came. On the far side, concealed in woods, the Louisiana Partisan Rangers from Port Hudson held their fire until the Federals had crossed the river—then let loose a shattering volley. Seven horses went down, three men were hit and five captured, the rest veering back across the bridge in panic.

Grierson's main column, alerted by the fusillade, came up at full gallop. Informed of the ambush, the Colonel ordered up the horse artillery and shelled the woods with an indiscriminate barrage. Then splitting his brigade three ways he led them in a hell-for-leather charge—one column across the bridge over the fallen Blackburn and Surby (Blackburn still yelling "On! On!"), the other two columns fording the river above and below the bridge for a flank attack from both sides. It was much the same maneuver by which John Hunt Morgan had stormed the bridge at Cynthiana, costly to both attackers and defenders. Remembered one of Grierson's men:

> We could hear the sound of galloping horses in front and soon a perfect chorus of yells arose from behind the brush, and then with a quick sharp rattle a little cloud of smoke arose, whiz, skip, cling, the bullets came howling past our heads, spattering the poor innocent trees unmercifully. Then suddenly came a quick flush in the face, a feeling at the small of the back as if a charge of electricity was passing through it, then a desperate attempt to keep cool, and whang went the carbines one after another all along the line. "Stand firm! Don't flinch! Hold your ground, men!"

By standing firm they broke and scattered the Confederates, who left their dead and wounded for the raiders to succor with their own. Blackburn and Surby were too severely hurt for further service; Grierson had Surby dressed in regulation uniform to prevent his being hanged as a spy, and left them at a neighboring farmhouse with the regiment physician. Then without pause the column galloped south.

Wall's Bridge was the first calamitous setback of the raid, which was turning now into a horse race for survival. Reported Grierson:

> The enemy were now on our tracks in earnest. We were in the vicinity of their stronghold [Port Hudson] and, from couriers and dispatches which we captured, it was evident that they were sending forces in all directions to intercept us. The Amite River, a wide and rapid stream, was to be crossed, and this was in exceedingly close proximity to Port Hudson. This I determined upon securing before I halted.

Captain Henry Forbes had vivid recollections of that all-night, sleepless ride to the Williams' Bridge over the Amite River, with the men dozing off in the saddle, heads nodding to the tired rhythm of the horses' hooves. This time a single scout, selected because he looked "as honest and harmless as a Presbyterian deacon," was sent ahead to check for Confederate pickets. He had them engaged in friendly conversation, when Grierson's vanguard arrived to take them prisoner.

"The best of the story is yet to be told," wrote Captain Forbes. An understatement—referring to one of those strange events, reported later, that change the course of battles and of history. A Confederate force of 2,300 infantry with field artillery, dispatched by General Gardner from Port Hudson, was en route to the Amite. Having an advantage in time, they bivouacked at the nearby town of Clinton where "the good citizens rejoiced at the foreseen capture of Grierson and his raiders, tendered a complimentary dance to the officers of the command."

So the music played and the Tennesseans danced; and as in Brussels fifty years before—on the eve of the Battle of Waterloo—"there was a sound of revelry . . . and bright the lamps shone o'er fair women and brave men." Just as during that most famous ball in history, when Napoleon stole the night's march from Wellington, Grierson's raiders slipped quietly over the Amite under Gardner's nose.

"While . . . we were stretching our legs for the bridge," wrote Captain Forbes, "the Confederate gentlemen were stretching theirs in the cotillion. After they had danced they marched. After we had marched we danced—when we learned they arrived at the bridge just two hours after we crossed it."

Ten weeks later General Gardner admitted with chagrin that the elusive raiders had caused his surrender of Port Hudson, "by cutting off communications and supplies." He later met Colonel Grierson and showed him a sheath of telegrams that had compounded his confusion. "Grierson was here; no, he was *there*, sixty miles away. He marched north, no, south, or again west." Confessed the outwitted general: "The trouble was, my men ambushed you where you did not go; they waited for you till morning while you passed by night."

They were now only twenty-five miles from Baton Rouge, less than that from the Union lines and safety. They had hoodwinked Gardner for the moment but were still in hostile territory and, as Captain Forbes observed, fatigue became the enemy:

> Men by the score were riding sound asleep in the saddles. The horses, excessively tired and hungry, would stray out of the road and thrust their noses to the earth in hopes of finding something to eat. The men, when addressed, would remain silent and motionless until a blow across the thigh or shoulders should awaken them, when it would be found that each supposed himself still riding with his company, which might perhaps be miles ahead.

As they passed the plantations of the rich Louisiana bottom lands, slaves by the score poured out to greet "the Yankees come to free the black folks." On overloaded mules and with wagons piled with household furnishings and children, they fell in behind the column, forming the sort of ragtail procession that would later follow Sherman on his march through Georgia. They too were headed for the Promised Land.

At one plantation three miles beyond the Comite, where the column stopped for food and rest, the men sprawled on the lawn, too tired to eat, and fell into oblivious sleep. Grierson himself was invited into the plantation manor where "I astonished the occupants by sitting down and playing upon a piano which I found in the parlor and in that manner I managed to keep awake."

He did not reveal what music he played, possibly something from his youth, but did recall his thoughts during that recital:

> Only six miles then to Baton Rouge and four miles would bring us inside the lines guarded by the soldiers of the Union. Think of the great relief to the overtaxed mind and nerves. I felt that we had nobly accomplished the work assigned to us and no wonder that I felt musical; who would not under like circumstances?

He was still playing when a scout rushed in with news that a large force with a battery of field guns had been sighted in the west. This close to safety, Grierson was dumbfounded. He had thought that Gardner's troops were twenty miles behind them. Mounting his horse he rode out alone to investigate. True! Both sides of the road to Baton Rouge were flanked by two companies of cavalry, dismounted and deployed, with carbines at the ready.

Grierson tied a white handkerchief to his saber, dismounted, and walked toward their captain, J. Franklin Godfrey, with the distinctive markings of the Louisiana Union Cavalry on his jacket. It took a good deal of fast talking to convince that Federal officer that he was indeed a bona fide commander of two regiments of Union cavalry that had crossed through all of Confederate Mississippi from La Grange in Tennessee.

Godfrey in turn explained the reason for his show of force. One of Grierson's orderlies who had dozed off in the saddle had been carried by his horse into the Union lines. He was taken for a spy and questioned by General Christopher C. Augur at Baton Rouge. Augur refused to believe that he was a wayward member of an Illinois Cavalry Brigade that had come from Tennessee. It was a trick, designed to lure his Federals into a trap. He sent Captain Godfrey to "ascertain the truth."

Once the matter was resolved, all of Baton Rouge turned out to greet the heroes. A triumphant parade was the last thing that the weary troopers wanted, but the residents demanded it. Bravely the brigade responded, forming a two-mile-long procession of mudstained men and horses followed by a tatterdemalion horde of blacks with their mules and wagons and boisterous children—surely one of the most raffish marches in Louisiana history.

One hundred ten miles to the north, Grant had crossed the Mississippi and was ready for the march on Vicksburg. Grateful to Grierson for having diverted Confederate forces from the site of his landing, the general was lavish in his praise. He reported to General-in-Chief Halleck that "Colonel Grierson's raid from La Grange through Mississippi has been the most successful thing of the kind since the breaking out of the rebellion. Grierson has knocked the heart out of the state [of Mississippi]." Grant's favorite corps commander and archcritic of cavalry, William Tecumseh Sherman, was, for him, effusive, calling Grierson's raid "the most brilliant expedition of the war."

In his own account, Grierson confined himself to the barest facts, noting that his troops had ridden over 600 miles in sixteen days and had lost 26 officers and men. "During the expedition we killed and wounded about 100 of the enemy, captured and paroled over 500 prisoners, many of them officers, destroyed between 50 and 60 miles of railroad and telegraph, captured and destroyed over 3,000 stand of arms, and other army stores and Government property to an immense amount; we also captured 1,000 horses and mules."

The most important service rendered, however, was the diversion of Confederate forces from the defense of Vicksburg; and Grant credited Grierson with being the first to demonstrate what Union cavalry could accomplish in raids on enemy communications. But Grierson was not alone in setting the example. To keep Bedford Forrest and Earl Van Dorn occupied in Tennessee, and to sever the Confederate supply line between Chattanooga and Atlanta, an equally daring and innovative raid was simultaneously under way, led by Colonel Abel D. Streight. . . .

CHAPTER

10

"FORWARD THE MULE BRIGADE!"

THE TAUNTING JIBE THAT FOOTSOLDIERS DELIGHTED IN SHOUTING AT passing cavalry—"Mister, where's your mule?"—derived from the simple observation that the mule was a comical creature; and a man who chose to ride instead of walk was just as well off on a mule, and just as ludicrous, as on a horse.

Yet the long-eared animal with the ornery reputation was an ever-present feature of the war. It was said at one time that "the South could not have been worsted . . . had it not been for the steady reinforcement brought to the Union side by the mule." In all, some 450,000 of these hybrids served in the Federal armies, compared with 650,000 horses, which gave the offspring of the horse and jackass a sizable share of the mobile branches of the service.

It was a curious coincidence (and probably nothing more) that, with Rosecrans' reorganization of his Army of the Cumberland cavalry in 1863, Kentucky became a statewide camp for the recruitment and training of the mounted troops. For Kentucky and Missouri were also the principal mule-raising areas of the Union, producing the largest and sturdiest of the species.

Rosecrans at the time was stalled at Murfreesboro, concerned with the Confederate cavalry of Forrest, Morgan, Earl Van Dorn, and Joseph Wheeler, which, by frequent raids on his outposts and communications, was disrupting his planned operations against Braxton Bragg at Tullahoma. One of these operations was to keep Bragg occupied in Middle Tennessee and prevent his sending forces to the aid of Vicksburg. To do this, he could use more cavalry if he could get the necessary horses and men competent to ride them.

So he was in a mood to listen to Colonel Abel D. Streight of the Indiana infantry when the forty-three-year-old soldier came to his headquarters with a proposition. Streight proposed a daring raid of, say, 2,000 men, deep into the heart of Confederate territory, through Alabama and into Georgia, to cut the Western & Atlantic Railroad supplying Bragg's base at Chattanooga.

Nothing could have tickled Rosey Rosecran's fancy more. This was the sort of thing the Rebels had been practicing for two years—men like Forrest and Morgan and Wheeler—and it was time to turn the tables. What pleased Rosecrans additionally was that Streight proposed, since the army was short of horses, he mount his infantry on mules. Mules were better adapted to rough terrain, could subsist on less forage, were more durable and "more intelligent."

Though Rosecrans might have disagreed on the intelligence, he promised Streight 800 mules from his quartermaster department; the colonel would have to get the rest by requisitioning the animals en route. As for men, in addition to Streight's own Indiana troops, he would be given three more regiments of Ohio, Illinois, and Indiana infantry, plus two companies of loyal Alabamans who would be familiar with the territory.

The idea of cavalry mounted on other than horses was not as outlandish as it might appear. Seven years earlier Jefferson Davis, then Secretary of War, had imported camels from Tripoli for use in mounted operations in the Southwest. The camels proved adequate for the desert country, but they "scared the daylights out of the horses" and the men who had to handle them. Abandoning the idea of a camel corps, the animals were turned loose in the desert and, presumably, hunted down and eaten by Comanches who were not particular about their diet.

There was precedent, too, for the raid on the Western & Atlantic Railroad. Exactly a year before, in April 1862, a Kentucky citizen named James J. Andrews had led 20 volunteers in a daring attack on the Western & Atlantic, starting in the neighborhood of Marietta, Georgia. Seizing a train, they proceeded up the track ahead of their pursuers, burning bridges and tearing up the rails behind them. In what became known as "the Great Locomotive Chase," the raiders were overcome near Ringgold, tried in Atlanta, and hanged or imprisoned as Federal spies.

Streight's expedition was to start from Nashville, travel by boat and overland to Eastport, Mississippi, and then by land through Alabama into Georgia. His force would aggregate 1,700 men, a modest number, but the mules would enable them to travel relatively fast and over unlikely, little-guarded byways. And at Rosecrans' suggestion, two brigades of infantry under General Grenville Dodge would march on a parallel course to the north of Streight, to screen the raiders from Forrest's Tennesseans should the latter pose a threat.

While Dodge effectively performed his mission on all counts, he gave generous credit to Streight and the mule brigade, writing later that "Colonel Streight was an officer peculiarly fitted for such a raid. He was active, clear-headed, determined, and of excellent judgment." These were not the sort of adjectives that one applied to a Forrest or a Stuart. But they suited the appearance of the stocky, soldierly, broad-shouldered man with the high forehead, well trimmed beard and firm-set mouth.

The self-styled "Independent Provisional Brigade for Temporary Purposes" got off on schedule, leaving Nashville on April 10 aboard eight transports. Before the boats reached the Ohio, men and mules disembarked for the overland trek from Palmyra to Fort Henry, where the vessels were to pick them up when they returned from the Ohio to the Tennessee.

The purpose of this cross-country detour was to get the men accustomed to the mules, and more importantly to scour the neighborhood for additional animals for those without mounts. It was a disillusioning experience. At Palmyra, men who had never ridden anything before were placed on mules who had never before been ridden. Many of the animals, wrote Streight, were "wild and unbroken," and the infantrymen "were at first very easily dismounted, frequently in a most undignified and unceremonious manner." It took a day and a half of trial and exercise to bring man and mule together in some sort of harmony.

A hundred mules were lost on the overland march, from exhaustion and distemper, but the foragers succeeded in obtaining 500 additional mules and horses from Union sympathizers on the way, giving them 1,250 animals for 1,700 men. They would pick up the balance as they raided through Alabama, thus "crippling the enemy by seizing the animals whose labor furnished subsistence for the rebel armies."

The vessels that had gone by way of the Ohio were a day late in arriving at Fort Henry, and the expedition did not get under way again until April 17, the day Grierson left La Grange for his celebrated raid through Mississippi. On April 19, three days behind schedule, the brigade reached Eastport, Mississippi, near which General Dodge had been expecting them.

Leaving the mules to be unloaded and corralled, Streight hurried to Dodge's camp at Big Bear Creek twelve miles to the southeast. Dodge himself had had difficulty keeping the rendezvous. En route from Corinth he had been attacked by Philip D. Roddey's brigade of Wheeler's cavalry, loosing 45 men and two pieces of artillery. If he was feeling testy, it was understandable. Streight had kept him waiting seventy-two hours, and Roddey was still skulking in the neighborhood.

Actually, Roddey was closer than he thought. While Dodge was conferring with Streight at Big Bear Creek, the Confederates overheard from a distance that most clarion of all sounds: the concerted braying of twelve hundred mules. It was a simple matter to follow that sound to Eastport, sneak up on the corral, open the gates, and with hoots and yells stampede the mules to all points of the compass.

A similar incident at another time in the war, when mules were stampeded by rifle fire and charged upon their fancied enemies, gave rise to a Tennyson-inspired poem that could have applied to this occasion:

> "Forward the Mule Brigade!"
> Was there a mule dismayed?
> Not when the long ears felt
> All their ropes sundered.
> "Forward the Mule Brigade!
> Charge for the Rebs!" they neighed.
> Straight for the Georgia troops
> Rode the two hundred.

Of the catastrophe Streight reported:

> Daylight the next morning revealed to me the fact that nearly four hundred of our best animals were gone. All of that day and part of the next was spent in scouring the country to recover them, but only about two hundred of the lost number were recovered. The remainder fell into the hands of the enemy.
>
> The loss of these animals was a heavy blow to my command, for besides detaining us nearly two days at Eastport and running down our stock in searching the country to recover them, it caused still further delay at Tuscumbia to supply their places.

Time and replacement of the missing mules were critical. According to Dodge, "I took horses and mules from my teams and mounted infantry and furnished [Streight] some six hundred head." According to Streight, Dodge gave him only two hundred mules but threw in a number of wagons and teams to make up the difference. The colonel found, too, that an inspection of his troops by the regimental surgeon revealed two hundred unfit for further duty. This not only delayed his schedule another two days, but reduced his command to 1,500 men.

Word of the raid, meanwhile, had reached Confederate General Braxton Bragg at Tullahoma. Bragg sent Bedford Forrest and Earl Van Dorn — the former "the best cavalry officer in the rebel army," in

Dodge's estimation—to join Colonel Roddey in pursuing and destroying the invaders. This news in turn reached Streight on the 26th as the mule brigade arrived at Tuscumbia, Alabama. "General Dodge informed me there was no doubt but Forrest had crossed the Tennessee River and was in the vicinity of Town Creek!"

"In his early battles," wrote Captain D. C. Kelley of Nathan Bedford Forrest, "he was so disregardful of ordinary rules of tactics, so reckless in personal exposure, that I felt sure his career would be cut short." It was almost cut short at Shiloh, when he returned to duty on April 29 still with a ball lodged against his spine, reactivated the near-mortal wound, and had to submit to painful surgery. But early in June of 1862 he was back in the saddle and reporting to General Beauregard at Tupelo, Mississippi.

Beauregard had been impressed with Forrest's conduct at Shiloh, in his qualities of natural leadership and the enthusiasm that his presence aroused among the troops. He sent him to Chattanooga "to take command of the several calvalry regiments in that vicinity and organize them into a brigade, for action as a unit."

It was Forrest's fate, more than any other calvalry commander in the war, to be relieved of his troops almost as soon as he had molded them into a well-coordinated fighting unit. At that point he would be given new recruits with which to do the same. It was the penalty imposed for his ability to organize, to train, and to inspire. Men would boast of riding with "Ole Bedford," but they never rode with him for long. Unlike Jeb Stuart with his constant Virginians and Wade Hampton with his faithful South Carolinians, he was never allowed time to feel that his command was composed exclusively of his, Bedford Forrest's, Tennesseans.

He turned over his old regiment to Kelley, now a lieutenant colonel, and set out for Chattanooga with a cadre of 20 men and his younger brother, Captain William Forrest. Here he organized half a dozen companies of untrained volunteers into a 1,000-man brigade; and on July 9, five days after John Hunt Morgan started on his first Kentucky raid, Forrest led his new brigade on a mission into Middle Tennessee. They were to get training and experience; they would also get, hopefully, needed weapons and equipment and additional recruits. Within three days he had added four more volunteer companies to his command, raising the total to 1,500.

His first target was Murfreesboro, where a Federal garrison equal in number to his own brigade was holding Confederate prisoners, some under sentence of death. At dawn of Sunday, July 13, the doomed men heard "a strange noise like the roar of an approaching storm" as Forrest's cavalry bowled into town, released the prisoners, then turned to do battle with the garrison. By day's end they had captured 1,200 officers and men and a quarter of a million dollars worth of arms, equipment, and Federal supplies.

Braxton Bragg, succeeding Beauregard as commander of the army called the action "a gallant, brilliant operation" and recommended Forrest for promotion. Within a month the Colonel was raised to brigadier general.

Meanwhile, Bragg prepared to shift his army from Tupelo to Chattanooga, and Forrest continued raiding in Middle Tennessee to screen the movement. Threatening Union-held Nashville and wrecking the Nashville-Chattanooga railroad, he kept thousands of Buell's troops occupied and off Bragg's back. The distraught Buell, chided by Halleck for not contesting Bragg's move to Chattanooga, explained that he was "constantly beset by a vastly superior cavalry force"—one newly-organized brigade!

Unable to catch up with Forrest, Federal leaders consoled their critics and their pride with fabricated reports of frequent "whippings" suffered by the rebel raiders. Forrest was "dispersed," then "routed," later "handsomely repulsed" at places he had long since voluntarily evacuated. The fact was, as one Federal commander confessed, "to chase Morgan and Forrest is a hopeless task . . . ," and as fast as the Tennessee railroads were repaired, the raiders ripped them up again.

But in late September as Bragg and Kirby Smith pursued their joint invasion of Kentucky, the familiar pattern had reoccurred. The brigade had proved itself; it had acquired the stamp and spirit of his personality; Forrest was relieved of his command and sent to Middle Tennessee to organize several more regiments, give them the Forrest touch, and prepare them for the field.

His new brigade numbered 2,100 men, many without weapons. To get arms and equipment from the enemy, and provide practical training for the raw recuits, Forrest led them on a raid that reached the environs of Nashville. His reputation by now was such that Federal officers cautioned their subordinates to exercise "extreme caution against Forrest's cavalry."

His force was always believed to be many times its actual number, and Forrest used every ruse to promote that misconception. He had his troops beat kettle drums at different points along their line of march, to suggest accompanying regiments of infantry; and when prisoners were interrogated, units of Forrest's calvalry circled back and forth through the surrounding woods, entering camp again and again from different directions. The prisoners, purposefully freed, would return to their commanders to report that Forrest had at least 10,000 troops and more arriving all the time.

In December, while Earl Van Dorn was raiding Grant's supply depot at Holly Springs, Bragg sent the new brigade deep into Western Tennessee to disrupt General Grant's supply lines as an aid to Pemberton's defense of Vicksburg. It was written of that fifteen-day foray by ill-equipped, poorly armed fledgling troopers under Forrest:

> They came out, armed and equipped with the best the Federal stock afforded, and with surplus equipment, a keen, veteran organization. They had killed or captured more men than they had; had taken or disabled ten guns; had carried off or destroyed stores and ammunition valued in millions of dollars; had kept more than ten times their own number frantically busy for a fortnight and, by destroying Grant's line of supply, had helped to compel the abandonment of his promising campaign against Vicksburg, saving that fortress for the Confederacy for yet another six months.

Only once was Forrest surprised and seriously threatened, and that was on December 31, the next to the last day of their swift return to safety. Caught between two superior forces at Parker's Cross Roads, a staff officer asked desperately, "General, what shall we do? What *can* we do?"

"Charge them both ways," Forrest reportedly replied.

They fought their way out of the trap and were back in camp at Columbia in mid-January 1863, where Bragg reported to Richmond that "the complete success which attended [Forrest's expedition] commends him to the confidence of the Government and the gratitude of the country."

Then, a new development. General Joe Wheeler had been placed in command of all Bragg's cavalry, which included Forrest and John Hunt Morgan. And in late January, Wheeler proposed that the cavalry recapture Fort Donelson as a means of obstructing Federal traffic on the Cumberland. Forrest protested vigorously. There was no need to storm a fort to disrupt river traffic; simply attack the transports on the river.

Wheeler was not dissuaded and the raid was a disaster. The cavalry was torn to pieces by the heavy guns and well-protected infantry at Donelson and nearby Dover. That night Forrest bearded Wheeler in his roadside quarters where the general was preparing his report of the catastrophe. Grimly he said:

> General Wheeler, I advised against this attack, and said all a subordinate officer should have said against it, and nothing you can now say or do will bring back my brave men lying dead or wounded and freezing around that fort tonight. I mean no disrespect to you; you know my feelings of personal friendship for you; you can have my sword if you demand it; but there is one thing I do want you to put in that report to General Bragg—tell him that I will be in my coffin before I will fight again under your command.

A gentleman by breeding, and more of a gentleman by nature, Wheeler replied softly: "Forrest, I cannot take your saber, and I regret exceedingly your determination. As the commanding officer I take all the blame and responsibility for this failure."

It was a fracture that would heal in time and with reciprocated admiration. For the moment it was resolved by Forrest being placed in the newly arrived corps of Earl Van Dorn, one of the South's most brilliant cavalry leaders whose career would be cut short in two more months by an assassin's bullet. He fought with Van Dorn in several engagements in Middle Tennessee, until Bragg ordered him southward to check the curious movements of General Dodge. Complying, Forrest quickly discovered that Dodge's maneuvers were simply a screen for the more menacing mule-mounted cavalcade of Abel Streight.

Of all enemy forces that Streight dreaded most to meet, Forrest, known now as "the Wizard of the Saddle," topped the list. If time had been precious before, it was now a matter of life and death. The colonel began a series of forced marches, some extending through the night, trusting Dodge to keep the enemy off his back. "It was understood that in the event Forrest took after me in the direction of Moulton, Dodge and his cavalry were to follow Forrest."

Dodge complied with this arrangement, assuring Streight that he "had Forrest on the run." He did, but not in the direction he anticipated. The man whom Dodge regarded as "the finest Cavalry officer in the rebel army" had reevaluated his priorities. Dodge had the larger force, 7,500 infantry, artillery, and cavalry, but Streight's column was more dangerous. Instructing Colonel Roddey to keep Dodge in check, Forrest slipped out from under Dodge's nose with a thousand of his riders and set out in pursuit of Streight.

In rain, mud, and darkness the mule brigade was pushing on toward Moulton, having covered eighty miles since leaving Eastport. Nearing Sand Mountain the weather improved, and unaware that Forrest had broken loose from Dodge and was hard upon their heels, the spirits of the expedition lifted. Wrote Lieutenant A. C. Roach, aide to Colonel Streight:

> On the morning of April 30, 1863, the sun shone out bright and beautiful, as spring day's sun ever beamed; and from the smouldering camp fires of the previous night the mild blue smoke ascended in graceful curves, and mingled with the gray mist slumbering on the mountain tops above. The scene was well calculated to inspire and refresh the minds of our weary soldiers.

Colonel Streight too had reason to be optimistic. Passing through a countryside of modest farms, his troops had foraged right and left, replenishing the mule supply. "Every man now was mounted," the colonel wrote, "and although many of the animals were very poor, nevertheless we had strong hopes that we could easily supply all future demands." Further:

> We destroyed during the day a large number of wagons belonging to the enemy, laden with provisions, arms, tents, etc., which had been sent to the mountains to avoid us. . . .
> I will here remark that my men had been worked very hard in scouring so much of the country, and unaccustomed as they were to riding . . . they were illy prepared for the trying ordeal through which they were to pass.

That ordeal began as they entered Day's Gap, a fairly narrow defile bisecting Sand Mountain. Half way through the gap the sound of shots behind him told the colonel that the rear of his column was under fire. He guessed rightly that Forrest had eluded Dodge and was following the mule brigade with his cavalry, which the colonel wrongly estimated as outnumbering his force by three to one.

Day's Gap was a made-to-order trap—for the mule brigade now a half mile into the defile, or for the pursuers entering the Western mouth of the ravine. Streight turned it into the latter. He sent word to his rear guard to turn and face the enemy, and slowly pull back, luring Forrest deeper into the defile. Then he dismounted the rest of his troops, concealing half in the woods on one side, the other half on ridges opposite. His two howitzers were masked; the mules were secreted in a crevice, safe from enemy fire.

The ambush worked to near perfection. Down through the gap, retreating as instructed, came Streight's rear guard. Hard in pursuit came Forrest's cavalry with orders to "Shoot at everything in blue, and keep up the scare." The dismounted Federals held their fire until Forrest's men were compressed in the trough beneath them. Then they loosed a downpour of lead on the concentrated target. As the Confederate cavalry reeled from this two-sided fusillade, Streight ordered his brigade to charge.

"The enemy, after a short but stubborn resistance," Streight reported, "fled in confusion, leaving two pieces of artillery, two caissons, and about forty prisoners, representing seven different regiments, a larger number of wounded, and about thirty dead on the field. Among the wounded was Captain William H. Forrest, a brother of General Forrest."

For his brigade to repulse Forrest's cavalry so decisively was an

exploit that almost justified the whole endeavor. And it was proportionately galling to Forrest, whose brother was out of commission
with a shattered thigh. He took his rage out, in part, upon Lieutenant
A. Willis Gould who had lost the guns—so vindictively that some weeks
later that officer tried to murder him. According to one description of
the irate Forrest at this moment of defeat:

> He rode in among the men with his saber drawn and accompanied
> his deft employment of this weapon with a series of remarks well
> calculated to increase the temperature of the mountain atmosphere.
> He told every man to get down and hitch his horse to a sapling. There
> would be no horse-holders in this fight; men were too scarce. Those
> guns had to be retaken if every man died in the attempt, and if they
> did not succeed they would never need their horses again.

Streight, learning that Forrest had been reinforced, skillfully slipped
out through the eastern end of Day's Gap and double-timed toward
the railroad until "the enemy was pressing our rear so hard I had to
prepare for battle." He selected a favorable position on a ridge commanding the approach of Forrest's cavalry. Again the mule brigade
held its ground, and Streight was able to report:

> The enemy strove first to carry our right; then charged left; but
> with the help of the two pieces of artillery captured in the morning . . .
> which were handled to good effect . . . we were able to repulse them.
> Fighting continued until about 10 p.m. when the enemy were
> driven from our front, leaving a large number of killed and wounded
> on the field. I determined at once to resume our march, and as soon as
> possible we moved out.

The country through which they rode was open woodland spotted
with clumps of undergrowth, perfect for ambushing pursuers. Mile
after mile, Streight concealed his men to wait for the enemy, fought a
fierce delaying action, then moved on to the next defensive ambush. It
was effective but exhausting. By the time they reached Blountsville on
the morning of May 1 "many of our mules had given out, leaving their
riders on foot, but there was very little straggling behind the rear
guard."

From Blountsville their projected route lay across a fork of the Black
Warrior River to the town of Gadsden, thirty miles west of the Georgia
line. Forrest's attempts to overtake them before they reached the river
were thwarted by Streight's rear guard hiding in "thick bushes by the
side of the road and firing at them at short range." But this running
battle of attrition could not be sustained. "Many of our animals and
men were entirely worn out and unable to keep up with the column;
consequently they fell behind the rear guard and were captured."

Ahead of them now, before they could reach Gadsden, lay Black Creek, a deep stream with precipitous clay banks. Too deep and wide to ford, the only means of crossing was a wooden bridge. Streight saw in that "fine wooden structure" a golden opportunity. If he could burn that bridge behind him it "would delay Forrest's forces long enough to enable us to reach Rome, Georgia, before he could again overtake us."

There was every reason for things to work out as he hoped. Reaching Black Creek early on the morning of May 2, Streight's rear guard kept the Confederate cavalry at bay until all had safely crossed the river. Then they set the bridge ablaze and watched the structure buckle and hiss into the water just as Forrest arrived in a cloud of dust, to draw up short before the blackened wreckage. But as the muleteers moved forward toward Gadsden, leaving Forrest presumably fuming with frustration, two significant but unrelated incidents occurred to seal the fate of the mule brigade.

On the west side of Black Creek stood the modest farmhouse of the Widow Sanson. An only son was serving with the Alabama infantry; and the widow and two teenage daughters were alone at the place when, wrote sixteen-year-old Emma Sanson, "a company of men wearing blue uniforms and riding mules and horses galloped past the house and went on towards the bridge." Some of the contingent stopped at the farmhouse for water and questioned the three female occupants.

Where were their men folk? Away at war. Do they think they have a chance of winning? "Of course," said the plucky Emma. "God is on our side and we'll win."

"Well, if you had seen us lick Colonel Roddey the other day," said one of the men in blue, "you would have thought God was on the side of the best artillery."

At that point an officer shouted from the roadway, "You men bring a chunk of fire with you, and get out of that house." The intruders snatched glowing firebrands from the wood-burning stove and hurried out. "In a few moments," wrote Emma, "we saw smoke rising and knew they were burning the bridge." Since the Sanson's fence connected with the bridge the women ran down to save the rails; but too late—the fence had been added to the fire, and the Yankees were now on the opposite side of the river watching the conflagration.

Returning to the house, the women saw a cloud of dust and a column of gray-clad cavalry approaching, and rejoiced that "we were now amidst our own men." Young Emma was flattered when the handsome but disheveled leader reined up at the gate, glanced at the burning bridge, and asked her, "can you tell me where I can get across that creek?"

Yes, said Emma, there was a trail on the farm that led to a ford that was shallow enough for the cows to cross. If the general would have a horse saddled for her, she could show the way.

"There's no time to saddle a horse," said Forrest. "Get up here behind me."

Emma swung herself up on the saddle behind the general—"Don't be uneasy," Forrest told the protesting mother, "I'll bring her back safe."—and the two rode off behind a screen of underbrush protecting them from the Union troops still ranged across the river. As they got close to the ford, Emma suggested:

"General, I think we'd better get off the horse, as we are now where we may be seen."

They got down and crept through the bushes on hands and knees, with Emma in front. As they reached the ford, Forrest pulled her behind him. "I am glad to have you for a pilot, but I'm not going to make a breastworks of you." Emma pointed out the best way to enter the water and to climb out on the farther bank, then returned to the house where she and the others listened with apprehension to the subsequent sound of fighting at the ford.

A short while later Forrest returned to the farmhouse. His cavalry had crossed the river, but one of his men, Robert Turner, had been killed in the attempt. "I want you to see that he is buried in some graveyard near here." Then he requested a lock of Emma's hair, and told her he had left a note for her on a bureau in the house. These amenities observed, he bade them goodbye and rode away. Emma and her sister watched over the body of the fallen soldier until daybreak, agreeing that "General Forrest and his men endeared themselves to us forever." Then Emma returned to the house to read the note:

> Head Quaters in Sadle
> May 2, 1863
>
> My highest Regardes to miss Ema Sanson for hir Gallant Conduct while my forse was skirmishing with the Federals across Black creek near Gadisden Allabama.
>
> N.B. Forrest Brig. Genl Comding N. Ala—

Deprived of the respite that he thought the burning of the Black Creek bridge would give him, Streight paused at Gadsden only long enough to destroy whatever arms and commissary stores were found there. Time was more than ever precious. He had not counted on the unlikely interference of a teenage farm girl. And there was another scene-stealer whom he had not counted on, and was too concerned with flight to notice.

Near Gadsden lived John H. Wisdom, forty-three, rural mail carrier for the county. Wisdom returned from his daily rounds to find his ferryboat sunk and a column of blue-coated soldiers on mule-back streaming eastward toward the Georgia border. "It was then three thirty in the afternoon," recorded Medorah Perkins. "Mr. Wisdom, still in his buggy, grabbed up the reins, urged his horse forward and set out with the most important message he would ever carry."

By the time John Wisdom reached his destination he had worn out five horses and a pony, and had covered sixty-seven miles, or triple the distance of that other indefatigable rider, Paul Revere. He galloped into Rome at midnight to arouse the population with the cry, "The Yanks are coming!" The alert spread by the grapevine clear down to Atlanta where Mayor James Calhoun called on the citizens to arm themselves and "prepare to defend their homes and property."

Unaware of this forewarning, Streight made final plans for seizing Rome and—the main purpose of the mission—moving against the Western & Atlantic Railroad. He picked 200 of the best-mounted men in the brigade, put them under the command of Captain Milton Russell, and ordered them to proceed at double time to the outskirts of Rome and secure the bridge across the Oostanaula River.

After Russell's detachment had sped ahead, the rest of the column struggled on toward the Georgia line. They had been fighting a running battle for the better part of three days, with little food and rest; men and mules were in a state of near collapse; and on top of all, their ammunition had deteriorated from exposure. Still determined, however, the colonel wrote:

> As a large number of the men were dismounted, their animals having given out, and the remainder of the stock was so jaded, tender-footed, and worn down, our progress was necessarily slow; yet as everything depended on our reaching Rome before the enemy could throw a sufficient force there to prevent our crossing the bridge, every possible effort was made to urge the command forward.

One more river, the Chattooga (not the "Chattanooga" as in Streight's report), remained to be crossed before they reached the Georgia border. There was a ferry which Streight counted on for transportation, but he found that this had been removed by the local citizenry a short time after Russell's men had commandeered it on their way to Rome. He learned, however, of a bridge some eight miles to the north, and the men—"so worn out and exhausted that many were asleep"—somehow managed to cover those grueling miles, cross the bridge, and burn it behind them, before Forrest's cavalry could overtake them.

They were now near Cedar Bluff within sight of the hills of Georgia, less than thirty miles from Rome. It was Sunday, May 3. In the East the

Battle of Chancellorsville was in its third and climactic day; the Confederates had evacuated Grand Gulf on the Mississippi in the West; everything in this war, someone observed, appeared to happen on a Sunday. Streight had his own grim Sabbath observations:

> It now became evident that the horses and mules could not reach Rome without halting to rest and feed. Large numbers of the mules were continually giving out. In fact, I do not think that at that time we had a score of the mules drawn at Nashville left, and nearly all of those taken in the country were barefooted, and many of them had such sore backs and tender feet that it was impossible to ride them; but . . . we struggled on until about 9 a.m., when we halted and fed our animals. The men, being unaccustomed to riding, had become so exhausted from fatigue and lack of sleep that it was almost impossible to keep them awake long enough to feed.

At the Cedar Bluff site Streight received two ominous reports. Russell's 200 men had not been able to secure the bridge at Rome. The hard riding postman, John Wisdom, had arrived ahead of them. After a brief period of panic, the citizens had rallied with shotguns and rifles, barricaded the bridge with bales of cotton, and put on such a show of force that Russell decided to wait for the rest of the mule brigade before proceeding further.

At the same time, Streight was informed that "a heavy force of the enemy was moving on our left, on a route parallel with the one we were marching on, and was then nearer Rome than we were." Then more adverse developments. The pickets surrounding his temporary halt were under attack, and the Confederates were closing in.

> The command was immediately ordered into line, and every effort made to rally the men for action, but nature was exhausted, and a large portion of my best troops actually went to sleep while lying in line of battle under severe skirmish fire. After some maneuvering, Forrest sent in a flag of truce, demanding the surrender of my forces.

The plucky Streight did not give up easily. Though, as he remarked, "our ammunition was worthless, our horses and mules in a desperate condition, the men overcome with fatigue and loss of sleep . . . in the heart of the enemy's country," he still wanted proof that his position was untenable.

Forrest craftily undertook to give him proof. As they conferred in a patch of woods between the lines, the Confederate general warned Streight that a whole (imaginary) column of fresh troops lay across his path to Rome and that he had "men enough right here to run over you." As Forrest embellished on these lies, his unit commanders led their men back and forth and in and out of the hills behind him, giving the impression that their 500 men constituted a vast horde on the move. His artillery captain did the same with the two small pieces of artillery until, according to Forrest, Streight exclaimed, "Name of God! how many guns have you got? There's fifteen I've counted already!"

"I reckon that's all that have kept up," said Forrest.

Convinced that he was hopelessly outnumbered, Streight presented the situation to his officers, and all agreed that surrender was imperative to avoid "the needless effusion of blood" that Forrest promised them if they resisted. The mule brigade lay down its arms, and were escorted under guard to Rome as prisoners of war, with Captain Russell's battalion captured on the way.

For Forrest, it was a triumphant entry into Rome where "the pathway of his gallant army was strewn with flowers," and where, by popular subscription, the citizens presented the general with "the finest saddle horse their county afforded" and a handsome saddle. Throughout the South as a whole his capture of Streight was hailed by press and public as his most brilliant exploit of the war, and the Confederate Congress tendered him a vote of thanks "for his daring, skill, and perseverance" against "the superior forces of the enemy."

Colonel Streight, by contrast, was spirited off to Richmond where he endured eight months in Libby Prison before managing to escape. He deserved more tribute from his countrymen than he received, partly because Grierson's simultaneous raid through Mississippi, successful in every way, tended to steal the limelight from the heroic struggles of the mule brigade—ending, as those struggles did, in capture.

Actually, however, Streight overcame greater obstacles than Grierson faced. His men were more constantly engaged; and it took one of the greatest cavalry leaders that the South possessed to catch him. He proved himself an able tactician and master of the ambuscade, and lost less men in battle than he did from exhaustion and the failure of their mounts. With regard to the latter, the colonel turned against the long-eared animals on which he earlier had pinned such faith.

"In reviewing the history of this ill fated expedition," he wrote, "I am convinced that had we been furnished at Nashville with 800 good horses, instead of poor, young mules, we would have been successful, in spite of all other drawbacks . . ."

Yet the mules, in their finest hour, would not be forgotten, as the anonymous poet recorded six months later:

> When can their glory fade?
> Oh, the wild charge they made!
> All the world wondered.
> Honor the charge they made!
> Honor the Mule Brigade,
> Long-eared two hundred!

11

CAVALRY AT THE CROSSROADS

IT WAS JUNE 1863 IN NORTHERN VIRGINIA, LOVELIEST OF SEASONS, when the sweet-scented clover stood ready for the scythe, ripe wheat carpeted the valley floors, and apple orchards blossomed with the promise of the region's favorite distillation, apple brandy. It was the drink that gave the village its name. The proprietor of a small store on the stagecoach route had displayed the sign BRANDY for the benefit of thirsty passengers. When the Orange & Alexandria Railroad replaced the stagecoach in 1856, the stop became known quite logically as Brandy Station.

It was already, in the spring of 1863, a name redolent of history, a crossroads for passing armies and the site of several cavalry engagements. It was here on August 20, 1862, in the campaign to regain his hat, that Stuart's Virginians had pushed back Buford's cavalry before marching on to Second Manassas. And it was near here on St. Patrick's Day of 1863, during an unsuccessful attack by Hooker's cavalry, that "the Gallant Pelham" had impetuously joined in leading a cavalry charge by the 3rd Virginians, and been mortally wounded by a Union shell.

Never quiet for long, Brandy Station had earned its reputation as a natural arena for the clash of cavalry.

Midway between the upper Rappahannock and the picturesque town of Culpeper, Brandy Station was about to make history again. For around Culpeper, Lee was assembling his Army of Northern Virginia for its most ambitious undertaking of the war, a second and more powerful invasion of the North. It would draw Hooker's army in pursuit and rid Virginia's soil of a large body of the enemy; or, if Hooker failed to stop him, Lee would penetrate deep into Pennsylvania, throwing panic into Washington, Baltimore, and Philadelphia and bringing the war to major centers of the North.

One thing above all was essential to success. Stuart's cavalry must throw a gray curtain over the operation, screening from Hooker's view the progress of the Confederate Army of Northern Virginia as it moved toward the Potomac in the shadow of the Blue Ridge Mountains. And the cavalry was in peak condition for the job, the largest, best-equipped force that Stuart had as yet commanded.

Of the five brigades, four were commanded by Fitzhugh and Rooney Lee, Beverly Robertson, and Grumble Jones. The fifth was led by Wade Hampton, Stuart's senior brigadier and rising star in the Southern cavalry. The force numbered 9,500 men in all, accompanied by five horse batteries aggregating 24 guns. Major R. F. Beckham had taken the place of the fallen Pelham as senior commander of artillery, and Captain Preston Chew was present with his battery to keep the legend of "Ashby's little gun" alive.

Lee planned to move out from Culpeper with one of his three-corps invasion force of 72,000 on June 10. Meanwhile, with the pardonable ego of the master showman, Stuart sought to put his magnificent cavalry on display. Never again, perhaps, would he have such a glittering force of horsemen to present, or such an arena in which to show them off to best advantage. The plains around Brandy Station were open and level. Stuart had pitched his headquarters tent on Fleetwood Heights overlooking Brandy Station from the northeast.

The demonstration was set for Friday, June 5, and formal invitations were sent out to draw such notables as former War Secretary John W. Randolph up from Richmond. Special trains were engaged to bring civilian spectators from the capital and Charlottesville, and nearer towns on the Orange & Alexandria Railroad, with carriages to meet them at the station. Tents were erected to house visitors for whom the small community had insufficient room.

If the troops complained of the added duties thus imposed—as Grumble Jones predictably did, refusing to change his homespun costume for dress uniform—they went about the preparations with a secret satisfaction, sharing in the general's pride. A hillock north of the railroad served as a natural reviewing stand, and, they were told, ladies would be present. So they greased their saddles, shined their boots, polished with wood ash their spurs and buckles and the metal on their scabbards.

The night preceding the review, Culpeper Courthouse, cleaned and scrubbed as it had never been before, was the scene of a military ball. By the light of all the tallow candles that the village could produce, ladies in crinoline waltzed to the music of a regimental band, and officers in elegant dress uniforms lent martial splendor to the fete. Only the lowliest cynic could have seen this extravagant affair as a hollow gesture to boost the spirits of a waning South.

Even the weather, on the morning of June 5, gave its blessing to the grand review. The skies were fair, the sun was bright, as General Stuart and his staff rode to the plains beneath the heights where the line of assembled cavalry stretched for a mile and a half. Trumpeters sounded flourishes. Battleflags fluttered in the breeze. Prancing steeds curvetted restlessly, flanks smooth as velvet, manes and tails twitching with excitement.

Sergeant George Neese of the artillery watched Stuart ride to the top of a knoll overlooking the field, there to sit his iron gray horse beneath the rippling Confederate battleflags. In Neese's eyes he was the epitome of the cavalry commander. "The trappings of his proud, prancing horse all looked bright and new, and his sidearms gleamed in the morning sun like burnished silver. A long, black ostrich feather waved gracefully from a black slouched hat cocked upon one side, and was held with a golden clasp which also stayed the plume."

The general signaled the buglers. The buglers raised their trumpets; and in column of fours the regiments majestically moved forward — then on signal, at a trot. As they neared the reviewing area sabers were drawn, and the buglers signaled "Charge!" Rank after rank, in clouds of dust, the cavalry swept past with a rebel yell that seemed to shake the skies. In the wings, the horse artillery let loose with a twenty-gun salute that reverberated from the heights and sent billows of smoke into the stands. In response to this thunderous climax, local belles politely fainted in their escorts' arms.

That night the dancing was resumed, this time *al fresco* on the smooth turf of the campground, by the light of swinging lanterns, with the music muted by surrounding groves. Thus they had danced complacently at Williams Bridge in Mississippi, just a month before, as Grierson's cavalry slipped over the Amite River and into Baton Rouge.

Only one thing marred the spectacle of the review. General Robert E. Lee, concerned with the logistics of the march to Pennsylvania, had not been able to attend. But the next day he sent word that he would be pleased to review the cavalry on the following Monday. So it had to be done all over again. Worse, it was announced that many notables, including General John Bell Hood would be on hand. With Stuart's permission, Fitz Lee had invited Hood to attend and "bring his friends." Hood's friends turned out be his division of infantry.

Knowing the ingrained resentment of foot soldiers for the cavalry, Stuart had cause for mild alarm. If raised, the infantry's traditional jibe of "Mister, where's your mule?" might cause his entire cavalry to charge the grandstand, and all hell would result. When he discovered Sergeant George Neese of Chew's battery astride a long-eared mule, he sent an aide to order Neese out of sight before the infantry caught sight of him.

All went well, although with less excitement. Lee, with more concern for saving energy and powder, requested that there be no charge, no firing of cannon. So the troopers simply walked their horses past the reviewing stand, a modest but commendable showing, and Lee wrote to his wife: "I reviewed the cavalry in this section yesterday. It was a splendid sight. The men and horses looked well. Stuart was in all his glory."

But to say that this exhibition, last of its kind on such a scale, was an unqualified success one would have to overlook the reactions from the capital, where Richmond papers ridiculed the "military foppery," and rumors were whispered of Stuart and his officers "rollicking, frolicking, and running after girls." Jefferson Davis received one not untypical letter reading in part:

> President, allow a rude Southern lady to say General Stuart's conduct since Culpeper is perfectly ridiculous, having repeated reviews for the benefit of his lady friends, he riding up and down the line thronged with those ladies, he decorated with flowers, apparently a monkey show on hand and he the monkey.

More to the point was the later-discovered fact that just across the Rappahannock, within sound of the display, the enemy cavalry was in attendance as silent, uninvited guests.

One of the first to use balloons for observation, Fighting Joe Hooker had been aware for several days that Lee was shifting his forces from Fredericksburg to the vicinity of Brandy Station, possibly in preparation for another invasion of Pennsylvania. Captured Confederates, moreover, had revealed that "Stuart is preparing a column of from 15,000 to 20,000 men, cavalry and artillery, for a raid."

Hooker summoned for conference his newly appointed cavalry commander, Brigadier General Alfred Pleasonton, who on June 7 had succeeded George Stoneman after the latter's disappointing raid in April. Pleasonton, thirty-nine, a West Point graduate, was the opposite of Stuart in all respects: modest, practical, unspectacular, and uninspiring. He had studied and was familiar with his Confederate opponent's strategy and methods.

Though he had served with distinction as a cavalry brigade and division commander on the Peninsula, at Antietam, Fredericksburg, and Chancellorsville, this would be Pleasonton's first assignment as chief of the army's mounted corps. Get up the Rappahannock, Hooker told him, and conduct a reconnaissance in force in the vicinity of Brandy Station. Raid Stuart's camp if you have to, but find out what the Confederates are up to.

Pleasonton arrived at Warrenton on June 8, in time to see the dust rising from the grand review and hear the sound of Stuart's trumpeters. That night, as music drifted across the river from the dancing on the green, the Federal troops crept closer to the Rappahannock to bivouac along the six-mile stretch between Beverly and Kelly fords. No fires were lit, no bugles sounded, and the troopers slept beside their horses with the reins hooked round their wrists.

Though they made no display of martial might contrasted to the Confederate troops across the river, they packed a lot of muscle. For this was a resurgent Union cavalry that had earned its spurs the hard way, in battle and defeat. It had learned some bitter lessons and had profited therefrom. If Stuart considered his graycoat cavaliers invincible, this newborn Union cavalry was not intimidated.

Virtually the entire corps, with infantry support, was present, 11,000 strong. Besides Pleasonton and his staff—the latter including a headstrong but brilliant young captain named George Armstrong Custer—were three divisions under men who were among the Union's most able commanders, John Buford, David McMurtrie Gregg, and the French-born Alfred N. A. Duffié, a graduate of St. Cyr who like St. Leger Grenfell and Heros von Borcke had come to America when war broke out to join the action. In Gregg's division was another foreigner, Sir Percy Wyndham, Ashby's former nemesis in the Shenandoah Valley, who after his capture on June 6 at Harrisonburg had been exchanged and had returned to serve with Judson Kilpatrick in Hooker's cavalry.

In addition to the five brigades, each with its batteries of horse artillery, were two brigades of infantry attached to the force on Hooker's order. Though the mounted troops looked somewhat askance at the 3,000 infantry, and resented slowing their pace to accommodate the men on foot, they secretly welcomed the support. When it came to holding ground or covering a retreat, a man with a rifle behind a rock or tree was a valuable ally.

Pleasonton's plan of action was one that he might have learned from Stuart, based as it was on surprise and on attack from several points at once. At daybreak Buford's division would initiate the thrust with a dash over Beverly Ford toward Brandy Station four miles distant. Once Buford had engaged the enemy on that front, Gregg would cross the river at Kelly's Ford, six miles south, and come upon the Confederate flank. Duffié would cross with Gregg, but continue with his division westward to Stevensburg, then cut north to strike at Stuart's rear. A three-pronged pincer movement whose outcome would depend on timing.

Just as the first gray light of June 9 filtered through the trees, Buford's division, 3,000 strong, splashed into Beverly Ford, drenching horses and riders with fountains of foam. The sleepy Confederate pickets on the farther bank had scarcely time to reach for their carbines before they were sabered down, captured, or scattered. In a flying wedge the Federal horsemen plunged into the 6th Virginia cavalry, as the Virginians, without time to saddle or dress, mounted their horses bareback in a fruitless effort to stem the charge.

In the vanguard of the Confederate rally was young John N. Opie, whose horse got out of control in the excitement, broke rank, and plunged toward the enemy. "I hallooed, 'Whoa! Whoa! Whoa!' but to no purpose, as her mouth was fixed against her breast. I thought of killing her, but I had nothing but a saber. . . . I thought of jumping off but that would never have done."

The Union cavalry must have viewed with astonishment this whirlwind countercharge by a lone Confederate on a frenzied horse. This was bravery in the honored cavalier tradition. The equally astonished Opie, still shouting "Whoa!" and hauling on the bit, saw the blue-coated cavalry raise their carbines, "then a line of smoke, then a crash; when, heels over head, both horse and rider tumbled through the air and fell, headlong, in a pile. . . . "

Opie leaped to his feet. Not a bullet had touched him, but his horse was killed. He waited for his fellow Virginians to reach him, then, as one of them was blasted from the saddle, leaped on the dead man's mount and joined the battle. Hailed later as the Murat of his company, Opie confessed, "Shucks, boys, my horse just ran away with me."

Buford's cavalry was scarcely slowed by the rallying Virginians. Their target now was Stuart's Horse Artillery straddling the road to Brandy Station. Caught unprepared, and on the brink of capture, the crews thought only of the safety of their battery. The fate of the day hung on the few seconds that it took to limber the guns, leap into the saddles, and whirl the field pieces to a rear position adjoining St. James Church.

Two South Carolina gun crews remained behind to cover the artillery's retreat, ready to be sacrificed if necessary. On came the Federal cavalry in unbroken stride. Artillery Captain James F. Hart sensed a feeling of admiration for that splendid charge. Of the Union cavalry's performance on that day he wrote, "Never rode troopers more gallantly than those steady Regulars, as under a fire of shell and shrapnel, and finally of canister, they dashed up to the very muzzles, then through and beyond our guns . . . "

By now all of Buford's division and its attached infantry were across the river, surging forward in the dust clouds of the lead brigade. At his headquarters tent on Fleetwood Heights, Jeb Stuart could not believe his ears and eyes. This was the sort of thing, complete surprise, that must never be allowed to happen to a cavalry commander. And this was *Union* cavalry he now saw driving back his own "Invincibles." Reacting quickly, he sent his wagon train rolling toward Culpeper and safety, while he prepared to reinforce Jones's brigade.

Near St. James Church, Confederate strength was rallying. From the north came Grumble Jones's Virginians, reins in their teeth, sabers and pistols in their hands, descending on Buford's right; while from the south galloped Rooney Lee's brigade, and from Brandy Station Wade Hampton's Carolinians were approaching. The triple pincers planned by Pleasonton was being turned against the Federals. The Federal general debated recalling his troops before being trapped.

For where were Gregg and Duffié, whose presence on cue would have splintered this resistance?

At Kelly's Ford, six miles south, there had been an hour's delay in crossing the river, a tardiness blamed on Duffié but never satisfactorily explained. Once both divisions were across, however, and the Confederate pickets had been taken by surprise, Beverly Robertson's bumbling defense offset this disadvantage.

Robertson had deployed his troops across the most direct approach to Brandy Station—a sensible enough position but one to which he seemed cemented. Gregg looked at the solid gray barrier, thought briefly of charging it, then simply bypassed it via a southerly road that led to Stevensburg. It was a roundabout way to Brandy Station, but it avoided the inconvenience of a fight. Where the roadway forked, Gregg turned his division northwest toward Brandy Station, while Duffié continued on to Stevensburg.

Inexplicably Robertson watched the two divisions pass and made no effort to intervene or follow. Equally inexplicably, he sent no courier to Stuart to inform him of this danger to his flank—or if he did, the couriers never arrived. It was Jones's scouts who saw the dust clouds rising in the south and rushed word of the approach to Stuart. Stuart could not believe the message. He had been surprised once; it was inconceivable that he could be surprised again. He told the scout:

"Tell General Jones to attend to the Yankees in his front, and I'll watch the flanks."

The courier brought the message back to Jones, whose irascibility exploded. "So he thinks they ain't coming, does he? Well, let him alone he'll damned soon see for himself!"

At the Confederate observation post on Fleetwood Heights, Stuart's aide, Major Henry McClellan, was standing a lonely watch when a scout brought word, "that the enemy was advancing from Kelly's Ford in force upon Brandy Station, and was now nearly in our rear." Incredulously McClellan leveled his field glass on the road:

> And so it was! Within cannon shot of the hill a long column of the enemy filled the road, which here skirted the woods. They were pressing steadily forward upon the railroad station, which must in a few moments be in their possession. How could they be prevented from also occupying the Fleetwood Heights, the key to the whole position? Matters looked serious!

Now came another singular, one-man engagement, as undesigned as Private Opie's lone charge on the New York Cavalry. At the foot of Fleetwood Heights was parked a six-pound gun, detached from Chew's Battery for want of ammunition. Lieutenant John W. Carter was guarding the gun as a matter of routine. Frantically McClellan signaled Carter: Bring up that gun! The lieutenant unlimbered the cannon, hauled it to the top of the hill, and under McClellan's direction stuffed the barrel with pieces of metal and substandard shells. There was enough powder for the chamber and the little gun would make a bang and send up smoke.

Approaching fast on the road to Brandy Station from the south, General Gregg kept covetous eyes on Fleetwood Heights, a position that, if taken, would give him command of the entire field. So far his march on Brandy Station, with Colonel Percy Wyndham in the lead, had been unopposed. Wyndham's brigade should be able to secure that hill.

Wyndham rose to the challenge, swept through Brandy Station and galloped full tilt toward the commanding ridge. Suddenly from the crest came a spurt of flame, a mighty bang, and a rising cloud of smoke. Wyndham signaled the brigade to halt. None of his men had fallen from the blast, but artillery was something he had not anticipated. Through his glass he saw only a single gun, but there must be more hidden on the ridge. Wyndham would wait for the rest of Gregg's division to arrive before he tried to storm the hill.

Perhaps no single gun in history has so greatly determined the course of battle. As the little gun flamed and spat until its ammunition was exhausted, Stuart had time to respond to McClellan's frantic call for help. Two units of Jones's brigade, which had been holding Buford's cavalry at bay, did an about-face and spurted toward Fleetwood Heights in a race to beat the Yankees to the top.

The 12th Virginia was first to reach the crest, just fifty yards ahead of Wyndham's cavalry. The Virginians should have stopped there, in possession of the hill, but over they went with the momentum of a tidal wave. Horses galloping too fast downhill collided head-on with the slower moving Union cavalry, sending their saber-wielding riders spinning through the air. Checked only momentarily by this downhill plunge of the Confederates, Wyndham's horsemen climbed over the fallen enemy to reach the crest of Fleetwood Heights, to await the rest of Gregg's division.

Pleasonton, though puzzled by Duffié's failure to appear with his division, saw victory within his grasp. Shortly after noon he informed Hooker by courier, "General Gregg has joined me, and I will now attack the enemy vigorously with my whole force." He added that Buford had driven the foe "out of their strongest positions," but did not mention that General Duffié had not arrived at all.

Through no fault of his own, Duffié would remain the little man who was not there. After he and Gregg crossed the Rappahannock at Kelly's Ford, and Gregg bypassed Robertson to take the next-best route to Brandy Station, Duffié led his division to Stevensburg as planned. Here he was almost five miles south of the battlefield, and in a position to charge in on Stuart's rear.

Stuart had belatedly covered this approach. At the last minute he asked Wade Hampton to send two of his South Carolina regiments, one commanded by Wade's younger brother Frank, to guard the road from Stevensburg to Brandy. It was too little and too late. Duffié met the two detachments and attacked them piecemeal. One brigade charged Frank Hampton's cavalry and, catching them at a disadvantage in entangling brushwood, cut the Confederates to pieces. Young Hampton was mortally wounded with a bullet through the chest.

The second Confederate regiment put up stiffer resistance, though its commander too was wounded by a saber swipe that severed an arm. Inspired, however, by their victory over Hampton's regiment, the Union cavalry rolled forward on its own momentum. Nothing could stop them between here and Brandy Station.

But something did. At this moment of victory, Duffié received an urgent summons from General Gregg. Go back the way you came and up the eastward road to join me here at Brandy. To the Frenchman with dreams of cavalry charges in Algeria and Senegal, and glorious victories in Austria and the Crimea, this was the cruelest of commands. Wrote Lieutenant William Kennedy in his recent record of the battle, "Duffié was on the point of scattering his badly hurt opponents when ordered to rejoin Gregg. . . . Had Duffié been kept where he was he most certainly would have broken through into the Confederate rear just when Gregg needed him most."

But orders were orders. Duffié withdrew his division to Stevensburg, then eastward along the road to Kelly's Ford to the point where the road branched off to Brandy. In this time-consuming maneuver he was riding himself right out of the battle; and though his troops were still fresh and itching for action, his would remain the only division not allowed to inscribe on its battleflag the illustrious name of Brandy Station.

On two levels, plateau and plain, the clash of cavalry at Brandy Station was rising to a climax. It was a grim game of King of the Mountain atop Fleetwood Heights. Following Wyndham to the crest came Federal artillery, but before the guns could be leveled on the plain below, Grumble Jones took his turn to storm the ridge. The 35th Virginia Battalion swarmed around the battery where the gunners tried to fight them off with pistols, jammers, sabers. They took possession of the guns, but only briefly. Judson Kilpatrick, his ginger whiskers flowing like a Viking's, was already coming up the other side.

Riding with Kilpatrick, Lieutenant R.B. Porter felt the blood surge through his veins, and asked himself, "Who can describe the feelings of a man on entering a charge? How exhilarating, and yet how awful! The glory of success in a charge is intoxicating! One forgets everything, even personal safety, in the one grand thought of vanquishing the enemy. We were in for it now, and the nerves were strung to the highest tension."

Half way up the slope they were met by a down-charging unit of Southern cavalry to engage them in hand-to-hand fighting for the hill. Recorded Porter:

> Then followed an indescribable clashing, banging and yelling. . . . We were now so mixed up with the rebels that every man was fighting desperately to maintain his position until assistance could be brought forward. The front squadrons broke to the right and the left to allow the rear squadrons to come upon the enemy fresh. Just then a big reb bore down on me with his saber raised. I parried the blow with my saber, which, however, was delivered with such force as to partially break the parry, and left its mark across my back. . . .

In difficulty, Kilpatrick summoned his rearmost regiment, the 1st Maine Cavalry, to come forward in countercharge. To downeaster Edward Tobie, who with the rest of the regiment had seen no action so far in the battle, the whole field surrounding the contested hill was a mass of rearing horses, clashing sabers, and dust so thick it was hard to distinguish blue from gray. It was a once-in-a-lifetime panorama, Tobie wrote, and worth all the risks of war to witness. And of the 1st Maine's charge upon the hill:

On they went, amid a perfect tangle of sights and sounds, filled with such a rare, wholesouled excitement as seldom falls to the lot of man to experience; and thoughts of danger were for the time furthest from their minds. Even the horses seemed to enter into the spirit of the occasion, and strained every nerve to do their full duty in the day's strange deeds, obeying the least motion of rein or spur with unusual promptness, as if feeling the superiority of their riders in this terrible commotion.

Aided by the 1st Maine Cavalry, which thought of its actions in nautical terms and "hove to" on the mountaintop, Kilpatrick and the bluecoat cavalry was in solid possession of Fleetwood Heights. On the plains below "a scene of the grandest description" unfolded before them as Buford's division, relieved of pressure by Gregg's arrival, was countercharging to regain the field. A thousand saber duels erupted such as might have been waged on the tournament grounds of medieval Bruges.

In this multiple confusion, Union Lieutenant Henry C. Meyer of Gregg's staff hardly knew which way to face. He saw a Confederate officer sabering a Marylander who had lost the power to defend himself. Meyer made a target of the executioner:

> I tried to shoot him, but the ball from my pistol missed him and hit the horse. This did not take immediate effect. . . . having only one charge left in my revolver, I had to allow the officer to ride up to and strike me, so to be sure of my aim. As I presented the pistol, it missed fire, and as soon as he could recover his seat in the saddle, he struck at me. I had, however, fallen down on the neck of my horse, so the point of his saber cut into my collar-bone but the weight of the blow cut a two-quart pail, that I had borrowed that morning to cook coffee in, nearly in two.

At which point the Confederate's wounded horse collapsed beneath him, and four of the officer's followers closed in on Meyer. Whereupon he deftly jumped his horse over a fence and escaped. Recounting the incident later to the owner of the life-saving coffee pot, the latter was highly indignant. "How do you suppose I am going to cook my coffee!" he demanded.

This was a time for giants, for men born to lead; the moment for Wade Hampton to take over. The blue-coated summit must be taken, Drawing his massive sword, Hampton led his South Carolinians, Georgians, and Mississippians in the last decisive charge up Fleetwood Heights, rolling back Gregg's Federals like a frothing tidal wave. With Gregg repulsed, Stuart redeployed his command along a line extending from Fleetwood Heights to Welford's Ford, confronting Buford's division.

It was now late afternoon. The battle had reached its final stages—the kind of fighting that allowed no pause for rest, a continuous slashing, firing, falling and remounting, of riderless horses swirling in panic, of screaming wounded and the bass din of rival horse artilleries. From this chaos only one fact was clear: Fleetwood Heights was again held by the Confederates.

As the opposing lines clashed on the crest, Captain William Blackford of Stuart's staff saw

> a passage of arms filled with romantic interest and splendor to a degree unequaled by anything our war produced. It was like what we read of in the days of chivalry, acres and acres of horsemen, sparkling with sabers, and dotted with brilliant bits of color where their flags danced about them, hurled against each other at full speed and meeting with a shock that made the earth tremble.

Silhouetted against the sky the giant figure of Wade Hampton, wielding his two-edged sword, stood out above all, and of that towering figure "nothing more superb could be imagined," wrote John Esten Cooke. "In the heady fight he was everywhere seen, amid the clouds of smoke, the crashing shell, and the whistling balls, fighting like a private soldier, his long sword doing hard work in the melee, and carving its way as did the trenchant weapons of the ancient knights."

The blue defenders of the hill were swamped beneath that tidal wave of gray. The artillerists spiked their guns, and joined in the hand-to-hand fighting, to be chopped down by Confederate sabers. The Federal cavalry countercharged, fell back, and charged again.

> *Morte à cheval, au galop* [as Edmond Rostand called it]—the cavalryman's fate. If a man must fall in battle, how meet death more gloriously than astride a galloping steed charging into the midst of the foe? So officers and troopers of the Gray and Blue died on Fleetwood Heights that afternoon as they joined combat in milling masses and desperate single encounters.

With the loss of Fleetwood Heights, the Federal force had shot its bolt. Both Buford and Gregg's divisions had fought with valor, but their troops were spent. Pleasonton called for a retreat. Via Beverly Ford the dust-coated, battle-grimed Federal cavalry and infantry streamed back across the Rappahannock, shelled by Stuart's battery now in possession of the hill. They were not pursued by the Southern riders, for these too had reached a point where they could fight no more.

The battle was over, and would be known as the greatest cavalry engagement on the continent of this or any century. Troops of both sides would cherish the inscription BRANDY STATION emblazoned on their regimental flags. It was a name to compare with Austerlitz or Waterloo or Balaklava. And if one left an arm or a leg on the battlefield, as all too many did, it was almost worth the price. The cavalry would never rise to such heights again.

Both sides claimed victory, though the conflicting assertions would add up to a draw. Stuart remained in possession of the field, but Pleasonton had accomplished what he came for. His cavalry had penetrated Stuart's screen, and spotted both the location and the probable direction of Lee's army. They had inflicted heavy damage on the enemy (and suffered heavier), and the withdrawal had been orderly; the corps was essentially intact.

But the true significance of Brandy Station was expressed by Major McClellan who had watched so much of the conflict from the top of Fleetwood Heights, and later wrote, "One result of incalculable importance certainly did follow this battle—it *made* the Federal cavalry. Up to that time confessedly inferior to the Southern horsemen, they gained on this day that confidence in themselves and in their commanders which enabled them to contest so fiercely the subsequent battlefields of June, July, and October."

Another of Stuart's biographers, John W. Thompson, Jr., came to a similar conclusion:

> For the first time in the war, blue cavalry had come over in dangerous force, provoked combat, inflicted heavy damage, and gotten away in good order. The gray troopers would no longer have it all their own way. Those Yankees, they conceded, could always fight: now they were learning to ride and fight at the same time.

Stuart himself would not, predictably, concede that much. Congratulating his troops, he told them that "the enemy's cavalry and artillery, escorted by a strong force of infantry, tested your mettle and found it proof-steel! Your saber blows, inflicted on that glorious day, have taught them again the weight of Southern vengeance."

Yet Stuart promptly removed his headquarters tent from Fleetwood Heights. For the signs of that dreadful carnage were too equally divided between blue and gray. The crest and slopes of the ridge were so heavily blanketed with corpses, men and horses grotesquely intertwined, that, even after the dead were buried, the buzzards haunted Brandy Station for months to come.

They did not linger on that battlefield, though Pleasonton withdrew his cavalry only as far as Warren Junction.

And on June 10 Lee set his three-corps army in motion toward Pennsylvania: Richard S. Ewell down the Shenandoah Valley with his own brigade of cavalry under Brigadier General Albert Jenkins; James

Longstreet moving east of the Blue Ridge Mountains; Ambrose P. Hill marching northwest from Fredericksburg to follow Ewell, all three to cross the Potomac west of Harpers Ferry.

It would be the double task of Stuart's cavalry, still groggy from the fight at Brandy Station, to screen this movement from the enemy and guard the mountain gaps against possible attack. Similarly it was Pleasonton's duty to penetrate that cover, keep track of Lee's invasion force, and screen the countermoves of Hooker's Army of the Potomac as it set off in pursuit. On parallel courses the two columns of cavalry, blue and gray, stalked one another, Pleasonton's scouts reaching out like highly tuned antennae for the vulnerable points in Stuart's line.

The first clash between the two came only seven days after Brandy Station, on the 17th, at the little crossroads town of Aldie. Here Judson Kilpatrick's brigade attacked Fitzhugh Lee's Virginians, under the contemporary command of Colonel T. T. Munford, protecting Ashby's gap; and here Captain Custer made his initial bid for fame. Assigned to deliver a routine message from Pleasonton to Kilpatrick, Custer arrived as the latter was ordering his formation to "Draw sabers! Trot! Gallop!—"

The concluding order "Charge!" struck Custer's reflex center like a jolt of benzedrine. Drawing his saber he galloped to the front of the brigade, ahead of Kilpatrick, shouting "Come on, boys!" As the rest of Kilpatrick's cavalry clashed with the Confederates, Custer, golden locks streaming in the wind, kept right on going, into the center of Munford's camp. Seeing this long-haired jackanapes, in faded uniform with sloppy slouch hat, the Southerners made no attempt to capture him. Whose side was he on? Custer trotted back to the Union lines to be rewarded shortly afterwards with the rank of brigadier general.

The Virginians were pressed back to Middleburg where two days later the blue horsemen struck again. This time the charge was led by the fiery Frenchman, Colonel Duffié, whose cavalry had been hobbled at Brandy Station. Duffié's string of bad luck held. He was hurled back, losing two-thirds of his regiment; and command of his division passed to Judson Kilpatrick. Duffié was banished to the Department of West Virginia.

Stuart, however, was forced to withdraw still farther west, and near Upperville lost the services of the gallant Heros von Borcke, shot through the neck by a Yankee sniper. Von Borcke recovered, but saw no further combat service. Attacked again at Upperville, Stuart held firm. Though Pleasonton's Union cavalry, still feeling itself the equal of the Southerners since Brandy Station, gave Stuart a hard time, they had not broken the screen protecting Lee's invasion force. Already the Army of Northern Virginia was crossing the Potomac toward Pennsylvania, and Hooker, confessing he was powerless to stop the movement ("I don't know whether I am standing on my head or feet"), was replaced on June 27 as commander of the Army of the Potomac by George Gordon Meade.

Now Stuart made a strange and controversial move. He requested Lee's permission to detach himself from the army and cross the Potomac to the rear of the Federal line, disrupting Union communications and raiding enemy supplies. He would take with him three of his five brigades, those of Hampton, Fitz Lee, and John R. Chambliss (replacing the wounded Rooney Lee), numbering roughly 2,000. Lee still would have almost twice that number, with Grumble Jones and Robertson's brigades, Jenkins's cavalry attached to General Ewell, and 2,000 horsemen under John Imboden, who had recently joined Lee from western Virginia.

Plenty of troopers, Stuart maintained, to guard the passes and screen the army's movements into Pennsylvania. And numerically, the argument was sound. But he might have remembered Napoleon's maxim, "In war *men* are nothing, *a man* is everything." And Stuart was the man whom Lee had always counted on for information on enemy movements, and the cavalry leadership it took to get that information. It was less spectacular service than independently conducted raids, but more essential.

It was probably pure coincidence, but John Mosby showed up at Middleburg that week to chat with his former commander. There is an indication that Mosby, like an impish Iago, might have put the idea in Stuart's head. If it is true that Mosby, as he claimed, inspired Stuart's ride around McClellan, there is reason to believe he might have promoted another ride around another army.

And Stuart's mind still rankled from the criticism directed at him, in Richmond and the press, for being surprised at Brandy Station. "The Richmond papers," noted the Union high command, "call upon him to do something to retrieve his reputation." This seemed to demand another daring exploit such as his ride around McClellan.

In agreeing to Stuart's proposal, Lee was cautious but indiscriminately vague. He suggested that Stuart might better follow the army across the Potomac near Shepherdstown, and cut behind the enemy near Frederick. He added: "You will, however, be able to judge whether you can pass around the army without hindrance, doing them all the damage you can, and cross the river east of the mountains."

The mountains meant, of course, the Blue Ridge—but *how far east* the general did not specify. He only cautioned his chief of cavalry to keep in touch with the army, "collecting information, provisions, etc.," and to remain, in effect, within calling distance.

Thus, on June 25, Stuart started out on what amounted to his own invasion of the North—leading his three brigades from Salem in a wide sweep to the east and north, far from the path of destiny that led to Gettysburg.

12

A SMALL TOWN IN PENNSYLVANIA

JUNE 30, 1863.

"My own darling wife," wrote Private William Christian of the Army of Northern Virginia: "You can see by the date of this that we are now in Pennsylvania, resting today near a little one horse town on the road to Gettysburg, which we will reach tomorrow . . . The country that we have passed through is beautiful and everything in the greatest abundance. You never saw such a land of plenty."

Little damaged by the war so far, Pennsylvania was indeed a land of plenty—of wheatfields and bulging granaries, herds of cattle and horses, and prosperous towns where the merchants were well supplied with boots and shoes, despite some depletion of these stocks by the vanguard of Lee's army, which had passed through earlier that week.

It was the shoes that attracted J. Johnston Pettigrew's brigade of North Carolinians, bivouacked with A.P. Hill's Third Army Corps near Cashtown. The march from Virginia had wasted shoe leather down to the skin, and many were practically barefoot. So they trudged toward the little town of Gettysburg, eight miles away. They didn't get the shoes, but they got some important information. Stretched along Willoughby Run, on the Chambersburg Pike, was a fringe of bluecoated cavalry; no telling how many more behind it. Prudently, they trotted back to report to their immediate commander, Major General Henry Heth, that there were Yanks at Gettysburg.

There were; three thousand of them representing John Buford's cavalry division. Square-faced, mustachioed Buford, a Kentuckian who would rather fight than eat, had arrived at Gettysburg on the orders of Alfred Pleasonton. He and Pleasonton had discussed the campaign on the way to Pennsylvania. Both agreed that contact with Lee would most likely occur in this vicinity, for all roads seemed to converge on Gettysburg.

So while General Meade was establishing a defense line south of Taneytown, Buford deployed two of his three cavalry brigades northwest of Gettysburg, their front covered by Willoughby Run. The enemy, he was convinced, would attack here; and his troops would "have to fight like the devil" until the infantry corps of General John Reynolds arrived to hold the town.

That night at Cashtown, General Heth was still concerned with footwear. He belittled the news of Yanks at Gettysburg, and so did Hill when told of the report.

"The only force at Gettysburg is cavalry, probably a detachment of observation," said Hill.

"Then," said Heth, "if there's no objection, I'll take my division tomorrow and go to Gettysburg and get those shoes."

"None in the world," said Hill.

Cue lines for the greatest battle ever to be fought in North America.

It was dawn of July 1 when Corporal Alphonse Hodges of Buford's division, on picket duty at Willoughby Run, saw shadowy figures approaching down the Chambersburg Pike. He crossed the stream for a closer look. Graybacks! A long column stretching back into the gloom! He whirled around and started to run, heard bullets whistle past him, turned to fire several shots, then raced back to report to his brigade commander.

The Battle of Gettysburg had begun, starting and destined to close with a cavalry engagement.

Far from surprised, Buford had hoped and looked for this attack. Since Brandy Station, the Federal cavalry had dogged Lee's steps, not penetrating Stuart's screen so long as Jeb was on the army's flank. But now Stuart had disappeared and every commander, from Meade down, knew that, of Lee's three corps, Hill was at Cashtown with Longstreet on the way and that Ewell was some miles to the north or northeast.

So these approaching Confederates would be units of Hill's corps, and Buford rushed word to Reynolds: Bring up the infantry! Then he dismounted his brigades, assigning one man in four to hold the horses. He would fight with his men on foot, taking advantage of the ridges that sliced through the Gettysburg area like herringbones. For two hot hours the dismounted cavalry held the attackers in check, retreating inch by inch up McPherson's Ridge, while Hill brought up more and more Confederates.

At midmorning Reynolds arrived, to relieve the hard-pressed cavalry and to plunge head-on into the Confederates. Though Reynolds himself was mortally wounded almost instantly, Hill's troops gave way until Ewell came down with reinforcements from the north. Then the Federal attack began to weaken. Though O. O. Howard's Eleventh Corps came up in support, one end of the line crumpled, then the other. The retreat became a rout, jamming the streets of Gettysburg so solidly as to block Confederate pursuers. By late afternoon the entire Federal force was installed on the fish-hook shaped heights of Cemetery Hill, Culp's Hill, and Cemetery Ridge.

The first day at Gettysburg was over. It had started with a shot fired by a trooper wearing the insignia of crossed sabers on his cap, and the stand made by Buford's cavalry had determined the site of the battle and prevented a Confederate takeover of the town. Yet as the opposing armies assembled, it did not shape up as a battle in which cavalry would play a major role. Statistical figures in this war were often questionable; but of Lee's estimated 75,000 men and Meade's 85,000-90,000, the cavalry available to each was roughly 12–15 percent of these respective totals. The numbers actually engaged would be considerably less.

But again, the numbers were deceptive. Meade had a seemingly slight advantage with eight brigades of cavalry compared with six brigades, along with Imboden's detached command, for Lee. But the Confederate brigades of Grumble Jones and Beverly Robertson were still far to the west, behind Lee's army, and would not arrive in time to be effective. The same with Imboden's command, which also had marched into Pennsylvania west of Lee's route and would not see action at Gettysburg.

Most important, the three strongest brigades were off somewhere with Stuart. Arriving in Cashtown the forenoon of July 1, Lee expressed his anxiety to General Richard Anderson:

> I cannot think what has become of Stuart; I ought to have heard from him long before now. He may have met with disaster, but I hope not. In the absence of reports from him, I am in ignorance of what we have in front of us here. It may be the whole Federal army, or it may be only a detachment.

Major Henry McClellan — paraphrasing Napoleon's concept that it is not the men who count in battle, but the man — expressed Lee's dilemma in a different way:

> It was not the want of cavalry that General Lee bewailed, for he had enough of it had it been properly used. It was the absence of Stuart himself that he felt so keenly; for on him he had learned to rely to such an extent that it seemed as if his cavalry was concentrated in his person, and from him alone could information be expected.

Thus the Confederate cavalry's role at Gettysburg was shaded by the simple, regrettable fact that it was not in the right place at the right time and its principal component, Stuart's battle-skilled brigades, were missing when they were needed most.

The Federal cavalry was reduced in strength on July 1 when Pleasonton withdrew Buford's two brigades from the scene of battle. They had been fighting all day, he told Meade, and needed a respite from constant combat. Actually, Buford's losses had been small; his men were tough and resilient; and Buford himself preferred fighting to resting any day. Yet Pleasonton shortly assigned the division to guard the army's supply depot southeast of town.

Gregg's smaller division did not arrive at Gettysburg until July 2, to take up a position on Meade's left. Kilpatrick's larger force, 3,500 strong, had been operating east of the army and was at Hanover, twelve miles from Gettysburg, when on June 30 Jeb Stuart's horsemen had suddenly appeared.

When Stuart left Salem, Virginia, the morning of June 25 to ride around the Union army on his way to Pennyslvania, he was still hazy about his instructions. Either that, or he slyly misinterpreted them to favor another spectacular raid that would restore a portion of the former glory he had lost at Brandy Station. In his own words he was simply "to proceed with all dispatch to join General Ewell's corps in Pennsylvania." Which gave him all the latitude an independent-minded officer could ask.

Heading east to circumvent the Union army he ran into his first snag in the form of General Winfield S. Hancock's corps crowding north along the road he planned to take. Rather than wait for the column to pass, he cut farther south and east, and wasted a day in reaching the Potomac, with time out to graze the horses. The three brigades, led by Hampton, Fitz Lee, and Chambliss, crossed the river at night at Rowser's Ford, two feet deeper than expected. The caissons and limbers were virtually submerged, and the men carried the ammunition over in hands held over head to keep it dry. "No more difficult achievement was accomplished by the cavalry during the war," declared one officer.

They were now in Maryland, with the troops exultantly chorusing:

> Oh, Bob Lee's heel is on thy shore,
> Maryland, my Maryland. . . .

But after 72 hours of marching they had lost all track of where Lee's army was. Stuart learned from obliging natives, however, that the vanguard of the Federal army had reached Frederick. He would have to avoid Frederick, then, and edge still farther to the east. By noon of June 28 he reached Rockville, 15 miles from Washington, and by cutting the telegraph line, direct communication was severed between the capital and the army—throwing the city into a state of panic.

They should have pressed on, but they fell victim to that most coveted of prizes, an enemy wagon train approaching from the capital. "The wagons were brand new, the mules fat and sleek," one trooper wrote. "Such a train we had never seen before and did not see again." The target was irresistible, and they chased the fleeing cavalcade back toward Washington, captured 125 wagons filled with army stores, 400 prisoners, and 900 mules. The action further delayed their progress, but the trophy was something tangible to take back with them as an evidence of their success.

Moving north they tore up the tracks of the Baltimore & Ohio Railroad connecting Washington with the West, and reached Westminster where they routed a plucky but outnumbered force of Delaware cavalry, taking more prisoners. Still no knowledge of Lee's whereabouts, but Stuart received reports that Ewell had reached Carlisle and was only sixteen miles from Harrisburg. Pricked by conscience and two days behind his schedule, Stuart, the next morning, pushed his column harder, finding the prisoners and the wagon train an increasingly embarrassing encumbrance.

Reaching Hanover about ten in the morning of June 30, the advance guard sighted a regiment of Kilpatrick's cavalry. Imprudently, without waiting for support, the contingent charged into battle, briefly driving back the Federals. A counterattack by General Elon J. Farnsworth's brigade hurled back the Confederates, and as at Verdiersville the previous summer Stuart was nearly captured.

He effected a hairbreadth escape by leaping his thoroughbred over a cavernous ditch, during which feat, a staff officer maintained, his horse covered a distance of twenty-five feet in the air. "I shall never forget the glimpse I then saw of this beautiful animal away up in midair over the chasm and Stuart's fine figure sitting erect and firm in the saddle." Once clear of his pursuers, Stuart rallied Chambliss's troopers, brought up Hampton's and Fitz Lee's brigades, and successfully held the Confederate position until nightfall.

He had no desire to renew the fight next morning; he was three days behind schedule. Bypassing Hanover, the column rode on to Carlisle in search of General Ewell. They found only Federal militia in Carlisle, and when these rejected an invitation to surrender, Stuart shelled the town and burned the Federal barracks. Where he might go next in his quest for the army was fortuitously settled when during the night a courier rode up from General Lee.

Lee had already recalled Ewell to Gettysburg, and had sent out several aides to track down his missing cavalry commander. Now two of them had luckily stumbled on the truant. They presented to Stuart the sealed orders carried by the others: Proceed in all haste to Gettysburg.

Stuart drove his exhausted cavalry down the Carlisle road and stopped a mile or two short of Gettysburg. Leaving Hampton in command, guarding the wagon train, he rode on south to contact Lee. The troops, half dead from lack of sleep, tumbled from their saddles and sprawled out beneath the trees. Wade Hampton, keeping a wary eye out for Yankees, rode forward to do a little reconnoitering.

It was a peaceful countryside of pleasant farms and fields and wooded knolls, and the battle five miles to the southeast, marked by the distance-muted sound of guns and fleecy clouds of smoke, seemed far away. He might have been stalking deer or raising a covey of grouse at Millwood in South Carolina.

Suddenly a bullet whispered past him. Startled, he tried to gauge its distance and direction, Then he saw the sniper: a bluecoated cavalryman standing arrogantly on a stump some hundred yards away and raising his rifle for another shot.

Hampton whipped out his pistol, and both fired simultaneously, the Northerner missing, Hampton's bullet sending splinters flying from the stump. As they prepared to fire again, young Frank Pearson of the 6th Michigan Cavalry raised his hand to signal for a truce. His powder-fouled gun had jammed. Hampton, true to the cavalier tradition, waited while the youngster cleaned the bore of his carbine and reloaded. Okay, Pearson signaled, ready.

Again both fired at once. Perhaps, since he rarely missed, Hampton's initial shot had been a warning to a gallant foe who refused to shelter behind a stump but faced his adversary upright. The bullet shattered Pearson's wrist and the carbine pitched muzzle-first into the ground. Hampton did not reload, but watched his wounded opponent stagger back into the trees—then noticed that his cavalry cape had been pierced just inches from his heart.

It had been a fair fight, and Hampton would have been content to leave it that way, had he been allowed to. But another Michigan cavalryman had been a witness to the duel. Creeping up from behind, his horse's hoofbeats muffled by the turf, he unsheathed his saber and swung the blade at Hampton's head. Only the general's felt hat and greater height saved him from a mortal wound. Even so, the saber cut a deep gash in his scalp.

Hampton whirled, blood streaming down his face, aimed the pistol at his new assailant and pulled the trigger. There was a harmless snap. The Yankee swung his horse around and fled. Hampton pursued, and together they raced across meadow, hill, and creek, the general press-

ing the trigger futilely and shouting uncustomary oaths at his opponent. When the Michigander finally plunged into a thicket, Hampton
hurled the useless pistol after him in resignation and rode back into
camp to have his wound dressed.

His head would ache for the rest of the day, while he waited for
Stuart to return. But the wound would be nothing compared with what
lay ahead of him.

Stuart, meanwhile, reached General Lee as the second day's fight was
roaring toward a climax. "Well, General Stuart, you are here at last,"
said Lee. He did not censure his chief of cavalry for the latter's absence
or his failure to communicate; but his tone of voice conveyed a lot more
than the words. When Stuart referred to the captured wagons, perhaps
as conciliation, Lee sadly shook his head. "Yes General, but they are
only an impediment to me now," he said.

There was yet time to resolve this battle, less than thirty-six hours old,
to Confederate advantage. By nightfall, both armies were extended to
the limits of endurance; both had suffered frightful casualties. As the
numerically weaker force, less able to sustain more losses, the South
would have to win tomorrow if it won at all; and Lee staked his bid for
victory on one desperate gamble. Having assailed both ends of the
Federal line, thus draining off strength from the center, he would, on
the following morning, hurl eleven infantry brigades at that center,
splitting the Federal defense asunder, and sending Meade's army
reeling back to Maryland.

In this conclusive action, Lee explained, Stuart would have a chance
to clinch the victory. He was to place his cavalry on the enemy's right
flank, east of Culp's Hill; and when the Federals broke before the
powerful Confederate offensive, Stuart would attack the rear of the
retreating army, adding confusion to the rout.

He had arrived late on the scene of battle, he had botched things up
so far; but there was still the opportunity for Stuart to add a crucial
cavalry engagement to the history of Gettysburg.

When, at 1:07 p.m. on July 3, the Confederate artillery on Seminary
Ridge began the 115-gun cannonade that would precede the great
assault, the Federal cavalry, Gregg's and Kilpatrick's divisions, were
positioned at two strategic points.

South of the battlefield beyond the Round Tops, Judson Kilpatrick
had two brigades, Elon Farnsworth's from his own division and Wesley
Merritt's of Buford's. His second brigade, under General Custer, had
been temporarily assigned to Gregg's division. Kilpatrick was serving a
dual role, protecting Meade's flank near Little Round Top, and
threatening Lee's right. His instructions were to attack Lee the moment

that the Confederate assault, which all knew was coming, failed—and the Confederates were thrown into confusion.

Gregg's division, raised to 5,000 in number with Custer's forces added, was guarding the right and rear of the Union line three miles northeast of Culp's Hill. Unlike Kilpatrick, who had nothing to fear from Confederate cavalry, Gregg was on the watch for Stuart, now known to be in the vicinity. He positioned his three brigades in a wooded area between Hanover and Low Dutch roads, from which he could watch both of these approaches, and placed a forward line of skirmishers across the fields that lay between the wooded area and Cress Ridge to the north. Then he waited.

Lee had concentrated virtually all his cavalry under Stuart, giving him Jenkins' newly-arrived brigade to increase Stuart's forces to 6,000 men. Robertson's and Jones's brigades were guarding trains and communication lines near Fairfield and John Imboden's command had not yet reached the battlefield. As the Confederate bombardment preceding Pickett's charge began, Stuart moved eastward on the York Road two and a half miles from Gettysburg, then turned south on a country lane to get to the rear of the Federal position.

From Cress Ridge he caught sight of a thin blue line of horsemen stretching from the Hanover Road to a patch of woodland farther east. That wooded area bothered him; no telling what the trees concealed. Since Jenkins' troops were found to have only ten rounds of ammunition in their belts, and would be useless in any extended fight, he sent a dismounted battalion forward to flush out any hidden enemy. They not only flushed them, they were decimated by the fire from the woods.

Stuart rushed Chambliss to their rescue and quickly brought forward Hampton's and Fitz Lee's brigades, with instructions to conceal themselves behind Cress Ridge. What he had in mind was unclear, but what happened dazzled the imagination. Either Fitz Lee mistook the order, or his men got out of hand and charged precipitously toward the sound of fire. There was nothing that Hampton could do but join the thundering herd. In a storm of hoofs and steel such as had not been seen since Brandy Station, the lines of cavalry swept across the open field.

Captain William Miller of the 3rd Pennsylvania Cavalry watched them come with admiration. "A grander spectacle than their advance has rarely been beheld. They marched with well-aligned fronts and steady reins. Their polished saber-blades dazzled in the sun. . . . Shell and shrapnel met the advancing Confederates, tore through their ranks. Closing the gaps as though nothing had happened, on they came."

Except for his impromptu one-man charge at Ashby's Gap two weeks before, George Armstrong Custer had not greatly distinguished himself in action. He had been raised to brigadier general, though, and having no proper uniform to fit the rank, he improvised a costume of black velvet jacket with gold braid to the elbows, black velveteen breeches with gold lace stripes, black soft-brimmed hat pinned up on one side by a silver star. "When I'm on the field," he said, "I want my men to recognize me."

He was recognized now as, shoulder-length tresses streaming in the wind, he led his 1st Michigan Cavalry forward to meet the Confederate attack, shouting "Come on you Wolverines!" Captain Miller, standing by in reserve with the Pennsylvanians, remembered:

> As the two columns approached each other the pace of each increased, when suddenly a crash, like the falling of timber, betokened the crisis. So sudden and violent was the collision that many of the horses were turned end over end and crushed their riders beneath them. The clashing of sabers, the demands for surrender, the firing of pistols and the cries of the combatants now filled the air.

The fighting was at such close quarters that those killed were found in pairs of blue and gray, pinned to each other by tightly-clenched sabers driven through their bodies. A farmer named Rummel, on a portion of whose field the fight took place, dragged thirty dead horses from his lane to find beneath them a Virginian and a Pennsylvanian: "Their fingers, though stiff in death, were so firmly imbedded in each other's flesh that they could not be removed without the aid of force."

Because of his height Wade Hampton stood out among the milling gladiators, a target for the enemy. Surrounded by a squadron of Michigan cavalry, he dueled with several at once, until an officer slashed at his scalp from behind, opening the earlier wound. Half blinded with blood, Hampton turned and cleft the man's skull in two. Two Confederates fought their way to his rescue.

"General, they're too many for us," gasped Sergeant Nat Price. "For God's sake, leap your horse over that fence."

Making one last effort, Hampton forced his horse to clear the fence. He was still in the air when a piece of shrapnel struck him down.

By now the rest of the Federal cavalry stormed from the woods to attack the Confederate flanks. Captain Miller's Pennsylvanians "cut off the rear of the rebel line and drove it back," then tried to charge Stuart's battery on Cress Ridge, a hundred yards away, "but my men were so disabled and scattered that they were unable to take it back." The flank attacks, however, forced Stuart's cavalry back to its original positions, and after nightfall they withdrew to the York Road to encamp.

"We lost many good men," wrote Stuart's aide, John Esten Cooke.

General Hampton was shot in the side, and nearly cut out of the saddle by a saber stroke. Ten minutes before I had conversed with the noble South Carolinian, and he was full of life, strength, and animation. Now he was slowly being borne to the rear in his ambulance, bleeding from his dangerous wounds. General Stuart had a narrow escape in this charge, his pistol hung in his holster, and as he was trying to draw it, he received the fire of barrel after barrel from a Federal cavalryman within ten paces of him, but fortunately sustained no injury.

It was the last great saber battle of the Civil War in which cavalry alone participated. Casualties had been severe, but neither side had been defeated. Both would claim victory. Stuart would write that the Federals "vanished" before his charging cavalry "like grain before the scythe," while Gregg would report that, "defeated at every point, the enemy withdraw." But the fact remained that Stuart's threat to Meade's rear had been thwarted. Yet even that was academic now. The massive assault on Cemetery Ridge, spearheaded by George E. Pickett's and Johnston Pettigrew's division, had been repulsed with dreadful losses.

The Battle of Gettysburg was over. Almost.

At the south end of the battlefield below Gettysburg, straddling the Emmitsburg Road, Kilpatrick's cavalry had fretted out the afternoon skirmishing with Confederate pickets. None was certain what their final mission would turn out to be. Screening Meade's withdrawal? Or pursuing fleeing rebels? Kilpatrick's orders from Pleasonton were "to press the enemy, to threaten him at every point, to strike at the first opportunity." Impatiently he waited for that opportunity. With the repulse of Pickett's charge, it came.

Guarding the Confederate right and facing Kilpatrick was a skirmish line of Texas and Georgia infantry, stretching from Emmitsburg Road to the base of Round Top, partially protected by a stake-and-rail fence. Two Vermont cavalry regiments under Farnsworth had tried to scatter that force with repeated sallies and suffered badly from enemy fire. Not only was that end of the valley unsuitable for cavalry maneuvers, unevenly strewn with boulders and chopped up with fences, walls, and ditches, but well-positioned infantry had a natural advantage over an exposed brigade of cavalry.

Kilpatrick had only Farnsworth's brigade, Merritt being stationed farther to the west. He sent word to Custer, temporarily assigned to Gregg's division, to rejoin him below Gettysburg, but Custer never came. ("Say you never got the message," Gregg told the curly-locked General, "I need you here.") With the Confederates demoralized after the failure of Pickett's charge, it was a now-or-never time to rout the Texans and Georgians and possibly roll-up Lee's right.

He directed Farnsworth to send the 1st West Virginia to break the Confederate line and open a door for the rest to follow through. Against withering fire they made it to the fence, and began yanking at the stakes and hacking at the rails with sabers. The Confederates picked them off at almost point-blank range. Forced back, they rallied and tried again. Not only did the Texans and Georgians hold firm, but Confederate regiments at the base of Round Top turned from facing the enemy on the hill to fire on this mounted enemy behind them.

Fearful of losing his one big opportunity to end the day with a triumph for his cavalry, Kilpatrick delivered an order to Farnsworth that had all the earmarks of an ultimatum. He was to take his last, undecimated regiment, and assault the Texans head on, break them up, then turn on the Confederates at the base of Round Top and destroy them too. In the face of what had gone before, an incredible demand to make, even of a man of Farnsworth's mettle.

Of the cavalry officers promoted by Pleasonton when he reorganized the cavalry, young Farnsworth, along with Custer and Merritt, had made the impressive leap from captain to brigadier general. In fact, the promotion had been so sudden, that Farnsworth had had no time to get a uniform to fit the rank, and Pleasonton had lent him his own blue jacket with the proper shoulder straps and stars. In Pleasonton's words, he was worthy of the honor:

> Gifted in a high degree with a quick perception and a correct judgment, and remarkable for his daring coolness, his comprehensive grasp of the situation on the field of battle and the rapidity of his actions had already distinguished General Farnsworth among his comrades in arms.

Captain H. C. Parsons, who had seen his companions cut to ribbons in the earlier assaults, was standing nearby when Kilpatrick delivered the order for the suicidal charge. Farnsworth looked unbelievingly at his commander. His voice choked with emotion.

"General, do you mean it? Shall I throw my handful of men over rough ground through timber, against a brigade of infantry? The First Vermont has already been cut to pieces. These are too good men to kill."

Kilpatrick looked at the other levelly. "Do you refuse to obey my orders? If you're afraid to lead this charge, I'll lead it."

Farnsworth rose in his stirrups, to look down on his commander. "Take that back!" he said.

Steel wills clashed like sabers in that confrontation. Briefly Kilpatrick tried to stare down his subordinate. Then his eyes lowered.

"I didn't mean it," he said. "Forget it."

For a moment there was silence while each man regained composure. Then Farnsworth said calmly, "General, if you order the charge, I'll lead it, but you must take the responsibility."

"Very well," said Kilpatrick gravely. "The responsibility is mine."

As Captain Parsons later wrote:

> I recall the two young generals at that moment in the shadow of the oaks and against the sunlight — Kilpatrick with his fine features, his blond beard, his soft hat turned up jauntily, and his face lighted with the joy that always came into it when the charge was sounded; Farnsworth, tall, slight, stern, and pale, but rising with conscious strength and consecration.
>
> Kilpatrick was eager for the fray. He believed that cavalry could "fight anywhere except at sea." He was justified by his orders and by results, and he was brave enough to withdraw the hot imputation, even in the presence of a regiment. Farnsworth was courage incarnate, but full of tender regard for his men, and his protest was manly and soldierly.

Captain Parsons led one of the battalions lined up for the charge. He remembered that "There was no encouragement from onlooking armies, no bravado; and each man felt, as he tightened his saber belt, that he was summoned to a ride to death."

On command they rode out in columns of four with Farnsworth at their head. Parsons remembered passing the wounded survivors of the previous attacks, and how they regarded him and his comrades with pitying eyes; remembered their own bluecoated pickets urging them to turn back before it was too late; remembered a half-crazed horse, with one leg missing, plunging in panic through their lines.

It was, he recalled, a swift, resistless charge over rocks, through timber, under close enfilading fire. They were almost immediately on the enemy, within thirty paces, when the first Confederate volley exploded. Farnsworth's horse fell; a trooper sprang from the saddle, gave the general his horse, and escaped on foot.

In numbers they were only half the famous Six Hundred of the Light Brigade that charged at Balaklava, but their valor and their fate were much the same. Smashing into the guns of the Texans and Georgians they went on through, then, with many saddles emptied, charged the two Alabama regiments prepared to meet them at the base of Round Top. The riderless horses of those who had fallen stayed with them as they circled back into the center of the field, their numbers reduced to 150 in the saddle. As they turned to charge the 15th Alabama from this opposite direction, there were men to the left of them, men in front of them; and only ten remaining at General Farnsworth's side.

Once again the general raised his saber, calling for a final effort, and five bullets, any one of them fatal, cut him down.

When they came for him later, searching among the wounded and the dead, they found him still with his arm upraised, still with the saber firmly in his grasp. A fellow officer knelt beside the body and cut the star from Farnsworth's coat. Someone must have a souvenir of this last gallant sacrifice at Gettysburg.

It would add up to only a footnote in history—but for a few, it was their finest hour. Of Farnsworth's role, Kilpatrick remarked, "For the honor of his young brigade and the glory of his corps, he gave his life. . . . We can say of him, in the language of another, 'Good soldier, faithful friend, great heart, hail and farewell!'" Why, then, had he sent him to his death? Because, he wrote, had the charge succeeded it would have resulted in "a total rout" of the Confederates. But who could have thought it might succeed?

Night had fallen over Gettysburg. General John Imboden, whose cavalry had finally arrived from Hancock, sought his commander for instructions. He found Lee after midnight, seated on Traveler, alone. "The moon shone full upon his massive features and revealed an expression of sadness that I had never before seen upon his face."

"General," Imboden ventured to remark, "this has been a hard day for you."

"Yes," said Lee, "it has been a sad, sad day to us." Then, after a moment of silence he remarked on the gallant performance of Pickett's division—"I never saw troops behave more magnificently"—and after another moment of silence, in a voice of agony: "Too bad! *Too bad*! OH! TOO BAD!"

They would now return to Virginia, the general said, recrossing the Potomac near Williamsport, and he would finally have use for Imboden's 2,000 troopers. They would escort the train of wounded, who would be evacuated first. It was no small assignment, for the wagons, when assembled, stretched for a distance of twenty-one miles. And while the wounded and dying cried out in agony—"For God's sake, will no one have mercy and kill me?"—vindictive Pennsylvanians attacked the train, hacking at the wheels with axes, trying to overturn the wagons.

In the following days, during which Meade was reluctant to follow up his limited victory with a vigorous pursuit of Lee ("He was within your grasp," wrote Lincoln, "and to have closed upon him . . . would have ended the war"), Pleasonton's cavalry snapped at the flanks and rear of the retreating army. Harass the enemy all you want, was the gist of Meade's instruction, but don't provoke a major engagement. As a result there was no battle, as had been expected, north of the Potomac, and Lee had time on July 13 to restore the pontoon bridge, and recross into Virginia.

So he passed over, but no trumpets sounded for him on the other side.

CHAPTER

13

RIDE TO OBLIVION

ALL THAT JOHN HUNT MORGAN KNEW, IN THE FIRST DAYS OF JUNE was that Lee seemed to be assembling his forces for another strike into the North, and that Vicksburg was in dire peril from Grant's forces at its eastern gates. These circumstances in themselves suggested a course of action: another raid deep into Kentucky to divert a portion of Grant's army from the siege of Vicksburg, and, that accomplished, a swift dash into Indiana, with the secret thought that he might join Lee if the latter again invaded Pennsylvania.

Morgan's commander Braxton Bragg went along with the Kentucky raid proposal, but for reasons of his own. It would screen from Rosecrans his planned withdrawal from Tullahoma to a more easily defended position behind the Tennessee River, covering Chattanooga. Go ahead, he told Morgan, but stay this side of the Ohio River. Though he acquiesced, Morgan had more ambitious plans. This was a time that called for daring. This would be, as Basil Duke later called it, "incomparably the most brilliant raid of the entire war."

There were other factors affecting Morgan's plans. It had been a grim winter for the 2nd Kentucky Cavalry, during which many had been released on furlough to go home to get new mounts. In the six months, January to June, there had been little action apart from minor raids and skirmishes launched from the cavalry camp at Alexandria in Middle Tennessee. Morgan's men had suffered from inaction; and with the success of Grierson's raid, there was a suspicion brewing that the Southern cavalry was being outmaneuvered.

Was the Morgan legend dying? Were Morgan's Terrible Men no longer to be feared? Not according to Blue Grass authoress Sally Rochester Ford, whose recently published *Raids and Romances of Morgan and His Men* was banned in Memphis and St. Louis. Though the book was largely fiction, it presented Morgan's raiders in a light seen only through cathedral windows, as crusaders of the days when knighthood was in flower. It was up to Morgan's cavalry to live up to the image.

But after this winter of their discontent, it was hard for the Kentuckians to measure up. "In this year," wrote Basil Duke, "the glory and prestige began to pass away from the Southern cavalry." Duke attributed the change not to the growing prowess of their Northern rivals—which was indeed a factor—but to "the greater scarcity of horses and the great difficulty of obtaining forage." The malaise, however, went deeper than that, and Morgan must have known it as did William Hardee, corps commander under Bragg.

"I learn that Morgan's command is in bad condition and growing worse," Hardee had written to Joseph Johnston in April.

> I judge from all I hear that he is greatly dissatisfied from being under Wheeler. His conduct, if this be true, cannot be justified and he has suffered and will continue to suffer in public estimation. I dislike to see his usefulness impaired and his reputation sullied by mistaken notions of pride and duty. Would it not be well for you to send for Morgan and have some talk with him?

Talk would do little good at this point. According to Duke, quoting however on hearsay, Bragg himself told Jefferson Davis that "General Morgan was an officer who had few superiors, none, perhaps in his own line, but that he was a *dangerous man*, on account of his intense desire to act independently." He could not have known how right he was.

For Morgan's mind was made up, and not in sympathy with Bragg's instructions. He would redeem his command, and his dwindling reputation, with the greatest raid yet undertaken in the Civil War. His men would not stop short at the Ohio River. They would cross that Rubicon into Indiana, striking deeper into the Union's vitals than any Confederate force had ever penetrated.

In preparation, he sent Captain Tom Hines and Sam Taylor, young Kentuckians who had been with him since the early days, on a secret mission to Indiana and Ohio to scout Ohio River crossings and, according to Duke, to "stir up any Copperheads" who might be useful to the raiders behind enemy lines. Then, near Burkesville south of the Cumberland, Morgan assembled his expeditionary force.

It numbered 2,460 men in all, along with a six-gun battery. Basil Duke commanded the larger of the two brigades, and four of Morgan's five brothers—Calvin, Thomas, Charlton, and Richard—would ride with the expedition, making it something of a family affair. St. Leger Grenfell, now affectionately known as "Old St. Lege," was sadly missing from the ranks. He had dropped out after Morgan's wedding.

The expedition started forth from Burkesville on July 2, 1863, in the buoyant spirits that usually prevailed at the beginning of a raid, the men "in high feather and full song," chanting:

> Here's to Duke and Morgan,
> Drink it down! Drink it down!

Even the rain-swollen Cumberland River, flooded to a half-mile width, did not damp their ardor, nor did the fact that the opposite bank was picketed by some of Frank Wolford's Federal Kentuckians. Grabbing everything that would float, they plunged into the turbulent wash, holding on to a plank or branch with one hand and their horses' bridles with the other. The artillery and wagons crossed by boat. Of their encounter with the Yankees on the farther bank, Private Bennett Young recorded:

> Those who had clothing on rushed ashore and into line, those who swam with horses, unwilling to be laggard, not halting to dress, seized their cartridge boxes and guns and dashed upon the enemy. The strange sight of naked men engaging in combat amazed the enemy. They had never seen soldiers before clad only in nature's garb.

Though Wolford's Kentuckians were easily brushed aside, it was a different story when they reached Green River two days later. Here, guarding the bridge, stood Colonel Orlando H. Moore with the 25th Michigan Infantry, stretched out behind formidable breastworks. Morgan resorted to his favorite game of bluff. Under a flag of truce he sent a courier to Moore demanding that officer's immediate surrender. Moore replied laconically: "Lieutenant, if it was any other day I might surrender, but on the Fourth of July I must have a little brush first."

Morgan opened up on the barricades with his battery, then hurled one of his two brigades against the enemy. The lead company was decimated as it charged across open ground into the fire of the Federals, and the two waves of assaulting troops that followed fared no better. "Many of our best men were killed and wounded," recorded Major James McCreary in his diary. "It was a sad, sorrowful day, and more tears of grief rolled over my weather-beaten cheeks on this mournful occasion than have before for years. *The commencement of this raid is ominous.*"

The underscoring was McCreary's, but the sentiment was warranted. The expedition lost 71 men killed and wounded in that three-hour futile fight; and when Morgan sent another flag of truce to Moore, it was to request permission to bury the dead. This granted, he decided to by-pass the fortified crossing, ford the river farther down, and head due north for Lebanon. They found Lebanon in the hands of Union infantry, and once again it was Kentuckian against Kentuckian.

Morgan sent word to evacuate women and children; he was going to shell the town. But the bombardment from the six light guns did little damage. The troops would have to move in and take the town house by house. And "a street fight," noted one of Morgan's scouts, "is one of the most desperate modes of warfare known to a soldier. The advantage is strongly against the storming party."

The defenders made the most of this advantage. Early in the assault "Poor Tommy Morgan ran forward and cheered the men with all the enthusiasm of his bright nature. At the first volley he fell, pierced through the breast." The nineteen-year-old lieutenant was the favorite of John Morgan's brothers, and he died in Calvin Morgan's arms. The raiders took the town, at a loss of about 40 killed or wounded, and Morgan wanted no more fighting for that day. Hearing that Union cavalry was approaching Lebanon, he hurried on via Springfield and Bardstown to the wide Ohio.

Tom Hines had scouted a likely place to cross the river: a steamboat landing below the hilltop town of Brandenburg. No armed garrison occupied the town; no Confederate raiders were expected this far north. Neither was there any ferry to carry the troops and guns across. By a schedule posted at the wharf boat, however, Morgan's men learned that a steamer made daily stops at Brandenburg. He posted lookouts above and below the town, and prepared an ambush for the vessel.

At noon the sidewheeler *John B. McCombs*, cheerily sounding its whistle, sidled up to the wharf boat. Like the pirates of an earlier day Morgan the ruffian-clad Confederates, armed to the teeth, swarmed over the rails and took possession of the vessel. A second steamer, the fast mailboat *Alice Dean*, followed in the wake of the *McCombs* to meet a similar fate. Morgan now had his landing craft, which he armed with his artillery, a gun on the bow and stern of each.

The following morning, July 8, men and horses marched aboard the vessels, and the amphibious invasion of the North was under way. A Federal gunboat named the *Elk*, on routine patrol, swept down the river and saluted the steamers with a friendly whistle. Morgan ordered his artillerists to turn their guns on the target, and the startled crewmen of the *Elk* found themselves under fire from innocent-looking vessels carrying the Stars and Stripes. The captain of the gunboat churned around and headed upstream to Louisville to sound the alarm and summon reinforcements.

On the Indiana shore, Morgan ordered the *McCombs* sent up to Louisville and the *Alice Dean* set afire. He was burning not his bridges but his boats behind him, and he had reached the point of no return. Wrote Basil Duke before their embarkation:

> On the other side of the great river . . . we would stand face to face with the hostile and angry North—an immense and infuriated population, and a soldiery outnumbering us twenty to one would confront us. Telegraph lines, tracing the country in every direction, would tell constantly of our movements; railways would bring assailants against us from every quarter, and we would have to run this gauntlet, night and day, without rest or one moment of safety, for six hundred miles. As we looked on the river, rolling before us, we felt that it divided us from a momentous future. . . .

Morgan himself was aware that events he had not foreseen had turned the odds against him. Vicksburg had fallen. Lee was retreating from Pennsylvania, and Morgan's plan to join that general in the east was thwarted. He would have to improvise a new route of withdrawal. Moreover, he had lost 200 men and many of his ablest officers. What was to have been his finest hour threatened to become a nightmare.

"We intend to live off the Yanks hereafter and let the North feel, as the South has felt, some of the horrors of war," wrote Henry Stone of Morgan's cavalry on first setting foot on Indiana soil. But the horrors of war were postponed for a time at any rate. "Some of the boys gave champagne parties that night," recorded another trooper, "which doubtless was taken from the stores of one of the steamers, as also were a few other luxuries that had so mysteriously come into their possession."

Early the next morning "Boots and Saddles" sounded, and the two brigades were on their way, ranging farther north than ever Confederate troops had ranged before. Their course lay north and east, and as Sergeant Stone had predicted, they would live off the country:

> Every morning the Captains of Companies would appoint a man for each mess to go ahead and furnish provisions. They would all go ahead of the command and scatter out to the farmhouses for miles on each side of the road, and by ten or twelve o'clock they would overtake us with sacks full of light bread, cheese, butter, preserves, canned peaches, berries, wine cordial, canteens of milk and everything good that the pantrys and closets of the hoosier ladies could furnish.

Thus laden, they marched through the cornfields and hamlets of Indiana to the sound of a curious, swelling beat. Everywhere bells. Bells ringing from steeples of churches, from town hall roofs, from firehouse towers, from the cupolas of village schools; often interspersed with shrieking whistles from the factories and mills. Village signaling to village, farm to farm. Morgan the raider was on the way. According to trooper Bennet Young, "Even rhyme was put under conscription to help tell how awful Morgan's men were." The lines of the ubiquitous ballad were more relevant than ever:

> I'm sent to warn the neighbors, he's only a mile behind.
> He's sweeping up the horses, every horse that he can find.
> Morgan, Morgan, the raider, and Morgan's terrible men,
> With Bowie knives and pistols are galloping up the glen.

Though Morgan had sent George "Lightning" Ellsworth to disrupt communications in their path, either cutting the wires or sending misleading information on the raider's whereabouts, Ellsworth had stumbled on some disconcerting news. Mounted troops under General Henry M. Judah were only twenty-four hours behind them; Wolford's Kentuckians were still in close pursuit; and the state militia in virtually every town and village in their path was mobilized to meet them. In Louisville all able-bodied men 20 to 45 had been ordered to report for duty; businesses were closed in Indianapolis; Cincinnati was under martial law.

At Corydon, on July 9, the home guard rallied to offer stiff resistance and "the fighting was very sharp for 20 minutes" before the town surrendered. And the same at Salem where they easily scattered the militia. In both towns, stores were pillaged, whiskey "confiscated," depots burned, and tracks destroyed. While Morgan himself discouraged plundering, there was an uncontrollable dedication in the hearts of the invaders. They were giving the North a taste of what the South had suffered over two long years.

Five days later, nearing the Cincinnati to Columbus railroad and hearing the whistle of an approaching locomotive, the scouts arrived in time to pile uprooted ties across the tracks—then stood by to witness the result. The engineer, seeing the gallery of Confederates on both sides of the roadbed, put on extra steam. "The train shot past us like a blazing meteor," recorded Lieutenant Kelion Peddicord, "and the next thing we saw was a dense cloud of steam above which flew large timbers."

> Our next sight startled our nerves, for there lay the monster floundering in the field like a fish out of water, with nothing but the tender

attached. . . . Over three hundred raw recruits were on board, bound
for Camp Dennison. They came tumbling and rolling out in every way
imaginable. . . . All submitted without a single shot, and were sent
under guard to the General.

Lexington, Paris, Vernon, Versailles . . . driving through home-
guard resistance like a dusty cyclone. Local militia tried to block their
return by felling trees across the roads that they were passing down,
which only impeded their pursuers. The men pillaged senselessly, "like
schoolboys robbing an orchard," Duke observed. "One man carried a
bird-cage, with three canaries in it, for two days. Another rode with a
chafing dish, which looked like a small metallic coffin, on the pommel
of his saddle. . . . Although the weather was intensely warm, another,
still, slung seven pairs of skates around his neck. . . ."

On July 13, when the raiders crossed into Ohio and neared Cincinnati, they heard again the church bells clanging and the whistles shrieking. Every able-bodied man in the neighborhood was called to arms.
The draft riots raging in distant New York were no less terrifying than
the news that Lightning Ellsworth circulated on the wires—that
Morgan and his Terrible Men were being followed by General Forrest
with two thousand of his Confederates.

The false report kept the local militia inside the city, which was just
what Morgan wanted. There was little truth in the rumor that "the
daring Morgan that night disguised himself, entered Cincinnati, and in
company with a friend there, actually attended a ball given by one of
the society ladies in the city." Under different conditions, it was the sort
of thing he might do; but Morgan, like the civilian residents, was in no
mood for dancing. He wanted only to sneak past the city without
interference. The daring raid had turned into a quest for safety.

An all-night ride, in which officers prodded men to stay awake,
brought them across the Little Miami River, heading east. There was
no refuge to the south of them, where the wide Ohio River was patrolled by Federals. The only escape lay into West Virginia, a hundred
and twenty-five miles or so away—light years away, to the exhausted
troops. They no longer sang as they marched, Duke noted, except for
one black servant strumming "The Hills of Tennessee," "making his
banjo ring like forlorn bells." His voice carried down the line of weary
riders like a lament for souls in purgatory:

> All up and down the whole creation
> Sadly I roam . . .

At Williamsburg on July 14 they had ridden for 35 hours without rest
and had covered a distance of ninety miles since leaving Indiana. It

would have been little comfort to know that news of their raid had spread new hope throughout the South, dispelling some of the gloom of Gettysburg and Vicksburg. "This bold raid," declared the Richmond *Enquirer*, "is the only real movement we are making toward a restoration of peace, for peace must be conquered on the enemy's ground, or it will not come at all."

But this bold raid had turned into a desperate effort to escape. South of their line of march the rain-swollen Ohio was patrolled by Union gunboats; ferries would be heavily guarded. Behind them pressed Wolford's Union Cavalry whose numbers they could only guess at. They might have guessed, too, that other mounted regiments from Ohio, Indiana, Michigan, and Illinois were joining in the chase, and that the home guards in Indiana and Ohio—numbering more than 120,000—were being mobilized to trap them.

"The enemy are now pressing us from all sides," wrote James McCreary in his diary on July 16, "and the woods swarm with militia. We capture hundreds of prisoners but, a parole being null, we can only sweep them as chaff out of our way." They wanted no part of guarding, feeding, and escorting captives.

Their own wounded were enough of a problem, and they found transportation for invalids in purloined vehicles of infinite variety: peddlers' wagons, farm carts, hackney coaches, omnibuses, elegant barouches. Morgan himself had taken to riding at times in an open barouche which carried "a pair of lady's fine kid boots suspended by their silk lacings from one of the posts"—no doubt a gift for Mattie. (When the carriage was later abandoned, it was found by Union troops to contain as well "a loaf of bread, some hard-boiled eggs, and a bottle of whiskey.") Other goods appropriated from village stores en route included a vast number of women's veils, deep blue in color, which the troopers wore as sunshades. To puzzled Ohioans who saw them pass, the cavalcade looked like a traveling carnival from Samarkand.

Even the horses had a circus touch. The smart mounts on which they had left Kentucky had been literally worn out, with no time for treating or shoeing a lame foot. Many had been exchanged in Indiana for farm horses, which the troops complained were "big-bellied, barefooted, grass-fed beasts." These too collapsed beneath them after a hard day's march, Henry Stone using up eight horses before he was captured.

Morgan, however, assured his staff that their troubles were behind them. He had plans for crossing the Ohio at Buffington Island near the river town of Portland, due east on their present line of march. Toward evening of July 18 they reached their destination, seeing through the dusk and mist the blue hills of Virginia. And seeing something else as well: that Buffington Ford was guarded by at least 300 Union infantry ensconced behind strong earthworks.

Morgan agreed with Duke that an immediate attack was risky. They could doubtless storm the breastworks with a minimum of casualties; but then to attempt to cross the river in the dark of night, unsure of its contours and currents, would be hazardous. They would wait till morning.

It was a dawn of heavy fog and startling surprises. Scouts reconnoitering the Federal position found that the barricades had been abandoned. Dismounted, the troops crept warily forward, down a narrow, valley-like depression leading to the ford. Then the fog lifted; and the sun revealed the glinting sabers, bayonets, rifle barrels of 6,000 Union cavalry and infantry, one brigade on the ridge to the left of them, another on the right; and on the river, two sleek gunboats with their rifled barrels leveled at the ford.

It was the gunboats that opened fire first; then the horse artillery of General Henry Judah on the nearer ridge; then the guns of General Edward Hobson's forces on the other flank. For a gentle Sunday morning in a soft Ohio valley, this was the closest thing to instant hell that mortal man could fashion.

Trapped in a three-way crossfire, there was no immediate escape. "The scream of the shells drowned the hum of the bullets," wrote Basil Duke. "and bursting between the two lines formed at right angles—a disposition we were compelled to adopt in order to confront both ground assailants—the air seemed filled with metal, and the ground was torn and ploughed into furrows."

A few men—it was hard to tell how many—plunged into the river, but exposed to the small-arms fire from the gunboats, barely thirty made it to the other side. The rest who tried to stand their ground were running out of ammunition, and with nowhere to gallop out of range, could only duck the shells which burst around them. Morgan and Duke met in hasty consultation. There was no escape for all, but Duke and Johnson would attempt to hold the enemy, while Morgan tried to lead as many as possible through a narrow gap in the valley that remained open.

By the time Morgan was on his way, confusion possessed the valley. Men dumped the encumbering loot they had been carrying, the skates, the kitchenware, the guitars and women's dresses. Bolts of calico, silk, and ribbons for the girls they had left behind them, garlanded the blazing field like bunting. The distracted troopers, wrote Duke, would find no shelter in the maelstrom and were "changing the direction in which they galloped, with every shell which whizzed or burst near them. . . ."

The upper end of the valley was filled with wagons and ambulances, whose wounded and terror-stricken occupants urged the scared horses to headlong flight. Often they became locked together, and were hurled over as if by an earthquake. Occasionally a solid shot, or unexploded shell would strike one, and dash it into splinters. . . . The remaining section of artillery was tumbled into a ravine, during this mad swirl, as if the guns had been as light as feathers. The gunboats raked the road with grape . . . In a moment the panic was complete, and the disaster irretrievable.

Duke hoisted a flag of truce and, with no alternative, surrendered. Approximately 700 men, some wounded, all without ammunition, were taken prisoner, including Duke, Tom Hines, and Morgan's brother Richard. But once the guns were silenced, a strange sort of fellowship took over. It had been a long chase in a long and drawn-out war. Both sides were tired of it; and as they took off their clothes to bathe and swim in the Ohio River, and get rid of the dust and grime of battle, you could not distinguish one man from another, friend from foe.

When the swimming was over, the men spread out on the grass, and the Union troops opened their haversacks and shared their provisions with the Southerners; then all tipped their hats over their eyes and fell asleep. Throughout the rest of that suddenly peaceful day there was little sign of life on the battlefield upon which, wrote a roving reporter from the Cincinnati *Gazette*, "one could pick up almost any article in the drygoods, hardware, house furnishing or ladies' or gentlemen's furnishing—linen, hats, boots, gloves, knives, forks, spoons, calico, ribbons, drinking cups, carriages, market wagons, circus wagons. . . ." And the most coveted of prizes, among civilian souvenir hunters, were buttons cut surreptitiously from the jackets of "Morgan's Terrible Men."

Morgan escaped from the battlefield at Buffington with roughly 1,100 of his troopers, riding up the north bank of the Ohio in search of a likely crossing. Close behind and thirsting for Morgan's blood, pressed the Union cavalry under Shackleford and Wolford—Wolford still pained by the wound he had suffered when surrounded and captured by Morgan's men at Lebanon twelve months before.

Fifteen miles upstream the river narrowed, not a promising place to ford, but every second counted. Morgan rode into the shallows, and ordered the troops to swim their horses across in column of fours, maintaining order in the ranks. More than 300 made it to the West Virginia side, when around the bend came one of the two gunboats that had followed up from Buffington, all barrels blazing. Those who had reached the farther shore could only watch helplessly as the floating hats of dying troopers marked the graveyard of a score of swimmers.

Morgan himself might have made it to the opposite bank before the gunboat got within range, but though half way across, he chose to remain with the 800 left on the Ohio bank. These he led in a swift flight farther up the river, until darkness retarded their pursuers.

Then, quickly, the men built a dozen large campfires at a likely site and, once these were blazing, rode silently on toward the northeast. The ruse worked. Wolford's troops crept up on what appeared to be the Confederate camp, surrounded it, and waited for morning to pounce upon their victims. But by morning Morgan's men were long gone; and once again Ohio was panicked by rumors and alarms. Morgan and his Terrible Men were still at large. "Never before in the war," wrote D. Alexander Brown, "had eight hundred poorly armed and badly mounted men frightened so many people over so large an area."

They had delayed their pursuers, but not eluded them. And for three days and nights it was touch and go, with the Union cavalry on their tracks, every turn in the road and each grove of trees a potential threat of ambush. On July 26 one bizarre incident gained them time. Skirting the town of Steubenville, known to be heavily guarded by militia, they bypassed the unsuspecting guards who were poised in line of battle, with rifles cocked, waiting for whatever came their way.

When Shackleford's cavalry came up the pike in a cloud of dust, the gallant defenders of Steubenville gave them all they had, including scrap iron hurled from an antiquated cannon. It was not until the smoke had settled that Shackleford sensed something wrong. He sent a courier with a white flag to ask the militia: "What are you damned fools shooting at?" By the time the matter was straightened out, Morgan's men were half way to Salineville, near the Ohio opposite Pennsylvania.

But time alone was not enough to save them. Exhausted men were dropping out, indifferent to what might happen to them, and at one point all of a hundred stragglers were rounded up by Union cavalry. At Salineville, with only 600 of the 1,100 left and the gunboat still tracking them from the river, they learned that two fresh regiments of cavalry had joined the chase, brought by rail from Cincinnati.

Briefly, Morgan thought of heading for Lake Erie, sixty miles away. But the Great Lakes route through Canada led only to oblivion. And if oblivion faced them anyway, why not a last stand here at Salineville, recalling the Macaulay lines "And how can man die better than facing fearful odds? . . . "

They did make one last stand near Salineville, with a comic-opera ending. As the vanguard of pursuing Union cavalry hove in sight, one remaining company of Morgan's forces rallied to attack. It was a far cry from the magnificent charges of the early days, when splendid steeds, manes and tails streaming in the wind, carried their saber-waving

riders into the heart of an intimidated enemy. They did their best —
viciously spurring their captured sag-bellied horses toward an intervening fence. But few of the farm animals could clear a fence. Head
over hoofs they went, tumbling their riders at the feet of the awaiting
enemy. Two hundred more of Morgan's men were prisoners.

With only 364 troopers left, Morgan offered to surrender to the local
home guard, hopeful of getting paroles for his officers and men. But
after this had been agreed to, the regular Union cavalry rode up under
Major George Rue, and he would not be cheated of his quarry. Rue
ordered the raiders disarmed, and pronounced them Federal prisoners. Shortly afterward, Colonel Frank Wolford arrived to take some of
the sting out of Morgan's humiliation. He invited the fellow Kentuckian and his troops to share a chicken and dumpling dinner with him at a
local inn. "Everthing is at my expense," he told his ranking prisoner
jovially. "Just do not go off the square in front of the hotel."

A week later, Morgan and his exhausted troops arrived by boat at
Cincinnati, to be escorted to the city jail by a regiment of Ohio infantry
and a marching band playing "Yankee Doodle." More than 5,000
turned out to watch the passing cavalcade, shouting "Hang the cut-
throats!" Morgan, noted a reporter, seemed "unconcerned." In the jail
they were reunited with Basil Duke and the prisoners captured earlier,
who had received a similar reception from the townsfolk. Duke, however, had responded to the shouts of "Shoot the rebels!" by courteously
waving his hat and bowing to the crowd.

Cincinnati was only a replacement center. At week's end, Morgan
and his officers were transferred to the Ohio State Penitentiary in
Columbus, to be treated not as ranking prisoners of war but as common
criminals. To crown their "degradation and humiliation," wrote one of
Morgan's officers, "our heads [were] shorn, and our beards taken
entirely off!" Basil Duke was shocked when he next confronted his
commander. "He was so shaven and shorn that his voice alone was
recognizable."

When all was said and done, what had the raid, so grandly conceived,
accomplished? Many years later, citizens raised a stone plaque on the
site of Morgan's capture, to mark "the Farthest Point North Ever
Reached by Any Body of Confederate Troops During the Civil War."
Statistics would show that Morgan's men had, since the start of the
invasion, ridden more than 700 miles at a rate of 24 hours a day, had
killed or wounded 600 Federals, paroled 6,000 prisoners, destroyed or
appropriated stores valued at $10 million, burned bridges, torn up
railroad tracks and telegraph lines, and engaged more than 100,000
men from three states in attempts to capture them.

But it came to more than that. Despite the calamitous ending, Basil
Duke considered the expedition a matchless feat of cavalry. "The

purposes sought to be achieved by it were grander and more important, the conception of the plan more masterly, and the skill with which
it was conducted is unparalleled in the history of such affairs."

Despite his grandiose view of the affair, Duke bewailed the sacrifice
of so many peerless Confederate cavalrymen, now dead or imprisoned,
and quoted one "sagacious" authority as saying that Morgan had recklessly ridden himself into oblivion. But had he, for a certainty?
Morgan's jailer had some doubts, believing that "the authorities at
Washington might as well turn Morgan's men out in a body, as they will
all get out singly, anyhow."

How right he was.

14

GOLDILOCKS

GEORGE ARMSTRONG CUSTER, BECOMING KNOWN IN THE NORTHERN press as "the Boy General with the Golden Locks," could trace the birth of his personal glory to the Gettysburg campaign. Up to that time he had been the youthful aide of McClellan on the Peninsula, then of cavalry commander Alfred Pleasonton ("Pleasonton's pet," he was considered by the troopers). Only after his June 1863 promotion to brigadier general did he have a chance to show his stuff—in Gregg's clash with Stuart east of Gettysburg, and afterwards. Mostly afterwards.

The Ohio-born Custer, twenty-three, who had never been west of the Mississippi, never fought Indians as other cavalry commanders had, never heard of a place in Montana called the Little Big Horn, and was in fact a neophyte, nonetheless thirsted for glory—of the martial kind. Most of his West Point demerits, which placed him at the bottom of his class, were for battling with his fists, and he was courtmartialed in his senior year for refereeing a scuffle between lower-class cadets. But he made it into the echelon of the cavalry by impressing Pleasonton with his innate ability and his do-or-die resolve.

He craved distinction not only for himself but for the girl of his dreams whom he had left behind in Monroe, Michigan; the onetime pert and pigtailed Elizabeth Bacon who, swinging on her father's gate, was wont to greet him with the taunting, never-varying, "Hiyuh, Custer boy!"

Since those puppy-love days, and after a formal introduction, he had courted Libby ardently. And she as ardently had turned him down. It was nothing personal, she explained as time went on. Her father, Judge Daniel S. Bacon, had a low regard for Custer's father and a dour opinion of a soldier's life. The risk of disability or death was too great. Besides, military men were known to drink and gamble. He counseled his daughter that she should "play and laugh to her heart's content, promenade, and walk in good weather." But lay off fast horses and "fast young men."

Young "Autie," as he was known in Monroe, did not give up on the judge. He hoped public acclaim of his feats in battle would bring the judge around, and cherished citations in the press as actors cherish first-night notices. "Did Judge Bacon think my promotion deserved or not?" he wrote to a confidante of Libby, since he was not allowed to correspond with her directly. "I am the youngest General in the U.S. Army by over two years, in itself something to be proud of."

His own official reports, subject to being leaked to Washington papers, were models of hyperbole if not of factual recording. As, for example, his summary of the clash with Stuart's cavalry at Gettysburg:

> I cannot find language to express my high appreciation of the gallantry and daring displayed by the officers and men of the First Michigan Cavalry. They advanced to the charge of a vastly superior force with as much order and precision as if going on parade, and I challenge the annals of warfare to produce a more brilliant or successful charge of cavalry.

If this sounded extravagant, it conformed to artillerist Major Charles Wainwright's maxim that "a man would hardly be a cavalry officer if he did not talk big." And it was not sheer puffery. General Kilpatrick, who had reason to be piqued at Custer's failure to rejoin him south of Gettysburg, forgave his subordinate enough to write, "To Gen'l Custer & his brigade . . . all praise is due," to which General Pleasonton appended his Amen.

So that, though Custer had been a brigadier general for only five days when Lee withdrew from Gettysburg, he had begun to feel his oats. While Meade dallied in his pursuit of Lee, Custer sought to reach the Potomac ahead of the Confederates, where, with his single cavalry brigade, he would pocket the whole Army of Northern Virginia. Kilpatrick, however, who may have begun to sense some competition from this "glory grabber," kept him on a tight leash, and Custer settled for capturing a Confederate supply train, taking 300 wagons and 1,300 prisoners.

Pleasonton's orders from Meade, as the opposing forces headed south from Gettysburg, were to halt his cavalry short of the Potomac and await the army. Which allowed Lee to cross the river to Virginia without major interference, leaving men like Custer fuming in the saddle. But two days later young Autie got a break. Judson Kilpatrick was granted sick leave, and turned over his command to Custer. From captain to brigadier general to division commander in less than a month! It might be only temporary, but Custer was off the leash and he would make the most of it.

He plunged across the Potomac on July 17 in pursuit of Lee, and six days later was beyond the Rappahannock, fifty miles deep into Virginia. Leaving two brigades at the river to watch out for Lee, he pushed on with the rest of his division thirty miles more, across the Rapidan. After a brief, scrappy encounter with units of A. P. Hill's corps, he retired to his camp at Amissville. When relieved by Gregg's division on July 30, Custer marched his troops to Warrenton Junction ("a dreadful place") to await the arrival of the army.

He used this interlude to assemble the personal staff to which his rank entitled him. Two cronies from Michigan days were appointed his aide and adjutant respectively, and a worshipful private named Johnnie Cisco became his tableboy and groom. A runaway slave, Eliza Brown, was engaged to cook for the mess, having "jined up with the gen'l to get a passel of this hyah freedom business." He rejected, however, a comely Miss Annie Jones who offered to act as "sister of mercy" to his troops, discovering, after a period of trial, that her services had been rendered willy-nilly to all soldiers coming down the pike, including the Confederate partisans of John S. Mosby.

When Kilpatrick returned from leave on August 4, to reassume command of the division, he appeared in Custer's eyes as a usurper, forcing him back to the rank of brigade commander. A certain coolness rose between them. Custer sought to cultivate support and popularity among the troops which were at first put off by his mannerisms, bizarre style, and flamboyant dress.

"The Boy General looked so pretty and so unlike the stern realities of war," wrote a captain in his division, "that he was certain to be quizzed and ridiculed unmercifully unless he could compel the whole army to respect him. There was envy enough about his sudden elevation as it was!" And his orderly Joseph Fought observed that "All the other officers were exceedingly jealous of him. Not one of them but would have thrown a stone in his way to make him lose his prestige."

But, noted Fought, "He was way ahead of them as a soldier," and while that generated some antagonism it also generated admiration and, in time, affection. While he was described as "one of the funniest-looking officers you ever saw," and "a circus-rider gone mad," many admired his "devil-may-care style." They remained amused at his outlandish garb and unshorn tresses, but conceded him respect.

Captain James Kidd of his brigade described the youthful General as "tall, lithe, active, muscular . . . with the fair complexion of a schoolgirl. Superbly mounted, he sat his charger as if to the manner born. . . . His golden hair fell in graceful luxuriance to his shoulders. . . . A keen eye would have been slow to detect in that rider with the flowing locks and gaudy tie, in his dress of velvet and gold, that master spirit that he proved to be." Probing further beneath the surface, Kidd observed:

> That garb, fantastic as at first sight it appeared to be, was to be the distinguishing mark which (like the white plume of Henry of Navarre) was to show us where, in the thickest of the fight, we were to seek our leader; for where danger was . . . there he was—always. Brave, but not reckless; self-confident, yet modest; ambitious, but regulating his conduct at all times by a high sense of honor and duty; . . . quick in emergencies, cool and self-possessed, his courage was of the highest moral type.

So that, while there were many who still lampooned him as "Crazy Curly," "Suicide Custer," and the "Mad Cavalier," most came to agree with the lieutenant who had been the general's roommate at West Point—that he was "a gallant soldier, a whole-souled generous friend, and a mighty good fellow." The troops began to cultivate his style and affectations. The flowing red-silk scarf, "Custer ties," became part of the Michiganders' uniform, as did the slouched hat pinned up on one side, Confederate-fashion. Some let their hair grow to shoulder length, and, perhaps with some difficulty, cultivated the extravagant mustache.

The camp at Warrenton Junction was at the edge of Mosby's Confederacy, and the balance of the summer was spent in futile pursuit of the Gray Ghost who seemed to exercise a greater hold upon that section of Virginia than the occupying Federals. To Custer, war was a highly personal matter. He saw the enemy not as Confederates in mass, but as individuals with whom he had a score to settle: Jeb Stuart, for one, and Texas Tom Rosser of Stuart's corps, who had been one of Custer's fellow cadets at West Point. Now Mosby moved to the top of the list, to become in time an obsession with the young commander.

More immediate was his friendly vendetta with Judge Bacon over Libby's future. He could do little to press his suit from this forbidding distance. He poured his heart out to Annette ("Nettie") Humphrey, Libby's confidante, with the understanding that his feelings would be passed on to his "Beloved Star." If the time ever came "for me to give Her up I hope it will find me the same soldier I now try to be—capable of meeting the reverses of life as those of war."

He met his first reverse of war in a forced reconnaissance of Jeb

Stuart's cavalry camp near Culpeper on September 13. In a charge on one of Stuart's batteries, his horse was shot from under him and he himself was injured in the thigh by a piece of flying shrapnel. The wound was sufficient to get him a 25-day leave of absence in which to visit Libby in Monroe.

Much had happened since they were last together. He wore the stars of a brigadier general, and his name had become a household word in Michigan. Libby could resist no longer; she would marry this "Flower of the Army." Judge Bacon assented to their corresponding, but when it came to marriage he was noncommital. Write me a letter, he said to Custer, stating your qualifications, and we'll consider it.

He arrived back in camp on October 8, glad to be again "among my little band of heroes, where I am loved and respected." But he had no time to compose the letter to Judge Bacon. The following day General Robert E. Lee, tired of the stalemate on the Rapidan, began a flanking movement to the west in an effort to get between Meade's army, and Washington. Meade pulled back to avoid entrapment, and both forces marched on parallel routes up the line of the Orange & Alexandria Railroad, looking for a chance to strike at one another.

Jeb Stuart and Fitzhugh Lee rode on the flank of the Southern army; Kilpatrick and Custer guarded the rear of the Federals. At Brandy Station, redolent of previous battles, Stuart saw a chance to slice between Kilpatrick and the infantry and block Kilpatrick's crossing of the Rappahannock.

He almost succeeded, placing his cavalry in battle line astride Beverly Ford, with scattered units on Kilpatrick's flanks and rear. Custer volunteered to charge and break that line, and Pleasonton consented. It was as if the Boy General stood aside and watched the unfolding of the drama, the sabers drawn, the bugles blowing, the colors flying, and the horses breaking from trot to gallop; for he wrote to Libby that he had never seen a more beautiful performance, "one of the most inspiring as well as imposing scenes of martial grandeur ever witnessed upon a battlefield."

Captain William Glazier saw the action in similar theatric terms: "Custer, the daring, terrible demon that he is in battle, . . . dashed madly forward in the charge, while his yellow locks floated like pennants in the breeze. . . . Fired to an almost divine potency, and with a majestic madness, this band of heroic troopers shook the air with their battle cry."

Though Custer had two more horses shot from under him, the Michigan regiments cut their way through Stuart's line and provided a passage across the river for the balance of Kilpatrick's cavalry. Once safe, Custer wrote to Libby: "Yesterday we passed thro' the greatest Cavalry battle ever witnessed on this continent. . . . Oh, could you but have seen some of the charges that were made! While thinking of them I cannot but exclaim, 'Glorious War!' "

Lee's Bristoe Campaign had fizzled.

Though advance units of his army under A. P. Hill were able to bring Meade's rear corps to bay at Bristoe Station, the attack was launched too hastily with insufficient preparation. Hill lost five guns and 1,300 men in fifteen minutes; and while Meade withdrew to Centerville, Lee started back the way he had come, with Stuart protecting his retreat.

Kilpatrick and Custer started in pursuit, down the course of the Orange & Alexandria Railroad as far as a stream called Broad Run. Here, at a place known as Buckland Mills, Custer found Stuart defending the south end of a bridge across the stream. The fact that the bridge had been left intact gave Custer food for thought. Though Stuart began retreating at the approach of the Federals, Custer for once did not pursue; he stood aside and let Kilpatrick lead the rest of his division in a dash across the bridge. Then he followed at his leisure.

It was, as Custer had suspected, a trap. Five miles beyond Broad Run, with Stuart still luring the Federals in pursuit, Fitz Lee's riders plunged from the surrounding woods to slice at Kilpatrick's cavalry on its left flank—a signal for Stuart to reverse direction and charge Kilpatrick's vanguard. Custer found himself suddenly in a millstream of stampeding bluecoats, swept along in a mad retreat that would later be known as "the Buckland Races." Custer lost his headquarters wagon, along with 250 of his troopers taken prisoner, and numerous ambulances captured.

The young brigadier general who had boasted to Libby of the relatively minor victory at Brandy Station ("the greatest Cavalry battle ever witnessed . . . ") was now obliged to write: "Yesterday [October 19] was the most disastrous this Division ever passed through." But some self-redeeming features could be noted, with a little fabrication, His single brigade, he implied, had faced "the entire Confederate cavalry" and had driven them from "a very strong position"—before he was subsequently attacked by two columns of infantry and was forced to make "an orderly retreat."

Reverses in battle seemed to make him more aggressive on another front, the pursuit of Libby's hand in marriage. Back in Gainesville, with the Bristoe Campaign ending on a sour note, he was ready to draft that letter to Judge Bacon. It was restrained but firm. He presented his qualifications without conceit. Surrounded by temptations since the age of sixteen, he had committed errors in judgment, but had never swerved from temperance and purpose. Now he wanted a definite answer on this marriage question. No more shilly-shallying. Yes or no?

The forthright approach was effective. "I consent to the Marriage," the judge wrote back in late November, "and would be proud to welcome you as my Son-in-law."

Now there was only the matter of obtaining leave for the return to Michigan to claim his bride, for the marriage must be held, with all the appropriate trappings and proprieties, in Monroe. Since the Buckland Races he and Kilpatrick were, as he put it, "on the outs." The fact that Custer had recognized the trap which Kilpatrick's division blundered into—and thus avoided some of the disastrous consequences—did not endear him to his immediate commander. Kilpatrick would not be inclined to grant him favors.

So for a while the impatient couple were limited to corresponding. In contrast to previous coquettishness, Libby poured her heart out. "Oh, how I long to see you! The worse about loving a soldier is that he is as likely to die as to live, and how should I feel if my soldier should die before I have gratified his heart's desire? My dear Beloved Star, if loving with one's whole soul is insanity, I am ripe for an insane asylum. . . . "

And to a friend, in similar vein: "My happiness is unspeakable! Oh, Rebecca, it is blissful beyond words to love & to be loved. I do not say that Armstrong is without faults. But he never touches liquor or tobacco, nor frequents the gaming-table. . . . " (At about the date of this letter, Custer wrote to his sister, "I lost $10 today I bet on a horse-race with Gen'l Kilpatrick.")

Custer's more intimate letters to Libby, during this ardent period, she kept to herself, never to be revealed to history. Surely he shared her impatience, and frustration at not being free to marry. He had heard that Kilpatrick might be ordered West, which would remove one obstacle to the desired furlough. But meanwhile: "Today Genl. Pleasonton sent me word that I cannot leave the army this winter, for he is going away, and we cannot both be absent at the same time."

Nevertheless, going over Kilpatrick's head, he continued to pester Pleasonton for a leave of absence. Not until we lick Jeb Stuart, said Old Whiplash.

As it turned out, Stuart was not the principal problem throughout fall and early winter. It was John Singleton Mosby, riding high and wide throughout his chosen territory between Warrenton and Alexandria. With the Federal army encamped for the winter north of the Rapidan, facing Lee's camps just across the river, Mosby's operations, centering on Warrenton, were a constant menace to Meade's rear.

It had been nine months since Robert E. Lee declared, after General Stoughton's capture, "Mosby has covered himself with honors." In the interval, besides scouting for Stuart before the cavalry started for Pennsylvania in June, the Gray Ghost had carried on an unremitting war on Union depots, railroads, and above all, wagon trains.

However, a shadow fell upon these operations. When it was reported that captured Federal property had been sold by Mosby's men at Charlottesville, for $30,000, the Confederate Congress began to raise some questions. Were the Partisans truly concerned with damaging the enemy, or with making money for themselves?

The whole independent service began falling into disrepute. Lee himself questioned whether Mosby exercised proper control over his battalion; and Tom Rosser of Stuart's command, though himself a man of independence, declared of the partisan movement generally:

> Without discipline, order or organization, they roam broadcast over the country . . . pillaging, plundering and doing every manner of mischief and crime. They are a terror to the citizens and an injury to the cause. Their leaders are generally brave, but few of the men are good soldiers and [they] have engaged in this business for the sake of gain.

The controversy led to a curious conclusion. By order of Congress the partisan service *per se* was abolished. General Lee made a list of all outfits operating in Virginia and North Carolina, advising that they be disbanded and their members absorbed into the Provisional Army. But he made an exception in the case of Mosby. "I recommend that this battalion be retained as Partisans for the present," he wrote. "Mosby has done excellent service." And he followed this up, on Stuart's recommendation, by promoting the Gray Ghost to the rank of Confederate lieutenant colonel.

To Custer, obsessed with war as a personal vendetta against personal opponents, Mosby supplanted Stuart as the arch antagonist. On November 1 he wrote to Annette Humphrey:

> I mentioned that Mosby had captured 2 of my orderlies. Yesterday, a party of my men, while scouting, came across the body of one, pierced in the back by a rifle-bullet. The Rebels had emptied his pockets of everything. . . . His horse, evidently killed first, lay near him.

The feud was on, though not to be climaxed for another year. Meanwhile he set out "to get that fox if it's the last thing I do." But Mosby fitted no pattern he could recognize and cope with. The Partisans were not apt to line up on an open field to await a saber charge from Custer's Michigan brigade. They were gone long before he reached the site of a carefully plotted encounter, leaving only the sound of mocking laughter in their wake.

Frustrated, Custer organized a *corps élite* of 300 of his troopers, drilled them in guerilla tactics, then combed Mosby's Confederacy to bring the fox to bay. All he accomplished, pursuing false leads and chasing wraiths, was to wear out scores of horses. He insisted that those supplied to his troops by the War Department were "of inferior qual-

ity" to begin with. But when he complained to the newly formed
Cavalry Bureau in Washington, now operated by George Stoneman,
Stoneman replied that all mounts were furnished from "the best the
Gov't has on hand," and added waspishly, "I understand that Custer's
brigade are great horse-killers." He was falling in the category of his
rival in command, "Kill-Cavalry" Kilpatrick.

Then two things happened in early February. John Singleton Mosby
went to Charlottesville to celebrate his promotion to lieutenant colonel
with his wife; and George Armstrong Custer headed on leave for
Michigan for another form of celebration with his wife-to-be. "I am
going to be married to Libbie Bacon," Custer wrote to his sister, Lydia
Reed. "Please have my shirts done up by the time I get home."

"The most splendid wedding ever seen in the State of Michigan,"
boasted Judge Bacon of the marriage which took place on February 9,
1864. "From one to two hundred more in the church than ever before
and as many unable to enter for want of room." Libby had insisted that
the bridegroom wear his full dress uniform; and she herself, according
to her friend Rebecca Richmond, "wore a rich white rep silk with deep
points and extensive trail, bertha of point lace. Veil floated back from a
bunch of orange blossoms fixed above the brow."

After the ceremony and reception at the judge's home the couple
took off on a peripatetic honeymoon, from Cleveland to Buffalo to
Rochester (where they saw *Uncle Tom's Cabin*), and on to New York City.
In the latter metropolis, Judge Bacon was sorry to learn that the
bridegroom, in civilian clothes, lacked the electric glamor that he had in
uniform. It was here that George Gordon Bennett's *Herald* had
apotheosized Custer as the "Boy General with the Golden Locks," and
at first, wrote the Judge, "all were disappointed in Armstrong's appearance." He had trimmed his hair for the wedding ceremony and
had taken to plastering down his unruly tresses with cinnamon oil.
However, on further acquaintance "he made a *most favorable* impression."

From New York they traveled to Custer's alma mater at West Point
where, recorded Libby, "the cadets who showed me Lovers' Walk were
like schoolboys with their shy ways and nice, clean, friendly faces."
Then via Washington to cavalry headquarters south of Brandy Station,
for Custer, though he lay down few rules for his wife, had made it
known that "She will come back with me to the Army."

Army wives were no novelty, and Libby, in smart green riding habit
trimmed with military braid, felt right at home. She found that other
married couples "live in the cutest little huts, opening one into the
other, surrounded by evergreens—all the work of soldiers." And,

"Such style as we go in! Most army officers' wives have to ride in ambulances, but my General has a carriage with silver harness that he captured last summer, and two magnificent matched horses (not captures). We have an escort of four or six soldiers riding behind."

However, she wrote to her parents, "in the Cavalry the men do not have nearly as nicely furnished quarters as the Infantry who are in winter quarters several months with no horses to care for." Moreover, "the wife of an Infantry General told me that she would not have her husband in the cavalry for all the world. Their work, like a woman's, is never done."

This was brought rudely home to her when, after less than three blissful weeks of honeymoon, Custer was enlisted in the first major Union cavalry raid in Virginia since Stoneman's abortive expedition of April and May of 1863. The project was exclusively Kilpatrick's idea. With Lee quiescent behind the Rapidan, and Richmond scantily guarded by militia, "Little Kil" felt the time was ripe for a swift-moving strike at the Southern capital, to free the 11,000 Federal captives held at Belle Isle and in Libby Prison.

There was a lot of Custer in Kilpatrick, and vice versa. They had been fellow cadets at West Point where their combative instincts earned them numerous demerits, Kilpatrick having thrashed an underclassman for 46 minutes for "insolent" behavior. Like Custer, according to his biographer, "his pulse quickened at the sound of martial music and the gleam of arms." His heroes were Alexander, Caesar, Charlemagne, and Napoleon, and "he strove to emulate their prowess and valor." In short, he hungered like Custer for military glory, and this raid was to be his bid for lasting fame.

He played his cards close to the vest, revealing his intentions neither to Meade, who he felt lacked imagination, nor to Pleasonton, who might steal the honor for himself. Instead, he communicated directly with Lincoln through the War Department, and was invited to Washington to discuss the proposal with the President and Secretary Stanton.

Politically, the timing was propitious. The war-weary North would soon be facing a national election. Lincoln was anxious for a psychological victory, for want of something better. A dash into Richmond, even if short-lived, would help to silence dissidence within the Union and deal a blow to Confederate morale. He gave the project his blessing and supplied Kilpatrick with propaganda leaflets to be distributed along the way.

While the raid was still in the planning stage, and being all too openly discussed, young Ulric Dahlgren, twenty-one-year-old son of Rear Admiral John A. Dahlgren, appeared at cavalry headquarters and asked to be included in the expedition. He had lost a leg in the Gettysburg campaign but had since been fitted with an artifical limb, and while he might be unsteady on one of his father's ships, he was more than able to sit a horse. He felt that this raid "will be the grandest thing on record. . . . I may be captured or I may be tumbled over, but it is an undertaking that if I were not in I should be ashamed to show my face again."

It was an approach that Kilpatrick found hard to resist. He not only accepted the peg-legged colonel; he had very special plans for using him.

He had special plans for General Custer too. It would be vitally important, on this sixty-five mile ride to the capital, to keep Stuart off his back. Custer would accomplish this by a diversionary thrust at Charlottesville, drawing off Stuart's forces in pursuit. Custer may not have relished serving as a pawn in Kilpatrick's operation, but anything that discommoded Stuart was inviting to the Michigan brigade commander. On the night of February 28, after Kilpatrick and Dahlgren had started southeast from Stevensburg, Custer said goodbye to Libby and led his 1,500 troops southwest toward Charlottesville.

It was the first time Custer had challenged Stuart in a one-on-one maneuver. It took Stuart a day to discover what was going on. Then he sent Hampton and Fitzhugh Lee to follow Kilpatrick, and took off after Custer. For once the Boy General had everything his own way. Pressing his troops at an arduous pace, through ice and snow and freezing rain, he approached Charlottesville at noon on Leap Year's February 29, well ahead of his pursuers.

Here he found Stuart's Horse Artillery bivouacked for the winter. Though the artillerymen were able to save the batteries, Custer burned their camp, captured 50 guards and 500 horses, and destroyed large stores of grain and flour. Wrecking behind him portions of the highway, he followed the route by which he had come, through Stannardsville and Madison. At the latter point Stuart's cavalry, frozen and weary after this exhausting chase, formed in line of battle to cut him off, and waited. Never had Stuart's Invincibles appeared less formidable. The Michigan horsemen sliced through them like butter and were on their way.

Though the actual damage done on this diversionary raid was relatively slight, Custer had fulfilled his mission admirably. He had diverted Jeb Stuart from Kilpatrick's operation, ridden a hundred miles in 48 hours, held off his pursuers without losing a man, and won General Pleasonton's "entire satisfaction . . . and gratification . . . at the prompt manner in which the duties assigned to you have been performed."

It was the only bright spot in Kilpatrick's harebrained operation. As the division's remaining 3,500 troopers crossed the Rapidan, following the shortest route to Richmond, Kilpatrick split his column into two wings. Ulric Dahlgren, with 500 troops, was to follow a westerly course to the James, cross that river, and come on Richmond from the south. Kilpatrick, with the rest of the cavalry, would assault the capital from the north, forcing the defenders to divide their strength.

Timing of course was all-important. Both wings must strike the city simultaneously, and Dahlgren had the longer route to follow. Reaching the James, he found the river severely swollen by winter rains, and was misdirected by a Southern spy to a nonexistent ford. Though they forthwith hanged the spy, the delay was costly and they still had no means of crossing over. Dahlgren gave up attacking Richmond from the south, and followed the north bank of the James River Canal toward the capital.

Meanwhile Kilpatrick, with Wade Hampton on his heels, reached the outskirts of Richmond on the morning of March 1. His direct march on the city had been relatively unopposed. There were perhaps 500 militia manning the outerworks, with a half a dozen cannon. Having six times that number in well-armed cavalry he should have been able to ride right over them, into the heart of the city and onto a pedestal of fame.

But something seemed to snap in Kilpatrick's normally stout fiber. The obstacles loomed larger than the goal. He wasn't certain of the number of defenders. He had had no word or sign from Dahlgren, who should be in the process of attacking Richmond from the south. And the marksmanship of the defending artillerists was proving singularly accurate. "They have too many of those damned guns!" he fumed.

So, he would later report: "Feeling confident that Dahlgren had failed to cross the river, and that an attempt to enter the city at that point would but end in a bloody failure I reluctantly withdrew." He led his troops east toward Atlee's Station where he was overtaken by Wade Hampton's cavalry. At this point, all visions of glory dissipated, his only concern was for survival. He managed to fight a successful rearguard action and escape to Williamsburg on the Peninsula, losing a number of men and horses, killed or captured, to the enemy.

Near Turnstall's Station he had been joined by 300 sad survivors of Dahlgren's detachment. They had become separated from the main force in the nighttime march along the marshy borders of the James, and thus had escaped the fate of their abandoned leader. Dahlgren himself, with less than 200 troops, had reached the outskirts of Richmond only to find Kilpatrick gone. He had turned northeast in an effort to reach Gloucester Point, and been ambushed by Fitzhugh Lee's dismounted cavalry. In a bold attempt to charge their lines, most of his men were killed or captured; Dahlgren himself was riddled with bullets and was dead before he hit the ground.

Dahlgren dead was a more inflammatory figure than he had been when alive. His body was tumbled into a shallow grave, stripped of personal possessions, and some said mutilated—an atrocity of propaganda value for the Union. But papers found by his side revealed some unsavory orders to his troops. They were, on entering Richmond, "to destroy and burn the hateful city and do not allow the Rebel leader Jefferson Davis and his traitorous crew to escape."

Though both Meade and Kilpatrick denied authorizing such a violation of the rules of war, the damage had been done. The South, in turn, had much-touted evidence of Federal barbarity.

Custer would have been less than human if he had not been secretly tickled by Kilpatrick's failure. After all Kilpatrick's boasting, he had not only failed to free the Richmond prisoners but had added 350 of his own men to the city's jails, in addition to losing 500 horses and being accused of abandoning Ulric Dahlgren in a time of crisis. As for Lincoln's propaganda leaflets, these had been jettisoned as so much excess baggage on the way.

For Custer, too, there was a gratifying aftermath to the affair. Kilpatrick was detached from the Army of the Potomac and sent by Grant to General Sherman, now opening his campaign for Atlanta.

If Custer had hoped for command of Kilpatrick's division, he was disappointed. The post went to Brigadier General James Harrison Wilson, two years his senior and a protégé of General Grant. He was also troubled to learn of Pleasonton's impending removal as chief of cavalry. His sobriquet of "Pleasonton's Pet" had had some grounding in their close relationship. He had written to Nettie Humphrey in October 1863:

> I do not believe a father could love his son more than Genl. Pleasonton loves me. He is as solicitous about me and my safety as a mother about her only child. You should see how gladly he welcomes me on my return from each battle. His usual greeting is, "Well boy, I am glad to see you back. I was *anxious about you*." He often tells me that if I risk my life so much he will place me in such a command that I shall never have the opportunity.

Now Pleasonton was going, to be replaced, it was rumored, by an unfamiliar Westerner named Philip Henry Sheridan. At the moment, however, Custer was rocked by a more bizarre crisis in the form of the near-forgotten Annie Jones. Miss Jones, it appeared, had been arrested as a Southern spy, taken to Old Capitol Prison in Washington, and grilled as to her alleged relations with Federal officers.

In her signed statement Annie asserted that it was all a mistake that originated when she went to the front as a "friend and companion" of Generals Custer and Kilpatrick, living in their quarters. Kilpatrick had become jealous of Custer's attentions to her, had gone to Meade's headquarters and had spitefully charged her with being a Rebel spy.

Custer was understandably outraged at the charge, and blamed Kilpatrick for having sent her to his camp five months before. He wrote a vigorous denial to the War Department, and the matter was wisely dropped with Meade's issuance of an order to the effect that "the employment of Females as officers' servants is, until further notice, prohibited." The rule happily exempted Custer's cook, Eliza Brown.

What Libby thought of the Annie Jones affair is not recorded. But she and her husband, in succeeding days, agreed that camp life was not harmonious with marriage. It was decided that Libby would be safer and more comfortable at a boarding house in Washington, and the last week in March the couple traveled to the capital to find suitable accommodations.

The visit turned into something of a hero's welcome for the curly-headed brigadier. Accompanied on the train by General Grant, the commander of all the Union armies even refrained from smoking his proverbial cigar in Libby's presence. Custer was welcomed on the floor of the House, where one member greeted him: "So you are the youngest General in the army. Well, I wish there were more like you." And both he and Libby attended a reception at the White House, where Lincoln greeted the couple with noticeable warmth.

After seeing the comedian Sleepy Clarke, brother-in-law of John Wilkes Booth, perform at Ford's New Theater ("simply killing!"), Custer said goodbye to his wife, and caught a special train to Brandy Station. "I will not attempt to tell you how lonely I am," Libby wrote to her parents some days later. "It was a far worse trial than I anticipated to part from my husband. And yet I am prouder by far to be his wife than I would be to be Mrs. Lincoln or a queen." And she added:

"Do you know Autie was on that car that was so nearly captured by Mosby?"

It was a question thrown in without preliminary explanation. But there was an explanation. . . .

CHAPTER

15

DUEL OF GIANTS

ONCE AGAIN, IN VIRGINIA, IT WAS THAT LOVELIEST OF SEASONS, WITH
the dogwood in early bloom, the scent of clover on the air, and a warm
sun powdering the roads with gentle dust. Even the Blue Ridge on the
west seemed fresh-born in the morning mist, foaled by a resurgent
earth.

History would little note and less remember the multiple drama that
took place near Warrenton that afternoon in late April, 1864.

Heading south across the Orange & Alexandria Railroad tracks flew
a column of horsemen in blue, their lathered horses straining at the bit,
riding as if the devil himself were after them.

A quarter of a mile behind, in a cloud of rising dust, came a second
column of gray-clad riders, whooping and hollering with the excitement of the chase.

And down from the northeast, over rickety rails, clattered a special
train from Alexandria, the tulip-shaped smokestack of the locomotive
spouting jets of sparks under an extra head of steam.

Seeing the curious steeplechase ahead of him, the engineer applied
his brakes. The train screeched to a halt at Warrenton Junction, with a
rattle of colliding cars. From the platform of one of those cars, chewing
the stub of an unlit cigar, the newly-appointed Lieutenant General of
the U.S. Army asked a lounger at the depot:

"What is the meaning of all that dust?"

"Just Mosby, chasin' Yanks, I reckon," he was told.

If Ulysses Grant gave little thought to Mosby, the engineer must have mopped his brow with infinite relief. For Mosby rarely let a train get near without seizing it lock, stock, and locomotive. Had General Grant been taken prisoner that afternoon — and it was pure luck that Mosby's men were chasing what they thought was bigger game — the course of history might have been considerably altered.

Grant, in the company of a young brigadier named Custer, was on his way back to Meade's Army of the Potomac which, as commanding general of the Union armies, he would now control. Though Meade would remain in nominal command, the war in the East was to become a duel of giants, Grant versus Robert E. Lee. And a duel of giants among cavalry commanders too. Though Richmond was the prize, Lee's destruction was the goal. "To get possession of Lee's army was the first great object," Grant wrote. "With the capture of his army Richmond would necessarily follow."

In Washington the General-in-Chief had discussed the coming campaign with Lincoln — one aspect of it in particular, noting in his *Memoirs*:

> In one of my early interviews with the President I expressed my dissatisfaction with the little that had been accomplished by cavalry so far in the war, and the belief that it was capable of accomplishing much more than it had done if under a thorough leader. I said I wanted the very best man in the army for that command.

Henry Halleck, now chief of staff, was present at the meeting. "How would Sheridan do?" suggested Halleck.

"The very man I want," said Grant.

In his own mind, Grant had already settled on Sheridan as the Army of the Potomac's chief of cavalry. Principally because of his "fiery spirit" and brilliant performance at Chattanooga in November. At the head of his division, Sheridan had been among the first to reach the top of Missionary Ridge, then over the top and down the far slope to pursue the Confederates as far as Chickamauga River. Though Sheridan had been commanding infantry, Grant had seen in the general "that quality so rare even in an illustrious soldier — the power to make the most of victory." And victory was what Grant wanted from his cavalry; not escort or picket duty, not screening and scouting for the army. Rather, the waging of what Grant referred to as "enlightened" war; which was another way of saying "total war."

Philip Henry Sheridan was not at first glance the prototype of the cavalry commander. "He is short, thick-set & common Irish looking," observed a colonel of artillery, while the flamboyant Custer found him "a broad-shouldered bantam with mossy black hair, piercing almond shaped eyes in his square head, with a trim fluffy beard and mustachios. . . . "

Sheridan himself confessed, "I was rather young in appearance — looking more under than over thirty-three years — but five feet five in height, and thin almost to emaciation, weighing only one hundred and fifteen pounds." Appended to this unprepossessing frame were over-long arms, and legs so short that they seemed hardly capable of straddling a horse. "One of those long-armed fellows with short legs," Lincoln observed, "that can scratch his shins without having to stoop over."

Like many people of small stature, "Little Phil" had a hairtrigger instinct for personal combat. At West Point, when a cadet sergeant gave him an order "in what I considered an improper tone," cadet Sheridan charged the man with lowered bayonet, checking himself just short of murder, but engaging the offender mercilessly with his fists. For this he suffered a year's suspension from the Academy and graduated in 1853 only thirty-fourth in a class of fifty-two.

Thereafter he wore two hats: one the dark-visored infantry kepi, the other with crossed sabers on the crown — serving first as lieutenant and captain of infantry; then colonel of cavalry; then back to brigadier general of infantry in Rosecrans' Army of the Cumberland. After the battle of Booneville, Rosecrans commended his subordinate to Henry Halleck as "worth his weight in gold," and Sheridan's appreciative troopers presented him with a big black gelding charger named Rienzi. Along with horses like Lee's Traveller, Jackson's Old Sorrell, and Grant's Cincinnati, Rienzi would earn a niche in whatever hall of fame Valhalla has reserved for steeds of battle.

It was from the Army of the Cumberland's winter bivouac at Loudon, Tennessee, that Sheridan was summoned to Washington to assume his new command. In the capital he "waited on" the President. "Mr. Lincoln received me very cordially, offering both his hands, and . . . saying that thus far the cavalry of the Army of the Potomac had not done all it might have done." The President spiced the comment with a facetious query often bandied throughout the war, "Who ever saw a dead cavalryman?"

Sheridan parted from Lincoln somewhat aggravated, hoping that the President "did not believe all that the query implied." After the interview he vowed to a friend at Willard's Hotel, "I am going to take the cavalry away from the bobtailed brigadier generals. They must do without their escorts. I intend to make the cavalry an arm of the service."

He arrived at cavalry headquarters around Brandy Station on April 5, replacing Alfred Pleasonton who was transferred to the West. While Pleasonton had been a respected leader and good organizer, Sheridan brought to his command the kind of cocky aggressiveness the troops themselves were starting to acquire. His bullet-shaped head was matched by bullet-like speech, interlarded with oaths and blasphemies that added spice to his commands. His instructions before a mission were simple. "Smash 'em up! Smash 'em up!" he would say, pounding his palm with his fist for emphasis. Confronting an enemy drawn up in line of battle, his orders were equally direct. "Keep moving, boys; we're going through. There isn't cavalry enough in the whole Confederacy to stop us." Their days of playing second fiddle to the men in gray were over.

Sheridan's three divisions comprising the cavalry corps and numbering nearly 13,000 sabers were commanded by brigadier generals Alfred Torbert, David Gregg, and James H. Wilson—the last a rising young officer, twenty-six, whom Grant had brought with him from the West. Brigades were led by men like Custer, Tom Devin, Wesley Merritt, and J. Irvin Gregg. Many of the troops were veterans of Brandy Station and the Gettysburg campaign. Sheridan found them men of "fine appearance" but "the horses very thin and much worn down by picket duty." On the latter point he consulted General Meade.

The interview was not congenial. Sheridan wanted relative independence for his corps, "to march where we pleased, for the purpose of breaking down General Lee's communications and destroying the resources from which his army was supplied." Meade held the traditional theory that the cavalry was subservient to the army and thus subject to his direction. He did however agree to relieve the corps, temporarily, from arduous picket service, "thus giving me about two weeks in which to nurse the horses before the campaign opened."

Grant's campaign for the spring involved a thrust from the vicinity of Brandy Station down through the Wilderness toward Richmond, drawing Lee's army from its winter quarters south of the Rapidan to counter the maneuver. Thus Grant would force Lee into battle, perhaps in the Wilderness, and beat him by sheer weight of numbers—knowing that if he suffered heavy losses, so would Lee, and Lee could less afford them. Grant's losses, the saying went, were always gains in the game of war.

As Meade, the first week in May, began the move toward the Wilderness, flanking Lee's army on the east, Sheridan's corps set out to clear the way to Spotsylvania. The first clash was not with the Confederates but between the Union infantry and cavalry. When Meade reached the vicinity of Todd's Tavern he found his foot soldiers snarled in a traffic bottleneck created by the presence of the mounted troops. He ordered Torbert's and Gregg's divisions to take different routes and keep the roads clear for his infantry.

As a consequence, Wilson's division, left without support as it reached Spotsylvania, was trapped by a superior force of Fitz Lee's cavalry and suffered heavy losses.

Learning that Meade had "interfered" with his instructions to the cavalry, Sheridan stormed into the general's headquarters demanding to know "by God!," whether Meade commanded the cavalry or he did. "I told him that he had broken up my combinations, exposed Wilson's division to disaster, and . . . that such disjointed operations as he had been requiring of the cavalry for the last four days would render the corps inefficient and useless before long." In conclusion, Sheridan wrote:

> Meade was very much irritated, and I was none the less so. One word led to another until, finally, I told him that I could whip Stuart if he . . . would only let me, but since he insisted on giving the cavalry directions without consulting or even notifying me, he could henceforth command the Cavalry Corps himself—I would not give it another order.

Such talk amounted to insubordination. Meade repeated the conversation to Grant, including Sheridan's boast that, left alone, he could whip Jeb Stuart.

"Did he say that?" said Grant delightedly. "Then let him go and do it."

He then issued, through Meade, new instructions to the cavalry commander. Sheridan was to cut loose from the Army of the Potomac, pass around the right of Lee's army, and attack his cavalry, then cut the two railroads supplying Richmond from the west. After that he was to proceed, for forage and supplies, to Benjamin Butler's camp on the north side of the James, and then return to the Army of the Potomac.

To the Confederates, the move would indicate a raid on Richmond, which was what, in fact, it might turn out to be. But in Sheridan's plans, Richmond was the bait and not the target. To threaten the capital was a sure way to draw Jeb Stuart in pursuit, and he saw this raid as "a challenge to Stuart for a cavalry duel behind Lee's lines, in his own country."

On May 8, immediately after receiving Grant's instructions, Sheridan convoked his officers and told them: "We are going out to fight Stuart's cavalry in consequence of a suggestion from me; we will give him a fair square fight; we are strong, and I know we can beat him, and in view of my recent representations to General Meade I shall expect nothing but success." By success he meant simply, "Smash 'em! Smash 'em!" His resolve was underscored by a later remark to one of his staff officers: "I have never taken any command into battle with the slightest desire to come out of it alive unless I won." The confrontation with Stuart, when it came, was to be a duel to the death.

For Jeb Stuart, headquartered near Orange Court House, April brought an end to a winter of near-domesticity. He had named his camp "The Wigwam." It was neither as devoid of amenities as Camp-No-Camp, nor as full of jollity as Camp Qui Vive. Rooney Lee had spent the winter in a Federal prison camp. Major von Borcke was recuperating from his wounds in Richmond. The banjo-playing Sweeny had died that winter of smallpox; and though Fitz Lee imported a minstrel troupe to keep alive the musical tradition, the singing was subdued. The troopers no longer belted out the old-time favorite, "If You Want to Have a Good Time, Jine the Cavalry," preferring such somber ballads as "When This Cruel War Is Over."

Stuart himself was absorbed in family and wifely matters. Providing a playmate for little Flora and Jeb Junior, Flora had given birth in October to a baby daughter. The couple named her Virginia Pelham Stuart, "a war-name, gallant as a cavalry saber." With the mother thus tied down in her temporary home at Beaver Station Dam, Stuart saw little of either, complaining that "every General and Colonel of infantry appears to have his wife along." To relieve his bachelordom he tried his hand at writing verse (for in every cavalier there was a hidden poet). One sample seemed to combine his love for Flora with his love of war:

> While Mars with his stentorian voice
>   Chimes in with dire discordant noise,
> Sweet woman in angelic guise
>   Gives hope and bids us fear despise.

His cavalry, which he took joy in reviewing almost every day, now numbered 8,000 sabers, organized in two divisions under Hampton and Fitz Lee. Besides the missing Rooney Lee, there had been some changes in subordinate commands. Grumble Jones had been transferred to southwest Virginia where he would shortly be killed in battle; Beverly Robertson had been reassigned to a South Carolina command. But Stuart still had veteran brigadier generals to rely on—among them the Texas-raised Tom Rosser, who had soundly whipped Custer at Buckland Mills the previous October and thereby made a dedicated enemy of his former classmate at West Point.

The only event to relieve the tedium of late winter was the Kilpatrick-Dahlgren raid on Richmond, which had accomplished little beyond indicating that the Federal horsemen were bent on taking the offensive. Now, early in May, there were signs that the Union cavalry, inspired by Sheridan, was on the move again. In fact, the signs were flaunted in Stuart's face, deliberately inviting his pursuit. On the very day, May 9, that Sheridan's three divisions left Todd's Tavern en route through the Wilderness to Richmond, Stuart took up the chase with three of his six brigades.

The fox and the hounds were unevenly matched. Against Stuart's 4,500 troopers Sheridan had some 10,000 cavalry equipped with the new Spencer seven-shot repeating carbines, greatly exceeding the fire power of the Southerners. Stuart could not afford a head-on confrontation. He could only nip at Sheridan's heels, attacking the rear of the Federal column, killing a few and taking some prisoners, suffering losses of his own in killed and captured.

Similarly, he was powerless to prevent Sheridan's destructions of Lee's stores at Beaver Dam Station—a disastrous blow to dwindling Confederate supplies—but he kept pressing hard on the enemy's flank and rear, trying to gauge Sheridan's intentions. When convinced that the goal was Richmond, his only thought was to get between the city and the raiders, close enough to the capital to have the support of the 4,000 infantry and artillery assembled there by Braxton Bragg.

The place he selected for this crucial stand was Yellow Tavern, named for an abandoned inn whose color had long since faded to dilapidated gray. Here two main roads to the city converged into a single highway, and by positioning his troops along both arms which formed the letter V, he could concentrate his fire on the enemy from two directions. Then he sent a message of reassurance to the anxious Bragg in Richmond:

> I intersect the road the enemy is marching on at Yellow Tavern, the head of the turnpike, six miles from Richmond. My men and horses are tired, hungry, and jaded, but all right.

The underscoring of "all right" was Stuart's. Though it expressed resolve—he was ready to hang on—it lacked the note of jubilant defiance common to his nature. He did not boast of whipping Sheridan, as Sheridan had talked of whipping Stuart; rather, as he told Henry McClellan, he hoped that "aided by a strong attack by the infantry in Richmond, he might be able to inflict serious disaster on the enemy's cavalry."

Possibly Stuart had begun to feel that time was running out, for himself and for the South. Riding beside him on the way to Yellow Tavern, McClellan later noted that "he was more quiet than usual, softer, and more communicative. It seems now that the shadow of the near future was already upon him."

Shortly before noon on May 11 the vanguard of Sheridan's column hove into sight. For a short while the two commanders sized up one another through their glasses: Stuart well positioned on the Union flanks, Sheridan with sufficient men and firepower to smash through Stuart's defense if it were worth the cost. Merely smashing through, however, was not Sheridan's objective. The destruction of Stuart and his legend of invincibility was still the goal, with Richmond a secondary target.

For two hours Sheridan sent one brigade after another to probe the Confederate lines, feelers that turned into bloody hand-to-hand encounters. Fitz Lee's troops bore and held the brunt of the attacks. Losses were costly to both sides, but by four o'clock Sheridan felt that he had found a weak point in the left of Stuart's line. He gave to Custer's four Michigan regiments the chance to deliver the finishing stroke, to plow through and come on Stuart's rear, blocking off all chance of his escape.

The assignment was meat and drink to Custer. But the performance must be orchestrated, so he signaled his drum major: Strike up the band!

"Custer's charge was brilliantly executed," wrote Sheridan. "Beginning at a walk . . . "

> Yankee Doodle is a tune
> Americans delight in . . .

" . . . he increased this to a trot";

> Good to fiddle, dance or sing,
> And just the thing for fightin'.

" . . . then, at full speed, rushed upon the enemy." The Confederates gave way grudgingly until the line had been rolled back some 500 yards.

"As he always did," wrote McClellan of Stuart, "the general hastened to the point where the greatest danger threatened, the point against which the enemy directed the mounted charge." Signaling Fitz Lee to circle behind the lines and seal off the gap that Custer was creating, Stuart ran to the wavering front.

"Shoot them! Shoot them!" he shouted.

In plumed hat and scarlet-lined cape, he was a conspicuous figure, blazing away with his revolver at the passing bluecoats. And now, as Fitz Lee turned his forces against Custer, the Federal cavalry began to pass in reverse direction. The whole force was turning back.

"Now," shouted Stuart. "Give it to them!"

Michigan Sergeant John Huff, dismounted during the fighting, was straggling rearward to safety, may have reacted to the call. Or he may simply have noticed the man on the gray horse who was such an easy target. He fired a single peevish shot at the brown-bearded officer, and hurried on.

Stuart slumped forward in the saddle. The plumed hat that had been the guidon of so many gallant charges fell to the ground.

"General, are you hit?" asked Private J. R. Oliver.

"I'm afraid I am," said Stuart calmly.

They lifted him down and placed him against a tree, while an ambulance was sent for. As Fitz Lee appeared on the scene, distressed at the sight of his wounded commander, Stuart called to him encouragingly "Go ahead, Fitz old fellow. I know you'll do what's right."

As the ambulance carried him to the rear it passed a group of Confederate stragglers still dazed by Custer's charge. Stuart raised himself painfully on an elbow.

"Go back!" he shouted. "Go back! Do your duty as I've done mine. I'd rather die than be whipped."

They took him to Dr. Charles Brewer's house in Richmond, where the physician diagnosed the wound as fatal; and on Stuart's insistence, told him so. "If it's God's will, then I'm ready," Stuart said, "I would like to see my wife, but God's will be done." A courier was rushed to the home where Flora was living, twenty-five miles away. Though in agony throughout that night, Stuart seemed sustained by the hope of seeing her again.

Around the house, appropriately hedged with red and yellow roses, a silent, tearful crowd kept vigil through the night. Once they gave way to a tall, slim gentleman arriving at the gate, and the whisper went around, "the President." Jefferson Davis remained at Stuart's bedside for a while; McClellan stayed with him; and the visiting Heros von Borcke, openly sobbing, consented to Stuart's request that they should sing together. The song they chose was "Rock of Ages, Cleft for Me".

Before dawn, Flora arrived at his bedside. But Stuart, fighting off death as he had fought off Yankees, could not wait.

In its next day's obituary the Richmond *Examiner* noted in part; "Major General J. E. B. Stuart, model of Virginia cavaliers and dashing chieftain, is dead . . . Of all our knights he was the flower." Before his death he bequeathed his sword to young Jeb Junior, his horses to his officers, and his gold spurs to Mrs. Lilie Lee of Shepherdstown.

At Yellow Tavern the fall of Stuart seemed to mark the climax of the battle, as if there were nothing left to fight for. Sheridan did not precisely withdraw into his corner after the defending champion was floored. But he decided, with a little futile probing here and there, that there was no point in continuing "this obstinate contest." He called his troops off and headed them down a pike that bypassed Yellow Tavern and continued on toward Richmond.

After marching all night they were still on the outskirts of the fortifications, five miles from Capitol Square, where the church bells clanged alarmingly. "We could see the lights and hear the dogs barking." There was no doubt in Sheridan's mind that he could plunge into the city, past the earthworks, through the defending lines of weak militia. It was, he wrote later, "the greatest temptation of my life." But there was the realistic question: if he took the city, could he hold it?

"It is possible that I might have captured the city of Richmond by an assault," he reported finally to Meade, "but the want of knowledge of your operations and those of General Butler, and the facility with which the enemy could throw in troops, made me abandon the attempt."

So he headed southeast for Meadow Bridges on the Chickahominy en route to Haxall's Landing on the James, and thence to rejoin Grant near Chesterfield Station. The only major problem encountered was the rebuilding of the highway bridge destroyed by the Confederates, and the only mishap, reported by Captain Charles D. Rhodes, "was the fall of a pack-mule from the bridge into the water thirty feet below. It takes much, however, to disturb the equanimity of an army mule. It turned a somersault in the air, struck an abutment, disappeared under water, came up, and swam tranquilly ashore without disturbing its pack."

On May 24 the cavalry corps was back with the army, having lost 625 men and 300 horses in the intervening sixteen days.

Sheridan had, he felt, fulfilled the purpose of his mission—damaged Lee's supply lines, destroyed enough provisions to feed the Confederate army for many days, and, more important than all, made good on his promise to whip Jeb Stuart: in his words, he "had inflicted a blow from which entire recovery was impossible."

The destruction of Stuart was, to a measurable degree, as important as temporarily investing Richmond would have been. To Lee it was comparable to the loss of Stonewall Jackson at Chancellorsville the year before.On hearing of Stuart's death the Confederate general retired to his tent in grief and confessed, "I can scarcely think of him without weeping."

Grant was quick to extol his new chief of cavalry: "Sheridan's first raid upon Lee's communications . . . attained in its brilliant execution and results all the proportions of an independent campaign." More specifically he wrote:

> Sheridan in this memorable raid passed entirely around Lee's army; encountered his cavalry in four engagements, and defeated them in all; recaptured four hundred Union prisoners and killed and captured many of the enemy; destroyed and used many supplies and munitions of war; destroyed miles of railroad and telegraph, and freed us from annoyance by the cavalry of the enemy for more than two weeks.

Two weeks was about what it amounted to.

Jeb Stuart's death was regarded in the North as marking the shift of supremacy from the Southern cavalry to the Union troopers. It was more than the death of a symbol, for other factors were at work. The supply of horses in the South was shrinking, and the loss of Vicksburg had cut off replacements from the Trans-Mississippi. The Union had all the horses that it needed, with ample reserves. And Sheridan had imbued the Federal cavalry in the East with a new élan and confidence, plus a sounder conception of the use of cavalry—plucked to some extent from Southern strategy—that had raised that branch of the service to a high potential.

The Southern cavalry struggled to adjust. As ranking major general of the three divisions of Lee's horsemen (Rooney Lee having been exchanged), the mantle of leadership fell unofficially on Hampton. He was taking over at a difficult time, and Stuart's were hard shoes to fill. Where Stuart was impetuous, Wade Hampton was calculating and deliberate. Where Stuart recklessly ignored the odds and plunged into battle against overwhelming numbers, Hampton favored a careful concentration of his forces and a calculated weighing of the odds before attack.

Lee admired him, but was reluctant to name him lieutenant general in Stuart's place. His seniority over the general's nephew Fitzhugh Lee was slight, just ten weeks really. And Fitz wanted the job. His uncle's hesitancy was not a concern with nepotism; he wanted the best man, and he wasn't sure. He would wait and see.

One thing bequeathed to Hampton by his predecessor was a smoldering urge to topple Sheridan and avenge Jeb Stuart's death. His first real opportunity came when word reached Lee that Grant was moving to flank his army from the east and had crossed the Pamunkey River near Hanover Town, with Sheridan's cavalry leading the advance. Lee ordered Hampton and Fitzhugh Lee to check this information and if necessary block the movement.

The two mounted legions clashed on May 28 near Haw's Shop, south of the Pamunkey, in the fiercest cavalry fight since Yellow Tavern. Though Hampton was breaking in fresh recruits—three uninitiated units of South Carolinians under Brigadier General Calvin Butler— they fulfilled all expectations. Their horses stampeded, but not the men, who fought dismounted and made up for lack of mobility with expert marksmanship. Sheridan's riders tumbled like tenpins from their saddles, including Michigan Sergeant John A. Huff whose bullet had brought down Stuart.

The battle lasted seven grueling hours, by which time reinforcements reaching Sheridan caused Hampton to withdraw. It was a qualified but satisfying victory. He had arrested Sheridan south of the Pamunkey. And his men had captured enough prisoners to give Lee the information he was looking for—the position and direction of the Army of the Potomac. In addition, it had given Hampton's troops the chance to take the measure of their leader.

"Up to this time," wrote Frank M. Myers of Rosser's Comanches,

> the Cavalry Corps had not learned the style of their commander, but
> now they discovered a vast difference between the old and the new,
> for while General Stuart would attempt his work with whatever force
> he had on hand . . . Gen. Hampton always endeavored to carry every
> available man to his point of operation, and the larger his force the
> better he liked it.

Myers concluded:

> The advantage of this style of generalship was soon apparent, for
> while under Stuart stampedes were frequent, with Hampton they
> were unknown, and the men of his corps soon had the same unwaver-
> ing confidence in him that the "Stonewall Brigade" entertained for
> *their* general.

Sheridan, however, remained a menace to Lee's right flank, and so of
course did Grant, with infantary and artillery that numbered about
105,000 at the start of the campaign. Throughout May and into the
first week of June it had been Grant's strategy to press toward
Richmond, meanwhile hoping either to catch Lee's army before it
could entrench or, failing this, to destroy the Army of Northern Virginia in a war of attrition. His losses had been frightful; but "I propose to
fight it out on this line if takes all summer," he averred.

It was threatening to take all summer. Each crab-like step he took
toward Richmond was matched by a similar southeast move by Lee.

Although Sheridan's cavalry occupied and held Cold Harbor on May
30, the Union was unable to exploit this success. Lee's veterans out-
marched the Federals and took up and fortified a strong line covering
Richmond between the Chickahominy and Totopotomoy. Grant
sought to bludgeon his way through in the battle at Cold Harbor, May
31 to June 1, and in later assaults during that first week of June
suffered frightful casualties without compensating progress.

Grant's idea from the start, he wrote to Henry Halleck, "has been to
beat Lee's Army north of Richmond," but there was no way to draw that
general into open battle, no way to get at him without risk of prohibi-
tively heavy losses.

He saw a key to the dilemma in the Shenandoah Valley and in the two
chief arteries, the James River Canal and the Virginia Central Railroad,
which supplied Lee's army with the vital produce of that valley. Grant
would use his cavalry to sever those supply lines, and both Lee and
Richmond would be starved into submission.

In May a Union force led by General Franz Sigel had marched up the
Valley to suffer defeat at New Market on the fifteenth. Now another

Union column commanded by General David Hunter was advancing up the Valley, and on June 5 at Piedmont had defeated the Confederates, killing Grumble Jones during the encounter. Three days later the column was joined by Generals Crook and Averell who had crossed the mountains from West Virginia to team up with Hunter.

At the same time Grant gave Sheridan new orders. He was to break up the Virginia Central Railroad, meet Hunter at Charlottesville, unite with him and return to the Army of the Potomac. On June 7 with two divisions of his cavalry Sheridan set out for Gordonsville, key point on the Virginia Central. The column was composed of Gregg's and Torbert's divisions, totaling eight-to-ten thousand troops in all. James Wilson's division remained behind to secure the army's flanks.

Just as Lee moved in counterpoint to Grant—and sent first John C. Breckinridge and then Jubal Early to the Shenandoah Valley to check Hunter—so Wade Hampton rode out with his cavalry corps of 5,000 to beat the Federals to the railroad. On June 10 Hampton's division was bivouacked near Trevilian Station with Fitz Lee's division farther south around Louisa Court House. At dawn of the following day Sheridan's advance guard stumbled on Hampton's pickets; both forces closed in; and the battle was engaged.

Hampton was holding Torbert's troops in check when he heard firing in his rear. This might be Fitz Lee coming up to join him from Louisa Court House or it might be something else, and he sent Tom Rosser to investigate. Rosser found that it was something else.

While Torbert and Hampton started hammering at each other, Custer saw a golden opportunity. He led his Michigan brigade on a sweeping detour east and south of Trevilian Station in a raid on Hampton's wagon trains, capturing 250 wagons, 350 Confederates guarding them, six caissons, and 800 horses Hampton was holding in reserve. This rich haul he sent back to his own camp two miles distant, just as Tom Rosser's Laurel Brigade struck him from the north.

Rosser was the perfect antidote for Custer's brashness. Ever since Buckland Mills the previous October, Texas Tom had been itching for another crack at his West Point classmate with the golden locks. Now Rosser's "Comanches" descended on the Michigan marauders with all the fury of an unleashed nest of hornets.

"Never has a brigade fought so long or so desperately," Custer later wrote to Libby. "I was fighting every man I had against two divisions [Rosser's one brigade] of enemy Cavalry. We were completely surrounded and attacked on all sides." In the melee, Rosser was wounded in the leg; Custer was twice stunned by spent bullets, but he was able to snatch and save the regimental flag as it fell from the hands of his dying color-bearer. By five o'clock, after three hours of fighting, the young general had had enough. "It's time to get out of here," he told his colonel of artillery, and the colonel observed later that "we lost no time."

It was not Custer's day. Returning to his wagon park, minus 400 men and horses, he found that Fitz Lee's cavalry, riding up to the sound of the action, had stumbled on his lightly guarded camp. They had released the captured Confederates, reclaimed the horses and wagons stolen earlier from Hampton's bivouac, made prisoners of Custer's guards, and then taken off with everything movable, including the black cook Eliza with the valise containing Libby's letters, which always accompanied Custer on his marches.

The Confederates had captured *everything except my toothbrush!"* Custer wrote to Libby. "They only captured one wagon from me, but that contained my all—bedding, desk, sword-belt, underclothing, and my commission as General which only arrived a few days before; also dress coat, pants, and one blue shirt. I regret the loss of your letters more than all else."

He could report, however, that Eliza escaped from her captors late that night and was able to return to camp, but without the valise which had been taken from her. Libby told him not to worry; no gentleman would violate a woman's correspondence with her husband. She forgot that chivalry diminishes as war prolongs. The captured letters were duly published in the Richmond papers, "and afforded some spicy reading." It was politely suggested that they came from Custer's mistress, since no wife would write in such a fashion.

The following morning, June 12, Sheridan found that Fitzhugh Lee had linked up with Hampton, and that both divisions had formed northeast of Trevilian Station, like the spread wings of an eagle sheltering its aerie, hooked talons ready for the fox. Assigning a portion of Gregg's troops to tear up the tracks for several miles below that point, Sheridan prepared to beat his brains out if he had to, to destroy that gray roadblock in his path.

Overnight the newly-arrived General Butler was put in charge of Hampton's division, perhaps to test his qualities of leadership. He and his green South Carolinians held that arm of the line that closely paralleled the railroad embankment and was thus most subject to attack. Dismounted, the troops threw up protective breastworks. Butler had two horse batteries of four guns each. He placed the guns at strategic points along the line, relying on his artillery to equalize the greater firepower of the Federals' repeating rifles.

After one o'clock the first thrust came, directed expectedly at Butler's tangent of the angled line. The South Carolinians held, and the Federals recoiled. After that, reported Butler, "five distinct and determined assaults were made upon us, and on the eve of every attack we could hear in the woods preparations for the onslaught, the sounding of bugles, words of command, etc." Toward the end of the afternoon:

Between sunset and dark, when the dusk of the evening was still further shrouded by the smoke of battle, and after six assaults had been repulsed, we heard the usual preparations for another, and, as I concluded, the last desperate effort.

Possibly Butler remembered that as ocean breakers hammer at the shore, the seventh of a series is the mightiest. Aided by semidarkness, the enemy would throw in everything he had. Butler took a chance. He concentrated his eight guns and focused them at the one point in the woods from which he guessed the Federals would next emerge. If he guessed wrong, he would have wasted part of his artillery support, and only God knew what would happen then.

With taut nerves the troopers waited in the gathering dusk. Then it happened—"just as I had anticipated," Butler gloated. From the precise spot he had targeted, the Federals charged from the woods and into the direct line of artillery fire, to be torn to pieces by canister and small-arms fire, and to fall back "for the last time." The battle of Trevilian Station was over.

Sheridan would report the day's fight as "by far the most brilliant one of the present campaign." In point of fact, though Hampton's troopers had been forced back several hundred yards, it was Sheridan's first defeat as Meade's chief of cavalry. He had lost twice as many men as in his earlier raid on Richmond; and although Confederate losses were proportionately heavy, Hampton and Fitz Lee still held the road to Gordonsville.

Sheridan abandoned plans for Lynchburg, Hunter, and their joint destruction of the James Canal and pulled back to rejoin Grant's army east of the Pamunkey. In his absence, Wilson's cavalry raid on the Weldon and Southside railroads had been generally unsuccessful.

"The expedition finished off disastrously," Colonel Charles Wainwright wrote of Wilson's defeat at Reams Station south of Petersburg. "They were caught by the enemy completely with their breeches down, attacked in front & flank, stampeded & driven to the 4 winds." Custer, so lavish with self-praise, was equally extravagant in damning "that imbecile Wilson who has brought disgrace upon our cavalry."

Lee's question of who should permanently lead his mounted troops was settled at Trevilian Station. The two brigades of his nephew Fitz had scarcely participated in the action. In fact, Rosser and Butler had complained to Hampton of Fitz Lee's sluggishness throughout the afternoon. Hampton allowed only that Fitz was "slow." He himself had ambivalent feelings on the battle:

We gain successes but after every fight there comes in to me an ominous paper marked "Casualties," "killed" and "wounded." Sad words which carry anguish to so many hearts. And we have scarcely time to bury the dead as we pass on in the same deadly strife. I pray for peace. I would not give peace for all the military glory won by Bonaparte.

Nonetheless, Robert E. Lee wrote to Jefferson Davis: "You know the high opinion I entertain of Gen. Hampton. In his late expedition he has displayed both energy and good conduct, and though I have feared that he might not have that activity and endurance so necessary to a cavalry commander . . . I request authority to place him in command."

In early August the appointment was confirmed: Major General Wade Hampton, commander of the Army of Northern Virginia's cavalry corps.

Grant's faith in Sheridan had not been shaken, though Federal cavalry operations around Richmond and Petersburg had been generally unproductive. Damage done to railroads, bridges, wagon trains, and depots was readily repaired. Supplies still reached Lee's army from the Shenandoah, where "Black Dave" Hunter had met his match in Jubal Early who was pushing down the Valley toward New Market.

Grant saw a solution to this Valley problem: to send sufficient forces to the Shenandoah, ably commanded, to destroy Early's army and that "granary of the Confederacy," depriving Lee of his food supply and forcing that general to detach additional troops from the Army of Northern Virginia before Petersburg to defend the Valley.

There was one man he could trust to do that job and that was Sheridan—a cavalry officer and infantry commander, and now, if Grant had his way, general of the about-to-be-created Army of the Shenandoah.

16

"THAT DEVIL FORREST"

"NO DAMNED MAN SHALL KILL ME AND LIVE!" VOWED NATHAN BED-
ford Forrest on June 14, 1863, as a doctor probed for the bullet in his
side. The bullet had been placed there by Lieutenant A. Wills Gould
whom Forrest had sharply rebuked at Day's Gap for the loss of his two
cannon during the pursuit of Streight. When Forrest later maneuvered
to have the officer transferred, the disgruntled lieutenant attacked him
with a pistol, and Forrest used the only weapon available, a pocket-
knife, to stab his opponent in the abdomen before collapsing.

Now told that his wound might be fatal, Forrest stumbled from the
doctor's office, grabbed a pistol from the nearest saddle holster, and
went after his assailant. He found him slumped on a bench off the
village green; shot at him and missed as Gould fled down an alley; and
finally found the lieutenant prostrate in a patch of weeds. He was about
to shoot him at close quarters when he realized this was needless. Gould
was bleeding to death.

The general summoned the doctor from his office. "Spare nothing
to save him," he bellowed. "And by God, when I give an order like that I
mean it!"

Gould died with Forrest at his side, each man pardoning the other.

The general, however, recovered from his wound in time to lead his
cavalry in screening Braxton Bragg's retreat from Tullahoma into
northern Georgia. At the Battle of Chickamauga circumstances required that he fight his troops dismounted—"a new sort of cavalry,"
one writer noted; not in the tradition of romantic charges by well-

mounted cavaliers, but rather that of "the hard, slogging, toe-to-toe fighting and dying that was the infantry's trade."

Forrest did not shirk, or even resent, this sort of service. But when Bragg refused to follow up the victory at Chickamauga in September and allowed the Union forces to entrench themselves in Chattanooga, he became disgusted with the general. "What does he fight battles for?" he asked. Others in the Army of Tennessee were asking the same question. In fact, a number of the army's senior officers signed a petition requesting Bragg's removal from command.

Forrest was not among the signers. His only personal grievance against the general was at having his brigades taken away from him as soon as he had adequately trained them. It was a tribute to his skill at recruiting and turning raw troops into veteran regiments, but he had had enough of it. The breaking point came with a curt message from Bragg's headquarters dated September 28, 1863:

> The general commanding desires that you will without delay turn over the troops of your command, previously ordered, to Major-General Wheeler.

Hard upon this came a second order from army headquarters stating that Wheeler was "assigned to the command of all the cavalry of the Army of Tennessee. . . . "

The fact that Forrest had vowed never to serve under Wheeler was only one cause of his indignation. That he should again be relieved of troops he had recruited, trained, and molded to his image, was more than he could stomach. Accompanied by his chief surgeon J. B. Cowan he stormed past the sentry into Bragg's tent, ignored that general's extended hand, and launched a withering barrage of words that struck the listener like bullets:

> You robbed me of my command in Kentucky . . . men whom I armed and equipped. . . . You drove me into West Tennessee in the winter of 1862, with a second brigade I had organized, with improper arms and without sufficient ammunition . . . and now this second brigade, organized and equipped without thanks to you or the government . . . you have taken from me. I have stood your meanness as long as I intend to. You have played the part of a damned scoundrel, and if you were any part of a man I would slap your jaws and force you to resent it. You may as well not issue any orders to me, for I will not obey them, and I will hold you personally responsible for any further indignities you endeavor to inflict upon me . . . if you ever again try to interfere with me or cross my path it will be at the peril of your life.

As Bragg retreated behind his desk, Forrest stalked from the tent with Cowan. "Now you're in for it," the surgeon told him. "No," said Forrest, "he won't do a thing"; but he might have added, "I will."

Forrest sent in his resignation from the army just as Jefferson Davis arrived to investigate the officers' charges againt Bragg. The President solved the immediate problem by transferring Forrest to Mississippi, promoting him later to major general, and authorizing the cavalry chief to raise his own force for operations in the West. He was allowed to keep a few selected units from his old command, which gave him a cadre of some 300 veterans. Around these he would build up his "army" as he'd built his previous brigade, by recruitment and by obtaining many of the needed weapons, horses, and equipment from the enemy.

During the last two months of 1863 Forrest, as commander of what he called the "Cavalry Department of West Tennessee and North Mississippi," made this twenty-thousand-square-mile area his own particular domain, much as Mosby had carved out his "Confederacy" in Virginia. It was mostly Union territory, but the people were largely sympathetic to the South. The general was familiar with the region from his boyhood days, and many of its residents knew the Wizard of the Saddle either personally or by reputation.

In secluded areas he established enlistment posts known popularly as "shebangs," oilskin tents erected over cut-branch frameworks, where he received from 50 to 100 new recruits a day. Some were men who had never served in any military force. Others were deserters from the infantry who had a predilection for the cavalry. Still others were Tennesseans or Kentuckians who had been enlisted into the Federal army and then decamped at the first opportunity. By the end of the year he had a force of roughly 3,500 men with whom to comb the countryside for horses, weapons, and supplies.

General Sherman, conferring with Grant at Chattanooga on their joint campaigns for early spring, at first paid little attention to Forrest's recruiting efforts in West Tennessee. When warned by an officer that, with Forrest back in the saddle, there would be "more dash in the rebel cavalry," he remarked derisively, "Forrest may cavort about the country as much as he pleases. Every conscript they now take will cost a good man to watch."

In mid-December, however, Sherman changed his tune. By that time, in addition to volunteers and conscripts, Forrest had accumulated forty wagonloads of bacon and other supplies, along with 200 head of cattle and 300 hogs, and was sending these back to Mississippi with 2,500 of his new, as yet unarmed, recruits. It was time to "get on his heels and chase him to the wall."

Five Union columns, from as many different points, took after the Confederate marauder. One was led by William Sooy Smith, Grant's chief of cavalry, another by Benjamin Grierson, still flushed with the triumph of his Mississippi raid. In all, the Federals numbered 15,000 or four times Forrest's 3,500, only a thousand of whom were well armed.

Forrest's chief concern, however, was for his wagon train of loot and captured livestock. Between these and safety in Mississippi lay the rain-swollen Wolf and Hatchie rivers, which temporarily blocked escape. With his personal escort of sixty men, he advanced across the Hatchie to engage six hundred of Grierson's cavalry under Colonel Edward Prince.

Outnumbered ten to one, Forrest, under cover of darkness on Christmas Eve, formed a line of battle in concealing woods, spacing his men ten paces apart to cover a distance of a quarter of a mile. As they advanced to within hearing distance of the Yankees, Lieutenant Nathan Boone shouted, "Brigade, charge!" And the command was repeated along the line, as the men went crashing through the dried stalks of a cornfield. With each reiterated order the horsemen shuffled and galloped noisily through the crackling stalks to create the din of a massive rallying of cavalry.

Colonel Prince was grateful for the darkness that enabled him to withdraw and escape to Somerville from this seemingly superior force which, judging by the racket, must have aggregated from four to six brigades.

The way across the Hatchie clear, Forrest on Christmas Day rode up to investigate the delay in getting the wagon train across the river. He found a big-mouthed recruit complaining that "he wasn't goin' to get down in that water, no sir, not for nobody he wasn't." The general picked him up by the neck and the seat of his pants and threw him in the river. There was no further trouble with the wagon train.

With the captured train and livestock safe, Forrest divided most of his remaining force, sending one unit in a feint toward Memphis, another in a diversionary raid toward the east, to siphon off the majority of his pursuers.

While the various columns of Union cavalry crisscrossed the area in his rear, bewildered as to his whereabouts, Forrest quietly withdrew to Como Station on the Mississippi & Tennessee Railroad, where during the next six weeks he shaped his heterogeneous gang of raw recruits into a disciplined cavalry force of four brigades, capable of coping with some unexpected trials to come.

William Tecumseh Sherman would never outgrow his distrust of cavalry. Put a man on a horse, be he Northerner or Southerner, and he became a glory chaser, obsessed with European myths of dragon-slaying feats of valor, knightly jousting before noble galleries, spectacular charges to the sound of bugles. All nonsense compared with the realities of war. He had strong opinions on the subject:

> Infantry can always whip cavalry . . . I have not seen in this war a cavalry command of 1,000 that was not afraid of a dozen infantry bayonets . . .

Which suggested a means of defeating "that Devil Forrest" in one brilliant stroke. He would use his infantry in a raid on the Southern Railroad, from Vicksburg to Meridian, challenging the Confederates to interfere, while Sooy Smith rode out from Memphis to swoop down on Forrest, wreck the Mobile & Ohio, and rendezvous with Sherman at Meridian—hopefully with Forrest's scalp hanging from his belt.

Smith assembled a force of 7,500 men, with Grierson second in command. The troops were well mounted, and many were equipped with the new breech-loading carbines, and accompanied by twenty pieces of artillery. He was ready, he told Sherman, "to pitch into Forrest wherever I find him." Sherman's advice was "to move quickly," and he cautioned Smith that Forrest "always attacked with a vehemence for which you must be prepared."

Perhaps Sherman overplayed the power of the adversary. Smith lost time double-checking his men and equipment and awaiting the arrival of an absent brigade that would bring his expedition up to full strength. Sherman's 20,000 infantry artillery and cavalry were near Meridian before Smith finally started out from Collierville on February 11 "resolutely bent on the destruction of the last vestige of Forrest's troublesome little army."

Informed of these operations, but uncertain of what route Smith would follow, Forrest withdrew his cavalry into east Mississippi. He would not precipitate a battle until circumstances favored his numerically weaker force.

Smith was heartened at first by Forrest's seeming retreat before his pursuing cavalry. Then he became assailed by doubts. Why didn't Forrest stand and fight? Was this a design to lure him into hostile territory, far from his base, where every wood and hollow held a threat of ambush? Rumors reached him of Forrest's growing strength, 8,000 to 9,000, matching or outnumbering his own. He was not, he later wrote, going to lead his command "into a trap set for me by the rebels."

In Meridian on February 14, Sherman looked in vain for signs of Smith's approach. "It will be a novel thing in war," he wrote "if infantry has to wait the motions of the cavalry." But wait he did, for seven exasperating days. Still no sign or word from Smith. Disgusted, he started back to Vicksburg having devastated the area and leaving Meridian in flames.

On that same day, Sooy Smith decided he had ventured far enough. He was too late to join Sherman anyway, and he feared the "disastrous effects" of a defeat by Forrest so far from home. He turned the expedition around and headed back for Memphis. Which was all the signal Forrest needed. "They are badly scared," he concluded, and he would not let them get away. At nightfall on the first day of the Federal retreat, he pushed half his force to the front of Smith's column while the other half attacked the rear.

"This was their first fighting under their new commander, Forrest," recorded Private J. P. Young of the 7th Tennessee Cavalry, "and his immediate presence seemed to inspire every one with his terrible energy, more like that of a piece of powerful steam machinery than of a human being." As the Federals stampeded to escape the trap, the pursuit was so close that Forrest was grazed by a bullet from one of his own men, an incident grimly reminiscent of the death of Stonewall Jackson in Virginia.

From then on, it was a chase across the state of Mississippi. Each time Smith paused to make a stand, Forrest, aware of facing superior numbers, applied a simple formula. "We can't hold them but we can run over them." It worked like magic at Okolona where the Federals were "forced to retire in haste" and where six of Smith's guns were captured in a five-mile running battle.

It worked again seven miles beyond Okolona at Ivey's Hill, but left a tragic scar. Young Jeffrey Forrest was killed by a bullet in the neck. The general paused to hold his brother in his arms, then rose, wiped the tears from his eyes, and ordered the attack resumed. In the next charge Forrest, bent on revenge, was so far ahead of his troops that few could keep up with him. He was in the center of the enemy, saber in one hand, pistol in the other, and had killed three of them before the Federals "broke to the rear and retreated with great speed."

Forrest called off the pursuit near Pontotoc and Smith's column, marching incessantly day and night, reached Memphis on February 26. "We were a worn and weary lot," wrote brigade commander Colonel George Waring, "broken in spirit . . . totally defeated." Smith reported in contrast that "we retired, fighting for over 60 miles, day and night, and had the fighting all our way except at Okolona."

Few of Smith's colleagues or subordinates agreed with him, one speaking of the "panic-stricken flight," while General Stephen A. Hurlbut, commander at Memphis, declared that the manner of Smith's retreat had "demoralized the cavalry very seriously." Sherman expectedly castigated Smith for "allowing General Forrest to head him off and to defeat him with an inferior force."

Lieutenant William Witherspoon of Forrest's cavalry had an explanation for Smith's rout by a third as many men. It was the difference between the troops who fought with Forrest and those who served with anybody else. He explained this after the war to a Union veteran who had been at Okolona:

"You made a formidable appearance, mounted, with your chargers well reined and sabers drawn," said Witherspoon. But before that charge, Forrest had gone down the Confederate line, identifying with each man in turn. "Hold this line for me," he said to each one individually. "So you see," said Witherspoon, "when you charged that line, it was

not one Forrest you were contending with, but every man in that line
was a Forrest."

On a visit to department headquarters in Alabama, in the winter of
1864, Forrest was given three Kentucky regiments and a brigadier
general named Abraham Buford. He reorganized his cavalry into two
divisions, one under Buford and the other under James R. Chalmers,
his second in command; and he wasted no time in putting them to
work.

For one thing, he was nagged by the thought of 3,000 potential
recruits he had left behind on his December 1863 expedition into West
Tennessee. For another, the new regiments were without mounts, and
the best place to get horses was Kentucky. These exigencies prompted a
West Tennessee-Kentucky expedition, beginning in mid-March.

Chalmer's division was left behind, to scour the state of Mississippi
for more recruits, to round up unattached companies of cavalry, and,
as a sensible disciplinary measure, to "destroy all distilleries." Buford's
division Forrest took north to Jackson, Tennessee, on the Mobile &
Ohio Railroad. Only one fortified post lay in his path, at Union City. He
detached a small force under Colonel W. L. Duckworth to "gobble up"
its garrison while he led the rest of his column up into Kentucky.

Duckworth had been a preacher and physician in civilian life, and
since that time a disciple of Forrest's histrionic talents. Approaching
the garrison at Union City, according to one account, he put those
talents into practice:

> By ingenious play acting, with horse-holders in the rear raising loud
> cheers at intervals, as if in welcome to arriving reinforcements, with
> much sounding of bugles from various points about the town, and
> with a judicious half-display of log "cannon" mounted on wagon
> wheels and maneuvered about in the bushes in the half-light of dawn,
> Duckworth managed to create the impression that he had artillery
> and that reinforcements were continually feeding in. Toward mid-
> morning he sent in his flag of truce with a demand for immediate and
> unconditional surrender, bearing the signature of "N. B. Forrest,
> Major-General commanding."

Colonel J. R. Hawkins in charge at Union City requested a personal
interview with General Forrest for the purpose of discussing terms. "I
am not in the habit of meeting officers inferior to myself in rank,"
Duckworth replied over Forrest's name, "but I will send Colonel Duckworth, who is your equal in rank and who is authorized to arrange

terms and conditions with you under my instructions." Face to face with Hawkins, and backed by the magic authority of Forrest, Duckworth gained the surrender of the city and its garrison of 500 troops, along with 300 horses and a quantity of arms and stores.

Twenty-four hours later Forrest himself was at Paducah on the Ohio River. Here the Federal garrison withdrew into Fort Anderson outside the town, leaving Forrest free to plunder the city for army stores and government horses. He remained in Paducah until midnight, then departed. He could have held the city longer, he reported, "but found the small-pox raging and evacuated the place."

In far-off Virginia, Ulysses Grant heard of the Paducah raid. "Forrest should not be allowed to get out of the trap he has placed himself in," he wired Sherman. "Send . . . all your cavalry with orders to find and destroy him wherever found." By the time Sherman received the message, Forrest was back in Jackson, Tennessee, pondering what he considered his essential mission in the war.

Forrest was far from psychic, but he was observant. He perceived in Sherman's movements, coupled with those of Grant, the shaping up of the Grand Design by which those generals hoped to consummate the war: Grant to move against Lee and Richmond, Sherman to move against Johnston and Atlanta, and most of the resources of the North to be confined to these two operations.

Only one outside factor could disrupt this plan. That was the threat to the vital railroads—notably the Nashville & Chattanooga—supplying Sherman at Chattanooga with war materiel, rations, and reinforcements. Forrest, along with John Hunt Morgan, posed this threat, and on April 6 Forrest wrote to Joseph Johnston, commanding the Army of Tennessee in Georgia:

> I am of the opinion that everything available is being concentrated against General Lee and yourself. Am also of opinion that if all the cavalry of this and your own department could be moved against Nashville that the enemy's communications could be utterly broken up.

Sherman was of the same opinion, urging that all Federal cavalry and infantry in the tri state area—Mississippi, Tennessee, Kentucky—be mustered to "throw a bombshell in Forrest's camp" and "make him pay dearly for his foolish dash at Paducah." None of these efforts succeeded, principally because Forrest could not be brought to battle. Forrest's scouts knew of the enemy's movements and how to avoid them; nobody knew where Forrest was at any given time.

Sherman even enlisted gunboats on the Mississippi and Tennessee in "the grand roundup of Forrest's force," perhaps calling Forrest's attention to this vital river artery—almost as important as the railroads. As Sherman was informing Grant, "The object of Forrest's move is to prevent our concentration against Johnston," Forrest was writing Leonidas Polk, Department commander, regarding the Mississippi: "There is a Federal force of five or six hundred at Fort Pillow, which I shall attend to in a day or two. . . . "

The day or two stretched into nearly a week, during which he divided his cavalry into several smaller units for diversionary raids on Memphis. The rest he led on April 10 due east from Jackson, Tennessee, to Fort Pillow on the Mississippi. The expedition was to become, regardless of whether the subsequent reports were true or false, the first project that would leave an ineradicable shadow on the general's reputation.

Built on bluffs overlooking the Mississippi some forty air miles north of Memphis, Fort Pillow was more a symbol of Federal dominance of the river than a bastion such as Vicksburg. The post was garrisoned by 557 officers and men, roughly half of whom were black, under the command of Major Lionel F. Booth. Besides the six guns on the nine-foot earthen parapets the gunboat *New Era* stood offshore to provide additional defense.

Marching from Jackson April 10, Forrest sent Chalmers ahead with two brigades to invest the fort. An outside line of pickets was driven back within the walls, and the dismounted Confederates occupied steep ravines on both sides, while marksmen were stationed on high ground commanding the Fort's interior. "We were as well fortified as they were," wrote Confederate Captain Charles Anderson, "the only difference was that they were on one side and we on the other of the same fortifications."

Unable to depress his cannon sufficiently to shell the troops in the ravines, Booth's position was already hopeless when he himself was killed by rifle fire from the bluffs. Forrest arrived at mid-morning and took time to study the situation—enough time for three horses to be shot from under him as he reconnoitered Fort Pillow through his glass. Then he sent a note to the deceased commander calling for unconditional surrender of the garrison, adding that if the demand were refused, he could not "be responsible for the fate of the command."

Major William Bradford, now in charge of the garrison, replied in Booth's name, asking for an hour to consult with his officers and with the captain of the *New Era*. About to concede, Forrest observed an approaching steamer, "apparently crowded with troops," and saw the smoke of three other boats behind it. Concluding that the request was a stall for time until these reinforcements could arrive, he shortened the hour to twenty minutes, and sent two detachments of cavalry to cover the landings where reinforcements might be put ashore.

When Bradford, still using Booth's name, sent back the answer, no surrender, Forrest signaled his bugler to sound the order to attack. For cavalrymen accustomed to the saddle, the charge was an extraordinary exhibition of gymnastics. While marksmen above the fort compelled the defenders to keep their heads down, the troopers swarmed from the ravines to the foot of the lofty walls and up the living ladders formed by one anothers' backs until they reached the summit. Wave after wave, they came over the parapets, firing into the garrison, then leaping inside the fort to finish the job with rifle butts and pistols.

The slaughter was quick and dreadful, aggravated, according to many reports, by the fact that half the garrison was drunk from whiskey later found inside the fort. True or not, none seemed able to restore some sort of organized resistance. Wrote Colonel Clark R. Barteau of Forrest's men regarding the defenders:

> . . . they made a wild, crazy, scattering fight. They acted like a crowd of drunken men. They would at one moment yield and throw down their guns, and then would rush again to arms, seize their guns and renew the fire. If one squad was left as prisoners . . . it was soon discovered that they could not be trusted as having surrendered, for taking the first opportunity they would break loose again and engage in the contest. Some of our men were killed by negroes who had once surrendered.

Without lowering the flag, Bradford signaled the gunboat New Era to stand by, and as many as could fled from the fort to escape by the river. Here they were slaughtered by Forrest's men already posted at the landings, while Captain James Marshall, fearing the capture of his gunboat, steamed off to leave them to their fate. Forrest found it impossible to calculate the number of Federals killed on the banks or in the water, beyond that "the river was dyed with the blood of the slaughtered for 200 yards."

When Confederates within the fort had the sense to lower the U.S. flag, signaling that the fight was over, Forrest gave the order to cease fire. The next several hours were spent in burying the dead and collecting the prisoners; and the following morning two vessels arrived from Memphis to carry off the wounded. A final tally showed that 231, or 40 percent of the garrison, had been killed, a disproportionate number of them black.

The fight for Fort Pillow was over, but not the bitter verbal battle that resulted; for the "massacre at Fort Pillow" was the first widely heralded "atrocity" of the war. As reported first by the Memphis *Bulletin*, and mentioned later in official army records, the storming Confederates had shouted "Forrest's orders!" and "No quarter!" as they shot down helpless Federals trying to surrender. There were infinite, shocking variations of this theme. Forrest himself was reported as trampling the wounded beneath his horse's hoofs as he urged his men on to the slaughter of the enemy.

There would later be a Federal investigation of these charges, never to be settled in an atmosphere of wartime frenzy. It seemed plain, however, that much of the slaughter had been needless, due partly to the fact that Bradford, in evacuating Fort Pillow, had never lowered the U.S. flag or formally surrendered. Both Grant and Sherman vowed swift retaliation if the charges could be proved. Significantly, there was no retaliation.

Time was growing short before the beginning of the great spring campaign —Grant and Meade against Lee in the East, Sherman against Johnston in Georgia. For Sherman, the one remaining obstacle was Forrest's likelihood of "interrupting my plans of preparations for the great object of the spring campaign." A strong force must be kept at Memphis, ready to strike at the Wizard of the Saddle whenever and wherever he should threaten Sherman's rear.

With this in view, Sherman placed General Cadwallader C. Washburn in command of the district of West Tennessee with head-quarters at Memphis. As his senior subordinate, Sherman sent Washburn General Samuel D. Sturgis, a florid-faced Pennsylvanian, forty-one, with a record of "gallant and meritorious conduct" so far in the war. After Sooy Smith's timid performance, Sherman no longer believed that cavalry alone could defeat Forrest. Washburn would have both the 3,500 footsoldiers now at Memphis plus 3,000 cavalry under Sturgis, "troops enough at Memphis to whale Forrest if you can reach him."

Reaching him was only half the problem. There was an intimidating aura of invincibility surrounding Forrest. He was the devil incarnate, weaving a spell of black magic over his opponents. "The very name of Forrest is a host in itself," wrote Confederate soldier J. Pugh Cannon, from recent experience. Cannon's company of infantry had "captured a cavalry detachment in the night by charging them under the battle cry of 'Forrest! Forrest!' " The Federals had quickly surrendered and, wrote Private Cannon, "were much surprised that 'General Forrest' had only 150 men, and they afoot. . . ."

Washburn was plainly a victim of the Forrest legend. He protested to Sherman, "I cannot venture to go in pursuit of Forrest unless I have more force." The Federal general had heard this all too often. He chided his new appointee: "Try and not exaggerate the force of the enemy or your own weakness, but use your force to best advantage. Don't let Forrest insult you by passing in sight of your command."

Thus goaded, Washburn launched his first expedition in pursuit of the Confederate marauder. A column of 6,500 cavalry and infantry, with twenty pieces of artillery, left Memphis on April 30 under the command of Sturgis. For a week they marched southwest to Ripley, Mississippi, in what Washburn called a "hot pursuit" but which involved only a minor skirmish with the enemy at Bolivar. The war-devastated countryside, however, and the hostility of the natives, gave them little comfort in the way of food, forage, or accommodation.

At Ripley on May 6 Sturgis found that Forrest's command had passed that place two days ahead of him. Due to "the utter and entire destitution of the country," he reported, "my horses had scarcely anything to eat, and my artillery horses nothing. . . . With the greatest reluctance . . . I decided to abandon the chase as hopeless." Returning to Memphis, he wrote to Sherman:

> My little campaign is over and I regret to say, Forrest is still at large. It is idle to follow him except with an equal force of cavalry, which we have not. . . . I regret very much that I could not have the pleasure of bringing you his hair but he is too great a plunderer to fight anything like an equal force, and we have to be satisfied with driving him from the state. He may turn on your communications and I rather think he will, but see no way to prevent it from this point and with this force.

Sturgis concluded, in self-justification, "Though we could not catch the scoundrel we are at least rid of him and that is something." But Sherman was far from being rid of Forrest. At Tupelo, Forrest continued to build up his mounted force, reaching an effective total of more than 9,000 men from which he selected a well-armed striking force of 3,500 for a thrust into Middle Tennessee.

As Johnston's army, fighting a skillful defensive war in northwest Georgia, was rolled back by Sherman's greater numbers, both Little Joe and Braxton Bragg, now serving as military adviser to President Davis, suggested immediate action by Forrest, while War Secretary Seddon considered a Congressional proposal:

> Now that the enemy are drawn far into Georgia would it not be a great move to order Forrest with his whole force to fall in behind the enemy and cut off his trains of supplies and make such a demonstration in his rear as will destroy his army.

Sherman was conscious of the likelihood of such a move. He would forestall it by sending another force from Memphis to strike Forrest first, "to prevent him from swinging over against my communications." Again he pinned his faith on Sturgis, a triumph of hope over experience. On the first of June, Sturgis led a new expedition out from

Memphis: 3,300 cavalry under Grierson, 5,000 infantry under General Ralph Buckland, 22 guns, and a train of 250 wagons of equipment, food, and ammunition. Of the three infantry brigades, one of 1,200 men under Colonel Edward Bouton was composed of blacks who "had taken an oath to avenge Fort Pillow and to show Forrest's troops no quarter."

On learning of this new campaign to bag him, Forrest abandoned his Middle Tennessee expedition to concentrate on Sturgis. His scouts kept him informed of the latter's movements, southwest from Memphis toward the Mobile & Ohio Railroad. He would let the Federals get deep into Confederate territory, far from their supporting base, then move out to meet them. Like a ship's pilot charting a collision course with an approaching vessel, he marked Brice's Cross Roads as the point of probable encounter. He would make certain that he got there first.

Only one Kentucky brigade, 800 strong, actually got there first, early in the morning of June 10. But Forrest knew the nature of this territory from his boyhood days — knew of its difficult thickets of scrub oak and blackjack, and the narrow roads, sometimes raised, sometimes submerged beneath mud and water, which approached the junction from the north.

The troops under Sturgis would greatly outnumber the Confederates, Forrest told brigade commander E. W. Rucker, "but the road along which they will march is narrow and muddy; they will make slow progress. The country is densely wooded and the undergrowth so heavy that when we strike them they will not know how few men we have." So, here was his plan of battle:

> Their cavalry will move out ahead of the infantry, and should reach the cross roads three hours in advance. We can whip their cavalry in that time. As soon as the fight opens they will send back to have the infantry hurried up. It is going to be hot as hell, and coming on a run for five or six miles, their infantry will be so tired out we will ride right over them.

After that, pursuit, capture, and possession of their wagons and provisions and artillery.

By 10 o'clock Grierson had brought up two of his brigades and spread them across the road in line of battle, with four pieces of artillery in position. Though he overestimated Forrest's strength, he had the Confederates outnumbered four to one. Forrest decided on a bluff, a quick show of strength to put the enemy off balance. He gave the order: Charge!

The "charge" was no more than a quick sting with a rebel yell attached — a dash forward, a barrage of small-arms fire, and an equally swift retreat—to be repeated until the rest of Forrest's cavalry arrived. The gamesmanship was psychologically effective. Grierson reported the first charge as "exceedingly fierce" and one of "three desperate attempts to take our position. We succeeded. however, in holding our own. . . . "

In less than an hour the balance of Forrest's cavalry arrived, raising the Confederate odds to a less unfavorable two to three. Now Forrest went after Grierson's cavalry in earnest. At the sound of the bugle the Confederates surged forward. "Such was their eagerness," wrote Forrest's follower, John Wyeth, "that the commands seemed to vie with each other as to which should first reach their antagonists." Simultaneously the Union troops pressed forward to grapple with the graybacks "in one of the most fiercely contested short engagements of the war. . . . "

> So close was this struggle that guns once fired were not reloaded, but used as clubs, and pistols were brought into play, while the two lines struggled with the ferocity of wild beasts. Never did men fight more gallantly for their position than did the determined men of the North for this black-jack thicket on that hot June day.

Hard pressed, Grierson sent back word to Sturgis: Bring up the infantry! Sturgis himself raced ahead to Brice's Cross Roads to size up the situation and to hear from Grierson that he could not hold on without support, that one of his cavalry commanders was "almost demanding to be relieved." Sturgis repeated the order to his foot troops. "Make all haste! Lose no time in coming up!"

The order was an invitation to disaster. As Forrest had noted, it was "hot as hell," and the infantry was hampered by the wagon train, the narrow sometimes boggy road, the suffocating atmosphere. Trotting or double-timing for six miles, some were overcome by heat prostration, all were exhausted. They were further disheartened to find, on arriving, that the situation at the front "was going to the devil as fast as it possibly could."

The Federal cavalry had, in fact, "partly by order, and partly without," withdrawn to the sidelines. Forrest had won his first phase of the fight as scheduled. He had whipped Grierson's cavalry. Now the second stage was starting as anticipated. The Union infantry was half-whipped by fatigue. He would give them no time to catch their breath, even though his own men were exhausted. When you rode with Forrest there was no such thing as standing still; one man in action was worth two waiting for the enemy to strike.

There was a moment of ominous quiet as the two contending armies faced each other: 3,600 Federal soldiers with 22 field guns, 2,000

Confederates with 12 pieces of artillery. On the face of it, critically adverse odds for the Southerners. Appearing in front of his troopers like "the very God of War," Forrest rode down the line. "When you hear . . . the bugle sounds," he said, "every man must charge—and we will give 'em hell!"

"Some people," wrote Sergeant William Witherspoon, "say that Forrest seldom cursed." Well, they were not present that day at the Cross Roads. "If we moved too slow he would curse, then praise, then threaten to shoot us himself if we were so afraid the Yanks might hit us. . . . He would praise in one breath, then in the next would curse us, and finally told us, 'Come on, I'll lead you.' We hustled, and across that narrow field was a race—double quick. . . . "

They charged the left of the Federal position, then the right, and as the line teetered like a seesaw on its fulcrum, struck the center. Then Forrest raised the cry of previous battles, "Hit the e-e-end!" Around the Union flank swept 250 hard-riding Tennesseans under Colonel C. R. Barteau, not stopping until well behind the enemy.

"I succeeded in reaching the Federal rear," reported Barteau, "just as the fighting seemed heaviest in front. I at once deployed my men in a long line, had my bugler ride up and down sounding the charge at different points, and kept up as big a show as I could . . . until their complete route [sic] was evident."

What amounted to little more than that, a big show, was enough to panic the battered Federals who rolled back as if the earth had tilted. Sturgis tried to bring the black brigade, guarding the wagon train, into action; they were caught in the tide of retreat and swept along as by a cataract.

Forrest had won the second phase: he had whipped the infantry. Now came the final stage: pursuit.

Sturgis was helpless to check the rout. "Everywhere the army now drifted toward the rear and was soon altogether beyond control," he officially reported. "Order gave way to confusion and confusion to panic. . . . The road became crowded and jammed with troops; wagons and artillery sank into the deep mud and became inextricable. No power could check the panic-stricken mass as it swept toward the rear."

Over the narrow bridge across Tishomingo Creek the fleeing troops congested, cavalry riding over infantry, the supply train blocking the passage, with some of the wagons abandoned as the drivers unhitched the teams and mounted the horses to escape. Colonel Bouton of the black brigade pleaded with Sturgis to make a stand.

"General, for God's sake, don't let us give it up so," he begged.

"What can we do?" asked Sturgis. "For God's sake, if Mr. Forrest will let me alone I will let him alone. You have done all you could and more than was expected of you and now all you can do is to save yourselves."

Colonel Benjamin Grierson, leader of the Union cavalry raid through Mississippi in support of Grant's campaign for Vicksburg in the spring of 1863. *(Harper's Weekly)*

Lieutenant General Joseph Wheeler, Confederate cavalry leader in the Atlanta campaign. He also aided Johnston's last stand in the Carolinas. *(Library of Congress)*

HARPER'S WEEKLY.
A JOURNAL OF CIVILIZATION

Vol. VII.—No. 334.] NEW YORK, SATURDAY, MAY 23, 1863. [SINGLE COPIES SIX CENTS.
$2.50 PER YEAR IN ADVANCE.

Entered according to Act of Congress, in the Year 1863, by Harper & Brothers, in the Clerk's Office of the District Court for the Southern District of New York.

MAJOR-GENERAL GEORGE STONEMAN, U.S.A.—[See next Page.]

Major General George Stoneman, leader of one of the first Union cavalry raids on Richmond, later fought under Sherman in the West. (*Harper's Weekly*)

Major General James Harrison Wilson who, like Sheridan in the East, led the Union cavalry to victory in the West. (*Library of Congress*)

MAJ GEN VOLS.

Major General Hugh Judson Kilpatrick, leader of a Union raid on Richmond, later fought in Sherman's campaign for Atlanta. *(Library of Congress)*

Kilpatrick's abortive cavalry raid on Richmond, February-March 1864, encounters hastily mobilized Confederate defenders. *(Harper's Weekly)*

Culmination of Sheridan's famous ride. The general arrives from Winchester to rally the demoralized Federal army at Cedar Creek. *(Library of Congress)*

Major General Philip Henry Sheridan, whose leadership helped the Union cavalry attain equality with the Confederates. *(Library of Congress)*

Major General George Armstrong Custer, flamboyant division commander of Federal cavalry until the last, conclusive days at Appomatox. *(Library of Congress)*

Wade Hampton duels with a Federal officer in the cavalry clash northeast of Gettysburg, July 3, 1863. *(Library of Congress)*

WADE HAMPTON'S CAVALRY FIGHT AT GETTYSBURG.

THE CAVALRY CHARGE AT WINCHESTER, VIRGINIA, September 19, 1864.—[See Page 653.]

Sheridan's Federal troopers strike outnumbered Confederates at Winchester, forcing Early's retreat up the Shenandoah, September 19, 1864. *(Harper's Weekly)*

GEN. WADE HAMPTON.

Lieutenant General Wade Hampton, C.S.A., who succeeded Jeb Stuart to the command of Lee's cavalry in the spring of 1864.
(Library of Congress)

MUSIC ON SHERIDAN'S LINE OF BATTLE.

As with many cavalry bands, Sheridan's mounted musicians rode with the troopers into battle, often playing throughout the fight. *(Battles and Leaders of the Civil War)*

Charge of Sheridan's cavalry on Lee's retreating army at Five Forks, Virginia, one of the last major battles of the war. *(Harper's Weekly)*

BATTLE OF FIVE FORKS. VA.

MOSBY'S GUERRILLAS DESTROYING SUTLERS' TRAIN.—[SEE PAGE 667.]

John Mosby's Virginia partisans raiding a Union sutlers' train, as depicted in a contemporary drawing. *(Harper's Weekly)*

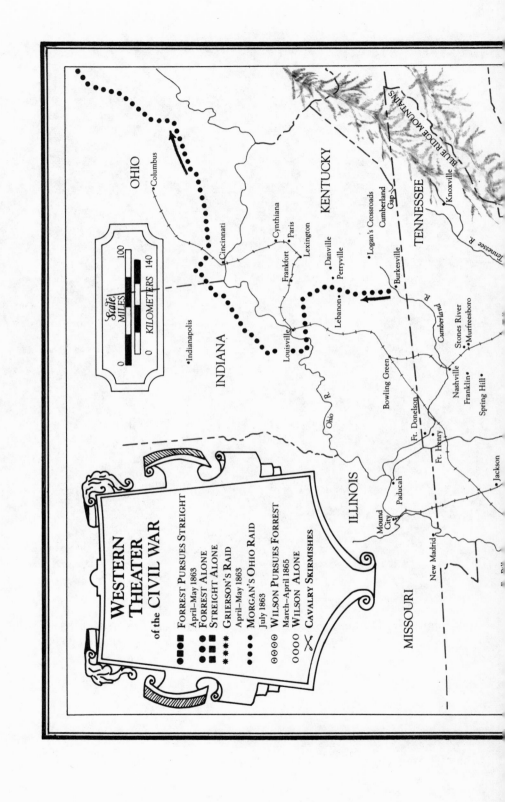

WESTERN
THEATER
of the CIVIL WAR

●■■ FORREST PURSUES STREIGHT
    April–May 1863
●●● FORREST ALONE
    April–May 1863
■■■ STREIGHT ALONE
**** GRIERSON'S RAID
    April–May 1863
●●●● MORGAN'S OHIO RAID
    July 1863
⊕⊕⊕⊕ WILSON PURSUES FORREST
    March–April 1865
○○○○ WILSON ALONE
✕ CAVALRY SKIRMISHES

Scale
MILES
0   100

0   KILOMETERS   140

OHIO

•Columbus

Cincinnati

•Cynthiana
•Paris
•Lexington
Frankfort•
      •Danville
      Perryville•

•Logan's Crossroads
Cumberland
Gap

KENTUCKY

TENNESSEE

Knoxville•

BLUE RIDGE MOUNTAINS

Tennessee R.

Burkesville•

•Lebanon•

Louisville•

Cumberland R.

Stones River
Murfreesboro•

•Indianapolis

INDIANA

Ohio R.

Bowling Green•

Ft. Donelson•

Nashville•
Franklin•
Spring Hill•

Ft. Henry•

ILLINOIS

Mound
City
Paducah•

•Jackson

MISSOURI

New Madrid•

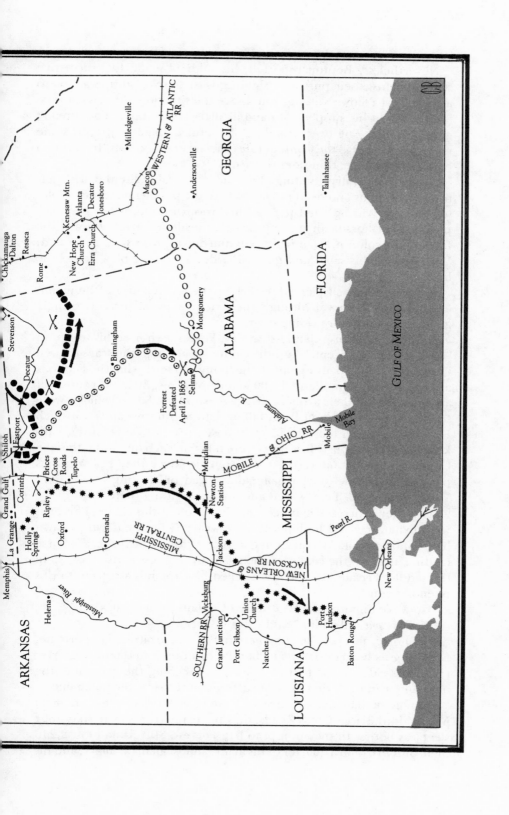

Nevertheless, Bouton reported, his soldiers made five successive stands against their pursuers, fighting with "terrible desperation" to avenge Fort Pillow. Nothing could save the situation, Sturgis confessing that as to his supply train and artillery, everything "had already gone to hell." The overturned or abandoned wagons offered some measure of relief as the Confederates paused to wolf down "fresh, crisp hardtack and nice, thin sides of bacon."

Grierson's cavalry, finding the road impassably littered with jettisoned weapons and dead horses, took to the paralleling woods. Colonel George Waring tried to keep his troops in line, when he saw a poncho-clad horseman pushing his way insubordinately toward the front of the column. "Damn him, cut him down!" his adjutant shouted; Waring drew his saber and gave the rider a stinging blow across the back.

He found himself pierced in turn by the startled eyes of Benjamin Grierson. "Who are you hitting?" the general inquired in a surprisingly gentle manner before riding on.

At the head of his relentless cavalry, Forrest exhorted his troops to "keep the skeer on 'em." And the Confederates kept the scare on well into the next day, pausing only long enough to seize what the Federals abandoned in their flight, 1,500 stands of arms, 300,000 rounds of ammunition, all their artillery, baggage, supplies. Some vehicles were set aflame to keep them from falling into Southern hands, to which Forrest reacted with orders to "put those fires out! Don't let the Yankees burn *my* wagons!" Prisoners were taken in such quantities that the Confederates lost interest. At the Hatchie River they saw Yankees perched like crows on partially submerged or floating logs, "more Yanks than logs." They waved and left them sitting there.

At Ripley, Forrest's main column abandoned the chase. The men were exhausted and he himself bone-weary from the dawn-to-dawn battle and pursuit. An officer and a trooper found the general's horse trotting along in the center of the roadway, Forrest himself asleep in the saddle. Private Mack Watson called his captain's attention to this phenomenon.

"Go wake him up, Mack," ordered Captain John C. Jackson.

"No, sir, *you* wake him," said Private Watson.

The horse, always an unsung hero in the war, arbitrated the dispute. Lowering its head defiantly, it charged head-on into the nearest tree, tossing its rider to the turf and rudely awakening the general to the only minor injuries that Forrest suffered in that long engagement.

Though it had taken Sturgis's troops nine days to march from Memphis to Brice's Cross Roads, they made the trip back in sixty-four sleepless hours. In the attempt to bag Forrest, Sturgis had lost 2,240 men, or more than a quarter of his army, almost all his artillery, and his entire wagon train. Over and above that was the deep chagrin of the commander and his troops. Wrote Adjutant E. Hunn Hanson of Waring's brigade:

> It is the fate of war that one or the other side should suffer defeat, but here there was more. The men were cowed, and there pressed upon them a sense of bitter humiliation . . . Upon a vague report that the enemy (who had given up pursuit fifteen hours before) had been seen in the rear, the weary men again took up the march toward Memphis, as though within its fort and under the shelter of its siege guns alone could they find safety.

"Yet there is some consolation," Sturgis wrote, "in knowing that the army fought nobly while it did fight, and only yielded to overwhelming numbers." He would never admit that the numerical advantage had been his, insisting: "The strength of the enemy is variously estimated by my most intelligent officers at from 15,000 to 20,000 men."

Sherman would never accept that excuse. Along with an unsubstantiated charge that Sturgis had been drinking during the engagement, starting with a whiskey breakfast, he was bewildered by the outcome of the expedition. "Forrest has only his own cavalry. . . . I cannot understand how he could defeat Sturgis with 8,000 men."

For Forrest, Brice's Cross Roads marked the apex of his vigorous career. Recorded Hanson, "If there was, during the war, another engagement like this it is not known to the writer; and in its immediate results there was no success among the many won by Forrest comparable to that at Guntown [Brice's Cross Roads]." Curiously, the battle would gain as much attention among foreigners as in America. Viscount G. J. Wolseley of Great Britain called it "a magnificent achievement," while French Colonel Kerbrecht of the Chasseurs d'Afrique extolled Forrest's feat in three words of his limited vocabulary. "Sapristi! God damn!"

Sherman, however, was unintimidated. "Forrest is the very devil," he wrote to War Secretary Stanton, "and I think he has got some of our troops under cower." But he himself would not give up. The fate of his campaign in Georgia rested on keeping Forrest off his back and clear of his supply lines.

He would turn the job over next to seasoned campaigner A. J. Smith and his hard-core veterans just arrived at Memphis from the Trans-Mississippi. "I will order them to make up a force and go out and follow Forrest to the death, if it costs 10,000 lives and breaks the Treasury. There never will be peace in Tennessee until Forrest is dead."

Four weeks after Brice's Cross Roads, Smith headed south toward Tupelo with a column of more than 14,000—cavalry, infantry, and artillery—"a force ample to whip anything this side of Georgia," declared General Washburn as he saw them off from Memphis.

In the subsequent battle at Tupelo on July 14, the Confederate cavalry was badly mauled, and Forrest himself severely wounded in the foot. Though a victory for Smith, the expedition was arrested and his troops, their ammunition exhausted, were sent scurrying back to Memphis with the Confederates in pursuit. "I bring back everything in good order; nothing lost," Smith reported to Washburn, which was the most that he could claim.

The next time Smith came after Forrest, with an expanded force of 18,000 men, the Confederate leader simply ducked around the column of invaders, and on August 21 raided Memphis in their absence. It was a daring foray, proving simply that Forrest's men could enter "Washburn's bedroom" any time they liked; and they brought out Washburn's uniform and his two best horses, as tokens of the raid, to prove it.

Four attempts, four failures, and That Devil Forrest was still riding free on Sherman's flank as Sherman closed in on Atlanta.

CHAPTER

17

HORSEMEN AT THE GATES

"WITH THE MONTH OF MAY CAME THE SEASON FOR *ACTION*," WROTE
William Tecumseh Sherman of that fateful spring of 1864. Grant was
to launch his final great offensive against Lee and Richmond in Virginia, "and I to attack Joe Johnston and push him to and beyond
Atlanta. This was as far as human foresight could penetrate."

Sherman assembled his three armies south of Chattanooga, facing
Rocky Face protecting the Confederate base at Dalton. His was a
formidable force: 100,000 men or more, with some 12,000 cavalry.
Three of the mounted divisions—under Judson Kilpatrick, Kenner
Garrard, and Edward M. McCook—were attached to General George
Thomas's Army of the Cumberland. A fourth division, George Stone-
man's, was assigned to John M. Schofield's Army of the Ohio.

It would be cynical to say that the West had become a place of exile
for Federal cavalry commanders. Yet perhaps because Sherman had a
low regard for cavalry, Grant sent him those who had been relatively
unsuccessful in the East: Kilpatrick after his abortive raid with
Dahlgren, Stoneman after his earlier, inconclusive raid on Richmond.
Both, it seemed, were being given a second chance, but under a commander who was difficult to please.

Edward McCook had a distinctive claim to fame. He was one of a clan
of fourteen brothers and cousins in uniform known throughout the
Union as "the Fighting McCooks." The youngest had fallen at seventeen at Bull Run. The oldest, father Dan McCook, had been shot in a
fight with Morgan's raiders in Ohio. His son, Colonel Daniel McCook,

would be killed in eight more weeks at Kennesaw, after reciting to his troops the family motto from Horatius's speech: "And how can man die better than facing fearful odds."

Kenner Garrard, making his debut as division commander, got more than his unwanted share of Sherman's spleen, becoming the butt of the general's sometimes waspish humor. When exasperated with his cavalry, which was often, Sherman would vent his wrath by shouting, "Gar'd! Gar'd! Where the hell's Gar'd?" When the brigadier responded, asking what he was supposed to do, the general would bellow at him: "Don't make a damn bit of difference what you do. Just get out of here! Go kill some rebels!"

Kilpatrick, of course, was a veteran of Meade's command at Gettysburg, and Stoneman had recently headed the Cavalry Bureau at Washington, filling the rising need for horses in the Union. "These cavalry commands," wrote Sherman, "changed constantly in strength and numbers, and were generally used on the extreme flanks, or for some special detached service . . . " He dismissed them too lightly: they were used for considerably more than that, but often with results that the campaign commander would rather not recall.

One of Sherman's concerns that spring, as the Grand Design got under way in East and West, was his long supply line, stretching more than 150 miles from Chattanooga to the principal Federal base at Nashville. It would get longer as he plunged deeper into Georgia. So long as Morgan and Forrest were free he could never feel certain of the operation of that railroad. Johnston's Army of Tennessee, which faced him now at Dalton was at least a measurable quantity, estimated now at 52,000 men. But numbers were only one factor, the commander something more. "No officer or soldier who ever served under me," wrote Sherman, "will question the generalship of Joseph E. Johnston."

Besides his three-corps army, Little Joe, commanding the Army of Tennessee, had General Wheeler's cavalry, 5,000 strong. Though battered and diminished in service under Braxton Bragg, Wheeler had with him William ("Red Fox") Jackson's division of 3,700 troopers (also quoted as numbering 4,400 and 5,200, such being the fluctuating nature of a cavalry command). Jackson had fought beside Forrest, and also under Forrest when the latter took over the cavalry from Van Dorn. He had that certain Western flare that Wheeler lacked.

Despite his nickname there had been nothing spectacular in "Fighting Joe" Wheeler's performance up to now, and little of the romance that seemed to go with the role of dashing cavalry commander. He was not the type. Five feet five in height and totally without humor—a combination that gave the impression of comic pompousness—his was not an arresting or magnetic personality. He obeyed orders, a trait endearing to his superiors. And he exacted strict obedience from subordinates, not a key to popularity among the troops.

Returning from a September-October raid into Middle Tennessee, pursued by Federal cavalry, his column had forded the river near the head of Muscle Shoals. It was a difficult crossing, with the horses stumbling over slippery boulders, and the men emerging dripping wet and shivering on the south bank. Nearby was a plantation manor, and Wheeler dispatched an aide to get permission for his troops to camp and build fires on the property. The aide was greeted at the door by Colonel Richard Jones, owner of the house.

"General Wheeler presents his compliments," said the aide, "and asks your permission for his men to camp here for the night."

As Jones nodded his consent, a gentle voice behind him asked, "General Wheeler, did you say? I'd like to see him."

"Well, ma'am," said the aide politely. "You won't see much when you do."

So it was that the diminutive general met his future wife, Daniella Sherrod, widowed daughter of Colonel Jones. It was love at first sight, and kept Wheeler and his cavalry camped on Jones's doorstep from October 9 to 20—for the reported purpose of shoeing horses and allowing tardy stragglers to catch up with the command. When the love-sick general refused to move—even though General Stephen Lee requested his presence in Middle Tennessee—Lee protested to Johnston that "up to the 9th instant General Wheeler declined to cross the Tennessee River with me, not deeming his command in condition to do so . . . "

When Wheeler finally, two months later, joined the Army of Tennessee at Dalton, there seemed some cause to doubt the cavalry's condition. The men were poorly clothed, some even barefoot; the horses undernourished and inadequately shod. But beyond their physical state, Johnston, on assuming command of the Army of Tennessee, found the cavalry dispirited. They had fought too long in a theater of retreat, been frustrated too often under Braxton Bragg. And under Wheeler, never one to inspire confidence and regimental pride, morale was at its nadir.

It was not altogether Wheeler's fault. In many ways he was an admirable leader; Jefferson Davis considered him one of the best cavalry commanders in the South. But he too had been a soldier of retreat too often, screening Bragg's discouraging withdrawals throughout 1863. Now he was about to join another long retreat, and Johnston, much as he admired Wheeler, would keep the cavalry close to the army, close enough to keep an eye out for the enemy, close enough to seal off breaks in the defenses if the enemy attacked. Wheeler would have little chance to exercise initiative.

Yet in the first few weeks at Dalton, Johnston did wonders in revitalizing both the cavalry and the infantry. He demanded and sometimes got from the quartermaster's office adequate equipment and provisions. He restored discipline; and as the men revised their habits, spruced up their uniforms, polished their weapons and groomed their horses, they recovered a sense of purpose and responsibility. A captain of Wheeler's cavalry wrote to his wife, "I doubt whether a volunteer army could be more perfect in its organization than the Army of Tennessee. General Johnston seems to have infused a new spirit into the whole mass, and out of chaos has brought order and beauty."

Along with this improvement, old branch-of-service rivalries returned. It is curious at this late point in the war, when Confederate cavalry had proven itself so often in both East and West, to find the infantry still prejudiced against the mounted arm. In one of the mock battles which Johnston staged as a means of drill and exercise, Lieutenant Andy Neal of Atlanta wrote to his father, "It was comic to see the cavalry splashing around and hear the taunts and jeers of the infantry. Cavalry never has and never will fight and is heartily despised by the men who do the fighting."

The first week in May, Sherman put his troops in motion and the two armies squared off in the valleys and ridges below Chattanooga, each general having settled on his strategy. Both would avoid an open battle far from the target, the "Gate City" of Atlanta. Sherman would flank positions seen as too strong to assault; Johnston would avoid encirclement by withdrawing to a previously fortified position, blocking further forward movement by the enemy—two master players in a mortal game of chess.

On May 8 Sherman made his first move, sending James McPherson through Snake Creek Gap to flank the Confederates at Dalton. Judson Kilpatrick's cavalry led the column through the gap, and were first to engage the Confederate troops at Resaca. "The General was never known to look so full of fight as on that day, while dashing to the front, his banner waving in the breeze," wrote army surgeon James Moore. But Moore found himself shortly treating Kill-Cavalry for a bullet in the groin, which sent the general behind the lines for two months of recuperation.

From Resaca on, it was a sort of dance of death between the opposing armies, a game of thrust and parry, with Sherman flanking Johnston on the right and then on the left, Johnston retreating to strategically prepared positions. Wheeler's cavalry delayed for four hours the thrust through Tunnel Hill, then fell back with the army down the line of the Western & Atlantic Railroad to Adairsville, Kingston, Allatoona, and Kennesaw Mountain.

Repulsed in a costly frontal assault on Kennesaw, Sherman again resorted to flanking Johnston's mountain stronghold, forcing Little Joe's retreat to Smyrna. Then, effectively using Kenner Garrard's and Stoneman's cavalry to keep the Confederate defense divided, he sent his infantry across the Chattahoochee River, last major barrier to Atlanta, Gate City of the South.

During this campaign, as in Virginia in 1864, the war was taking on a new dimension. Battles had heretofore been field affairs, fought in the relative open, where the swiftness of cavalry charges was sometimes decisive. Now the forces of both sides were taking to the rifle-pits, and trench warfare became the rule instead of the exception. More often than not, Wheeler's cavalry fought dismounted beside the footsoldiers, subjected to the tactics and the status of the infantry. To what extent this bred dissatisfaction and resentment it was hard to say. Certainly some of the cavalry's esprit de corps was lost.

By mid-July Johnston had formed a new line south of the Chattahoochee overlooking the valley of Peachtree Creek, eight miles above Atlanta. He was closer, he felt, to ultimate success. Sherman had extended his supply line by a hundred vulnerable miles; he had suffered heavy losses and left many men behind to guard the railroad; his army was consequently less formidable. Johnston, on the other hand, was close to his base in his strongly fortified Atlanta — to which he could withdraw to offer incontestable resistance to the Federal invaders.

Then Jefferson Davis intervened. Johnston's Fabian policy had not sat well in Richmond. Few recognized the strategy behind it, and saw only the retreats; and Davis on July 18 replaced Johnston with the aggressive, reckless John Bell Hood.

Sherman, for one, was grateful for the move. "At this critical moment the Confederate Government rendered us most valuable service," he recorded. "The character of a leader is a large factor in the game of war, and I confess I was pleased with this change. . . . "

Hood, Sherman knew, would be apt to abandon Johnston's cautious policy, and expose his outnumbered troops to open battle. Precisely what Sherman wanted. With only a single-track railroad line to Chattanooga, down which must come all essential supplies — food, guns, and ammunition — he could not sustain a long siege of Atlanta. "I was willing to meet the enemy in the open country, but not behind well-constructed parapets."

Hood obligingly met him in the open country and in nine days of late July, was successively defeated at Peachtree Creek, in the Battle of Atlanta, and at Ezra Church. Then he withdrew his badly mauled army into the city's fortifications, while Sherman brought up his guns to batter down the gates.

Artillery alone, however, would not be enough. The city could quicker be brought to its knees by severing the single-track lines, especially the Macon & Western railroad, supplying Hood's army and Atlanta's population from the south. ("Pile the ties into shape for a bonfire, put the rails across and when red hot in the middle, let a man at each end twist the bar so that its surface becomes spiral.") This was a job ideally suited—or so he thought—to the cavalry now on his flanks: Garrard's and Stoneman's two divisions at Decatur, Edward McCook's division west of Campbelltown.

It was to be a simple pincers movement. Garrard and Stoneman with 5,000 troops between them would ride down through Covington to strike the Macon & Western railroad from the east. At the same time, McCook's division of 4,000 men would circle the city on the west and close in on the railroad from that direction. These two forces would lock together somewhere around Lovejoy's Station and slam the door on Atlanta's lifeline, leaving the city dying on the vine.

Stoneman had a project of his own that he suggested to the general. There were more than 34,000 Federal prisoners in the infamous stockade at Andersonville. The cavalry chief proposed that, after wrecking the Macon railroad, he take his troopers on to Macon and then Andersonville, liberating the prisoners at these two points. Provided with arms, this vengeful host would present a terrible threat to the already apprehensive heartland of the South. It would also, in Stoneman's mind, offset the failure of his 1863 Richmond raid and make him a hero in the North. Sherman subscribed to the proposal:

> There was something most captivating in the idea, and the execution was within the bounds of probability of success. I consented that after the defeat of Wheeler's cavalry, which was embraced in his [Stoneman's] orders, and breaking the road he might attempt it with his cavalry proper, sending that of General Garrard back to its proper flank of the army.

Both officers understood their orders, Sherman wrote, and "entertained not a doubt of perfect success." But did Stoneman take those orders to heart? The provisions were that he first defeat Wheeler's cavalry, then wreck the Macon & Western Railroad, and only after these goals were achieved proceed to the liberation of Andersonville.

The two task forces, those of Stoneman and McCook, got off according to schedule on July 26. Following whatever secret plan he had in mind, Stoneman sent Garrard's division to the little crossroad town of Flat Rock, twelve miles south of Decatur. He explained this as a diversionary tactic, to screen his own advance to Covington. Later the two would meet at Flat Rock and proceed together to Lovejoy Station, there to link up with McCook's division coming from the west.

Wheeler learned of their initial movements the following morning. The greatest cavalry race in Georgia's history was under way.

Like Stoneman, Wheeler had something to prove in this engagement. His cavalry had been lately used to fight dismounted, in rifle-pits, behind barricades. The men were disgruntled; they had lost a great deal of their former verve. And Wheeler's relations with Hood were opposite to those he had shared with Johnston. His obedience and loyalty to Johnston were absolute. With Johnston gone, he felt to some extent liberated from his conscience. He was free to go off on his own, and his cavalry was free to act as cavalry.

This refreshing attitude was catching to the troops. Racing to Flat Rock on word of Garrard's presence there, the Confederates vigorously attacked the town, dislodged the Union cavalry from its hastily constructed breastworks, and drove the Federals some miles back to Latimer's, with Garrard still wondering where Stoneman was.

Stoneman never showed up, and Wheeler's cavalry kept the pressure on Latimer's defenses until Garrard decided to adhere to orders and rejoin the army. This he did on July 31, reporting to a bewildered Sherman that he had got only as far as Flat Rock, been apparently abandoned by his colleague, and been forced to retreat when Stoneman failed to keep their rendezvous.

Wheeler had taken care of one division of Sherman's cavalry with very little trouble. But like Garrard he wondered where Stoneman was and what part Stoneman was playing in this cavalry charade. Dividing his forces at Latimer's, he sent three brigades under Alfred C. Iverson to hunt down the Federal general who might be headed for the Macon railroad. Wheeler himself swung west to link with Jackson's cavalry and form a tight chain of defense across the all-important railroad, for word had reached him that McCook was on the move.

Cavalry seemed to be chopping up the countryside around Atlanta. General McCook had given the slip to Jackson's riders when he crossed the Chattahoochee, and was following Sherman's orders to the letter: Smash the Macon railroad near Lovejoy's Station, then rendezvous with Stoneman and push on to Andersonville. En route to Lovejoy's, he sliced up sections of the intervening West Point Railroad, then met and confiscated several Confederate supply trains, burning 1,160 wagons and slaughtering 2,000 mules—all badly needed by Hood's forces in Atlanta.

At one point a wagon train blocked their progress, the mules sleeping on the road. An officer jabbed the nearest animal with his sword. The mules "came to life with loud snorts and other uncouth noises," according to one account. "With tails in the air, the whole train stampeded and went rushing down the road, scattering units ahead and strewing packs through the woods on either side. It was hard to straighten this out."

At Lovejoy's Station, McCook was puzzled to find no sign or word of Stoneman. After waiting awhile he gave up on the appointed rendezvous, tore up several more miles of track along the Macon & Western

Railroad, then headed back west toward Newnan on the West Point line—wondering, as Garrard had wondered, where was Stoneman? His troopers slaughtered a few hundred additional mules, burned several score wagons, and took 300 Confederate prisoners who proved more trouble, even under guard, than they were worth.

In Newnan, a hospital town for Atlanta's wounded, was General Philip D. Roddey's cavalry, 600 strong. Roddey had been on his way from north Alabama to join Hood's forces at Atlanta when he learned that the Yankees had chopped up sections of the railroad near Palmetto. His troops were stranded until the line could be repaired.

Newnan itself was in a state of shock and panic over reports of McCook's approaching Federals. The streets were clogged with refugees from the surrounding country communities where McCook, "by his unparalleled cruelty, had made his name a horror." Many had lost their homes and families and possessions, and were seeking shelter before moving farther south.

In the Newnan hospital, nurses Kate Cumming and Fanny Beers shared the general apprehension. What would happen to their wounded patients when McCook arrived? Would they be taken prisoner, or shot, or what? The incoming refugees, women especially, told harrowing tales of the unconscionable raiders. "They go into houses and what they do not carry away they destroy. They have a dreadful antipathy to crockery, and break all the poor people's dishes."

By mid-afternoon of July 30 McCook was at the gates and skirmishing flared on the fringes of the town. The Union colonel had expected little opposition, but he had cut his throat when he cut the Atlanta & West Point Railroad. He had trapped Phil Roddey's small but gallant cavalry inside the town.

Now Roddey leapt on his horse, "without taking time to saddle the animal or don his uniform," according to nurse Cumming. Like a modern Pied Piper in a Hamelin besieged, he mustered behind him the young, the maimed, the halt, the hospital convalescents and attendants—anyone capable of bearing arms—and led them out to battle. Nurses Beers and Cumming climbed to the hospital roof to see the charging Yankees brought up short at the foot of an intervening hill.

"Evidently they expected to surprise the town," wrote Fanny Beers, "but, finding themselves opposed by a force whose numbers they were unable to estimate, they hastily retreated up the hill."

Startled by the sheer numbers of men at arms in Newnan, and unable to tell from a distance that half were frightened adolescents and hospital wounded who could barely stand, McCook withdrew into an unexpected trap. Joe Wheeler, having split from the rest of his division, which was watching out for Stoneman, was coming at him from the east. Jackson, having recovered the scent, was closing on him from the west. His troops were exhausted from two days of riding without decent food or rest. Their officers were too befuddled by fatigue to make decisions.

McCook put every man on his own, releasing his troops to fight their way out of the trap as best they could.

Some of them, including McCook himself, made it back to Sherman's camp. Others were killed or captured, with scores of their injured taken to the Newnan hospital. Here one of the Confederate patients, a captain, volunteered to help attend to the Union wounded. He started, with the first man to arrive, by taking him outside and shooting him. Though he claimed it was in revenge for the atrocities committed by the Federal cavalry, he was removed from further duty.

In Atlanta, Hood was informed by a dispatch from Wheeler:

> We have just completed the killing, capturing, and breaking up of the entire raiding party under General McCook—some nine hundred and fifty (950) prisoners—two pieces of artillery, and twelve hundred horses and equipments captured.

Sherman, in turn, got his report from the chagrined McCook himself. The general felt he had fulfilled his mission. In addition to property destroyed and prisoners taken, he had mangled the West Point and Macon railroads. Sherman smoldered silently. His worst suspicions of cavalry were confirmed. "They have not the industry to damage a railroad seriously," he wrote. "Usually it can be repaired faster than they can damage it." He was right; the roads were back in operation within forty-eight hours.

And, Sherman wanted to know further, where was Stoneman?

In Stoneman's mind there was nothing illogical in his procedure. Thinking things over before he left to meet Garrard at Flat Rock, intending to join forces later with McCook at Lovejoy's Station, he decided these intermediate steps could be dispensed with. His ultimate goal was Andersonville and the liberation of the Union prisoners. This single act would embellish his career, so far branded a "distinguished failure," with a crown of glory. Why bother with the preliminaries? Garrard and McCook could take care of demolishing the Macon & Western Railroad.

He swept wide to the east to avoid detection, through Covington and on toward Macon, confident that Garrard, whom he was ignoring, was unwittingly protecting the right flank of his column. He planned now to bypass Macon, maybe hurling a shell or two into the city for good luck. But no more, for Major General Howell Cobb, playing host to Joe

Johnston, was there with his Georgia Reserves and militia, and the town was fortified. To try to capture it would simply hold things up.

At Macon, hearing from scouts of the approach of Federal cavalry, Cobb led his Georgia Reserves out from the city and into Stoneman's projected path. Around the only bridge across the Ocmulgee River the citizen soldiers erected barricades and waited. Stoneman could not ignore them without a tedious and time-consuming detour. He made a mistake; he ordered his artillery to shell the town.

The first shell (which did not explode) was like a rock thrown at a wasps' nest. Out from wherever they worked or lived, in stinging fury, came old and young, schoolboys, clerks, mechanics, doctors, lawyers, even convalescents from the Macon hospitals. They broke open the arsenal for rifles and ammunition, wheeled out some ancient artillery, and raced to join their comrades at the bridge.

Surprised at this resistance, Stoneman's dreams of glory turned to apprehension and alarm. Rumors reached him that Alfred Iverson with three brigades of Wheeler's cavalry was descending on him from the neighborhood of Latimer's. He thought briefly of seeking refuge near Pensacola on the Gulf, then chose a disastrous alternative. He retreated north toward Decatur and ran squarely into the arms of Iverson, who had entrenched his dismounted cavalry across the Federals' escape route.

Goaded by fury and frustration, Stoneman on July 31 made no attempt to slip past Iverson by one side or the other. He charged the Confederate line head-on, was driven back, and tried again. The seesaw battle continued for six hours, until Stoneman was falsely told that troops were coming up from Macon to attack his rear. His situation, he deduced, was hopeless.

The general told his troops that he, with 500 volunteers, would hold the Confederates in check while the rest of the cavalry made good their escape. Two of the three brigades took off through the woods, eventually to reach the Union lines above Atlanta, while Stoneman surrendered himself and his sacrificial band to Iverson. Though he believed he had no alternative, there was actually no enemy in his rear. His troops, before they dispersed, outnumbered Iverson's. Had he continued the fight it might have gone the other way.

But as it was, he was hailed in the North as a self-sacrificing hero. He fostered the image, writing to Sherman from a Southern prison camp that he preferred to be in captivity "rather than among those who owe their escape to considerations of self-preservation."

That the 500 surrendered troopers agreed with him is open to some doubt. In Sherman's mind there was no doubt whatever. The twin cavalry probes had ended in unqualified catastrophe. When, on August 4, the last surviving members of Stoneman's command straggled into camp, Sherman had lost over 2,000 troopers, almost half of the army's mounted force. Never again, he wrote, would he orient his plans on "the motions of the cavalry."

Back in Atlanta, still invested by Sherman's armies, Hood shared Wheeler's satisfaction with the cavalry's performance. If Wheeler's confidence in his troops had risen, so also had Hood's—to a dangerous degree. As he recorded:

> Wheeler and Iverson having thus thoroughly crippled the Federal cavalry, I determined to detach all the troops of that arm that I could possibly spare, and expedite them, under the command of Wheeler, against Sherman's railroad to Nashville ... and also that General Forrest be ordered, with the whole of his available force, into Tennessee for the same object. . . . I intended General Wheeler should operate, in the first instance, south of Chattanooga.
>
> I was hopeful that this combined movement would compel Sherman to retreat for want of supplies, and thus allow me an opportunity to fall upon his rear with our main body.

If the fight for Atlanta was as critical to the South as the battles around Richmond in Virginia, as indeed it was, Hood had learned nothing from Lee's unfortunate experience with Stuart in the Gettysburg campaign. A general in crisis does not let his cavalry get far afield, beyond the reach of his command. Johnston had known that, and had kept Wheeler close to the army, leaving it to Forrest and Morgan to threaten Sherman's lines in Tennessee. Now Hood, ignoring this basic principle, was playing into Sherman's hands.

"I could not have asked for anything better," wrote Sherman, "for I had provided well against such a contingency, and this detachment left me superior to the enemy in cavalry."

First the Confederate high command had relieved Sherman of Johnston's formidable presence; now they were relieving him of Wheeler.

Following orders, Wheeler left Covington on August 10 with 4,000 troops and, as one writer expressed it, "literally rode himself out of the war." He would be heard from again—from time to time, and from different places—but over the racket he raised as his men destroyed the Western & Atlantic railway could be heard the whistle of the locomotives riding down the tracks that Sherman's men repaired as fast as Wheeler could demolish them. Though Hood would later credit Wheeler and Forrest with success (having "accomplished all but the impossible with their restricted number of cavalry"), all that really resulted from this madcap ride was the loss to Hood of several thousand mounted troops that could better have been used to guard Atlanta's gates.

The campaign in Georgia was dispersing in a number of directions, Wheeler moving north to attack the enemy's supply lines, Sherman looking south for ways to isolate Atlanta, by destroying the railroads on the city's rear. Kilpatrick was back with the mounted troops, having violated doctor's orders and rejoined the army before his wound was fully healed. With Stoneman in a Southern prison, Sherman made him his chief of cavalry.

Despite his distrust of cavalry commanders, Sherman liked Kilpatrick. The tempestuous Celt was, in his words, "a hell of a damned fool," but for just that reason might accomplish what others had failed to do; cut the two critical railroads and force Hood to evacuate Atlanta.

As Kilpatrick moved against the railway line with acceptable success, Wheeler began running out of steam in northern Georgia. On August 14 he captured Dalton but was unable to hold the town. For one thing, the country between Chattanooga and Atlanta had been laid bare by the war. Johnston's and Sherman's armies had stripped the land of forage and provisions. Wheeler's cavalry was forced to live on green corn that had half-way ripened since midsummer.

"I went into a cornfield," wrote one trooper, "gathered twelve ears from the growing stalk; gave my horse eight and kept four to roast for my dinner. I took two from him to help my dinner, but gave him the shucks from all, so I claimed to have been generous."

Under pressure of hunger Wheeler's orders against pillaging were tossed aside. The troops stole everything that they could get their hands on. They plundered barnyards for chickens and eggs, orchards for fruit, truck gardens for vegetables, smoke houses for meat. The Yankees, they reasoned, had lived off this land before them; they were entitled to what was left.

As Wheeler on September 2 crossed the Tennessee River into Alabama, hoping to join Bedford Forrest in compliance with Hood's wishes, Robert Toombs, former Confederate presidential nominee, breathed a sigh of relief. He wrote to Vice President Alexander Stephens that Wheeler was proving no asset to the Cause. The enemy was indifferent to his depredations; the damage done to Federal communication lines was negligible; Wheeler had "avoided all depots where there were as much as an armed sutler."

"Now that he has gone," wrote Toombs, "I cannot say he has done no good, for he has relieved the poor people here of his plundering, marauding bands of cowardly robbers. . . . I hope to God he will never get back to Georgia."

The raid, in fact, was a costly failure. Some tracks on the Western &

Atlantic railroad had been torn up, 1,300 government horses and mules had been captured, and the inhabitants of towns along the railway line had been intimidated. But Wheeler had suffered substantial losses. One whole brigade under Major General William T. Martin had set off on a foraging expedition and never returned, apparently disappearing from the surface of the earth. Brigadier General John H. Kelly had been killed by a Yankee marksman in a minor skirmish. So when Wheeler reached Tuscumbia, Alabama, to rendezvous with Forrest, he was minus two valuable officers and almost half his troops.

The meeting between Forrest and Wheeler must have had overtones of previous antipathy. If so, Wheeler suppressed his feelings enough to subscribe to a joint raid into Middle Tennessee. This was not in accord with Hood's instructions but, he wrote to the army commander:

> General Forrest thinks that the aid of my force for ten or twelve days would be of great service to him and materially affect the success of his expedition. . . . However, unless I hear from you, will start [back] as directed as soon as possible. General Williams being absent with half [sic] my command, I will only be able to bring back 2,000 men.

A letter from Forrest gave a somewhat different slant to their encounter:

> I met Major-General Wheeler to-day at Tuscumbia. . . . He claims to have about 2,000 men with him; his adjutant-general says, however, that he will not be able to raise and carry back with him exceeding 1,000, and in all probability not over 500.
>
> One of his brigades left him and he does not know whether they are captured or have returned, or are still in Middle Tennessee.
>
> His whole command is demoralized to such an extent that he expresses himself as disheartened, and that, having lost influence with the troops, and being unable to secure the aid and co-operation of his officers, he believes it to the interest of the service that he should be relieved of command.

It was a low point in Wheeler's years of loyal service. Though he never offered to resign, as Forrest seemed to anticipate, his depression was not raised by subsequent events. Shortly after Wheeler left on his desultory foray into Tennessee, Kilpatrick's cavalry cut the Macon railroad, and Sherman's armies all but surrounded Atlanta from the west. On September 1 the city surrendered and Hood withdrew his forces farther south.

In late September, however, Hood instituted plans for regaining the initiative. He would march back north, retracing Johnston's route to

Dalton, wrecking the Western & Atlantic Railroad on the way and cutting the Union army off from its supplies. If Sherman pursued him, well and good. He would entice the general out of Atlanta, out of Georgia, and back to Tennessee. If Sherman refused to take the bait, then Hood was free to operate in the enemy's rear, destroying his bases, reoccupying Middle Tennessee and possibly Kentucky. Possibly from there to Virginia, to join Robert E. Lee in the defense of Richmond.

With this decision came a back-handed slap at General Wheeler. When and if Hood invaded Middle Tennessee, he would rely on "Red Fox" Jackson's division and Nathan Bedford Forrest's corps for cavalry support. Wheeler would return to Georgia as a minor threat to Sherman.

If Hood's plan was sound, things failed to work out quite as he expected. Leaving Atlanta in flames, Sherman led his army in four separate columns toward Savannah, escorted by Kilpatrick's cavalry. But he first sent Generals Thomas and Schofield with two corps of the Army of the Cumberland to take care of Hood in Tennessee. In disastrous defeats at Franklin and Nashville in November and December, Hood saw his once magnificent Army of Tennessee all but destroyed.

Forrest missed the fight at Nashville, having been sent by Hood on a pointless mission to Murfreesboro. But he returned to form the rear guard of the sad Confederate retreat—the men trudging to a dirge-like ballad improvised for the occasion:

> So now I'm marching southward,
> My heart is full of woe;
> I'm going back to Georgia
> To see my Uncle Joe.

Uncle Joe Johnston would replace Hood in another month or so; but the Army of Tennessee—one of the finest cohesive fighting units of the war—could never be replaced.

As for Joe Wheeler, he followed Sherman to the sea, skirmishing with Kilpatrick on the way and almost capturing "Little Kil" in a delaying fight at Waynesboro, half way to Savannah. But his diminished, hard-worn cavalry was not sufficient to deter the Sherman juggernaut. "My marching columns of infantry don't pay the cavalry any attention, but walk right through it." The early, invincible days of the Southern cavaliers—when Union infantry scattered at the cry of "Black Horse!"—were indeed past. And the roads that the riders in gray patrolled were growing shorter.

CHAPTER

18

SHERIDAN ALL THE WAY

UNTIL PHILIP SHERIDAN ARRIVED TO TAKE COMMAND OF FEDERAL forces in the Valley, Confederate General Jubal Early since mid-June 1864, had been having a field day in the Shenandoah. Detached from Lee's army to take care of David Hunter, he had driven Hunter into West Virginia, then crossed the Potomac virtually unopposed to scare the daylights out of Washington and Baltimore—invading Maryland not once but twice, and exacting a tribute of $200,000 from the town of Frederick.

At one point President Lincoln himself had ridden to Fort Stevens to appraise the danger to his capital. In stovepipe hat and frock coat he surveyed the enemy through his field glass until an exasperated colonel told him, "Keep down, you damn fool!" The President stepped back obligingly, but what he had seen disturbed him. He sent for Grant. The Shenandoah Valley must be cleared of the enemy once and for all, he told his commander in chief; Washington could not tolerate repeated threats to its security.

If Grant was certain that Sheridan could clear the Valley—"put himself south of the enemy and follow him to the death"—not all in Washington agreed. Secretary of War Stanton and Henry Halleck thought the former chief of cavalry, thirty-three, was too young for the job. So that when Sheridan arrived at Harpers Ferry the first week in August 1864, to take command of what was to become the Army of the Shenandoah, he felt under a certain necessity to prove himself.

He had the material or soon would, with which to do it: seven divisions of infantry aggregating more than 30,000 men, and one division of cavalry under General Alfred Torbert numbering close to 12,000 troopers. He had seasoned division commanders in Wesley Merritt, James H. Wilson, and William Averell, and able brigadiers in men like Thomas Devin and George Armstrong Custer.

Custer's normally aggressive spirit was honed by stimulating animosities. Having briefly tasted the joys of commanding a division after Gettysburg, he chafed under the divisional command of Merritt, and resented the fact that Wilson, "that upstart ass," also commanded a division. Among his Confederate enemies, and everything was personal with Custer, he bore a particular grudge against his former West Point classmate, Thomas Rosser, who would soon be joining Jubal Early.

Early's forces that first week in August numbered roughly 10,000 infantry and 3,000 cavalry, the latter in one division under Lunsford Lomax. Shortly after Sheridan took command, however, the Union general learned that Early had been reinforced by Lee. Two divisions of infantry and several brigades of cavalry had raised the Confederate force to 23,000—wrongly estimated by Sheridan as 40,000—which made Little Phil uncharacteristically cautious for a man whose motto had been "Smash 'em up!"

As a result, the next six weeks were a period of restless stalemate, Sheridan pushing Early back from Winchester to Cedar Creek, Early following Sheridan north to Harpers Ferry, then both reversing direction and marching back to Opequon Creek, a seemingly neutral, unprovocative position. A lot of movement on Sheridan's part, with nothing much accomplished. When Lincoln complained to Grant of this seeming "deadlock," Grant visited the Valley on September 15 to prod Sheridan to action.

Grant had with him a plan of campaign to submit to his major general, but he found that Sheridan had his own precisely formulated plan, based partly on secret communications with a loyal Winchester girl named Rebecca Wright. Written on thin tissue, the messages were smuggled through enemy lines by a black civilian courier who was prepared to swallow the papers if intercepted. The latest of these dispatches contained the number and disposition of Early's troops, where they were weakest, all that Sheridan would need to know.

Finding Sheridan "so clear and so positive in his views and so confident of success," Grant kept his own plans in his pocket, slapped his general on the back, and told him to "go in!"

Sheridan started going in two hours before dawn, September 19. As a former chief of cavalry he knew, as few generals before him had understood, the effective use of mounted troops. They were the sharp, pointed spearhead of the army, first to attack from flanks and rear, piercing, stinging, and so demoralizing the enemy that the muscled infantry could close in for the knockout blow.

So it was at Opequon Creek, with Wilson's horsemen charging at daybreak through a narrow ravine to slash at Early's right while Torbert with the other two divisions struck simultaneously at his left. As the Confederates turned from the front to face these side attacks, Sheridan's infantry steamrolled to and through the center. For five hours Early's troops stubbornly resisted, giving ground grudgingly, slipping back toward the south.

It was the last of several charges by Merritt's cavalry that helped seal Early's fate that afternoon. Three brigades abreast, under Custer, Devin, and Charles Lowell, plunged into the enemy's heart, "sabers slashing and pistols cracking—an onrushing, crushing tidal wave of snorting, half-crazed horses and yelling troopers. Guns were overrun, wagons overturned. Confederate soldiers, wounded and unwounded, fled in all directions as defeat turned into rout and rout into panic."

Lieutenant William Harrison, a captured Union officer, was a sidelines witness of this final action. "The confusion, disorder, and actual rout produced by the successive charges of Merritt's division," he reported, "would appear incredible did not the writer actually witness them." Sheridan himself, writing of the battle, declared modestly, "I claim nothing for myself. My boys Merritt & Custer did it all."

The Confederates had staggered back to Fisher's Hill, south of Strasburg, leaving behind 2,000 prisoners, five pieces of artillery, and most of their wounded—a loss in men of almost 4,000 or a good fourth of Early's army. From his headquarters Sheridan wired Grant that night:

"We have just sent them whirling through Winchester, and we are after them tomorrow." Grant wired back, "If practicable, push your success and make all you can of it."

It was the first decisive Federal victory in the Valley, and Sheridan's first triumph in the Shenandoah. True to his promise he pressed after Early, and three days later prepared to dislodge the Confederates from Fisher's Hill. It was the same battle plan with opposite results. Using his infantry to assault the front, he sent Averell's mounted division to flank the enemy left, while Torbert with Merritt's and Wilson's divisions circled round to cut off their line of retreat at New Market.

This time around both cavalry commanders failed him miserably. Torbert ran into two brigades of Fitz Lee's troopers—minus Lee himself, who had been wounded at Opequon Creek. Sheridan was "astonished and chagrined" to learn that Torbert had failed to reach his prescribed position. Averell had performed no better, even worse. Claiming that his troops were tired after a hard day's fighting, he simply bivouacked by the roadside for the night while the Confederates safely retreated farther down the Valley Pike.

Both Averell and Wilson were, with Grant's approval, relieved of their commands. For Averell, thirty-two, it was the end of a career that had never really begun for one who "lacked the fighting heart that marks the true Cavalry commander." For Wilson the results were just the opposite. Transferred to George Thomas' forces in the West, he caught his second wind and began a new career that followed an almost level path to glory.

For George Armstrong Custer, who in his own mind had been leading warrior hosts to victory since the age of ten, this shift in officers confirmed a dream. A week after the Fisher's Hill engagement he wrote to Libby in Washington that he had been given command of "a division [Wilson's]. Mine is the largest." He had been allowed to keep his cook Eliza; to keep his marching band some of whom "threatened to break their horns" if not permitted to accompany their general; and on top of all "I have a tent almost as large as a circus tent." In short, he concluded, his every wish was gratified.

Though Fisher's Hill counted as Sheridan's second victory in the Valley, and won him the plaudits of Lincoln, Stanton, Grant, and Halleck, he was not completely satisfied. During the week he had lost 5,000 men, a costly price to pay, and despite great numerical advantage had failed to eliminate the enemy. Early himself wrote of the engagement, "with the immense superiority in cavalry which Sheridan had . . . [he] would have destroyed my whole force and captured everything I had. . . . I can but attribute my escape from utter annihilation to the incapacity of my opponent." Professional jealousy, however, surely colored that remark.

As Early withdrew his battered army through New Market and Harrisonburg as far as Brown's Gap, Sheridan sent his cavalry to raid Staunton and Waynesboro, destroying army stores and sections of the Virginia Central Railroad. Grant wired him: "Keep on, and your good work will cause the fall of Richmond." Sheridan was not so sure of keeping on. "My judgment is that it would be best to terminate this campaign by the destruction of the crops, etc., in this Valley, and the transfer of the troops to the armies operating against Richmond."

In point of fact, he felt uneasy this far up the Valley. Early had been driven out, for now at any rate. But far behind Sheridan, in Loudoun and Fauquier counties, was John Singleton Mosby. Throughout his pursuit of Early, the general had looked over his shoulder for signs of the Gray Ghost on his rear. Now he turned back to countermarch down the Valley, conforming to Grant's earlier instructions that, in passing through that region, "it is desirable that nothing should be left to invite the enemy to return. Do all the damage to railroads and crops you can. Carry off stock of all descriptions, and Negroes, so as to prevent further planting. If this war is to last another year we want the Shenandoah Valley to remain a barren waste."

For nine terrible days, as Custer's and Merritt's cavalry ranged down the Valley to Fisher's Hill, the scorched earth reeked of that destruction. Clouds of smoke, from burning farms and fields and granaries, shrouded the wake of the horsemen. "The atmosphere from horizon to horizon has been blackened by a hundred conflagrations," a war correspondent wrote, "and at night a gleam brighter and more lurid than sunset has shot from every verge . . . The completeness of the devastation is awful."

Sheridan himself reported to Grant that a crow could not fly down the valley without carrying its own provisions. "I have destroyed over 2,000 barns filled with wheat, hay, and farming implements; over 70 mills filled with flour and wheat; have driven in front of the army over 4,000 head of stock, and have killed not less than 3,000 sheep . . . When this is completed the Valley, from Winchester up to Staunton, 92 miles, will have little in it for man or beast."

Not far behind, however, the first week in October, was a surprisingly resurgent army under General Early. The Confederates had been reinforced with another division of infantry and a battalion of artillery to make up for the losses suffered in September. Early's deficient cavalry had also been revitalized. From Richmond came Thomas L. Rosser's famed Laurel Brigade which had routed Custer's cavalry at Buckland Mills a year ago, and Rosser, replacing Wickham as commander of Fitz Lee's brigade, was being welcomed as "the Savior of the Valley."

For the past week Wickham and Lomax had been nipping at Sheridan's heels, and by October 9 the bandy-legged Irishman had had enough. At Tom's Brook south of Strasburg he ordered Alfred Torbert to turn his cavalry loose on the pursuers—"whip the enemy cavalry or get whipped himself." To Custer the order was a stimulating challenge, a chance to get even for the Buckland Races of the year before and to settle the grudge he bore against his former friend and West Point classmate.

It was the classic cavalry battle, reminiscent of the earlier years when the saber was the honorable weapon and men crossed swords in face-to-face encounters. And in this case it was something of a grudge duel, introduced with a flourish. According to eyewitness Frank A. Burr, Custer rode to the front of his well aligned troopers, took off his hat, bowed to his antagonist, and shouted across the intervening gap:

"Let's have a fair fight, boys! No malice!"

To this Quixotic proposal, Rosser responded only to the men around him:

"You see that Yank down there, bowing? Well, that's Custer that the

Yanks are so proud of, and I'm going to give him the best whipping he ever got — see if I don't!"

Again Custer raised his hat, this time as a signal to his men, and led the Federal cavalry forward from trot to gallop, from gallop to charge. The Confederate horsemen waited in disciplined formation . . . till the two lines came together with a clash of sabers that rang out in silver notes across the valley.

Sheridan had ridden to the crest of Round Top Mountain for a better view, recording later:

> In the center the Confederates maintained their position with much stubbornness, and for a time seemed to have recovered their former spirit, but at last they began to give way on both flanks, and as these receded, Merritt and Custer went at the wavering ranks in a charge along the whole front. The result was a general smash-up of the entire Confederate line, the retreat quickly degenerating into a rout the like of which was never before seen. For twenty-six miles this wild stampede kept up, with our troopers close at the enemy's heels . . .

In his official report of the engagement, General Torbert noted: "There could hardly have been a more complete victory & rout. The cavalry totally covered themselves with glory, and added to their long list of victories the most brilliant one of all & the most decisive the country has ever witnessed. Brig.-Gen'ls Merritt & Custer . . . particularly distinguished themselves." Custer wrote that nothing as brilliant had been seen "since the opening of this war."

During the retreat, which flowed through Woodstock to Mount Jackson, dubbed "the Woodstock Races" by the Federals, the Confederates lost 330 prisoners, eleven guns, and 47 wagons containing the personal possessions of the officers. Custer tried on Rosser's dress jacket and, finding it too big for him, sent it to Libby as a souvenir. At the same time he wrote a note to Rosser, leaving it with a family in the Valley:

> Dear Friend:
>   Thanks for setting me up in so many new things, but would you please direct your tailor to make the coattails of your next uniform a trifle shorter.
>
> > Best Regards,
> > G.A.C.

After the Tom's Brook steeplechase Early held the balance of his army at New Market, refusing to follow the cavalry's retreat, letting the disaster flow around him. "God knows," he wrote to General Lee, "I have done all in my power to avert the disasters which have befallen this command; but the fact is that the enemy's cavalry is so much superior to ours, both in numbers and equipment, and the country is so favorable to the operations of cavalry, that it is impossible for ours to compete with his."

It was a far cry from 1861 and the days before and after First Manassas, when Federal officers were saying practically the same about the Southern cavalry. The pendulum had swung in a full half-moon, from gray to blue.

With Averell and Wilson gone, and command of the mounted troops tightened under Custer, Merritt, Powell, and Torbert, Sheridan had no complaint about his cavalry. But he was deeply concerned with another situation that had plagued him in the Valley since the start of the campaign. Despite repeated victories, he still had Mosby on his rear—threatening his communications, intercepting orders, seizing trains bringing him supplies from Washington, killing or capturing Federal pickets left behind to guard the Valley Pike. And above all, limiting Sheridan's actions against Early.

Without mentioning Mosby specifically, he noted:

> The difference of strength between the two armies at this date was considerably in my favor, but the conditions attending my situation in a hostile region necessitated so much detached service to protect trains, and to secure Maryland and Pennsylvania from raids, that my excess in numbers was almost cancelled by these demands . . .

Mosby had missed capturing Grant when he failed to seize the special train bearing the general from Washington to Culpeper that spring. He almost made up for it by nearly capturing Sheridan the first week Little Phil took over in the Shenandoah. On August 9 the Gray Ghost led a furtive band to the outskirts of Sheridan's camp, located the general's quarters in the hotel, and sent one of his men, John Hearn, to determine the strength of the surrounding guard. Hearn was detected by a Federal picket who alarmed the camp, and Mosby and his followers were chased back into Fauquier County, pursued by Federal cavalry until the trail grew cold.

On the following day, as Sheridan moved toward Early's forces south of Cedar Creek, a supply train of 525 wagons—one of the largest of the war—left Harpers Ferry with provisions for the Army of the Shenandoah. The immense train, three miles long, was guarded by 3,000 troops, spread strategically along the line.

Nothing that large could escape detection by Mosby's scouts. The next day, on heights overlooking the road to Berryville, Mosby stationed his little howitzer, deploying his rangers on both sides of the pike. A blast from the howitzer would signal the attack. Only one thing nearly wrecked the venture. As the howitzer was being readied, a host of yellow jackets swarmed out of their disrupted nest and attacked the gunners with stinging fury. Mosby's horse reared and almost threw its rider; the men scrambled for safety; and the rangers below waited vainly for the signal. The day was saved when artillery Sergeant A. G. Babcock blindly dashed through the swarm of wasps, beating at them with his hat, and yanked the halyard. A boom sounded over the valley and the attack was on.

As the Rangers swarmed over the wagon train from two directions, the Federal guards took refuge wherever they could find it. Wagons were overturned and looted of valuable stores, 75 vehicles were burned, 200 prisoners taken, and 600 horses and mules with 200 head of cattle captured. Minutes later the Rangers were on their way through Snicker's Gap to safety.

The raid on the wagon train was a body blow to Sheridan—not only in the loss of provisions, but in the damage to his pride and reputation in this first week of command. Nor did the news sit well in Washington, where the *Star* disparaged the "futile efforts of the Federal cavalry to catch these marauders," adding: "About the only aggressive enemy in [this neighborhood] is Mosby, and the only dangerous place appears to be the rear of our army on its line of communications . . . "

Grant was as disturbed as Sheridan, wiring the latter on August 16: "The families of most of Mosby's men are known and can be collected. I think they should be taken and kept . . . as hostages for the good conduct of Mosby and his men. When any of Mosby's men are caught, hang them without trial." He followed this up with another suggestion: "If you can possibly spare a division of cavalry, send them through Loudoun County, to destroy and carry off the crops, animals, Negroes, and all men under 50 years of age capable of bearing arms. In this way you will get many of Mosby's men."

Grant was sowing the seeds of a bloody crop of corpses in the Valley, and defining a new and ruthless code of warfare. Chivalry, becoming fragile with the prolongation of the war, was dying out. Causes and principles were yielding to blind fury and a craving for revenge.

Sheridan chose Custer to implement Grant's order for the rape of Loudoun County and extermination of the partisans. The Boy General took to the task with relish, ordering that "every barn and farmhouse in this immediate area be burned to the ground." A grim group of Mosby's Rangers watched the holocaust that blazed on one plantation, then opened fire on the arsonists. Before the partisans slipped away, eighteen of Custer's veterans lay dead.

Grant's no-mercy edict had, if anything, a catalyzing influence on Mosby. His partisans ranged everywhere, towing with them the little howitzer that Stuart had given Mosby when he organized the cavalry battalion. The howitzer blasted railroad tracks and locomotives, wagon trains, Federal camps and depots, and anything in blue that moved. The Union commander at Fairfax confessed that it was futile to try to catch the raiders. "The cavalry at my disposal is too cowed to be of use."

Robert E. Lee, who had exempted Mosby from his disbandment of guerilla groups and later raised the sandy-haired partisan to the rank of lieutenant colonel, saw the wisdom of both moves. He publicly praised Mosby's latest operational report, which showed, said Lee, "the skill of Colonel Mosby and the intelligence and courage of the officers and men in his command . . . "

> With the loss of little more than twenty men, he has killed, wounded and captured during the period embraced in the report about 1,200 of the enemy and taken more than 1,600 horses and mules, 230 beef cattle and eighty-five wagons, without counting smaller operations. The services rendered by Colonel Mosby in watching and reporting the enemy's movements have also been of great value.

As Sheridan pushed farther up the Valley, driving Early from Winchester and Fisher's Hill, his supply line back to Harpers Ferry became longer and more vulnerable. It would take 4,000 to 5,000 troops to guard the route effectively, he estimated, and no contingent fewer than 500 cavalry could pass in safety. Mosby, in late September, recognized the opportunity. He had been wounded in a recent skirmish, and sent Sam Chapman in his stead, with 120 hand-picked men, to attack a wagon train discovered approaching Front Royal from the Luray Valley.

Chapman, one-time divinity student, underestimated the train's escort. Two hundred guards, he thought. Actually, an entire brigade of Merritt's cavalry led by Colonel Lovell was following just behind. When Chapman attacked, so did Lovell's brigade, and in a furious battle to escape, six of Mosby's men were captured.

Remembering Grant's no-mercy order, the Federal officers knew what to do with them.

"The 'dark day' of 1864 is indelibly photographed in my memory," wrote Mrs. Davis-Roy of Front Royal, for it had been so arranged that the whole town should remember and be warned. The band marched slowly through the town, playing the death march. In front of the church, two of the six prisoners were shot. Farther along the route another was executed. Then down the street came two mounted troopers lynch-dragging a seventeen-year-old Mosby volunteer behind them. The boy was a native of Front Royal, and as the townspeople tried to free him, an officer put the lad out of his misery by emptying his pistol into him.

Two others still marched behind the band to their place of execution, and Mrs. Davis-Roy remembered:

> One of them was a splendid specimen of manhood—tall, well-knit frame, and a head of black, wavy hair floating in the wind. He looked like a knight. While I was watching them, General Custer, at the head of his division, rode by. He was dressed in a splendid suit of silk velvet, his saddle bow bound in silver or gold. In his hand he had a large branch of damsons which he picked and ate as he rode along. He was distinguished looking with his yellow locks resting on his shoulders.

Beneath a tree at the edge of town the two men were hoisted on horseback and the nooses placed around their necks. They were asked if they had anything to say.

"Mosby'll hang ten of you for every one of us," said William S. Overby, the wavy-haired man with the look of a knight.

The whip cracked; and when the suspended bodies had ceased twitching, a placard was attached to one, inscribed: "This will be the fate of Mosby and all his men."

Recovered from his wound, Mosby was back with his battalion when word came that the Manassas Gap Railroad, supplying Sheridan's army in the Shenandoah, was being rebuilt and repaired. With that news came an order from Lee, "Do all in your power to prevent construction of the road." All in his power was applied. The howitzer blasted great gaps in the tracks, work crews were killed or scattered, lumber and rails were destroyed—until all work was suspended.

When Grant agreed that these attacks could not be stopped, Sheridan shifted the burden of supplies to the Baltimore & Ohio Railroad north and south of the Potomac. Mosby zeroed in on the new target. At 9:15 P.M., October 13, an express train left Baltimore with nine passenger coaches and a car containing U.S. Army payroll money. Between Harpers Ferry and Martinsburg it rolled through a gap in the mountains and came to a resounding halt, derailed by the obstacles placed in its path.

Down from steep banks roared Mosby's rangers, surrounding the train and setting fire to the coaches when the passengers refused to leave. In the express car they pried open the paymaster's box containing $173,000 in greenbacks destined for the army. This was divided among the raiders, with Mosby, as was his custom, declining to accept his share.

In reporting on the "Greenback Raid" and other recent operations, Mosby wrote to General Lee that, in retaliation for the execution of his men at Front Royal, "It is my purpose to hang an equal number of Custer's men whenever I catch them." Lee sent the letter to War Secretary Seddon, endorsing the proposal in the light of "the cruel conduct of the enemy." Seddon in turn declared, "General Lee's instructions are cordially approved."

A few days later a grim ritual took place in the Village of Rectortown. Thirty Federal prisoners who had fallen into Mosby's hands drew slips of paper from a hat. Six of the seven who drew unlucky numbers were marched as close as possible to Sheridan's headquarters where their execution would get maximum notice. Unlike Custer, Mosby could not bring himself to watch the hangings, declaring later it was "the most loathsome act of his career." To one of the bodies was attached a note:

> These men have been hung in retaliation for an equal number of Colonel Mosby's men hung by order of General Custer at Front Royal. Measure for measure.

One week later Mosby sent a note to Sheridan via a courier who himself barely escaped being hanged by Custer's men, despite a flag of truce. The message, which explained that the prisoners had been executed as a consequence of the hangings at Front Royal, added:

> Hereafter any prisoners falling into my hands will be treated with the kindness due to their condition, unless some new act of barbarity shall compel me reluctantly to adopt a course of policy repulsive to humanity.

There were no further acts of barbarity against his men, Mosby noted in his *Memoirs*. Sheridan, in fact, advised his cavalry commanders that Mosby should be left alone — for now.

While Jubal Early's wounded army bivouaked at Fisher's Hill, Grant suggested that Sheridan move still farther south and cut the James River Canal and the Virginia Central Railroad feeding Lee and Richmond. Sheridan strongly objected. The fight at Tom's Brook had been a signal triumph for his cavalry; but the main body of Early's army was still intact and coming toward him down the Valley. Grant suggested that he come to Washington and talk it over.

On October 16 Sheridan started for the capital with a sizable cavalry detachment, leaving General Horatio Wright in charge of the army encamped at Cedar Creek. On the way to Washington he was handed a disturbing bit of information — a supposedly secret message his signal corps had intercepted from the Confederate semaphore station on Three Top Mountain in the Valley:

TO LIEUTENANT-GENERAL EARLY:
  Be ready to move as soon as my forces join you, and we will crush
Sheridan.
                        LONGSTREET, Lieutenant-General.

He suspected that the message was a plant, designed to scare him off.
Still, the words haunted him. If, conceivably, the dispatch were valid,
Longstreet's corps could double the size of Early's forces, to a point
outnumbering his own. He sent some of his cavalry back to camp, with a
warning to Wright: "Look well to your ground and be well prepared."
He advised the surrogate commander that he would be back Tuesday,
October 18, "if not sooner."

Early had not been reinforced by Longstreet; the semaphore message had been a ruse. But his hand was being forced by circumstance.
So well had Custer, Merritt, Powell, and their troopers destroyed the
crops and produce of the Valley, that his army could not survive by
standing still. "I was now compelled," he wrote, "to move back for want
of provisions and forage, or attack the enemy in his position with the
hope of driving him from it, and I determined to attack." Lee gave him
encouragement in this hope. "With your united force it can be accomplished."

Early had an advantage in the Confederate semaphore station on
Three Top Mountain from which he could view the enemy's deployment north of Cedar Creek. He could see Custer's cavalry far to the
west and rear, Merritt's division on the opposite side and also to the
rear, and Powell's division still farther to the right. This gave him hope
for a surprise attack on the Union left; and shortly after midnight of
October 19 he started his army rolling forward, men and officers
constrained to silence, leaving behind canteens and swords that could
rattle.

The cavalry was to synchronize with this forward movement, Rosser
on the left for a surprise attack on Custer, Lomax on the right to
pounce on Merritt. Rosser, detected by Custer's pickets, was again
intimidated, finding the enemy cavalry so well alerted that "all he could
do was watch it." Lomax, in turn, drove so far to the east and so deep
into Federal territory that he rode himself out of the battle altogether.

But the advancing infantry took the Federals by surprise, "the men
and officers driven from their beds, many of them not having time to
hurry into their clothes, except as they retreated half-awake and
terror-stricken from the overpowering numbers of the enemy. Their
own artillery, in conjunction with that of the enemy, was turned on
them, and long before it was light enough for their eyes, unaccustomed
to the dim light, to distinguish friend from foe, they were hurrying to
the rear intent on safety."

As each scattered unit of the camp broke to the rear, groggy with sleep and stunned by surprise, the Valley Pike to Winchester overflowed with men in blue. Units of Merritt's and Custer's cavalry formed a line across the road to block the stream of refugees, but nothing short of a miracle could stop them. More practically, Devin's and Lowell's brigades rode forward to form a defensive line to protect the fleeing infantry from Confederate pursuit.

But the pursuit was stalled by an epidemic common to victorious armies. All over the field Confederate troops were engaged in plundering the Union camps, breaking open chests and scrapping for the contents, looting wagons, stealing everything that they could get their hands on. "I got two nice tent flies, two fine blankets, a fine rubber cloth, two new overshirts and two pair of new shoes," wrote a Georgia private who also noted that many of the plunderers, possibly surfeited with liquid loot, "simply went to sleep."

Exasperated at this precious loss of time enabling the Federals to escape, Early ordered one battalion "to clear the camps and drive the men [back] to their commands." One battalion was not enough to distract the frenzied looters. Finally, "I sent all my staff-officers who could be spared to stop it if possible, and orders were sent to the division commanders to send for their men."

Singularly, throughout this fighting and confusion, one Federal unit stood like a granite cenotaph in the center of the field, General George Getty's division of the Sixth Corps. Positioned well back of the foremost line, the men had had time to close ranks and prepare for the attack. Assaulted from all sides they stood their ground as if encased in armor plate. General John Gordon suggested to Early a mass assault on the position.

"No need for that," said Early. "They'll go with the rest of them." And added, "We have had glory enough for one day."

For the moment his triumph was complete. He was in possession of the field, had captured almost all the enemy's artillery and supplies, and thousands of Federals were in retreat, down the Winchester pike, as far as eye could see.

Which, however, was not far enough.

Sheridan returned to Winchester the night of October 18, expecting to rejoin the army at Cedar Creek "at my leisure" the next day. He slept only fitfully if at all, perhaps remembering the spurious (or were they?) words, "Be ready when I join you, and we will crush Sheridan . . . crush Sheridan . . . crush Sheridan." He was alerted at six by the sound of artillery fire from the direction of Cedar Creek and asked the officer on picket duty what it meant. Probably some morning reconnaissance, the officer told him, simply banging away at the enemy to see what he was up to.

Aroused by a sense of foreboding he breakfasted quickly, ordered his black horse Rienzi saddled, and set off with his mounted escort for Cedar Creek. As they rode through the streets of Winchester they got a curious reception. "I noticed that there were many women at the windows and doors of the houses, who kept shaking their skirts at us and who were otherwise markedly insolent in their demeanor." He attributed this peculiar action to "their well known and perhaps natural prejudices. . . . "

But as the group reached the Valley Pike, the shaking skirts began to assume an ominous meaning. The artillery fire was increasing and coming closer, suggesting that the women of Winchester had learned by the "grape-vine telegraph" of some major development of which he was unaware. He pressed forward with the escort as far as Mill Creek, a half mile south of town where —

> . . . just as we made the crest of the rise beyond the stream, there burst upon our view the appalling spectacle of a panic-stricken army — hundreds of slightly wounded men, throngs of others unhurt but utterly demoralized, and baggage-wagons by the score, all pressing to the rear in hopeless confusion, telling only too plainly that disaster had occurred at the front. On accosting some of the fugitives, they assured me that the army was broken up, in full retreat, and that all was lost . . .

Be ready . . . and we will crush Sheridan.

His first thought was to check and rally the retreating army when it reached Winchester and form a new line of defense. But that was to accept defeat at Cedar Creek. So: "I was fixing in my mind what I should do. . . "

> I was sure the troops had confidence in me . . . and as at other times they had seen me present at slightest sign of trouble or distress, I felt that I ought to try now to restore their broken ranks, or, failing that, to share their fate because of what they had done hitherto.

It was a big gamble, to stake everything on one's ability to quell a panic and reverse the course of a stampede. But, noted Wesley Merritt, the effect of Sheridan's appearance was electric. As he passed the first band of broken, frightened men stumbling toward the rear, he raised his hat in greeting. And they in turn, wrote Sheridan, "threw up their hats, shouldered their muskets, and as I passed along turned to follow with enthusiasm and cheers." And one by one the other groups he passed fell in behind him — a martial Pied Piper leading his children back to the gates of Koppenberg Hill.

Getting closer to Newtown, where the panic was more intense, the flight more precipitous he waved his cap at the stragglers and shouted, "Face the other way, boys; face the other way! We are going back to our camps! We are going to lick them out of their boots!" With several more miles to go the General spurred Rienzi to a gallop, shouting to all he passed, "Face the other way!"—until he reached the shattered front where cavalry commander Torbert greeted him with "My God! I am glad you've come," and the impetuous Custer threw his arms around Little Phil and kissed him on both cheeks.

Getty's division, though pushed back, still stood as a solid monument on which to rally. Ignoring enemy fire Sheridan rode to the crest of a hill, in full view of the mass below and waved his hat. Backward, forward, backward, forward. There were cheers from below, and then a silent, more spectacular response. A flag arose, and then another. All over the field the battleflags sprouted like a magic crop—blues, oranges, purples, pinks, and golds—as the regimental standard bearers, who had lain beside their staffs to escape artillery fire, stood erect to signal their units to fall in and take their places.

What happened next was summarized by Wesley Merritt, writing of Sheridan:

> He rapidly made the changes necessary in the lines, and then ordered an advance. The cavalry on the left charged down on the enemy in their front, scattering them in all directions. The infantry, not to be outdone by the mounted men, moved forward in quick time and impetuously charged the lines of Gordon, which broke and fled. It took less time to drive the enemy from the field than it had for them to take it.

A bottleneck formed on the bridge over Tumbling Run as the fleeing Confederates jammed across it, but worse awaited on the other side. Wrote war correspondent Whitelaw Reid:

> Custer charged down in the fast gathering darkness to the west of the pike, Devin to the east of it, and on either flank of the fleeing rout they flung themselves. Nearly all the rebel transportation was captured, the camps and artillery were regained; up to Fisher's Hill the road was jammed with artillery, caissons, and ambulances; prisoners came streaming back faster than the provost marshal could provide them. It was the end of Early's army; the end of campaigning in the beautiful Valley of the Shenandoah.

It was indeed the end for Early. He had lost all that he had captured in the morning, and all his own artillery and wagon trains besides. His army had suffered more than 3,000 casualties, dead and wounded, with some 1,200 of its number taken prisoner. The Confederates limped back to New Market, thirty miles down the Pike, and except for minor incidents and skirmishes, the Valley would hear little more of Jubal Early for many months to come. "Had my cavalry been sufficient to contend with that of the enemy," he would always maintain, "the rout [of the Federals] in the morning would have been complete."

George Armstrong Custer would, expectedly, take the lion's share of credit for the victory, but he included his troops in telling them, "Your conduct throughout was sublimely heroic and without a parallel in the annals of warfare. . . . You have surrounded the name of the Third Cavalry Division with a halo of glory as enduring as time."

Though Sheridan received "the thanks of the nation" from President Lincoln, he gave Custer the honor of taking the captured battle flags to Washington. There was a triumphant ride down Pennsylvania Avenue, of which the *Star* reported: "Washington has not had many such sensations. The soldiers in the city were jubilant, and when they met Custer in the street would give him a hug; and some of the old soldiers would kiss Custer's hand." Secretary Stanton was considerably less ecstatic. He refused to let the crate with the battle flags be stored in the War Department, for fear it contained explosives designed to blow him up.

Sheridan was above the ordinary paeans of the press, the apotheosizing headlines, and the songs and ballads written in his honor. One of the latter, however, written by Thomas Buchanan Read, paid overdue credit to the horse Rienzi as much as to the general who had saved the day. An excerpt:

> With foam and with dust the black charger was gray;
> By the flash of his eye, and his red nostril's play,
> He seemed to the whole great army to say:
> "I have brought you Sheridan all the way
> From Winchester, down to save the day!"
> . . . .
> And when their statues are placed on high,
> Under the dome of the Union sky,
> The American Soldiers' Temple of Fame,
> There with the glorious General's name,
> Be it said, in letters both bold and bright,
> "Here is the steed that saved the day,
> By carrying Sheridan into the fight,
> From Winchester—twenty miles away!"

19

TWILIGHT OF THE WESTERN
CAVALIERS

IT WAS MORE THAN THE SEASON OF SHORTENING DAYS AND EARLY nights beyond the Appalachians. It was the twilight of hope for the Confederacy in the West. Not yet despair, for the names of Forrest and Morgan still streamed like banners in the sunset sky. But Forrest, whether or not he knew it, had left Tennessee forever. And Morgan? To pick up Morgan's story, one must go back a year—to November, 1863.

"MORGAN, 6 OTHERS, FLEE PRISON" read the newspaper headline that elated the South and shocked the North:

> Columbus, Ohio, Nov. 28—Confederate Gen. John Hunt Morgan and six of his captains, held prisoner at the penitentiary here, escaped early yesterday morning, virtually four months to the day after they had been captured at New Lisbon, Ohio.
>
> Following a plan conceived by Capt. T.H. Hines, the group began digging a tunnel from beneath the floor of Hines' cell on Nov. 4, according to a taunting note which the escapees left Warden N. Merion. Even though the cell was inspected daily, no jailor thought to check the carpetbag which hid the hole in the cell floor.

The escape sounded so superbly simple that many could not accept the given explanation. It was rumored that they had bribed the jailers with money brought to them by rebel visitors; that they had had accomplices inside the jail and out; that they had been slyly released through the machinations of the Copperhead conspiracy, with which

Tom Hines was known to be connected, and in which St. Leger Gren-fell was later implicated. None of these charges could be substantiated, and Basil Duke's account was generally accepted.

Ever since they had arrived at the Penitentiary in mid-summer of 1863, Morgan's men had thought of nothing but escape. But how to circumvent the barred cells, the courtyard guarded by police dogs, and the surrounding wall 25-feet high? It was Tom Hines who came up with a solution, suggested by his reading of Les Miserables. The concrete floor of their ground-level cells remained dry even in the dampest weather, indicating the likely existence of an air chamber underneath. Dig down into that chamber, and tunnel out from there.

Using blunt table knives stolen from the mess, and working in shifts, the men scraped a hole through the flooring, and for twenty days burrowed like moles through the earth beneath the cell until they reached a point below the courtyard. The excavated earth was hidden inside the mattresses, and the hole concealed when guards threatened to inspect the cell, which was fortunately seldom. Choosing the rainy night of November 27 when the dogs would be in their kennels, the handful of prisoners, led by Hines and Morgan, crept through the tunnel, and scaled the outer wall with a rope comprised of interwoven sheets.

Outside they separated, Morgan and Hines slipping aboard a pas-senger train bound from Columbus to Cincinnati. There was nothing about their prison garments that differed greatly from civilian clothes, and for double deception Morgan sat next to a uniformed Federal major whose company would help divert suspicion from himself. As the train passed the outlying penitentiary, the Union officer identified the building to his traveling companion.

"Over there is where they put the Rebel General Morgan for safe-keeping."

"I hope they'll always keep him as safe as he is now," said Morgan.

Nearing Cincinnati the two fugitives went to the rearmost car, pulled the emergency cord, and dropped off as the train slowed down. Min-utes later they were on the banks of the Ohio, the river nemesis of their July raid. They found a willing and obliging urchin with a skiff who rowed them across to the Kentucky shore, back to familiar, sometimes friendly territory.

On stolen horses they made their way south toward Tennessee. Not to jeopardize their freedom by an attempt at mass escape, Basil Duke had remained in the penitentiary, but Duke continued to follow Mor-gan's movements through second-hand reports. As Morgan traveled across Kentucky:

> Everybody vied with each other as to who should show him the most attention—even to the negroes; and young ladies of refinement

begged the honor of cooking his meals. He assumed more than one disguise, and played many parts in his passage through Kentucky — now passing as a Government contractor buying cattle, and again as a quartermaster or inspector.

By now, of course, news of the escape had led to massive Federal pursuit. Jerry Boyle, who had smarted so often from Morgan's trickery, took up the chase. "Morgan is believed to be in Kentucky," he told his superiors. "If so — and it is possible — I will catch him." But Morgan and Hines were already at the Tennessee River, and approaching the south bank by ferry.

But trouble awaited them across the river. Hines sighted a sizable Federal patrol arrayed to meet them. Signaling Morgan to make his escape, he galloped up to the approaching Federals, shouting that he was a Home Guard with information on the fleeing prisoners. He offered to lead the patrol to "Morgan's hideout," misleading them up a rural cul-de-sac. At this point Hines was arrested as a spy and threatened with hanging, but miraculously talked his captors into letting him survive.

A week later Morgan himself, alone but aided by Southern sympathizers as he journeyed through East Tennessee, arrived at Columbia, South Carolina, in time to spend Christmas with his wife; and after the holidays he took Mattie with him on a triumphant entry into Richmond. Though Braxton Bragg was now adviser to the President, and had never forgiven Morgan for ignoring orders and crossing the Ohio in this latest raid, the capital gave him a rousing welcome.

"Morgan, our escaped hero, is here," wrote Mary Chesnut in her diary. "I went off to see the parade, and hear the music, and listen to Mayor M. introduce Morgan to the crowd." Mayor M. followed the playing of the "Marseillaise" with a speech describing Morgan as "the Marion of the Second Revolution" and "a gift from Providence," and castigating his Ohio jailers who "in their futile efforts to degrade you, have only elevated you in the estimation of all Confederate citizens, and the whole civilized world." Morgan replied modestly with thanks for this reception, and "the hope that my future career will prove that I am not unworthy of the honor you have done me."

Among the dignitaries on the platform was J. E. B. Stuart; it was the first time these two great cavalry leaders had appeared together. According to the Richmond *Examiner*, Stuart rose to say for himself and Morgan that

> some people had gotten up the idea that they were rivals. If a desire to harm the enemy most and advance the Southern Cause could be called rivalry. . . . He was glad to know that the sleepless blade of the gallant Kentuckian would soon again be flashing. . . . He must express the gratification he felt at the honor done to the gallant Morgan.

Attending the ceremonies also were two unexpected luminaries. Captain Tom Hines had not only talked his captors out of hanging him, but had engineered another escape to join his chief at Richmond before slipping away to become involved in the Northwest Conspiracy. And suddenly too appeared George St. Leger Grenfell. Old St. Lege had overcome his earlier prejudice against the married Morgan, and had arrived to serve again under "the only Cavalry Officer except Forrest in the Service."

Morgan would need him. For his goal now was to reassemble and reconstitute his old command, as many of them as were left, and get enough new recruits to rebuild his brigade. It would not be easy. With Bragg and the War Department holding a dim view of his disregard for orders (and Bragg negotiating to have his former subordinate court-martialed), he would need Grenfell's diplomacy to smooth things over. He appointed the Englishman his agent, to remain in Richmond to lobby for money, horses, and provisions for his future cavalry.

Morgan himself went to Decatur, Georgia, to set up his cavalry command post. At Decatur, the first week in February, he published a proclamation:

> Soldiers! I am once more among you, after a long and painful imprisonment. I am anxious to be again in the field. I therefore call on all the soldiers of my command to assemble at once at the rendezvous established at this place. . . . Come at once, and come cheerfully, for I want no man in my command who has been sent to his duty by a provost-marshal. The work before us will be arduous, and will require brave hearts and willing hands. Let no man falter or delay!
>
> JOHN H. MORGAN

They came from all parts of East and West, singly, in isolated groups, in companies: more than 300 of those who had escaped the trap at Buffington, another 300 who had been left behind in the Ohio raid because of illness, a surviving battalion of the famed Second Kentucky Regiment, and virtually all those who had fought under Forrest at Chickamauga. By early May, Morgan's new command had expanded to roughly 2,200 to 2,400 men.

A third of the men, however, were still without mounts, inadequately uniformed, and poorly armed. Grenfell had been able to accomplish little. In a warm letter to his chief, St. Lege had written "I only hope, General, that our Rulers will . . . not again place you, the most esteemed Cavalry Officer of the Confederacy, under the orders of any cavalry commander who . . . would cramp your energies and render you powerless to carry out any measure of importance with success."

Officially, Morgan was attached to Joseph E. Johnston's Army of Tennessee, now facing Sherman's "army group" in northwest Georgia.

And technically that put him under General Wheeler, Johnston's chief of cavalry. Possibly that was what Grenfell was referring to—but who could tell? As abruptly as he had reappeared in Richmond, Grenfell disappeared again, taking a boat to Cuba by which route he would return to the United States, accept amnesty from the Federal government, then go to Chicago to join a conspiracy to undermine that government.

If Morgan were to have the needed horses, his men would have to get them, preferably in Kentucky. Once before, he had proposed another raid into that state, and the War Department turned him down. Now, in late May, he would not ask again, but simply go. Assembling his brigade at Wytheville, Virginia, he informed the Confederate War Department on May 31 that he was starting out for Kentucky, this time ostensibly to take the pressure off Johnston in Georgia by disrupting Sherman's communications.

He did not wait for a reply. The next day the brigade was on its way through the Cumberlands into Kentucky, increased in numbers to 2,700. Only about a third of this total would have qualified as "Morgan's men," of the caliber of the early Second Kentucky Cavalry. They were not the same eager, hard-riding youths, anxious to serve under Morgan and to prove themselves in battle. As in other parts of the Confederacy, as well as in the North, the recruits of 1864 were looking for an acceptable alternative to serving with the infantry, believing that the cavalry lived better, under less stringent discipline, with a greater chance of material gain.

Morgan himself appeared to have changed in some respects, more than in the fact, as noted by Confederate Chief of Ordnance Josiah Gorgas, that "His hair has not quite recovered from the cropping it received in the Ohio penitentiary." Some of his confidence seemed cropped as well. He led with a less sure hand, less purposeful direction. Aware now that General Stephen Burbridge, Union Commander of the District of Kentucky, was on the watch for him in the vicinity, he was not anxious to force an encounter. True, Burbridge's cavalry had him outnumbered by two to one, but up to now Morgan had never bothered much about the odds.

Basil Duke, of course, was not with him. Duke was still languishing in prison, although about to be exchanged. But following by hearsay his commander's fortunes, he wrote of this period that "the great esprit of the Kentucky cavalier" diminished after his imprisonment.

For the next seven days, over rocky roads and along inhospitable trails, the column trudged westward, averaging thirty miles a day and reaching the town of Mount Sterling on June 8. The 300-man Federal garrison, hopelessly outnumbered, surrendered at the first shot; and the troopers poured into Mount Sterling with the cheering arrogance of conquerors. Perhaps it was the long trudge over the mountains, with insufficient food and rest, that provoked the lawless plundering that followed. Houses and stores were entered and food and clothing taken.

The crowning outrage occurred when a Confederate officer, described as having a blond beard and a German accent, entered the Farmer's Bank of Kentucky and presented a note with Morgan's adjutant's signature demanding the surrender of all money on deposit—$72,000, as it turned out—on the threat that the town would be otherwise destroyed. Told of the incident, Morgan was duly angered; the signature was a forgery; and the officer, later identified as Surgeon R. R. Goode, had disappeared with the loot—leaving Morgan with a stain upon his reputation that would never be erased.

There was no time to straighten out the mess or bring some order back to the brigade. General Burbridge, with a large force of mounted Federals, had heard of the raid and was already within striking distance of Mount Sterling. Rallying as much of his expeditionary column as he could, and leaving behind some 800 unruly troopers to divide the spoils (and to be themselves divided and many captured by Burbridge's pursuing Federals) Morgan swung north to Lexington, thirty-three miles away.

Here, in his home town, he found enough horses in Federal depots to mount those of his troopers still on foot. And here he drew more infamy upon his head. "Though the stay of Morgan's command in Lexington was brief," reported the local paper, "he made good use of his time—as many empty shelves and pockets will attest." According to another account:

> Once more looters took over, and this time veterans joined the pillage. Another bank was robbed, though more forthrightly than the one two days ago; the celebrants simply put a pistol to the cashier's head and made him open the vault, from which they took $10,000. Several buildings were set afire and whiskey stores were stripped, with the result that a good many troopers, too drunk to stay on a horse, had to be loaded onto wagons for the ride to Cynthiana, thirty miles northeast. Morgan had learned there were supplies and a 500-man garrison there, and he was determined to have or destroy them both.

The Cynthiana raid, disastrous in the end, had a temporary tinge of victory. No sooner had Morgan's men taken possession of the town on June 11 than Morgan's old enemy, Edward Hobson, with 1,200 of Burbridge's troops was seen approaching. Briefly Morgan became the master strategist again. Dividing his forces, he sent one regiment charging the front of Hobson's column, while two other units circled around to attack the flanks and rear. Facing annihilation, Hobson surrendered—a surrender sweet to Morgan who had lost so many men to Hobson's troops at Buffington the year before.

But his satisfaction was short-lived. Following in Hobson's wake came Burbridge's main force of cavalry, 5,200 strong. Morgan's troops, after the losses at Mount Sterling, were down to 1,400, many out of ammunition. When the latter shortage was pointed out to Morgan, he responded with old-time bravado, "You hold your position at all hazard. We can whip them with empty guns."

It was an empty promise. When Burbridge attacked at dawn, the gray riders held their positions valiantly until the cry of "out of ammunition!" sounded, to be echoed down the line. As one of Morgan's men recalled, "Our whole command was soon forced back into the streets of the town, routed and demoralized. The confusion was indescribable. . . . There was much shooting, swearing and yelling—some from sheer mortification were crying."

An attempt at an orderly retreat collapsed, and the men were ordered to escape as best they could. One fifth of the division was killed or captured; the rest fled with their commander. Wrote Private George Mosgrove: "While falling back on the town I saw General Morgan, on his step-trotting roan horse, going toward the Augusta road. He was 'skimming' along at an easy pace, looking up at our broken lines—and softly whistling. I was glad to see him getting away, for had he been captured he would doubtless have fared badly."

He would fare badly no matter what. Arriving at Abingdon, Virginia, on June 20, he was minus half the troops that he had started with three weeks before; was out of favor with the War Department for having taken off without authority; and his reputation had been badly tarnished by the atrocities committed on the raid, the Mount Sterling bank robbery in particular. Needing a lift in spirits, he gave himself one of dubious authority, issuing at Abingdon two days later his General Order Number One: "I hereby assume command of the Department of Southwest Virginia and Eastern Tennessee." Whatever they might say of him, they could not hold him down.

On August 30, 1864, after two cheerless summer months that saw Atlanta tottering and Petersburg invested, the order came from Richmond that "Brig-Gen. J. H. Morgan be suspended from command and a court of inquiry . . . be at once constituted and convened, to meet at Abingdon, Virginia, on the 10th day of September next." It was charged, among other things, that Morgan had authorized the theft at the Mount Sterling Bank, and that the money taken had been misappropriated by the culprits. Further, that Morgan himself had taken no steps to investigate the matter. All true. And though Morgan shrugged off the charges as not "thoroughly sifted," he was a sorely troubled man.

What hurt him most was that his own state of Kentucky had begun to see him as a renegade, and some of his officers supported Richmond's charges. Colonel R. A. Alston of Morgan's division and former editor of the *Vidette* declared that "the conduct of our command was such as to cause a man to blush at the name of Confederate soldiers." It was not Morgan's fate alone. Throughout the Confederate States, divided and shrunken since the fall of Vicksburg, the cavalry had, in certain quarters, fallen into semi-disrepute. The shortage of mounts and provisions had turned them into "horse thieves, robbers, plunderers"—discipline, it was charged, had all but disappeared. To a degree, Morgan's decline was part of this disintegration, which in turn was a symptom of the waning of the South.

During that summer Basil Duke—having been finally released from prison and exchanged—had rejoined his chief at Abingdon where Morgan was living with his wife. Duke was dismayed at the Kentuckian's appearance. "He was greatly changed. His face wore a weary, care-worn expression, and his manner was totally destitute of its former ardor and enthusiasm." Among Morgan's enemies, former begrudging admiration turned into contempt, Burbridge reporting of the rout at Cynthiana, "General Morgan, when he learned the tide of battle had turned against him, had ignominiously fled with his choicest troops."

Though he had been suspended from command, his appointed successor, General John C. Echols, had not yet arrived from the Valley. And during these few days of grace before the hearing on September 10, word came of a Union expeditionary force approaching Bull's Gap, Tennessee. Whether or not Morgan saw this as a chance to thwart the Richmond proceedings, his duty appeared clear. In Echols's absence, he must take steps to check this threatened invasion of Virginia.

On August 29, again acting without authority, he led his depleted column of 1,600 troops toward Bull's Gap and five days later arrived at Greeneville, a town of divided loyalties in the shadow of the Smoky Mountains.

At Greeneville, pickets were placed at all likely approaches and the troops were bivouacked on the fringes of the town. The general and his staff put up at the home of Mrs. Catherine Williams, whom Morgan had visited in the past. Mrs. Williams was believed to be pro-Confederate in her sympathies, but had played host to transient officers of both sides in the war. She had two sons in the Confederate service, another in the Union army; and the wife of the latter, Lucy Williams, was living with her now. The stage was set for one of the saddest episodes in the tragic drama of the war.

Precisely what happened that evening can only be pieced together from conflicting versions. It was a hot night, brewing up a thunderstorm, and as Morgan and Major Charles Withers and others of Morgan's staff sat in the parlor with Mrs. Williams, chatting and sipping wine, Lucy Williams offered to ride to the nearby farm to get some watermelons for the guests. She left the house by buggy (some said on Morgan's borrowed horse), and disappeared into the misty world of legend. By the time she returned, where she went and why would hardly matter.

When Lucy failed to reappear, Morgan and his staff retired to their second story chambers for the night. It was a restless night for Morgan, who appeared more taciturn than usual, paced the floor, and peered through the window to see that the pickets were keeping their positions in the rain. At dawn, he instructed Major Charles Withers to send couriers to the troopers' bivouac, alerting the men to be ready to march again at seven. That would give them another hour to get their small-arms dry.

Suddenly, rifle fire—from one direction, then another. Morgan hastily pulled on boots and trousers over his nightshirt, and he, Withers and Major C. W. Gassett rushed to the window. The street, though covered with a layer of morning mist, was solid blue. The house was surrounded by Union cavalry, rifles at the ready. Withers and Gassett suggested surrender as the better part of valor.

"It is no use for me," said Morgan. "They've sworn never to take me prisoner again."

There was no sign of the sentries; no way to signal or get word to Morgan's cavalry outside the town. Morgan told Withers to cover him with a pistol, while he made a dash for the horses in the stable.

As the Federal troops began pounding on the door, Withers saw Morgan slip out the back and race across the yard. His white nightshirt was a perfect target. A dozen rifles snapped at once. Withers heard the cry, "My God!" and saw the general's body pitch into the bushes. Then another hoarse cry with the Yankee rasp: "I've killed the damned horse thief!"

Gassett escaped but Withers and the rest of Morgan's staff were taken prisoner. Union soldiers carried the general's body with some respect into Mrs. Williams's house. In the Confederate camps, Morgan's troops had heard the shooting, and prepared to storm the town and extricate the general, unaware that he was dead. Their impulsive charge was repulsed by General Alvin Gillem's Union Cavalry, with discouraging losses. Retreating to Rheatown 14 miles away, they sent back a patrol to see what had happened. They found the Federals gone, and the general's body laid out for burial.

It was hard for the troops to accept the fact of Morgan's death. Many had ridden with him since the beginning of the war; he had seemed shining and forever young, and indestructible. Any minute, they felt, he must return, perhaps on Black Bess, with the jaunty feather in his cap. True, he had changed greatly in the last few months, become waspish, moody, and unpredictable. But they would remember him as he was in Kentucky when the war broke out, and the Lexington Rifles took a vow that "Morgan's law is our law."

Wrote Lieutenant Kelion Peddicord:

> Any one of us—all of us—would gladly have died in his defense, and each one would have envied the man who lost his life defending him. So much was he trusted that his men never dreamed of failing him in anything that he attempted. In all engagements he was our guiding star and hero.

Basil Duke would always believe that it was Lucy Williams, wife of a Union soldier, who had ridden that night to the nearest Union outpost to inform the Federals of Morgan's presence in her mother-in-law's house. No one would ever know for sure, and Lucy herself was happy to become and to remain a Mata Hari type of legend—riding the roads of Tennessee in her black riding habit with bugle-trimming, her hat with a long blue plume—a woman of enduring mystery.

To Duke the tragedy of the betrayal, if indeed that was what it was, lay in the loss of "the greatest partisan leader the world ever saw"; and in Richmond, where all pending charges against Morgan vanished with the wind, the *Examiner* proclaimed: "This is a distressing blow to the Confederacy . . . The pride of the people was very much interwoven with the achievements of Morgan."

If the people of backwoods Tennessee professed to see, on moonlit nights, the figure of Lucy Williams riding like a witch across the countryside, black cloak streaming in the wind, how many people in Tennessee, Kentucky, Indiana, and Ohio, would see in their nightmares the ghost of Morgan, and Morgan's Terrible Men, with Bowie knives and pistols, galloping up the glen?

With Morgan gone, the Confederate West pinned much of its hopes on Nathan Bedford Forrest. Hood's defeat at Nashville on December 15 and 16 had not been a defeat of Forrest, who had been dispatched with most of his troops to Murfreesboro. According to General James Wilson, "The fortunate absence of Forrest, with a large part of his cavalry, relieved the operations of the Federal cavalry from the great peril it would otherwise have incurred . . . Had his whole cavalry force advanced against me, it is possible that it would have succeeded in driving us back."

And in screening Hood's retreat from Nashville, Forrest had shown that rare facility for highlighting a defeat with glints of victory. Whenever a chance presented, his cavalry turned on their pursuers with bared fangs, countercharging and slashing at their tormentors as they had on their retreat from Shiloh. They fought until they reached the Tennessee and Hood's army had crossed to safety.

To Hood's Army of Tennessee, "ragged, barefoot, bloody, without food and without hope," Forrest and his rear guard were a tonic for despair. In this hour of trial, the infantry noted, the general "spoke in his usual cheerful and defiant tone. . . . Not a man was brought in contact with him who did not feel strengthened and invigorated. . . ." Wrote Captain Walter Goodman of Chalmer's staff, "At no time in his whole career was the fortitude of General Forrest in adversity, and his power of infusing his own cheerfulness into those under his command, more strikingly exhibited than at this crisis."

Leave it to the enemy to have the final word. Federal General Thomas, who reported the Army of Tennessee as a "disheartened rabble" unable to rally to any organized resistance, added the underscored sentence: *The rear-guard, however, was undaunted and firm, and did its work bravely to the last.*"

After crossing the Tennessee River on December 27, Forrest established a temporary camp at Corinth, later to shift to the vicinity of West Point, Mississippi. When Hood relinquished command of the Army of Tennessee to General Richard Taylor, the Wizard of the Saddle found himself alone, "left to defend as well as can be done this section of the country." But there was one recompense. On February 28 Forrest was promoted to lieutenant general, commanding all Confederate cavalry in General Richard Taylor's Department.

Yet any elation he might normally have felt was tinged with gloom. Talking with Major Powhatan Ellis of his staff, he remarked that it "will only be a question of time" before General Lee would be forced "to leave Virginia or surrender." He had earlier stated: "To my mind it is evident that the end is not far off."

To some extent, he reflected bitterly, his cavalry had been sacrificed, on the long retreat from Nashville, to the survival of the army. His command which had numbered 6,000 troops when joined by Jackson the month before, was down to a scant 3,000, many without shoes, mounts, or decent weapons. So at year's end he gave those who were native to the region a 20-day furlough to return home for horses and new clothing. There would be a bonus for those who brought back a deserter or a new recruit.

During this interval, meanwhile, Federal cavalry leader James H. Wilson reorganized and strengthened his cavalry corps to make it, as generally admitted, one of the finest mounted forces in the Western hemisphere—five divisions totaling 22,000 men. Wilson's personal stature in the West was assuming the proportions of Sheridan's image in the East, both usurpers of Confederate superiority in the cavalry arena of the war. Less flamboyant than Sheridan but equally aggressive and resourceful, Grant had considered Wilson just the man to reorganize and vitalize the Western cavalry, and Sherman had agreed.

Wilson's ordained target was Forrest, as it had been during Hood's campaign in Tennessee. "I would like to have Forrest hunted down and killed," wrote Sherman from Savannah, "but I doubt if we can do that just yet." Wilson believed otherwise. He set his sights on the city of Selma on the Alabama River, a railroad town and a key Confederate manufacturing center with foundries, arsenals, and workshops. A thrust at Selma would draw Forrest to the city's defense, and force a final showdown between Union and Confederate cavalry in the Southern Heartland.

For this expedition Wilson assembled three of his five divisions numbering 12,500 men, all, he reported, "in magnificent condition, well armed, splendidly mounted, perfectly clad and equipped." They would be accompanied by three batteries of horse artillery, canvas pontoons for crossing rivers, and a train of 250 wagons of supplies—for this was to be something new in cavalry: a massive, juggernaut-type invasion.

Forrest responded as Wilson had expected, directing his scattered brigades to rendezvous, and heading for Selma with his mounted escort the last week in March. The two commanders made indirect contact through a meeting at Rienzi, called under a flag of truce to discuss the treatment and exchange of prisoners. Captain Lewis Hosea, representing Wilson at the rendezvous, left a verbal impression of the Wizard of the Saddle in these final days:

> . . . the rich gray uniform with its embroidered collar (a wreath of gold on black ground enclosing three silver stars) added much to the effect produced. His habitual expression seemed rather subdued and thoughtful, but when his face lighted up with a smile, which ripples all over his features, the effect is really charming. . . . He speaks of his success with a soldierly vanity, and expresses the kindliest feelings toward prisoners and wounded.

On March 31 an initial clash of arms occurred at Montevallo, on the railroad north of Selma, where Wilson found that "Forrest was in our front. We were face to face at last. True to his own rule, he was striving . . . to strike the first blow." Wilson guessed wrong. Only a part of Forrest's command was on his front, Roddey's brigade and fragments of other units. Forrest was hoping to avoid a fight until Chalmers's and

Jackson's division could catch up with him. But time was running out. Wrote Robert Selph Henry:

> The last battle had begun—a running fight which was to last forty-eight hours, almost without intermission, and to stretch from Six Mile Creek, below Montevallo, back to Selma, fifty miles away, in which Wilson's men went at their work with a dash and a power that knew no stopping. As their commander gleefully commented, they "had the bulge on Forrest and held it to the end . . . fairly turning his own rules of war against himself."

The battle spilled south the next day, April 1, to the banks of Bogler's Creek, where Forrest's cavalry turned to make a stand. When the Federals charged with raised sabers, the general ordered his men to draw their revolvers but hold their fire till the attackers were upon them. There resulted, according to John Allen Wyeth, "one of the most terrific hand-to-hand conflicts which occurred between cavalry soldiers during the war. It was a test between the saber in the hands of as brave a lot of men as ever rode horses and the six-shooter in the hands of experts that were just as desperately brave."

Forrest's headquarters flag, near which he stood, made him a conspicuous target for the enemy. Wrote one of his escorts, Lieutenant George Cowan, "I saw General Forrest surrounded by six Federals at one time, and they were all slashing at him." From one of these attackers, Captain J. D. Taylor, Forrest received his fourth wound in combat, a gash on his arm from the captain's saber before he could shoot his adversary dead (his twenty-ninth and next to last hand-to-hand victim of the war). Forrest himself would have been killed, he later reported, "if that boy had known enough to give me the point of the saber instead of the edge."

Again Forrest withdrew, this time behind the fortified lines around Selma, hoping to hold this position until the greater portion of his cavalry arrived. To strengthen his limited force, Forrest reportedly ordered that every able-bodied male in Selma "must go into the works or into the river." He placed this citizen soldiery in the center of his defenses, flanked on both sides by his cavalry. The latter numbered less than 1,500 men, his mainstay against an attack force of 9,000 which Wilson was prepared to hurl against him.

The assault came at dusk of April 2—Forrest's last battle of the war and fought without the support of his two principal divisions. For the defenders, as the Federal cavalry steamrolled into town, it was hopeless from the start. According to Wilson's account, the militia broke first, allowing the Federals to plunge through the gap and come on Forrest's forces from the rear. Forrest and Roddey barely escaped capture, to flee with a small body of their troopers across the river and to the east.

Total rout, utter defeat. No note on which to end four years of bitter fighting from which Forrest's cavalry had never flinched and during which Forrest had become, in Grant's words, "about the ablest cavalry general in the South." He and Wilson would meet again, but only as reconciled opposites, with nothing left to fight for. And that, for Forrest, was the essence of the tragedy.

20

"A FINAL BLAZE OF GLORY"

SPRING NORMALLY COMES EARLY IN VIRGINIA. EARLIER THIS YEAR OF 1865, it seemed, than formerly, perhaps to compensate for an exceptionally bitter winter and one pregnant with anticipation. "By the first of February," Grant wrote, "all preparations were completed for the final march"—Sherman from Savannah to the Carolinas to pursue Joe Johnston to the death, Grant to launch his last great effort against Lee and Richmond.

"Winter quarters in the Valley had been, on the whole, of an attractive character for our cavalry," wrote Frank Burr with Sheridan's forces in the Shenandoah. "The six weeks of needed rest . . . in the crisp, cold winter days of that delightful region." But by the last week in February, Sheridan was on the move again. Wesley Merritt had replaced Torbert as chief of cavalry, with his two divisions headed by Tom Devin and George Armstrong Custer.

On March 2 the cavalry descended upon Jubal Early making his last stand of the war at Waynesboro west of the Blue Ridge. Strongly entrenched, Early had boasted that Sheridan would not penetrate the positions held by his two brigades of infantry and Rosser's cavalry. But, wrote Burr, "Custer was in his front, sweeping all before him, and without waiting for support, the golden-maned trooper fell upon Early's lines. Some fierce fighting ensued, the Union troopers charging boldly up to the earthworks and leaping their horses over them. The Confederates met them as boldly . . . but the invincible Michiganders and others of Custer's following, swept onward, actually wiping out Early's command."

It was not only the end of Early's little army but the end of his career, with the added humiliation of seeing virtually all his men taken prisoner. To Custer's gratification it was the last appearance of Tom Rosser in the Shenandoah, after his boastful arrival five months earlier as "the Savior of the Valley." But Rosser would challenge him again when "Texas" Tom, with what remained of Early's cavalry, joined the Army of Northern Virginia defending Petersburg against Grant.

Sheridan, too, pushed south, his mission completed in the Shenandoah. Breaking the James River Canal and the Virginia Central Railroad—to make certain Lee would get no further sustenance from the ravaged Valley—Little Phil joined Grant before Petersburg on March 26.

The cavalry barely had time to catch its breath and have the horses shod. Three days later Grant launched his last campaign, leading down a road of destiny to Appomattox. He commanded, with Sheridan's forces, an army of 125,000 veterans.

Lee retained less than half that many, stretched in a tenuous line from the James to slightly west of Petersburg. The weakly held right of that line was critical. If forced to abandon Petersburg and Richmond, Lee planned to join Joe Johnston in North Carolina. With that in mind he had sent his chief of cavalry, Wade Hampton, to join the forces resisting Sherman in the Carolinas, placing Fitzhugh Lee in command of the mounted troops with the Army of Northern Virginia. Meanwhile, if the enemy occupied the strategic intersection of Five Forks and cut the South Side Railroad, he was trapped.

Which was what Grant had in mind—block Lee's chance of teaming up with Johnston. "I intended to close the war right here, with this movement." The next day, March 29 he sent Sheridan's cavalry, 12,000 strong with the addition of George Crook's division from the Army of the Potomac, to Dinwiddie Court House, from there to take possession of Five Forks five miles to the northwest. It was a dismal sixteen-mile ride in torrential rain, over roads sometimes bottomless with quicksand. Men sank to their waists and horses to their bellies. "If anyone asks us have we been through Virginia," the troopers joked, "we can tell 'em, 'yes, sir—in a number of places.' "

At the Court House, Sheridan and his staff took refuge in a ramshackle tavern, to find themselves guests of two lovely but bedraggled female refugees from Petersburg and Richmond. "You No-then gentlemen won't do any fighting heayah at the Cote House?" the ladies asked pleadingly. Assured there would be no violence in their presence, the women boiled coffee for the officers, and later one of the two sat down at a piano while the men gathered around to sing "The Battle Hymn of the Republic" and "When This Cruel War Is Over." The singing went on for a large part of the night.

The next morning, with Custer's men assigned to bringing up the wagon train, Sheridan sent Devin's division, supported by one of Crook's brigades, up the road to occupy Five Forks. Lee had anticipated the maneuver by a day, sending George Pickett's division of infantry with Fitz Lee's cavalry to take possession of the junction. As a result Devin found himself confronted by a wall of cavalry, while Pickett's foot soldiers charged from the surrounding woods to strike his flanks. Though Devin countercharged stubbornly, his troopers found themselves outmaneuvered — and infantry was something that he had not counted on.

In the midst of the battle Grant's aide Horace Porter, arriving with dispatches from the general, observed Sheridan's regimental band, "under heavy fire, playing 'Nellie Bly' as cheerily as if it were furnishing music for a country picnic." Lively music, Sheridan believed, inspired lively fighting; and wind instruments were capable of drowning out the rebel yell. Back and forth the musicians trotted, moving with the tide of battle, flinching only at the sound of bullets striking brass. But though their performance had "great effect on the spirits of the men," it failed to stop the Confederate surge.

By sundown Devin and Crook had been rolled back to Dinwiddie Court House. Only Custer's last-minute intervention saved them from disaster. The blue cavalry had lost 800 horsemen in the fight, due largely to the unexpected presence of Confederate infantry. Sheridan brewed up a storm of Irish fury. He told Porter to inform Grant that he must have infantry support — preferably Horatio Wright's Sixth Corps which had held the field so valiantly at Cedar Creek.

Grant replied quickly. Five Forks must be taken at all cost. The Sixth Corps was too far away; he was sending instead General Gouverneur Warren's Fifth Corps which was closer, along with General Ranald Mackenzie's cavalry division from the Army of the James. Sheridan was satisfied. With Warren and Mackenzie he would have a total force of 30,000, half infantry, half cavalry, with which to redeem, the following day, the afternoon's defeat.

At the same time, Grant made a significant decision. Hitherto Sheridan had been a cavalry corps commander, then leader of the Army of the Shenandoah. He now placed Little Phil at the head of all the Union cavalry in Virginia. The bandy-legged Irishman was back in his element, a horseman among horsemen, with the rank of major general awarded to him for his service in the Shenandoah.

There was no more singing at Dinwiddie Tavern, where Sheridan worked out his plan for the first day of April. Everything was carefully figured and precisely timed. Devin's cavalry would march up the road to Five Forks to attack the enemy's front; Custer's division would swing wide to the left to block Pickett's western exit and attack his flank;

Warren's infantry corps, approaching on Grant's promised schedule, would assault the enemy's left and rear—the whole operation functioning like a purse-string net, to be drawn closed with the enemy inside. Mackenzie's division would remain mounted in reserve, ready to charge in as needed. "We attack at dawn," the order went out to Merritt, Devin, Custer, and Warren.

Precisely at daybreak Devin moved up the turnpike, driving back the Confederate pickets, and closed in on Five Forks. Ahead of him lay forbidding earthworks guarding the intersection, to be charged when Warren's infantry attacked the flank.

There was no sign or sound of Warren. By 10 o'clock, Porter found Sheridan on the Dinwiddie road consumed with fury. "He . . . paced up and down, struck the clenched fist of one hand into the palm of the other, and fretted like a cage tiger." Where was Warren?

At mid-morning Warren rode leizurely up, with two of his three divisions still far behind. "His manner," Sheridan wrote when he had calmed down, "gave me the impression that he wished the sun to go down before disposition for the attack could be completed." As during the afternoon Warren continued to dally in the deployment of his troops, Sheridan again exploded—this time to Porter:

> This battle must be fought and won before the sun goes down. All the conditions may be changed in the morning: we have but a few hours of daylight left. My cavalry are rapidly exhausting their ammunition, and if the attack is delayed much longer they may have none left.

Anticipating Sheridan's assault on April 1, Pickett reportedly called on Lee for reinforcements. If he did, Lee could not spare additional men from other endangered sections of his line; but "Hold Five Forks at all hazards," he replied. It was asking a lot of the man who had given so much, so futilely, at Gettysburg, and who on March 31 commanded a considerably smaller force: an infantry division of 6,600 men and Fitz Lee's 5,700 cavalry.

Pickett put the troops to work building two miles of earth-and-timber breastworks stretched across the roads approaching Five Forks from the south, with additional earthworks and rifle pits at either end. He positioned the infantry and artillery in the rifle-pits, and the cavalry on the flanks, Rooney Lee on the right and Thomas Munford on the left. Tom Rosser's troopers were positioned behind the center, some distance to the rear.

All were braced for an attack at dawn. Except for some skirmishing with Sheridan's cavalry on the front, nothing happened. The hours passed, and by eleven a feeling of relief and relaxation settled on both officers and men. Sheridan, it appeared, had postponed the action to another day.

Rosser was not at his fighting best that morning. His troopers complained of saddlesores, men and horses had eaten nothing but green corn for a week, and he himself had been nicked by a sniper's bullet just the day before. To appease their hunger some of the men had fished the Nottoway River for shad, returning with a "handsome catch." Rosser decided to treat his fellow officers to a fish fry, first asking Pickett's permission and inviting the general to attend. Pickett assented, and on the way to Rosser's camp they encountered Fitzhugh Lee. Fitz agreed to join them, leaving Tom Munford in charge of the cavalry, and soon all three were grouped with their staffs around the fire.

The affair was a marked success. For three hours the soft air was fragrant with the scent of roasting shad and burning charcoal, the fish washed down with surreptitious applejack obtained from neighboring plantations. Shortly after noon, General Munford approached Fitz Lee with news of a Federal force on the White Oak Road east of Five Forks. The generals listened for the rap of rifles or the bark of cannon, but no sound appeared to penetrate the piny forrest. "We concluded," Rosser later wrote, "that the enemy was not in much of a hurry to find us at Five Forks."

Sheridan had been in a hurry since dawn's early light, with nothing he could do about it. Toward noon, one of Warren's three infantry divisions reached its assigned position on the east, Warren meanwhile disappearing. Sheridan decided to make do with what he had; and at 4 P.M. he gave the order to advance: the cavalry charging Pickett's front, Warren's infantry flanking the Confederates on the left. Only one senior Confederate officer commanded the defenders, Thomas Munford—wondering where Pickett was. And Fitzhugh Lee. And Rosser, supposed to be protecting Pickett's rear. He dispatched two couriers to track down the absent leaders, but the scent of roasting shad can carry only so far.

As the Federal forces closed around Five Forks like a contracting circle, infantry and cavalry became inseparably mixed. Though Mackenzie's troopers remained in the saddle, most of Sheridan's horsemen fought dismounted, using their rapid-fire carbines. The reporter George Alfred Townsend arrived on the battlefield in time to see the Confederates making one last desperate stand before retreating to their waist-high breastworks. As the Federals charged:

> It was an awful instant; the charging column trembled like a single thing, but at once the Rebels, with rare organization, fell into a hollow square, and with solid sheets of steel defied our centaurs. The horse-

men rode around them in vain; no charge could break the shining squares until our dismounted carbineers poured in their volleys afresh, making gaps in the spent ranks, and then in their wavering time the cavalry thundered down. The Rebels could stand no more; they reeled and swayed, and fell back broken and beaten.

By late afternoon every Confederate soldier and artillerist was behind the breastworks. Sheridan had dismounted his horsemen to charge the front of their entrenchments, then turned his attention to Warren's infantry, with the impatience of the cavalry commander used to speed. They were slow in mounting the attack. He rode over to stir them up. "Mounted on his black pony, the same which he rode at Winchester, Sheridan galloped everywhere, his flushed face all the redder, and his nervous figure all the more ubiquitous."

"Come on, men!" he shouted to the foot troops. "Smash 'em up!" An infantryman toppled beside him, writhing, screaming "I'm killed!" "You're not hurt a bit," said Sheridan. "Pick up your gun, man, and move right on to the front." The soldier struggled to his feet obediently, took a dozen steps forward, and fell dead.

As the infantry wavered in the face of fire from the breastworks, Sheridan seized his white and crimson battle flag from the hands of the sergeant color bearer, waved it above his head, and signaled the men to charge the breastworks. On his left Custer followed his example, waving the red and blue silk banner Libby had created for him. Horace Porter saw Federal pennants of every size and color closing in on the entrenched Confederates.

He remembered: "All this time Sheridan was dashing from one point of the line to another, waving his flag, shaking his fist, encouraging, threatening, praying, swearing, the very incarnation of battle. It would be a sorry soldier who could help following such a leader." They followed, "and with fixed bayonets and a rousing cheer dashed over the earthworks, sweeping everything before them. . . ." At the same time:

> The cavalry commanded by the gallant Merritt made a final dash, went over the earthworks with a hurrah, captured a battery of artillery, and scattered everything in front of them. Here Custer, Devin, and the other cavalry leaders were in their element, and vied with each other in deeds of valor.

Sheridan leaped Rienzi over the breastworks and landed in a clutch of astonished Confederate prisoners. His manner turned from insensate fury to calm consideration when they asked him apprehensively: "Where do you want us-all to go?"

"Go right over there," he said politely, pointing to the rear. "Get right along now. Drop your guns; you'll not need them any more."

Colonel Walter Harrison of Pickett's mauled division, seeing redeeming glory in the performance of Rooney Lee's horsemen in holding Custer at bay, called the battle "one of the most brilliant cavalry engagements of the war." Brilliant perhaps, but disastrous to the South. Sheridan's troopers rounded up 5,200 prisoners, close to half of Pickett's army, and chased the rest across Hatcher's Run and the South Side Railroad until darkness ended the pursuit.

At 7 P.M., after the battle was over, General Warren was finally discovered, sitting beneath an oak and sketching a map of the day's engagement. Sheridan told him he was relieved of his command and being replaced by Charles Griffin.

"Won't you reconsider?" Warren pleaded.

"Reconsider? hell!" said Sheridan, "I don't reconsider my determinations!"

From now on, reports from the front to General Grant would be compiled and signed by Sheridan. The pronoun "I" that Sheridan used included no acknowledgment of Meade. Officially, Little Phil was only chief of cavalry, not a commander of an army. Unofficially, and very positively, he was taking over. Grant might be commander of the armies, but "the Inevitable Sheridan" would lead the final bid for victory. And Grant, to a large degree, would let him.

With the defeat at Five Forks, Lee was forced on April 2 to abandon his Richmond-Petersburg position—"the line has been stretched until it is broken"—and the long Confederate retreat began. The projected path of that retreat led west to Amelia Court House, thirty miles away. Here Lee expected to find 350,000 rations sent from Richmond to keep his army going. Instead he found only crates of ammunition he no longer needed. The troops would have to beg for food, or forage, or go hungry. Most went hungry; more and more were beginning to desert.

Shadowing the Confederate army to the south was Sheridan's cavalry, so close that the Confederates could hear the music of the Union bands. And wherever the gray army paused, or lowered its guard, the Federal horsemen struck at its flank with short, swift punches, throwing the Confederates off stride. It was plain to Grant and Sheridan now that Lee was planning to join Joe Johnston in North Carolina, and a major effort should be made to cut him off.

A golden opportunity came on April 6 at Sayler's Creek, a tributary of the Appomattox River two-thirds of the way between Petersburg and Appomattox Station. On that "Black Thursday," Lee's column became divided as it moved across the marshy valley of the stream. Lee and Longstreet were ahead with two thirds of the army; the two corps of Richard Ewell and John Brown Gordon with the wagon trains had lagged behind; and Sheridan saw the gap between them. He would slice through that gap, and isolate Ewell and Gordon and the wagons, and with the help from the infantry would bag the lot of them.

Colonel Henry Tremain was with the Union forces at the creek that day, and remembered "the spring flowers smiling coyishly through the grass were literally trodden under the iron hoof of war; they carpeting the fields for Sheridan's squadrons" as they formed in line of battle. Facing the formation, and pounding his fist on the palm of his hand, the general gave the only command he felt was necessary. "Smash 'em up!" he shouted at his three divisions. "Smash 'em up!" And so, wrote Tremain, the charge began:

> A bugle sounded, and as bugle after bugle echoed "the charge" along that line of cavalry, there was one grand jump to conflict. All was dust and confusion; horses and men fell dead across the rebel works. Every firearm might have been discharged, but on one side all was desperation, horror, and dismay, while on the other, confidence, enthusiasm, and victory. The rebel line was gone, and squads, companies, and regiments were flying over the hills. [Union] horsemen were among them, and turned them back . . . as prisoners.

There were isolated pockets of Confederate resistance, noted Colonel Walter Harrison of Pickett's division. "It was the decimated few of a noble command who hung on to the last, fighting for survival in a final blaze of glory." Harrison was among those few:

> A squadron or more of cavalry were riding directly down upon us, at about one hundred yards distance, when we succeeded in rallying a mere squad of men, who delivered a last volley in the faces of these horsemen, which checked them for a moment, and we escaped by the speed of the horses.

By day's end Sheridan's forces had rounded up 6,000 prisoners, including General Ewell, and had burned or captured most of the wagon trains. General Lee, who had been forward of the battle zone with Longstreet, looked back upon it from the high ground west of Sayler's Creek. He witnessed a scene, described by General William Mahone who stood beside him, "that beggars description—hurrying teamsters with their teams and dangling traces, retreating infantry without guns, many without hats, a harmless mob, with the massive column of the enemy moving orderly on."

"My God! Has the army been dissolved?" Lee asked Mahone, incredulously.

"No, General," said Mahone. "Here are troops ready to do their duty."

"Yes, General," said Lee, "There are some true men left."

But they were only two-thirds of the 43,000 troops that he had led from Petersburg and Richmond only seven days ago. He still had Gordon's, Longstreet's and A. P. Hill's old corps, and Fitzhugh Lee's exhausted cavalry on battle-weary horses; they might add up to 30,000 in all. And at Appomattox Station thirty-five miles ahead, he would find four trainloads of provisions waiting, ordered down from Lynchburg. If he could only shake loose from Sheridan's cavalry, he still might make it to North Carolina.

Though Harrison considered the battle of Sayler's Creek the "death struggle" of Lee's army, it was not the final blow, the *coupe de grâce*, that Sheridan had hoped for. But, he wired Grant that night, "I am still pressing on with both cavalry and infantry. If the thing is pressed I think Lee will surrender." Grant referred the dispatch to Lincoln aboard ship at City Point. "Let the thing be pressed," replied the President.

The following day, April 7, Grant sent the first of a number of notes to Lee, pronouncing the Confederate position "hopeless" and calling for the surrender of the Army of Northern Virginia. Lee rejected the word hopeless, and stalled on the demand. Most highways leading south were closed to the Confederates, but the road to Lynchburg remained open, and the mortally wounded army struggled on in that direction, heading for Appomattox Court House.

"I shall fight as long as I can wield my saber," Wade Hampton wrote Texas Senator Louis Wigfall before leaving in mid-January on Lee's orders, for South Carolina. He took with him General M. Calbraith Butler and Butler's division of 1,500 troopers, veterans of many saber clashes in Virginia. Though Lee was reluctant to let his chief-of-cavalry go, it was vital that Sherman be stopped in the Carolinas before he could join Grant before Petersburg.

The bearded, patrician major general, forty-six now, was no longer the calm professional soldier he had been a year ago, practicing the art of killing only as a duty. His son had died in his arms from a Yankee bullet. Another son lay seriously wounded. His beloved South Carolina had been invaded, and his home and possibly his wife in peril. He had heard what Sherman, with Kilpatrick's cavalry, had done to Georgia. This was no longer a gentleman's war, but a back-alley brawl for survival. He would give no quarter and would ask for none.

Sherman had left Savannah in late January 1865, ploughing into South Carolina at ten miles a day, with Kilpatrick's cavalry crisscrossing in front of the army as it had in Georgia. And as in Georgia, it was a "smoky march," with burning and pillaging on an even larger scale — for South Carolina was damned as "the hell-hole of secession," the state that had started the whole bloody mess. "Here is where Treason began," a Federal colonel told his troops, "and, by God, here is where we end it."

Kilpatrick and his troopers were in prime condition. Even when

dismounted you could distinguish cavalrymen from infantry by looking at their legs—the footsoldiers scrawny of limb from constant
marching, the horsemen well-rounded from riding and foraging almost at their leisure; for until Hampton took over the Confederate
cavalry Kilpatrick had only Wheeler to contend with, and Wheeler was
not strong enough to give him serious trouble.

As chief of raiders and marauders Little Kil was in his element. The
cavalry was apt to be first on the scene when a village or plantation
offered opportunities for loot and arson. "There'll be damned little for
you infantrymen to destroy after I've passed through," he told the
envious footsoldiers as they crossed into South Carolina. His only
complaint concerned the "infernal bummers," licensed by Sherman to
forage for the army, who "managed to plunder every hamlet and town
before the cavalry came up."

Since the cavalry rode in advance of the army, Sherman told Kilpatrick to signal his location from time to time by "burning a bridge or
something" to send up smoke "like the Indians do on the plains."
Kilpatrick sent up so much smoke, wrote a newspaper correspondent,
that the sky at high noon "was black and gloomy." Though Sherman did
not sanction wholesale pillaging—defining the targets as depots,
granaries, mills, and produce useful to the enemy—he was reluctant to
restrain his headstrong army "lest its vigor and energy should be
impaired."

To light the nighttime marches of the army, Kilpatrick's troopers set
fire to the resin-coated Carolina pines, and the troops marched
through long corridors of climbing fire. A brigade of cavalry, crossing a
stream beneath an arch of flame, found "the water so infernally hot
from the heated air of that mighty cauldron that it took the hair off the
horses' legs as they went through it on the double-quick."

Joe Wheeler, whose Southern cavalry was no less arson-minded in
seeking to keep Confederate property from falling into Federal hands,
tried to negotiate a deal, writing to Sherman that he would quit burning
cotton if Sherman would "discontinue burning houses." Sherman replied readily: "I hope you burn all cotton and save us the trouble. . . .
All you don't burn I will."

Writing in his *Memoirs* of Wade Hampton's arrival in South Carolina
"with a great flourish of trumpets, and extraordinary powers to raise
men, money, and horses," Sherman added, "I had a species of contempt for these scattered and inconsiderable forces, knew that they
could hardly delay us an hour." Contempt was not what Hampton held
for Sherman, who was now invading his Palmetto State and forcing his
wife to flee their home. He hated the man, even more than Sherman
hated him.

He reserved, however, a portion of his venom for Kilpatrick, whose cavalry outnumbered his own troopers three to two—not a formidable margin. He had routed Kilpatrick before, at Atlee's station for example, but the score was still unsettled. With Sheridan, Kilpatrick represented all the unsheathed Union sabers east of the Appalachians; and to an increasing degree the final engagements of this waning war were devolving on the cavalry of both sides, Sheridan versus Fitzhugh Lee in southern Virginia, Hampton against Kilpatrick in the Carolinas.

Hampton arrived at Columbia, South Carolina, the day before the Confederates abandoned the city to concentrate all available forces on stopping Sherman. And it was the following day, February 17, that "Sherman's dashing Yankee boys" marched into Columbia, singing:

> Hail Columbia, happy land,
> If I don't burn you, I'll be damned.

Reportedly, Hampton had ordered all merchants to pile their stores of cotton in the streets and be ready to burn them if the Union army threatened to take over. True or not, cotton was the tinder that turned the city into an inferno. Helplessly, Hampton could only watch as his beloved home of Millwood—among the first to go—was consumed in the flames, along with its priceless library, its imported furnishings, the two-story wine cellar, barns and stables.

The burning of Columbia was regarded in the South, as the Fort Pillow Massacre was regarded in the North, as one of the war's most inexcusable barbarities. And both in some degree were attributed to cavalry, Sherman publicly declaring: "The fire was originated with the imprudent act of Wade Hampton in ripping open bales of cotton, piling it on the streets, burning it and then going away." Hampton denied the charge; and more impartial witnesses attributed the holocaust to soldiers carrying too much whiskey and too many matches.

The last week in February, Robert E. Lee, previously appointed General-in-Chief of the Armies of the Confederacy, reinstated "Uncle Joe" Johnston in command of all the scattered Confederate forces in South Carolina, Georgia, and Florida—some under Beauregard, some under Hardee, some with Braxton Bragg, and some representing remnants of Hood's former Army of Tennessee. These Johnston struggled to bring together in a united front against Sherman, meanwhile looking forward to the time when either Lee would join him in North Carolina or he would join Lee in Virginia.

Against Sherman's army of 60,000, the most Johnston could hope to assemble was some 20,000 infantry. With Butler's and Wheeler's cavalry divisions, Hampton's mounted forces numbered roughly

5,000, though more and more—in these years of emergency adjust-
ments, shifting logistics, and mounting desertions in the South—
figures were unreliable.

As Sherman marched northeast from charred Columbia toward
Fayetteville, North Carolina, Hampton assembled his and Wheeler's
troopers for a stab at Kilpatrick's cavalry riding on the Union flank. It
was easy to capture Federal stragglers, loitering behind the rest for
purposes of plunder, and Sherman was glad to be rid of them. But
from these Hampton learned, on March 9, that Kilpatrick was
bivouacked at Monroe's Cross Roads on the route to Fayetteville.
Creeping up on the camp, he deployed his troops for the attack.

At dawn the following morning Butler's division swarmed over the
Federal camp from opposite directions, slashing at the sleep-drugged
Federals with sabers, emptying their pistols into startled clusters of
half-clothed Union cavalry.

The surprise was complete; and for Kilpatrick somewhat similar to
Mosby's invasion of General Stoughton's quarters in Virginia. He was
sleeping in a nearby farmhouse with an accomodating lady when the
shots aroused him. "My first thought was: four years' hard fighting for
a major general's commission gone up with surprise!" Without waiting
to don jacket or trousers he fled in his night clothes to the yard where a
Confederate trooper shouted at him, "Where's Kilpatrick?"

"There he goes on that black horse!" yelled the general, waving the
man on.

Mounting the nearest horse Kilpatrick, still pantless, rallied his
forces on a nearby rise from which, with the horse artillery, they
peppered the Confederates with rifle shot and shrapnel. Hampton's
cavalry galloped into the cannons' mouths, killing the gunners and
silencing the battery, in what Kilpatrick described as "the most formidable cavalry charge I have ever witnessed." But what had begun as a
rout concluded as a draw.

It was a small engagement as such things go, known locally as the
"Battle of Kilpatrick's Pants" or "Kilpatrick's Shirt-tail Skedaddle."
And the next day, as Johnston's infantry evacuated Fayetteville in the
face of advancing Union troops, the bluecoats got a measure of revenge. Hampton, preparing to follow Johnston, was breakfasting at the
Lafayette Hotel when the sound of small-arms fire brought him to the
street. There were bluecoats everywhere, thirsting for his blood.
Hampton was able to round up a handful of troopers, and with typical
audacity gave the order: "Charge!"

The valiant eight plunged headlong at the startled enemy. Hampton
cut two down with his saber, shot two more with his revolver, and as the
rest of the band discharged their pistols at the swarm of bluecoats the
Federal cavalry closed in behind them.

"General, we're surrounded," cried seventeen-year-old Hugh Scott. "Stand still. Pick them off one by one," said Hampton.

The Confederates fired with such accuracy that nine more Federals fell dead. As the rest began to withdraw, some of them wounded, the Hamptonites captured a dozen of them—then retreated to rejoin Johnston's column on the road to Smithfield.

Despite the adverse numerical odds, Johnston hoped to lure Sherman into open battle at a place of his own choosing. But it was Hampton, according to the Carolinian, who chose the site near the little hamlet of Bentonville some miles south of Smithfield. Here the crest of a wooded ridge overlooked an open field across which Sherman, to avoid the thick, surrounding woods, would have to pass. Hampton sent word to Johnston that he would hold the position with his cavalry until the infantry arrived. The next morning, March 19, Johnston's forces were deployed on both sides of the village in a V-formation with one flank resting upon Mill Creek.

Of the Battle of Bentonville, well planned and poorly executed, staff officer Alexander C. McClurg of Sherman's army wrote:

> When Johnston, with skillful strategy . . . massed his scattered troops near the little hamlet of Bentonville, and placed them, unknown to his great adversary . . . across the road upon which two [Federal] divisions were marching, he proposed to . . . sweep these two divisions from the field, in the first furious onset. . . . Then, with half his army destroyed, with supplies exhausted, and far from any base, he believed General Sherman . . . would no longer be a match for his elated and eager troops.

McClurg was probably right in saying of Johnston that "never before, in all the long struggle, had fortune and circumstance so united to favor him, and never before had hope shone so brightly," Hampton later contended that the Battle of Bentonville could have been won had all of Johnston's separate forces moved in consort. But they had never fought side by side before, and tended to improvise as things progressed. Time after time the Confederates attacked—"their onward sweep," wrote McClurg, "was like the waves of the ocean, resistless"—and the Federals were driven back, to regroup and counterattack, until both sides were too exhausted to continue after sunset.

The following day was a repetition of that costly, seesaw action; and the third day, the 21st, when one of Sherman's division commanders saw a gap in the Confederate defense and plunged through, Johnston had no choice but to withdraw. Federal infantry rushed to bar the bridge across Mill Creek. Hampton summoned all the cavalry that he could find, some sixty or eighty men of the 8th Texas Cavalry, and deferred to William Hardee commanding that section of the line.

Hardee ordered the cavalry, supported by a brigade of infantry, to charge.

"The attack was so sudden and so impetuous," wrote Hampton, "that it carried everything before it, and the enemy retreated hastily." With the bridge secure, Hardee turned to Hampton, "his face bright with the light of battle," to exclaim exultantly:

"That was Nip and Tuck, and for a while I thought Tuck had it."

Then Hardee's face clouded as a team of stretcher bearers passed with a mortally wounded soldier. Just hours earlier William Hardee, Jr., sixteen, had arrived at Bentonville and pleaded with his father for permission to join the army. Reluctantly, "swear him in," the general told captain "Doc" Matthews of the 8th Texas Cavalry—and young Willie had ridden to his death in the charge his father ordered.

Johnston and Hampton crossed Mill Creek, and marched up to Raleigh, taking with them, wrote McClurg, "the last hopes of the Southern Confederacy." Sherman did not pursue believing "enough blood had been shed already." Johnston had lost more than 2,600 men in the engagement, and "had nowhere to go"—so, let him go. Sherman's next stop was Goldsboro where another 26,000 Federal troops awaited him. With his army reinforced to nearly 90,000, he planned to join Grant in Virginia for the knockout blow against Robert E. Lee.

Aboard ship at City Point on April 8, Lincoln received a gift of the enemy's battleflags captured by Sheridan's cavalry at Five Forks in Virginia. The President hefted the staves and shook the pennants out. "This is something I can see, feel, and understand," he said. "This is victory."

21

AVE ATQUE VALE

THE SUN HAD SET THREE HOURS BEFORE. IT WAS DARK OUTSIDE THE candle-lit cottage, but Sheridan could still hear small-arms fire to the northeast where Custer's cavalry fought for control of the Lynchburg road. He finished his last dispatch of the day to Grant:

Cavalry Headquarters
April 8, 1865, 9:20 P.M.

General:
I marched early this morning . . . on Appomattox Station, where my scouts had reported trains of cars with supplies for Lee's army. A short time before dusk General Custer, who had the advance, made a dash at the station, capturing four trains of supplies with locomotives. . . .

Custer then pushed on toward Appomattox Court House, driving the enemy, who kept up a heavy fire of artillery, charging them repeatedly. . . .

If [the infantry] can get up tonight we will perhaps finish the job in the morning. I do not think Lee means to surrender until compelled to do so.

P. H. Sheridan
Major-General, U. S. Army, Commanding

This sixth day of a seventy-mile pursuit of Lee's retreating army had been relatively uneventful—until sundown. "The cavalry are doing well," Grant observed that morning. "I'm hoping General Lee will continue to fight them. Every hour's delay lessens his chance of escape." But Sheridan's horsemen were less concerned with fighting Lee than with beating him to Appomattox Station, cutting the South Side Railroad, and blocking his last highway of retreat to Lynchburg.

The drive was given added incentive when one of Sheridan's scouts reported four trains of Confederate supplies approaching Appomattox Station. "If those trains can be taken," Sheridan told Custer, "it will be work enough for one day." Custer led his Third Cavalry Division at a gallop down the sandy roadway, with Devin's and Crook's divisions following at an easier pace, and reached Appomattox Station around four o'clock.

The trains were there all right, with wagons drawn alongside for unloading the supplies. Only a squadron of General Martin Gary's South Carolina Cavalry Brigade were guarding the operation. The blue horsemen, greatly superior in numbers, drove them back into the woods and took possession of the cars. Custer then polled his cavalry. Who in civilian life had been a locomotive engineer and could conduct the trains to safety?

A surprising number of engineers volunteered and, Sheridan noted from his cottage, "seemed delighted to get back to their old calling. They amused themselves by running the trains to and fro, creating much confusion, and keeping up such an unearthly screech with the whistles that I was on the point of ordering the cars burned. They finally wearied of their fun, however, and ran the trains off to the east. . . . "

If weariness hadn't stopped the locomotive frolic the Confederates were ready to. Masked by woods northeast of the station was most of Lee's artillery reserve under General R. Lindsay Walker. Walker had been shaving when the South Carolina Cavalry alerted him to Custer's presence. With a beard of white lather on his face he raced to the artillery park, and ranged his guns in line of battle—three batteries, twelve gleaming barrels leveled at the depot. When his gunners were in position with the Carolina Cavalry on their flanks, Walker gave the order: Fire!

The blast caught Custer by surprise. As men and horses disintegrated, the situation was dramatically reversed. Artillery was generally backed up by infantry. If so in this case, all the advantage Custer had gained, along with the captured trains, was lost. Then the old adrenalin began to flow. There was one rule that universally applied to cavalry: when in doubt, attack. He drew his saber, signaled the bugler, and gave the order; Charge!

Lieutenant Edward Boykin of the 7th South Carolina Cavalry was astonished at the sight, the artillery ablaze, the thunder deafening, the whole world incandescent—and the curly-haired general leading his

wild horsemen into the barrels of the ubiquitous cannon as if the guns
were spouting nothing more than cotton. He remembered:

> They made three distinct charges, preluding always with the bugle,
> on the right, left and center, confusing the point of attack. . . . Amid
> the flashing and the roaring and the shouting rose the wild yell of a
> railroad whistle, as a train rushed up almost among us, as we were
> fighting around the depot, sounding on the night air as if the devil
> himself had just come up and was about to join in what was going on.

A devil of sorts had just come up in the form of Tom Devin and his
First Division; he had arrived to fill the gaps where many of Custer's
saddles had been emptied by the shrapnel. A moment before, Lieutenant W. F. Robinson of Walker's artillerists had spotted Custer on his
white horse, calling on his men to press the charge, that there was only a
handful of Confederates opposing them. "I urged my men to take
good aim and shoot at General Custer, and I shot at him a number of
times myself."

Custer had always borne a charmed life under heavy fire. Now with
Devin beside him, and Cook's and Mackenzie's divisions on the way, he
could see the Confederates starting to haul their batteries to safety.
One more charge, and almost half the Confederate guns were sur-
rounded by the Union cavalry. The South Carolina horsemen suc-
ceeded in getting one battery rolling up the Lynchburg road, when
Custer called off the pursuit, after capturing more than twenty of
Walker's guns.

It was long after dark now, and Sheridan had his cavalry precisely
where he wanted them, straddling the road to Lynchburg, blocking any
possibility of Lee's escape — provided the infantry arrived as scheduled
to back him up. That night he ordered the cavalry to hold their places,
keep their mounts saddled, and sleep on their arms beside the horses.
Tomorrow would be Palm Sunday and it seemed, as Stonewall Jackson
had once piously deplored, everything important happened on a Sunday.

For a while Lee rode alone along the Lynchburg road, preferring
solitude, wrapped in thought as heavy as a blanket. At one point he
caught up with Martin Gary's brigade of South Carolina Cavalry on its
way to protect the supply trains at the Appomattox depot. They had
paused to water their horses; but now sprang to attention and
saluted — with the special reverence in which heads are bared before
cathedral alters. Lee was not just their leader; he was the army, the
country, the Cause for which they fought. As the general saluted and

passed on, the South Carolinians rode with lighter hearts than they had known for many weeks.

Would that Lee's heart had been less heavy. Grant's armies were not his only nemesis, nor even his principal concern. He was down to only two corps of infantry under Gordon and Longstreet, and Fitz Lee's depleted cavalry. Yet he had battled Grant for eleven months, from south of the Rapidan to Petersburg, with insufficient forces. Though the Union general had the numbers to outflank him, and was doing so, he could still slip to the southwest and join Johnston in North Carolina. They could then unite to whip Sherman and then turn on Grant, together.

There was the shadow of a nightmare on this dream, and it was cast by Sheridan. Though numerically small, perhaps 12,000, the Union cavalry—once held in contempt by the Confederates—gave the Armies of the Potomac and James new dimensions. Time was one of them. Sheridan could move swiftly to break Lee's line as he had at Five Forks and again at Sayler's Creek, destroying his wagon trains, biting off straggling units of his army, severing the South Side Railroad bringing him supplies. Some newspapers, South as well as North, were snidely hinting that Grant commanded the Army of Northern Virginia, controlling its every move by the moves he made himself. More accurate to say that Sheridan's cavalry was dictating the course of events, and with an almost unobstructed hand.

The mounted troops under Fitzhugh Lee, reduced to less than 2,500, were no longer able to cope with Sheridan. The spirit was willing, but the flesh of men and horses both was weak. The general summoned his nephew from the rear to the front of the column, and for awhile they rode together toward Appomattox Court House. The hitherto unspoken matter of surrender, growing with every exchange of notes with Grant, was uppermost in both their minds. At one point, Fitz told his uncle:

"Before there's a surrender, will you notify me? I would want to unite with Johnston in North Carolina, and fight on."

Lee nodded. "All right," he said. Men like Fitz and Rosser and Wade Hampton were the headstrong centaurs for whom a war would never end; it was only fair to let them go. But later he told Rooney Lee, in a tone that was almost pleading: "Stay with us. I will see you through."

By late afternoon that Saturday, April 8, the Confederate army was telescoping in the valley east of Appomattox Court House. It was a scene, observed by Lieutenant J. F. Caldwell, of total confusion "exceeding anything I had ever witnessed." Men dropped in their tracks from exhaustion, sleeping where they fell. Others straggling in with haggard faces wandered around in search of their regiments. Wagons and artillery were scattered everywhere; horses and mules collapsed beside them. "A horrible calm brooded over everything," wrote Caldwell—the calm of resignation and despair.

Lee had counted on the four supply trains, waiting at Appomattox Station, to keep his army moving. Now he learned that the Union cavalry had seized the trains and a number of Lindsay Walker's cannon. That night he summoned Fitz Lee, Gordon, Longstreet and his staff for a conference. They reached a fatal decision. Since only Sheridan's cavalry appeared to block the road to Lynchburg, with numbers roughly equal to their own, they would attempt to break through.

Fitz Lee's cavalry, supported by Gordon's infantry, would spearhead the attack, punching a hole in the center of the Union line. Gordon would hold the gap open with his infantry. Longstreet would follow with what was left of wagons and artillery—and the Army of Northern Virginia would be on its way again, to join Joe Johnston or, this failing, to seek sanctuary in the Blue Ridge Mountains of Virginia.

There was nothing to wait for; the cavalry rode out at break of dawn. In the half light, stretched across the Lynchburg road, Sheridan's horsemen waited, Mackenzie's and Crook's divisions behind barricades in front, Custer on the flank. The Union troopers saw the Confederates advancing with their tattered regimental flags aloft, "like marching gardens blooming with cockscombs, red roses and poppies."

There would always be contention as to which Confederate cavalry unit led that final charge. Fitz Lee was at the head of his troopers; Rooney Lee was also in the vanguard; but Tom Rosser's Laurel Brigade claimed to be first to reach the Union lines. The distinction hardly mattered, for the line of Federal cavalry withdrew and melted into the woods on either side, like a blue curtain parting in the middle. "The Lynchburg road was cleared," wrote war reporter Morris Schaff, "and the tattered forces that had cleared it burst into cheers."

The cheers died in their throats. The Union horsemen who had taken to the woods had not, as the Confederates thought, been routed. Having lured the Confederate cavalry to charge, they had simply stepped aside to reveal a threefold line of infantry, 24,000 strong, stretched across the roadway farther down.

Fitz Lee looked upon that mass of blue, bayonets gleaming in the sunrise, with despair. "I cannot budge them," he told Gordon. "Your boys will have to take them on." But Gordon had expected only Sheridan's cavalry to contend with. "My men are worn to a frazzle," he said. "I cannot attack without support from Longstreet." He sent word to that effect to Lee, knowing that Longstreet was assigned to bringing up the rear and was in no position to support him.

Lee seemed to have foreseen that dismal message and all that it portended. He was dressed that morning in a new Confederate-gray uniform, red silk sash with jewel-hilted sword and scabbard, gold spurs on polished boots, white buckskin gauntlets. After reading Gordon's dispatch, Lee told his staff, "There is nothing left me to do but to go and see General Grant," he said, "and I would rather die a thousand deaths."

As the white-haired general rode beneath a flag of truce toward the designated meeting place in the village, rumors of imminent surrender swept through the armies like an April wind. Informal cease-fires were agreed on, and finally an hour's truce. To men like Sheridan and Custer the white flags were like red capes to an angry bull. "Hell!" said Sheridan, summoned to join Grant at the conference with Lee. "Why couldn't they have held on longer? Damn it, we could have finished them off!"

To Custer, stationed on a rise above the Lynchburg road, in perfect position to charge anything that tried to pass, this lull in fighting was a personal affront. He was not going to wait for Lee and Grant to thrash things out. The Union cavalry had won this war, his own division in particular, and he would see that they got the honor due them. He tied a white towel to a staff—there was general wonder as to where he got a white towel in the army—and rode toward the assembled enemy. As General Gordon later wrote:

> A cavalry officer came to me from Sheridan with a flag of truce. He was a handsome fellow and very polite. Saluting with his saber he said:
> "I am General Custer and bear a message to you from General Sheridan. The General desires me to present you his compliments, and to demand the immediate and unconditional surrender of all the troops under your command."
> I answered, "You will please, General, return my compliments to General Sheridan and say to him that I shall not surrender my command."

Custer retaliated by quoting Sheridan to the effect that the Federal cavalry had Gordon surrounded and, in the event of a refusal to surrender, were prepared to "annihilate your command in an hour." Then he rode off.

One rebuff was not sufficient to discourage Custer. Longstreet and his staff were to the rear of Gordon's corps, awaiting developments, when, as that commander wrote, "General Custer, flaxen locks flowing over his shoulders, galloped up and in a brisk, excited manner said:

"'General Longstreet, in the name of General Sheridan and myself I demand the unconditional surrender of this army.'"

"I'm not in command," Longstreet said curtly. "General Lee is, and he's gone back to meet General Grant in regard to our surrender."

Custer, Longstreet noted, seemed satisfied, and rode back to his command. He had not personally received the surrender of the Army of Northern Virginia, which undoubtedly was what he hoped for, but at least he had been the first to personally demand it.

In the parlor of Wilmer McLean's house, chosen for the meeting between Grant and Lee, the Confederate commander had only his aide, Colonel Charles Marshall, at his side. Grant had a dozen or so officers, distinguished by his cavalry commanders, Sheridan and Merritt. Sheridan, if one credits Colonel Burr's report, seemed in character and presence to dominate the Federal assembly, "as marked a figure, in face, pose, expression, dress, as was Lee himself."

Burr painted a last wartime picture of the chief-of-cavalry who had done so much in just eleven days to clinch the Union victory.

> He wore the full uniform of his rank, with sash, belt and sword. Cavalry boots, rusty and soiled, covered half his short, sturdy limbs. His short, broad, sturdy form stood posed in strength. The head and face were remarkable. Beardless, except a close, dark mustache . . . . The expression was that of a set, fixed force and determination. . . . Sheridan was indeed the embodied vigilance of the Union army.

After polite discussion, Lee noted that the proposed surrender terms did not permit the Confederates to keep their horses, which would be helpful in the transition period. Grant verbally agreed to the concession. "This will have the best possible effect upon the men," said Lee. Other terms were more than fair, more than generous, as Lee himself acknowledged; and the conference concluded with Grant's promise to supply the half-starved Southern army with provisions from the Union commissary.

The Confederate general and his aide were first to leave when the conference ended, and Sheridan had one last glimpse of his opponent through the parlor window. Lee was standing below the porch holding his gray charger by the bridle. For a moment he gently stroked Traveller's forehead, as if horse and man were sharing some inviolate communion. Then he wearily mounted and rode down into the valley.

When Wilmer McLean had left his home near Manassas Junction after the battle of 1861, and moved to Appomattox Court House, he had hoped to escape the ravages of war. Now he found his house a center and a victim of the war. Relic-hunters tore the place apart for souvenirs, making off with candlesticks, ink stands, chairs and pieces of chairs, and ripped-up patches of upholstery. Sheridan claimed for twenty dollars (which McLean indignantly refused to take) the oval-topped table on which Grant had written the surrender terms.

He presented the table to Custer as a gift for Libby. To go with it, the Federal cavalry chief composed a note for Custer's wife:

. . . permit me to say, Madam, that there is scarcely an individual in our service who has contributed more to bring this [surrender] about than your very gallant husband.

Grant's terms to Lee at Appomattox had prescribed that all Confederate officers and men would be paroled with their promise not to take up arms against the government. A later broadside of dubious origin declared that, "The guerilla chief Mosby is not included in the parole." Grant himself would not have endorsed that statement. Whatever he thought of Mosby at the moment, he had a warrior's respect for warriors, writing some time later:

> Since the close of the war, I have come to know Colonel Mosby personally, and somewhat intimately. . . . He is able and thoroughly honest and truthful. There were probably but few men in the South who could have commanded successfully a separate detachment, in the rear of an opposing army and so near the border of hostilities, as long as he did without losing his entire command.

Still, Mosby presented a thorny problem to the Washington authorities. Having always held himself aloof from any command beyond his own, it was improbable that he would voluntarily lay down arms or submit to Grant's surrender terms. General Winfield S. Hancock, commanding the Middle Military Division, believed that, "It is quite as likely that Mosby will disband as that he will formally surrender, as all his men have fine animals and are generally armed with two pistols only."

Nevertheless, Mosby was approached through intermediaries on the matter of surrender—none of the Federal authorities knew where he was—and the partisan leader sent back a reply to Hancock, "I am ready to agree to a suspension of hostilities . . . until I can obtain sufficient intelligence to determine my future actions." The intelligence he wanted was Joe Johnston's plan for continuing the war. If Johnston held out against Sherman, the Rangers would join him as Lee had hoped to do. Otherwise, as some of Mosby's men proposed, they would ride to Mexico where the Emperor Maximilian was seeking men of their experience.

Mosby even questioned, through an intermediary, General Robert E. Lee who was on parole in Richmond. Should the Rangers surrender or fight on? Lee's counsel was the same as given to the Army of Northern Virginia, in essence: "Go home . . . and help to rebuild the shattered fortunes of our old state."

Perhaps because of this advice, rather than the warning that—if he failed to surrender—his men would be hunted down and offered no quarter, Mosby agreed to a temporary truce and a meeting with Hancock's representatives. What might have resulted from that April 20 conference at Millwood would never be known. In the midst of things a scout brought word to Mosby that the town was surrounded by Federal troops preparing for his capture. Aristides Monteiro, one of the Rangers with Mosby at the time, recorded the colonel's reactions to this treachery:

> With a look that I shall never forget, Mosby sprang to his feet, instantly grasping one of the murderous weapons in his belt and glaring upon the Yankee officers with an expression that reminded me more of a tiger crouching to spring upon his prey than anything I have ever seen . . . He said in a loud and sharp voice: "Sir, if we are no longer under the protection of our truce, we are, of course, at the mercy of your men. We shall protect ourselves."
>
> With that inimitable sign and gesture that so often had sent his gallant followers like a thunderbolt into the serried ranks of the foe, he led the way with long and rapid strides to the door. . . . It was a scene difficult to describe, but never to be forgotten. Every Partisan was well prepared for instant death and more than ready for a desperate fight. Had a single pistol been discharged by accident, or had Mosby given the word, not one Yankee officer in the room would have lived a minute. . . . His only word of command was "mount and follow me." We galloped rapidly from Millwood to the Shenandoah River, closely followed by a cloud of Yankee cavalry.

Another reported version of the incident maintained that Mosby had been misinformed; that there was no trap prepared for him at Millwood; the Union troops around the village had been simply picketing the place. It hardly mattered. Mosby had made up his mind on what to do.

The following morning, April 21, the townspeople of Salem in the heart of Mosby's Confederacy, witnessed an impressive gathering. From all directions came men on horseback, superbly mounted, dressed in rich Confederate gray with polished pistols in their belts. On the village green their commanders lined them up by companies, about 200 men in all, and there they sat in the saddle patiently and waited.

Promptly at noon arrived John Singleton Mosby, clean-shaven, neatly uniformed, boots polished to a high sheen. He spoke no greeting, gave no orders, and no roll was called. Instead, the colonel simply rode to the end of the column, and then proceeded down the line, the eyes of each man meeting his in mute communion. This silent ritual over, Mosby rode to the front of the formation, turned, and spoke:

> Soldiers: I have summoned you together for the last time. The vision we cherished of a free and independent country has vanished, and that country is now the spoil of a conqueror.

I disband your organization in preference to surrendering to our enemies. I am no longer your commander. After an association of more than two eventful years, I part from you with a just pride in the fame of your achievements and grateful recollections of your generous kindness to myself. . . . Farewell!

With no more words between them, the assembly dissolved as if scattered by an April wind, the men riding off to whatever destiny their conscience counseled, leaving behind the equally scattered graves of fallen comrades, these to be remembered in some future April by Virginia's poet-historian A. Churchill Gordon:

> And song of birds and hint of bloom
> Are gay and bright, as when
> Those gallant lads rode to their doom
> Long since with Mosby's men.

General Sherman, pressing heavily on Johnston in North Carolina, was particularly gratified to hear that Mosby had disbanded the partisan Rangers. After Lee's surrender, he had written to Grant, "I now apprehend that the rebel armies will disperse and . . . we will have to deal with numberless bands of desperadoes, headed by such men as Mosby. . . . " Now his worries remained, but were concerned with different desperadoes. Writing to his wife he noted, "There is great danger of the Confederate armies breaking up into guerrillas, and that is what I most fear. For such men as Wade Hampton, Forrest, Wirt Adams, etc. never will work and there is nothing left for them but death or highway robbery."

Both Forrest and Hampton would have preferred death to highway robbery, but neither was considering the choice. After Forrest's defeat at Selma, the Confederate general recalled his troopers to Gainesville, Alabama, to await developments. He refused to listen to rumors of Lee's surrender in the East and advised his troops on April 25 to disregard them. "It is the duty of every man to stand firm at his post and true to his colors. A few days more will determine the truth or falsity of all the reports now in circulation."

Those days saw Wilson's formidable cavalry riding east from Selma to raise the Stars and Stripes above the 1861 Confederate capital at Montgomery, Alabama. Then, reminiscent of the days when Forrest and Morgan had raided so freely through Tennessee, Wilson's unconquerable horsemen occupied Columbus, Macon, and Augusta, Georgia. General Richard Taylor tried, despite the Federal capture of Mobile, to cling to a Southern enclave in the Gulf states—Alabama, Mississippi, and Louisiana—but finally surrendered at Citronelle, Alabama, the first week in May.

Two days later, on a contemplative ride with his adjutant Charles

Anderson, Forrest paused at a fork in the road.

"Which way, General?" Anderson asked.

"Either," said Forrest. "If one road led to hell and the other to Mexico, I would be indifferent as to which to take."

His troops had been talking much of going to Mexico, anything rather than surrender. Forrest himself was sorely tempted; surrender was no more appealing to him that it was to Mosby, Hampton, Wheeler, or Fitzhugh Lee. Yet, before the war he had been something of a pillar in the South, a man of substance in Memphis, a public servant of influence in Tennessee. There was much work ahead if the South was to survive, work less to his liking than fighting but essential nonetheless.

The following day he spoke to his troopers in the Gainesville camp. He told them that they were the last remaining troops of the Confederacy east of the Mississippi, a distinction in itself, but that any further resistance was hopeless, and "would be justly regarded as the very height of folly. . . . It is your duty and mine to lay down our arms . . . and to aid in restoring peace and establishing law and order throughout the land, divesting ourselves of feelings of animosity, hatred and revenge." Then his voice quavered slightly with emotion:

> I have never on the field of battle sent you where I was unwilling to go myself, nor would I now advise you to a course which I felt myself unwilling to pursue. You have been good soldiers, you can be good citizens.

Jefferson Davis, fleeing Richmond with most of his cabinet and $275,000 from the Confederate treasury, had counted on the support of men like Forrest. He counted too, though with diminishing expectations, on Joe Johnston's holding out against Sherman in North Carolina. Reaching Greensboro, he summoned Johnston for a meeting — ironically turning for last-minute advice and help to the man he had removed from command in the crucial days before Atlanta.

Johnston harbored no illusions. Another division of infantry had bolstered Sherman's forces around Raleigh to over 80,000 men. To continue the fight would not be gallantry but murder. Halfheartedly Davis acquiesced to Johnston's getting the best surrender terms he could. Davis himself, however, would not yield; he would gather around him what loyal troops remained and ride to the Trans-Mississippi Department and perhaps from there to Mexico to continue a government-in-exile. He had been encouraged by a message from Wade Hampton:

> Give me a good force of cavalry and I will take them safely across the Mississippi — and if you desire to go in that direction it will give me great pleasure to escort you.

I can bring to your support many strong arms and brave hearts—
Men who will fight to Texas, and who, if forced from that state, will
seek refuge in Mexico.

Hampton, however, was given the more immediate assignment of
delivering a note from Johnston to Sherman proposing that they
negotiate—the word surrender was avoided. On April 17 the two met
at a farmhouse near Durham Station to discuss terms, "while outside
the house," wrote a Federal cavalryman, "Kilpatrick and Hampton
exchanged boasts and threats." Inside the house a pall of gloom hung
over the meeting, with the news of Lincoln's assassination on the night
of April 14. Though the South as well as the North deplored the
murder, peace would be more difficult to come by. The generous terms
which Sherman offered Johnston—the same as Grant had offered
Lee—were now hotly opposed and bitterly debated in the North,
delaying the final surrender until April 26.

Neither Wade Hampton nor Joe Wheeler felt bound by that
decision—"South Carolinians never surrender" was the virtual motto
of Hampton's cavalry. Both would attempt to join Davis in his flight to
exile. Wheeler left at once with 600 volunteers. Hampton rode off
alone, swimming the swollen Catawba River to catch up with Wheeler.
The two met at Yorkville on May 1, below the South Carolina border,
where Mary Hampton had been staying since the burning of Columbia.
Though Hampton stopped only to say farewell to Mary, both she and
Wheeler dissuaded him from going further. His wife and children
needed him; the South needed him to chart and shape its future. He
bowed to the obligation; and Wheeler rode on without him, hoping to
join the President at Washington, Georgia.

Jefferson Davis and his escort were by then in Georgia, and Basil
Duke had joined the troop with remnants of Morgan's Terrible Men,
and several skeletal brigades of Morgan's former cavalry. "Three
thousand brave men," the Confederate President boasted, "are enough
for a nucleus around which the whole people will rally." Yet Duke
doubted that Davis believed what he said or that he really intended to
escape. It was "flight for flight's sake." A few days later Davis paid off
and disbanded his cavalry escort, to spare them the indignity of capture, and was himself overtaken by James Wilson's cavalry at Irwinsville
on May 10.

As at Appomattox the Union cavalry was writing the last sad chapter
of the war. Both Stoneman's and Wilson's horsemen had been chasing
Davis, with Wheeler a secondary target. Near Conyers, Georgia—the
approximate scene of Fighting Joe's victories over Union cavalry
around Atlanta—Wheeler and his exhausted men were surprised
while asleep by Federal troopers "who had been pursuing us more
closely than we knew."

Yet ironically Wheeler and Davis kept their rendezvous — first at Athens and then in Savannah harbor, aboard the prison ship *William P. Clyde* which set sail on May 16 for the Federal bastille of Fort Monroe, Virginia.

It was a day of soft sunshine and calm waters as the steamer left the harbor. Leaning with his arm against the guard rail, Wheeler watched the receding shoreline while his mind rebelled against the sight. This was not the way that things should end — not with this finality. And in his imagination he devised a better ending . . .

The steamer was a large three-decker, and the sixty-man guard patrolled the upper deck. When the guards went below for meals, they stacked their weapons and left two sentinels at the companionway. It would be easy for Wheeler and the other prisoners to overcome the sentinels, seize the guns, and take possession of the ship.

And what then?

Turn south, to the Florida coast. Or to the Bahamas. Or to Cuba, if necessary. Not enough fuel to get that far? They would tear up the decks and burn the planking. He let his imagination soar until the dream took substance. In some pleasant, sub-tropical climate redolent of Georgia, he saw the capital of a new South rising, perpetuating the Confederacy forever. The more he thought about it, the more certain it became.

The flat blade of a saber slapped against his wrist. He turned with shock to face the blue-clad officer of the guard.

"Take your arm off that rail!" the officer barked. "No leaning on the rail!"

"I'm sorry," said the general softly. "I did not know the rule."

Philip Henry Sheridan, with all his fondness for parades and bands, was cheated of marching in Washington's Grand Review of Grant's and Sherman's armies the last week of May. Grant hurried him off to Texas to keep an eye on Maximilian in Mexico; and later the Secretary of War appointed Little Phil commander of the Fifth Military District of the Gulf, embracing Texas and Louisiana. Sheridan's rigid enforcement of Reconstruction measures raised an outcry for his removal. Transferred to the Department of the Missouri, he was back in the saddle chasing Indians, an occupation more in character.

In 1870 he was sent abroad as United States observer with the Prussian armies warring with Napoleon, and witnessed the final charge of the French cuirassiers against the Germans at Sedan. At the conclusion of that decisive battle, Sheridan warmly shook Otto von Bismarck's hand.

"Let me congratulate you, count," said Little Phil. "I can only compare the surrender of Napoleon to that of General Lee at Appomattox Court House."

Returning to America, Sheridan succeeded Sherman as commanding general of the United States Army in 1884, and four years later
received the highest military honor of the nation, the rank of full
general. He had already started writing his two-volume *Memoirs*, completed just before his death in August 1888. . . .

"I came out of the war pretty well wrecked," said Nathan Bedford
Forrest, "completely used up, shot all to pieces, crippled up . . . a beg-
gar." He returned to Sunflower Landing, Mississippi, to the only
plantation he had left, and tried to make a comeback planting corn. In
the front yard grazed his horse King Philip, still imbued with memories
of battle. When a Federal cavalry unit rode past the house, King Philip
instinctively charged the bluecoats, "teeth bared and front feet flail-
ing." As Forrest tried to restrain the horse, the captain remarked:

"General, now I can account for your success. Your . . . horses fight
for you."

It would be too much to expect that life for men like Forrest would go
smoothly in this postwar period. Without slaves to work the plantation,
he was bankrupt within two years, and forced to sell the land to pay his
debts. Then came a curious development, the details shrouded in
contemporary secrecy. Sometime around 1867, at a clandestine meeting of ex-Confederates in Pulaski, he was elected Grand Wizard of the
Klu Klux Klan. He claimed later to have renounced (and even to have
disbanded) the organization when its sinister purposes became apparent to him.

From then on it was all downhill for Forrest. Broken in health, a
victim of army dysentery, he tried to make a go at railroading, found
himself bankrupt again, and in desperation conceived a scheme for
conquering Mexico in six months with 30,000 volunteers. That bubble
burst with all the rest. In the fall of 1877, sixteen years after he had
ridden to war as lieutenant colonel of his own battalion, he died, with
his wife and ex-President Jefferson Davis at his side.

Like Forrest, Wade Hampton lost his entire fortune in the war,
including his beloved Millwood, burned by Sherman's troops. He returned to a new home in Columbia presented to him by the people of
South Carolina. From this base he waged a vigorous war against the
repressive Reconstruction measures of the radicals in Washington. His
uncompromising fight to retain the traditions of the Old South, white
supremacy for one, were both a handicap and asset in his public life.
Defeated in his first bid for governership of South Carolina, he was
elected to that office in 1876 and later to the United States Senate,
dying the year after his first term had ended.

Fitzhugh Lee, the one-time "Flower of Cavaliers," turned to farming
in Stafford County, Virginia, in the immediate postwar years, finding it
as hard to get corn from the soil as from a quartermaster's office ("but I

did it!"); then turned to politics to be elected Governor of Virginia in 1885. Named consul-general at Havana ten years later, he walked a tightrope between the United States and Spanish governments. When war with Spain broke out, he was commissioned a major general of U.S. Volunteers. Retired three years later, he died in the spring of 1905. His cousin, Rooney Lee, also divided his postwar interests between politics and farming, serving in the Virginia state senate and later in the U.S. House of Representatives until his death in 1891.

James Harrison Wilson, a late riser to cavalry stardom in the Civil War, emerged from the conflict with the admiration of both fellow officers and former foes. He had gained for the Union cavalry in the mid-South the same prestige which Sheridan had imparted to the horsemen of the East. Volunteering for service in the Spanish-American War, he was commissioned a major general and served in both Cuba and Puerto Rico. His biographer noted that up to his death in 1925, at eighty-eight, "he still walked like a cavalry commander."

There is no record that Wilson met Fighting Joe Wheeler when they fought on the same side in Cuba. But Wheeler was not one to hold a grudge or cling to a lost cause. Released from prison by the War Department, he worked wholeheartedly for reconciliation between North and South, and on this platform was repeatedly elected to the U.S. House of Representatives. When the bugles called him to the war with Spain, he again found himself leading a cavalry division charge up the slopes of San Juan Hill. Retiring as brigadier general in the army, he died in 1906 at the age of seventy.

For many years after the war, Tom Rosser found it hard to make a living for his family at a peacetime occupation. Modest training as an engineer got him some railroad construction jobs, the most notable with the Northern Pacific. He was surprised in 1873 to find his survey-ing crews guarded from marauding Indians by U.S. cavalry com-manded by George Armstrong Custer, the "Ol' Curly" he had whipped at Buckland Mills in the fall of 1863. The hatchet of their early feuds was buried congenially on the Dakota plains.

Three years after that reunion, Custer met a more implacable enemy who ended his decade's career as lieutenant colonel of the 7th U.S. Cavalry. Leading a punitive expedition against the Sioux in June of 1876, the general (with still flowing locks) found himself and his troop-ers cut off and surrounded near the Little Big Horn by 4,000 braves under Sioux Chief Crazy Horse.

Custer and 246 of his immediate command were overwhelmed and killed in the attack. General Nelson Miles, who had known the Boy General in the march to Appomattox and now investigated the misfor-tune for the War Department, wrote an epitaph of sorts: "Custer's flag went down in disaster, but with honor." Armstrong's former commander Phil Sheridan, when told of Custer's death, reacted with a comment that was typical and in a way prophetic: "Nonsense! Don't believe it!" Men like Custer didn't die. And in fact, a century later, Custer's Last Stand was more real and living to the schoolboys of America than all his achievements in the Civil War combined.

In mid-August of 1865 a Northern journalist reported from Virginia:

> A solitary man was seen beside the grave of Stuart in Hollywood Cemetery, near Richmond. The dew was on the grass, the birds sang overhead, the green hillock at the man's feet was all that remained of the daring leader of the Southern cavalry, who, after all his toils, his battles, and the shock of desperate encounters, had come here to rest in peace. Beside this unmarked grave the solitary mourner remained long, pondering and remembering. Finally he plucked a wild flower, dropped it upon the grave, and with tears in his eyes, left the spot. This lonely mourner at the grave of Stuart was [John Singleton] Mosby.

With this last mission completed, the former partisan leader returned to Warrenton, one-time center of Mosby's Confederacy, to become a struggling smalltown lawyer. A controversial figure in Fauquier County, whose countryside he had ravaged of necessity, he became more controversial still by his vigorous support of Grant for President in 1872.

It was a curious friendship that developed between the Confederate raider and the Union general he had almost captured eight years earlier. After his reelection Grant welcomed Mosby to the White House and pressed upon him government appointments, which the ex-Confederate turned down. But the fact that they were offered to him made him suspect in the South. Charged with being a turncoat, he was so fond of defending his honor with fists or pistols, that Grant got him out of the country—having him sent to Hong Kong as American consul in the Crown Colony.

The years that followed his return from service in Hong Kong might, for Mosby's sake, be better forgotten. He was an anomaly; time had passed him by. The Old South was a vanished dream. Men were no longer ten feet tall and women were no longer gentle Daphnes on vine-garlanded verandas.

He grew irascible and touchy. His health failed, and an accident damaged his sight and hearing. Though he tried to revive his legal practice, he became too difficult to get along with. Death in battle would have fitted his image better than death through the senility that stalked him. But he rallied enough to attend, as guest of honor, a reunion of the veterans of the Forty-Third Battalion in January 1895.

Addressing the hundred and fifty survivors of the band that he had parted from in Salem thirty years before, Mosby's words were something of an epitaph for the men of the Civil War cavalry whose like would never come again:

> Modern skepticism has destroyed one of the most beautiful creations of Epic ages, the belief that the spirits of dead warriors meet daily in the halls of Valhalla, and there around the festive board recount the deeds they did in the other world.... A man who belonged to my command may be forgiven for thinking that, in that assembly of heroes, [he] ... will not be unnoticed in the mighty throng.

NOTES

CHAPTER 1

RALLYING OF THE SABERS

No single source provides a comprehensive picture of the organization and operation of the Civil War cavalry. The story, for the most part, must be pieced together from the biographies of cavalry leaders, accounts of individual engagements, and regimental histories. There are two good works of reference, however: Miller's *Photographic History of the Civil War*, volume 4 of which is devoted exclusively to the mounted troops of both sides; and Kerr and Wallace's *Story of the U.S. Cavalry*, chapters 5 and 6 on the Confederate and Union cavalry respectively. One finds additional comments and information from such sources as Burr's *Life of Sheridan*, chapter 24 on "The Confederate Cavalryman," and Fairfax Downey's excellent book on the battle of Brandy Station, *Clash of Cavalry*, in which the author prefaces and footnotes his account with background material on the cavalry of both sides. Otherwise, virtually every history of the Civil War touches at different points on cavalry operations, and these have been inserted in this chapter where and if they seem to fit.

CHAPTER 2

GOLD SPURS AND ROSES

John Esten Cooke, Virginia historian and novelist who fought all through the war as a staff officer under Stuart, gives a sympathetic and personal first-hand character sketch of the cavalry commander in his *Wearing of the Gray*, chapter 1, pages 2–43. A retrospective view of Stuart's character by a modern novelist is provided by Joseph Hergesheimer in *Swords and Roses*, pages 267–96, from which the title of this chapter partially derives. John Thomason's biography of Stuart supplied much of the material here presented. A history of the famed Black Horse Cavalry, already a legend by the end of 1861, appears in *Annals of the War*, pages 590–98.

CHAPTER 3
HELLION ON HORSEBACK

John Allen Wyeth, army surgeon throughout most of the war and later author of *With Sabre and Scalpel*, never fought under Forrest but frequently crossed paths with him. His authoritative *Life of General N. B. Forrest*, along with Ralph Selph Henry's *"First with the Most" Forrest*, provided much of the material for this chapter. And again, Joseph Hergesheimer paints a sympathetic portrait of the Western cavalry commander in *Swords and Roses*, pages 205–31. Forrest's role at Fort Donelson is noted in *Battles and Leaders*, volume 1, pages 417, 418, 425, and 426.

CHAPTER 4
A TEAR FOR ASHBY

The quoted words of John Esten Cooke regarding Turner Ashby ("fact and fancy were so intertwined that no one bothered to try to separate them. He became a phantom.") apply to some extent to the material presented here. The saga of Ashby is so larded with superlatives, and with so much conflict in the accounts of eyewitnesses, that one is assailed with doubts as to what precisely happened. One can only present Ashby as his contemporaries saw him, and they saw him through rose-colored glasses even in the heat of battle. Most of the material herein comes from James B. Avirett's *The Memoirs of General Turner Ashby*, the memoirs being Avirett's own. Also from two biographies: Frank Cunningham's *Knight of the Confederacy*, and the *Life of Turner Ashby* by Thomas Almond Ashby, a kinsman of the general. Henderson's two-volume biography of Stonewall Jackson gives an excellent account of Ashby's part in the Valley campaign, and Julia Davis gives a briefer, more readable version in *The Shenandoah*. More can be found in Cooke's *Wearing of the Gray*, Dabney's *Life of Jackson*, and Dufour's *Nine Men in Gray*. It is unfortunate that space does not permit including the figure of Lieutenant Harry Gilmor and his brief role in Ashby's cavalry. It is recounted in his little-known book *Four Years in the Saddle*. Marylanders deserve more recognition for their role in the Civil War, and Gilmor provides it as that role pertained to cavalry.

CHAPTER 5
KENTUCKY CAVALIER

Basil Duke is Morgan's most readable and creditable Boswell, and George St. Leger Grenfell the most fascinating of the many characters the cavalier attracted. Both deserve chapters of their own, yet their auxiliary roles forbid it. As Morgan's brother-in-law and one who fought beside him throughout all of Morgan's up-and-down career, Duke does full justice to his subject in his *History of Morgan's Cavalry*. Grenfell never wrote a line about Morgan; but he served as a sort of Greek chorus to Duke's presentation of the general, with perceptive comments on Morgan, the war in the West, and Confederate cavalry in general. Ever in search of action, Grenfell later teamed up with Thomas Hines and the Northwest Conspiracy, and almost brought off the storming of Camp Douglas in Chicago and the release of its Southern prisoners. Betrayed by an associate, Grenfell was captured and sent to Fort Jefferson in the Gulf, where he shared a cell with Dr. Samuel Mudd, one of the several prisoners implicated in Lincoln's assassination. St. Leger slid out of Fort Jefferson on a stormy night aboard a stolen fishing vessel and was reported lost at sea. More fittingly, he is alleged to have surfaced from the gulf near Tampa, Florida, walked to the home of one A. W. McMullen for breakfast, and regaled the family with the same tales of derring-do that had thrilled the campfire caucuses of Morgan's cavalry.

CHAPTER 6

RING AROUND AN ARMY

Colonel W. T. Robins commanded the advance guard in Stuart's ride around McClellan's army and gives a first-hand account of the feat in *Battles and Leaders*, volume I, pages 271–75. John Esten Cooke offers an equally authoritative version in *The Blue and the Gray*, pages 129–34. John Singleton Mosby, in his memoirs, claims to have been more than a scout for the expedition, but its progenitor as well—the man who gave Stuart the idea in the first place. If true, Mosby shares the blame for a later, unfortunate raid during the Gettysburg campaign, which he also claims to have proposed. Stuart, on the other hand, while he put great confidence in Mosby, is nowhere quoted as granting this much influence to his protégé.

CHAPTER 7

THUNDERBOLT OF THE CONFEDERACY

Basil Duke's history of Morgan's cavalry and John Wyeth's biography of the Kentuckian are the principal sources for this chapter. But much light on this period of Morgan's operations is reflected by St. Leger Grenfell's comments and recollections. Anyone interested in Morgan will be equally interested in Stephen Starr's *Colonel Grenfell's Wars*. Though Grenfell left Morgan's command shortly after the latter's marriage, he drifted in and out of Morgan's life in subsequent years, and rejoined him in a subordinate position before Morgan's death.

CHAPTER 8

THE GRAY GHOST

The life and career of John Singleton Mosby are portrayed by Virgil Carrington Jones in *Gray Ghosts and Rebel Raiders* and *Ranger Mosby*. Mosby's own account of the raid on General Stoughton's camp is reprinted in *Battles and Leaders*, volume 3, pages 148–51. Going only by official records, the three empty champagne bottles found under Stoughton's bed the following day suggest that the general had been numbed by alcohol. However, the Brattleboro (Vermont) Public Library has documentary evidence of the visit to Stoughton's room that night by his mother and sister. While New England ladies of the period were not known as heavy imbibers, it is charitable to assume that they drank a bottle apiece, and that the third was hardly enough to render the general unfit for duty.

CHAPTER 9

THE YANKS ARE COMING

The siege and capture of Vicksburg was more fatal to the South than the reverse at Gettysburg or the fall of Atlanta. In general, the cavalry of both sides played only peripheral roles in the campaign which began with Farragut's entering New Orleans in the spring of 1862. Grierson's diversionary raid, however, contributed significantly to Grant's operation, as Grant himself admitted. Grierson's official report of his ride through Mississippi is given in *The Blue and the Gray*, volume 2, pages 656–62. A more full and detailed account is provided by Dee Alexander Brown's *Grierson's Raid*, which includes a day-by-day map of the expedition.

CHAPTER 10

''FORWARD THE MULE BRIGADE!''

The pursuit and capture of Streight's mule-mounted raiders is best told by John Allen Wyeth in *That Devil Forrest*, pages 169–99. General Grenville Dodge gives his version of the affair in *The Battle of Atlanta and Other Campaigns*, pages 111–26, and appends Streight's official report, which is more to the point.

CHAPTER 11

CAVALRY AT THE CROSSROADS

There is an epic account of the Battle of Brandy Station, and that is Fairfax Downey's *Clash of Cavalry*. Downey details every move before, throughout, and after the June 9 battle, yet the details never clog the narrative or sacrifice the human story of this military classic. It was certainly the high point of cavalry encounters in the Civil War. There would be other major engagements, but from this point on, with the ascendancy of the riders in blue and the decline of the Confederates, none would be so evenly matched or ably contested. Wade Hampton's important role in the fight is given in Manly Wellman's *Giant in Gray*, pages 106–10.

CHAPTER 12

A SMALL TOWN IN PENNSYLVANIA

The debate continues. Who was at fault? Jeb Stuart, for too freely interpreting his orders and being absent during the first two crucial days at Gettysburg? General Lee, for not giving his cavalry commander more specific instructions? Or was neither at fault, and Stuart's circuitous raid a sensible diversionary tactic that suffered some ill luck in execution? John Mosby in his *Memoirs* takes the third view, claiming to have masterminded the affair. His defense of Stuart appears in *Battles and Leaders*, volume 3, pages 251–52. Regardless of the argument, the cavalry of both sides made up for earlier relative inactivity with sharp engagements on July 3. For background there is "The Confederate Cavalry in the Gettysburg Campaign," *Battles and Leaders*, volume 3, pages 251–53; and "The Union Cavalry at Gettysburg," *Annals of the War*, pages 373–79. Regarding specific battles: Gregg's encounter with Stuart on July 3, *Annals of the War*, pages 527–35, and *Battles and Leaders*, pages 397–406; Farnsworth's charge and death, ibid., pages 393–96. Wade Hampton's personal duel with the Union sniper, one of the more dramatic incidents in this dramatic battle, appears in Manly Wellman's *Giant in Gray*, pages 115, 116.

CHAPTER 13

RIDE TO OBLIVION

Basil Duke gives a full account of Morgan's raid to the Ohio in his *History of Morgan's Cavalry*, pages 344–461. A more summary account is given in *Battles and Leaders*, volume 3, pages 634–35; Morgan's pursuit and capture, ibid., volume 4, page 415. Also see Howard Swiggett's *The Rebel Raider*, chapter 5; and Commager's *The Blue and the Gray*, pages 678–84, for eyewitness accounts by participants in the adventure.

CHAPTER 14

GOLDILOCKS

Custer is most revealing in his letters to Libby Bacon, many of which are printed in Marguerite Merrington's *The Custer Story*. Though he exaggerates the facts and even twists statistics, the personality comes through. D. A. Kinsley's *Favor the Bold* offers a readable but somewhat fictionalized account of Custer's Civil War career, Jay Monaghan's *Custer* a more definitive biography.

CHAPTER 15

DUEL OF GIANTS

Brigadier General (formerly captain) Theophilus F. Rodenbough gives an account of Sheridan's Richmond raid in *Battles and Leaders*, volume 4, pages 188–93. Jeb Stuart's death as seen by a private of the Virginia cavalry follows on page 194. Rodenbough's account of the cavalry fight at Trevilian Station appears in ibid., pages 233–36, followed by General M. C. Butler's version of the encounter, pages 237–39. Combining Frank Burr's *Life of Sheridan* with Sheridan's *Personal Memoirs* gives a pretty complete picture of the foremost of Federal cavalry commanders. Grant's reasons for selecting him as chief of cavalry are given in Grant's *Memoirs*, volume 2, pages 133 and 134. Perhaps the most sympathetic if somewhat idolatrous portrait of Wade Hampton is given by John Esten Cooke in *Wearing of the Gray*. As a member of Hampton's staff and a novelist and historian in private life Cooke gives a vivid personal picture of the South Carolinian. For a more full biography there is Manly Wade Wellman's *Giant in Gray*.

CHAPTER 16

"THAT DEVIL FORREST"

In their memoirs, both Sherman and Grant reflect the concern of these generals over Forrest's threat to their respective plans in Georgia and Virginia. Cowan's account of Forrest's quarrel with Bragg is given in Ralph Selph Henry's *"First with the Most" Forrest*, pages 199, 200; Smith's unsuccessful pursuit of Forrest is related in ibid., pages 214–34, and in *Battles and Leaders*, volume 4, pages 416–18. The Fort Pillow Massacre is discussed at length in Henry's *"First with the Most" Forrest*, pages 248–68, including the dispute that raged long afterwards. John Allen Wyeth's description of the battle at Brice's Cross Roads is included in William Webb's *Crucial Moments of the Civil War*, pages 281–304.

CHAPTER 17

HORSEMEN AT THE GATES

The circumstances of Johnston's removal from command of the Army of Tennessee, which so greatly affected the outcome of the campaign for Atlanta, are discussed by the general himself in his *Narrative of Military Operations*, pages 348–70; how this affected cavalry operations, and Johnston's appraisal of these operations, ibid., pages 360–62. Cavalry encounters around Atlanta in July and August of 1864 are recounted in *Battles and Leaders*, volume 4, pages 341, 342; and in Samuel Carter's *Siege of Atlanta*, pages 239, 249, 256–64.

CHAPTER 18

SHERIDAN ALL THE WAY

Much of the material in this chapter comes from E. J. Stackpole's *Sheridan in the Shenandoah*, and from Sheridan's *Memoirs*, volume 1, beginning with page 414, and volume 2, through page 59. A contemporary account of the battle of Cedar Creek and Sheridan's famous ride from Winchester is reprinted in Webb's *Crucial Moments*, pages 305–14, along with Buchanan's ode to the event, partially quoted here. Roughly the same material is in chapters 18 and 19 of Burr's *Life of Sheridan*. Since the horses of the Civil War cavalry were given more credit by their riders than by latter day historians, it is worth noting that Sheridan's charger "Rienzi"—which the general renamed "Winchester" after this event—passed a comfortable old age with his master until the horse's death fourteen years later, after which his "lifelike remains" (how preserved is not made clear) were presented to the Governor's Island Museum in New York City.

CHAPTER 19

TWILIGHT OF THE WESTERN CAVALIERS

Accounts of Morgan's imprisonment and escape appear in Basil Duke's *History of Morgan's Cavalry*, pages 471–89, and in Swigget's *Rebel Raider*, pages 190–201. Duke also reports on Morgan's activities in 1864 in *Battles and Leaders*, volume 4, pages 422–24. There are many accounts of Morgan's death at Greeneville, but none solves the mystery of his betrayal, if betrayal it was. Swiggett's *Rebel Raider*, pages 260–88, goes into the matter at more length than most. Forrest's screening of Hood's retreat from Tennessee is narrated in Henry's *"First with the Most" Forrest*, pages 412–17; and in Wilson's *Under the Old Flag*, volume 2, pages 119–42. Forrest's surrender in Alabama, Henry's *"First with the Most" Forrest*, chapter 26, and Wilson's *Under the Old Flag*, pages 240–45.

CHAPTER 20

"A FINAL BLAZE OF GLORY"

The retreat and pursuit from Richmond to Appomattox saw more concentrated cavalry action than any other week of the war, and an excellent chronological account is given in Burke Davis's *To Appomattox: Nine April Days, 1865*. Sheridan's *Memoirs*, volume 2, also cover the period, beginning with page 134; and Tremain's *The Last Hours*, all thirteen chapters, is devoted exclusively to this campaign. Concerning the two principal cavalry engagements of the nine days, Horace Porter's account of the battle of Five Forks appears in *Battles and Leaders*, volume 4, pages 708–22, and covers the subsequent pursuit of Lee and the fight at Sayler's (here called "Sailor's") Creek. Hampton's and Wheeler's combined operations in the Carolinas are reviewed in Johnston's *Narrative*, pages 371–93; the terms of surrender proposed by Sherman, and the resulting contention, ibid., pages 397–417. A fuller account, and one more properly stressing Wade Hampton's role in these events is given in Wellman's *Giant in Gray*, pages 166–211.

CHAPTER 21

AVE ATQUE VALE

General James Longstreet's detailed account of the events at Appomattox on July 9 are given in his *From Manassas to Appomattox*, Chapter 43; the incident of Custer's demand for his surrender, page 359. A readable account of the events leading up to Lee's surrender is given in Davis's *To Appomattox, Nine April Days*, pages 307–409. Wade Hampton's own report of the Battle of Bentonville is given in *Battles and Leaders*, volume 4, pages 700–05. In the same volume Horace Porter provides an eyewitness account of the surrender at Appomattox Court House, pages 729–46. Chapter 13 of *E. A. Pollard's Southern History of the Civil War*, volume 4, gives details and circumstances of Lee's and Johnston's surrenders, as well as of other events of April–May 1865 leading to the conclusion of the war, as seen by the editor of the Richmond *Examiner*.

BIBLIOGRAPHY

Annals of the War. Philadelphia: Times Printing Co., 1879.

Ashby, Thomas A. *Life of Turner Ashby*. New York: Neale Publishing Co., 1914.

Avirett, James B. *Memoirs of General Turner Ashby*. Baltimore: Selby & Dulaney, 1867.

Bagby, George W. *The Old Virginia Gentleman and Other Sketches*. Richmond: Dietz, 1943.

Barrett, John G. *Sherman's March Through the Carolinas*. Chapel Hill: University of North Carolina Press, 1956.

Battles and Leaders of the Civil War. Edited by R. U. Johnson and C. C. Buel, 4 vols. New York: Century, 1887.

Blackford, William W. *War Years with Jeb Stuart*. New York: Scribners, 1945.

Brackett, Albert G. *History of the United States Cavalry* (reprint of 1865 edition). New York: Argonaut Press, 1965.

Brown, D. Alexander. *The Bold Cavaliers*. Philadelphia: Lippincott, 1959.

———. *Grierson's Raid*. Urbana: University of Illinois Press, 1954.

Brownlee, Richard J. *Gray Ghosts of the Confederacy*. Baton Rouge: Louisiana State University Press, 1958.

Bryan, T. Conn. *Confederate Georgia*. Athens: University of Georgia Press, 1953.

Burr, F. A., and Hinton, R. J. *The Life of Gen. Philip H. Sheridan*. Providence: J. A. & R. A. Reid, 1888.

Butler, Lorine L. *John Morgan and His Men*. Philadelphia: Dorrance, 1960.

Carter, Samuel III. *Siege of Atlanta*. New York: St.Martin's Press, 1973.

Catton, Bruce. *The Coming Fury*. New York: Doubleday, 1961.

———. *Never Call Retreat*. New York: Doubleday, 1965.

———. *Terrible Swift Sword*. New York: Doubleday, 1963.

Chesnut, Mary Boykin. *A Diary from Dixie*. Edited by Ben Ames Williams. Boston: Houghton Mifflin, 1949.

Commager, Henry S. *The Blue and the Gray*. 2 vols. Indianapolis: Bobbs-Merrill, 1950.

Connell, Thomas L. *Autumn of Glory*. Baton Rouge: Louisiana State University Press, 1971.

Cooke, John Esten. *Wearing of the Gray*. New York: E. B. Treat, 1867.
Cunningham, Frank. *Knight of the Confederacy: Gen. Turner Ashby*. San Antonio: Naylor Co., 1960.

Davis, Burke. *Jeb Stuart, the Last Cavalier*. New York: Rinehart, 1957
_____ . *To Appomattox: Nine April Days, 1865*. New York: Rinehart, 1959.
Davis, Julia. *The Shenandoah*. New York: Farrar & Rinehart, 1945.
Dodge, Grenville M. *The Battle of Atlanta and Other Campaigns*. Council Bluffs, Iowa: Monarch Printing Co., 1911.
Dodson, William C. *Campaigns of Wheeler and His Cavalry*. Atlanta: Hudgins Publishing Co., 1899
Downey, Fairfax. *Clash of Cavalry*. New York: David McKay, 1959.
_____ . *The Guns at Gettysburg*. New York: David McKay, 1958.
DuBose, John W. *General Joseph Wheeler and the Army of Tennessee*. New York: Neale Publishing Co., 1912.
Dufour, Charles L. *Nine Men in Gray*. New York: Doubleday, 1963.
Duke, Basil W. *A History of Morgan's Cavalry*. Reprint. Edited by C. F. Holland. Bloomington: Indiana University Press, 1960.
_____ . *Reminiscences*. New York: Doubleday, Page, 1911.
Dyer, John P. *"Fightin' Joe" Wheeler*. Baton Rouge: Louisiana State University Press, 1941.

Eckenrode, Hamilton J. *Life of Nathan B. Forrest*. Richmond: B. F. Johnson, 1918.

Fiske, John. *The Mississippi Valley in the Civil War*. Boston: Houghton Mifflin, 1900.
Foote, Shelby. *The Civil War*. 3 vols., New York: Random House, 1958–74.
Fremantle, Arthur J. L. *The Fremantle Diary*. London: Andre Deutsch, 1956.

Garrett, Franklin M. *Atlanta and Environs*. Atlanta: University of Georgia Press, 1969.
Gilmor, Harry. *Four Years in the Saddle*. New York: Harper, 1866.
Grant, Ulysses S. *Personal Memoirs*. 2 vols. New York: Webster & Co., 1886.

Haskell, Frank A. *The Battle of Gettysburg*. New York: P. F. Collier, 1910.
Henderson, G.F.R. *Stonewall Jackson and the American Civil War*. 2 vols. London: Longmans, Green, 1913.
Henry, Robert S. *As They Saw Forrest*. Jackson, Tenn.: McCowat-Mercer Press, 1956.
_____ . *"First With the Most" Forrest*. Indianapolis: Bobbs-Merrill, 1944.
Hergesheimer, Joseph. *Swords and Roses*. New York: Knopf, 1928.
Herr, J. K. and Wallace, E. S. *The Story of the U. S. Cavalry*. Boston: Little, Brown, 1953.
Hood, John Bell. *Advance and Retreat*. Reprint. Bloomington: Indiana University Press, 1969.

Johnson, Adam R. *Partisan Rangers of the Confederate States Army*. Louisville, Ky.: G. G. Fetter, 1904.
Johnston, Joseph E. *Narrative of Military Operations*. New York: Appleton, 1874.
Jones, Virgil C. *Gray Ghosts and Rebel Raiders*. New York: Holt, Rinehart & Winston, 1956.
_____ . *Ranger Mosby*. Chapel Hill: University of North Carolina Press, 1944.

Kinsley, D. A. *Favor the Bold: Custer, The Civil War Years*. Kansas City: Promontory Press, 1967.

Lee, Robert E., Jr. *Recollections and Letters of General Robert E. Lee*. New York: Doubleday, Page, 1904.

Leech, Margaret. *Reveille in Washington*. New York: Harper, 1941.
Lever, Charles J. *Charles O'Malley, the Irish Dragoon*. Philadelphia: Carey and Hart, 1841.
Lewis, Lloyd. *Sherman, Fighting Prophet*. New York: Harcourt, Brace, 1932.
Long, E. B. *The Civil War Day by Day*. New York: Doubleday, 1971.
Longstreet, James. *From Manassas to Appomattox*. Philadelphia: Lippincott, 1896.
Luvaas, Jay. "Cavalry Lessons of the Civil War." *Civil War Times Illustrated*, vol. 4, no. 9, Jan. 1968.

McClellan, H. B. *The Life and Campaigns of Major General J.E.B. Stuart*. Boston: Houghton Mifflin, 1885.

Merrington, Marguerite. *The Custer Story*. New York: Devin-Adair, 1950.
Meyer, Henry C. *Civil War Experiences under Bayard, Gregg, Kilpatrick, Custer*. New York: Raulston & Newberry, 1911.
Miers, Earl S. *The General Who Marched to Hell*. New York: Knopf, 1951.
Miller, Francis T. *Photographic History of the Civil War*. The Cavalry, vol. 4. New York: A. S. Barnes, 1911.
Monaghan, Jay. *Custer*. Boston: Little, Brown, 1959.
Moore, James. *Kilpatrick and Our Cavalry*. New York: W. J. Widdleston, 1865.
Mosby, John S. *Stuart's Cavalry in the Gettysburg Campaign*. New York: Moffat, Yard & Co., 1908.
———. *War Reminiscences of Colonel John S. Mosby*. New York: Dodd Mead, 1887.
Myers, Frank M. *The Comanches: a History of White's Battalion, Virginia Cavalry, Laurel Brigade*. Baltimore: Kelly, Piet, 1871.

Neal, Andrew Jackson, personal letters, 1861–1864. Special Collections, Robert W. Woodruff Library, Emory University, Atlanta, Ga.
Neese, George M. *Three Years in the Confederate Horse Artillery*. New York: Neale Publishing Co., 1911.
Niles, Blair. *The James*. New York: Farrar & Rinehart, 1939.
Nye, W. S. "Cavalry Fight at Gettysburg." *Civil War Times Illustrated*, vol. 2, no. 4, July 1963.

Opie, John N. *A Rebel Cavalryman with Lee, Stuart, and Jackson*. Chicago: W. B. Conkey Co., 1899.

Patten, G. W. *Cavalry Drill and Sabre Exercises*. Richmond: West & Johanston, 1862.
Pollard, E. A. *The Lost Cause*. New York: E. B. Treat, 1867.
Porter, Horace. *Campaigning with Grant*. New York: Crown, 1961.
Pratt, Fletcher. *Ordeal by Fire*. New York: Smith & Haas, 1935.

Rowell, John W. *Yankee Cavalrymen*. Knoxville: University of Tennessee Press, 1971.

Sheridan, P. H. *Personal Memoirs*. 2 vols., New York: Webster, 1888.
Smith, Thomas W. *The Story of a Cavalry Regiment*. Chicago: W. B. Conkey Co., 1897.
Stackpole, Edward J. *Sheridan in the Shenandoah*. Harrisburg: Stackpole Co., 1961.
———. *They Met at Gettysburg*. New York: Crown, 1956.
Starr, Stephen Z. *Colonel Grenfell's Wars*. Baton Rouge: Louisiana State University Press, 1971.
Stephenson, W. H. and Coulton, E. M. *A History of the South*, vol. 7. Baton Rouge: Louisiana State University Press, 1950.
Swigget, Howard. *The Rebel Raider*. Indianapolis: Bobbs-Merrill, 1934.

Thomason, John W. *Jeb Stuart*. New York: Scribner's, 1934.

Tremain, Henry E. *Last Hours of Sheridan's Cavalry*. New York: Bonnell, Silver & Bowers, 1904.

Tucker, Glenn. "The Cavalry Invasion of the North." *Civil War Times Illustrated*, vol. 2, no. 4, July 1963.

U.S. War Department. *The War of the Rebellion; A compilation of the Official Records of the Union and Confederate Armies*. Washington: Government Printing Office, 1880–1901.

Van de Water, Frederic. *Glory-Hunter, a life of General Custer*. Indianapolis: Bobbs-Merrill, 1934.

Vandiver, Frank E. *Jubal's Raid*. New York: McGraw-Hill, 1960.

_____ . *Their Tattered Flags*. New York: Harper's Magazine Press, 1970.

Warner, Ezra J. *Generals in Gray*. Baton Rouge: Louisiana State University Press, 1959.

_____ . *Generals in Blue*. Baton Rouge: Louisiana State University Press, 1964.

Webb, Willard, ed. *Crucial Moments of the Civil War*. New York: Crown, 1961.

Wellman, Manly W. *Giant in Gray*. New York: Scribner's, 1949.

Wiley, Bell I. *Embattled Confederates*. New York: Crown, 1964.

_____ . *The Life of Billy Yank*. Indianapolis: Bobbs-Merrill, 1951.

_____ . *The Life of Johnny Reb*. Indianapolis: Bobbs-Merrill, 1943.

_____ . *They Who Fought Here*. New York: Crown, 1959.

Wilson, James Harrison. *Under the Old Flag*. 2 vols. New York: Appleton, 1912.

Wyeth, John A. *That Devil Forrest*. Reprint of 1899 edition. New York: Harper, 1959.

INDEX